FLOURISHING

POSITIVE PSYCHOLOGY AND THE LIFE WELL-LIVED

Edited by COREY L. M. KEYES
and JONATHAN HAIDT

AMERICAN PSYCHOLOGICAL ASSOCIATION

WASHINGTON, DC

Published by
American Psychological Association
750 First Street, NE
Washington, DC 20002
www.apa.org

To order
APA Order Department
P.O. Box 92984
Washington, DC 20090-2984
Tel: (800) 374-2721
Direct: (202) 336-5510
Fax: (202) 336-5502
TDD/TTY: (202) 336-6123
Online: www.apa.org/books/
Email: order@apa.org

In the U.K., Europe, Africa, and the Middle
East, copies may be ordered from
American Psychological Association
3 Henrietta Street
Covent Garden, London
WC2E 8LU England

Typeset in Goudy by World Composition Services, Inc., Sterling, VA

Printer: United Book Press, Inc., Baltimore, MD
Cover designer: Anne Masters, Washington, DC
Project Manager: Debbie Hardin, Carlsbad, CA

The opinions and statements are the responsibility of the authors, and such opinions and
statements do not necessarily represent the policies of the American Psychological
Association.

Library of Congress Cataloging-in-Publication Data
Flourishing : positive psychology and the life well-lived / edited by Corey L. M. Keyes,
Jonathan Haidt.—1st ed.
    p. cm.
  Includes bibliographical references and indexes.
  ISBN 1-55798-930-3 (alk. paper)
  1. Psychology—Congresses.   I. Keyes, Corey L. M.   II. Haidt, Jonathan.

BF20.F57 2003
158--dc21   2002033219

British Library Cataloguing-in-Publication Data
A CIP record is available from the British Library.

Printed in the United States of America
First Edition

CONTENTS

CONTRIBUTORS

Paul B. Baltes, Max Planck Institute for Human Development, Berlin, Germany

Gwen Bennett, University of Pennsylvania, Philadelphia

Vincent J. Cassandro, Buffalo State College, Buffalo

Edward C. Chang, University of Michigan, Ann Arbor

Mihaly Csikszentmihalyi, Claremont Graduate University, Claremont, CA

Robert A. Emmons, University of California–Davis

Alexandra M. Freund, Max Planck Institute for Human Development, Berlin, Germany

Shelly L. Gable, University of California–Los Angeles

Jonathan Haidt, University of Virginia, Charlottesville

James K. Harter, The Gallup Organization, Lincoln, NE

Corey L. M. Keyes, Emory University, Atlanta, GA

Jeanne Nakamura, Claremont Graduate University, Claremont, CA

Christopher Peterson, University of Michigan, Ann Arbor

Jane Allyn Piliavin, University of Wisconsin, Madison

Harry T. Reis, University of Rochester, Rochester, NY

Paul Rozin, University of Pennsylvania, Philadelphia

Carol D. Ryff, University of Wisconsin, Madison

Frank L. Schmidt, University of Iowa, Iowa City

Martin E. P. Seligman, University of Pennsylvania, Philadelphia

Dean Keith Simonton, University of California–Davis

Burton Singer, Princeton University, Princeton, NJ

Elaine Wethington, Cornell University, Ithaca, NY

Amy Wrzesniewski, New York University, New York

ACKNOWLEDGMENTS

We are grateful to the Gallup Foundation for hosting and supporting the first Summit of Positive Psychology. This summit was cochaired by Donald Clifton, Ed Diener, Corey Keyes, and Martin Seligman, and it was held at the Gallup Organization in Lincoln, Nebraska, September 9–12, 1999. The purpose of the first summit was to begin mapping the key elements of a positive life; many of the chapters in this volume are based on presentations given at this summit. We wish to thank our colleagues Robin Simon, Amy Wrzesniewski, Jennifer Janovy-Meyer, and Ashby Walker for their assistance and reviews of chapters. Also, Sam Oliner, Jon Schooler, and Kristine Enderle provided invaluable reviews of the manuscript; we are grateful for such genuine colleagues. Susan Reynolds and Kristine Enderle at the American Psychological Association were patient and helpful shepherds of this project. We especially thank the authors, who contributed their time, energy, talents, and insights; without them, neither this book nor the movement called *positive psychology* would be possible. May you all flourish.

FOREWORD:
THE PAST AND FUTURE
OF POSITIVE PSYCHOLOGY

MARTIN E. P. SELIGMAN

As the volume editors noted in the Acknowledgments, this book is based on the first Summit of Positive Psychology sponsored by the Gallup Foundation. At that gathering, one of our colleagues asked a pointed question: "If we were a business, would we invest in positive psychology and positive social science?" In one form or another, that is the question to which all of the contributors to this volume have responded. Is this movement in science worth the investment of time, energy, and research effort? I believe that it is, because I believe that psychology should be about more than repairing what is wrong. It should also be about identifying and nurturing what is good.

Historically, however, this has not been the case, because when nations are troubled—when they are at war, in social turmoil, or impoverished, or when their citizens suffer famine—their natural concern is defense and the repair of damage. Accordingly, the sciences these nations underwrite, the art they appreciate, and the novels they understand are about defense and repair of damage. This is not meant to deny that human virtue often appears in deeply troubled societies. In fact, great turmoil makes the exercise of virtue more difficult and therefore more heroic. But most of the history of humankind has unfolded in difficult circumstances, and if such societies focus only on repairing what is wrong, then the best result that even a utopianly successful program can achieve is to attain *zero*.

A shift occurs, however, when societies are in surplus and not in social turmoil. These societies lift their eyes up from preoccupation with damage and its victims and inquire instead into what makes life worth living. What are the best things in life? How can we go from zero to plus two, or even to plus six?

History provides a few examples of such societies: Greece in its Golden Age was the cradle of democracy and philosophy; Victorian England enshrined honor, duty, and valor; and Florence in the 1450s became enormously wealthy based on its wool trade and then its banking prowess. Although it considered the option of becoming the most important military power in Europe, Florence decided instead to invest its economic surplus in beauty. The suggestion that positive psychology makes to the world is not that we build an aesthetic monument but rather that we create a humane scientific monument—that we bring the light of science to bear on the question of what are the best things in life and how human beings might achieve them.

Since September 11, 2001, I have pondered the role of positive psychology in a time of trouble (Seligman, 2002). Positive psychology has three pillars: First is the study of positive emotion. Second is the study of the positive traits, foremost among them the strengths and virtues but also the "abilities" such as intelligence and athleticism. Third is the study of the positive institutions, such as democracy, strong families, and free inquiry, that support the virtues, which in turn support the positive emotions. The positive emotions of confidence, hope, and trust, for example, serve us best not when life is easy but when life is difficult. In times of trouble, understanding and shoring up the positive institutions—such as democracy, strong family, and free press—are of immediate importance. In times of trouble, understanding and building the strengths and virtues—among them, valor, perspective, integrity, equity, and loyalty—may become more urgent than in good times.

Times of trouble are times of suffering, and we may ask if the understanding and alleviating of suffering trumps the understanding and building of happiness. This is a different way of asking if positive psychology becomes irrelevant in times of trouble. I think not. Positive psychology holds that one of the best ways to help suffering people is to focus on positive things. People who are impoverished, depressed, or suicidal care about much more than just the relief of their suffering. These people care—sometimes desperately—about virtue, about purpose, about integrity, and about meaning. Experiences that induce positive emotion cause negative emotion to dissipate rapidly. The strengths and virtues function to buffer against misfortune and against the psychological disorders, and they may be the key to building resilience. Thus, positive psychology may become still more important in times of trouble, even though a bleeding nation may not easily see that, in the long run, building strength and virtue effectively stanches wounds.

THE BIRTH OF POSITIVE PSYCHOLOGY

Corey Keyes writes in this volume about languishing. We usually think about the languishing of individuals, but I believe that a field or discipline can languish in the same way as an individual. Psychology has, for the past 50 years, been almost entirely about remediation, about repairing the worst in life. It has turned its back on the goals of understanding what makes people happy, what builds positive character, and what makes life worth living. When psychology ignores these goals, it can languish just as the social sciences and many individuals are languishing.

The notion of positive psychology began for me at a moment in time in 1997, shortly after I had been elected president of the American Psychological Association (APA). Before this moment, I had been floundering. I had thought my theme as APA president was going to be prevention, so I gathered together a dozen of the leading scholars on prevention, including Mike Csikszentmihalyi. We held a meeting that I found dull; it was nothing more than a routine application of the medical model delivered proactively. Not only did I think that a disease model of prevention would not work, but I also thought the approach was too mechanical and uninspiring to capture the imaginations of the best young scientists and clinicians. On the way out of the meeting Mike said to me, "Marty, this has to have some intellectual backbone; this has to be a lot more interesting."

Shortly afterward, I was in my garden weeding with my daughter Nikki, who had turned five a few weeks earlier. I first must admit that, even though I write books about children, I am really not very good with them. I am too goal-oriented and time-urgent. When I am weeding in the garden, I am really focused on getting the weeding done. Nikki, however, was throwing weeds in the air and dancing around. So I yelled at her. She gave me a look and walked away. When she returned, she said, "Daddy, I want to talk to you." "Yes, Nikki?" "Daddy, you may not have noticed, but do you remember how I was before my fifth birthday? From the time I was three until I turned five, I was a whiner. I whined every day. But when I turned five, I decided not to whine anymore. And that was the hardest thing I've ever done—but I did it. So if I can stop whining, Daddy, you can stop being so grumpy!"

Nikki's declaration was an epiphany for me. That day I learned something about Nikki, something about raising kids, something about myself, and a great deal about my profession. First, I realized that raising Nikki was not about stopping her whining. She had accomplished that herself. Rather, raising Nikki was about taking the strength she had shown—her marvelous gift of seeing into the soul—and amplifying it. Raising children, I realized, involves more than simply fixing what is wrong with them. It is about identifying and nurturing their strongest qualities—what they already possess and are good at—so that they can use them as buffers against the troubles life will bring.

As for my own life, Nikki was exactly right: I was a grouch. For 50 years I had walked around being grumpy, despite being surrounded by a wife and children who are all rays of sunshine. I had no good reason for my grouchiness, and anything I had ever accomplished in my life had probably been in spite of my grouchiness. So I resolved, at that moment, to change, just as Nikki had. And yes, that has been the hardest thing I have ever done.

But the broadest implication of Nikki's lesson was about the science and practice of psychology. The message of positive psychology is to remind our field that it has been half-baked. We have made real progress on the study of mental illness and the repair of damage. But we have made little progress in so many other areas. Psychology is not just the study of disease, weakness, and damage. It is also the study of happiness, strength, and virtue.

The next day I called Mike Csikszentmihalyi and said, "Mike, I don't know what your plans are for New Year's, but I'd like you to cancel them and come to Mexico with Mandy and me, to discuss the notion of creating a field of positive psychology." I then called Ray Fowler and asked him the same thing. We all met in Mexico for a week of walking, talking, and thinking about the past and future of psychology. We asked how psychology got labeled as a "healing" profession, concerned almost exclusively with identifying and fixing what is wrong with people. What follows is our diagnosis.

HOW PSYCHOLOGY GOT NARROWED

Before World War II, psychology had three distinct missions. The first was to cure mental illness. The second was to make everyone's lives happier and more productive and fulfilling, with the burgeoning of industrial psychology as the paradigm example. The third was to identify and nurture high talent and genius.

Right after the war, however, psychology got derailed, and two of its three missions were forgotten. Two events, both economic, caused this derailment. The first occurred in 1946 with the passage of the Veterans Administration Act, when thousands of psychologists discovered that they could earn a living treating individuals with neuroses in Omaha. The second and complementary event occurred in 1947 with the founding of the National Institute of Mental Health (NIMH). Based on the disease model, the NIMH is more accurately described as the "National Institute of Mental Illness," because it concerns itself only remotely with mental health. But with the founding of the NIMH, academics, myself included, discovered that they could obtain grants if they described their research in terms of curing mental illness.

Still, I think these economic changes also produced two great victories: In 1947, none of the so-called major illnesses was treatable. They were all shrouded in superstition, shadow, and fog. But now 14 of the major mental illnesses are treatable, and two are curable by either psychotherapy or psychopharmacology (Seligman, 1994).

The second great victory was that a science of mental illness developed. Scientists were able to take fuzzy concepts (e.g., depression, anger, alcoholism, schizophrenia, and impotence) and define them. We were then able to operationalize them and measure them in valid and reliable ways. Later we were able to evaluate their causes using experimental methods and sophisticated longitudinal designs. And, best of all, we developed both biological and psychological interventions, which we then rigorously tested for efficacy. As a result, we were able to build a science of mental illness that actually works.

But the cost of these victories was that psychology forgot its other two missions. It forgot that it is also about making the lives of normal people more fulfilling, more productive, and happier. It also forgot that one of its tasks is to nurture genius, to identify our most precious resource—talented young people—and find the conditions under which they will flourish. *Genius* and *talent* have become almost dirty words now, and it is incumbent on psychologists to make them respectable concepts once more.

THE DISEASE MODEL OF PREVENTION AND WHY IT DOES NOT WORK

Prevention was the theme of the 1998 APA meeting in San Francisco. We asked how we can prevent problems such as depression, substance abuse, and schizophrenia in young people who are genetically vulnerable or who live in worlds that predispose them to these problems. We asked how we can prevent murderous school-yard violence by children with access to weapons, with poor parental supervision, and with, perhaps, a mean streak. The answer does not lie in the disease model (Catalano, Berglund, Ryan, Lonczak, & Hawkins, 1998).

What we have learned over 50 years is that the disease model does not move us closer to the prevention of these serious problems. Indeed, the major strides in prevention have resulted from a perspective focused on systematically building competency, not on correcting weakness. Positive psychologists have discovered that human strengths act as buffers against mental illness (Keyes & Lopez, 2002). Much of the task of prevention in the 21st century will be to continue this fruitful line of work and create a science of human strength, the mission of which will be to understand how to foster these virtues in young people (Bornstein, Davidson, Keyes, & Moore, in press).

I have worked in prevention for more than 15 years. When I started, my view of prevention was just the disease model done proactively. But then, as the emerging prevention literature highlighted what worked and what did not, it became clear that little of what I had learned about the biology of mental illness or psychotherapy for mental illness was applicable to prevention. Prevention was not about repairing damage. My own work on "learned optimism" supports this view (Seligman, Reivich, Jaycox, & Gillham, 1995). In teaching learned optimism to children and adults, we do not repair damage but instead teach skills. We teach participants to accurately attribute causes for bad events. We change the ways they interpret bad events, regarding them as local and temporary, not pervasive and permanent. In so doing, we find that we cut the rate of depression by about 50% in both children and adults. The focus of prevention, then, should be about taking strengths—hope, optimism, courage, interpersonal skill, perseverance, honesty, work ethic, future-mindedness, capacity for insight, to name a few—and building on them to buffer against depression. But because psychology has been a profession and a science focused on what was wrong and what was weak, we know almost nothing about the strengths and virtues. So if we want to succeed in prevention, we need a science to illuminate strengths and virtues.

THE THREE PILLARS OF POSITIVE PSYCHOLOGY

Here is how I parse the science of positive psychology. The first pillar of positive psychology is about the positive subjective experience of the past, present, and future. Positive subjective experience about the past is contentment, satisfaction, and well-being. Positive subjective experience about the present is happiness, flow, ecstasy, and the sensual pleasures. And positive subjective experience about the future is optimism and hope.

The second pillar of the science is the investigation of positive individual characteristics: the strengths and the virtues. If we want to get the public, U.S. Congress, and the medical profession thinking about how to assess positive lives, then we need to move away from the DSM model (American Psychiatric Association, 1994). We need an alternative that is essentially the opposite of the DSM. In other words, we need a sensible classification of the strengths. One such classification was pioneered in 1999 by Don Clifton and is now being expanded by Chris Peterson. This effort, funded by the Mayerson Foundation, has identified 24 strengths and virtues that appear to be important across cultures and historical eras. The final product will allow us to assess how an individual is doing on such strengths and virtues as future-mindedness, leadership, kindness, integrity, originality, wisdom, and intimacy.

The third pillar of positive psychology is the study of positive institutions and positive communities. Sociology has languished in the same way as psychology; it has been mostly about disabling conditions, the "isms"—racism, sexism, and ageism—and how the isms ruin lives. Even if we were able to get rid of all those isms, we would still only be at zero. So positive psychology and positive sociology need to ask, "What are the institutions that take human beings *above* zero?"

Understanding incivility is a good example of where social science needs to head. Incivility makes you angry with the person who is uncivil to you, it makes you want revenge, and it causes your blood pressure to rise. But civility is not just the absence of incivility. Civility leads to what Barbara Fredrickson (1998) called the broadening and building of positive emotions. Civility moves you out of a defensive mode of arguing and into a creative, tolerant, and expansive mindset in which both parties benefit.

THE APPLICATIONS AND AIMS OF POSITIVE PSYCHOLOGY

Three applications will foster the three pillars of positive psychology. The first is assessment. The Gallup Foundation took the list of strengths and virtues that Clifton's group first offered and created Gallup-like questions for all of them. This 107-item questionnaire, called "Wellsprings," is about psychological health. It can be used to assess the health of an individual, a community, or even a nation. This approach holds the promise of augmenting economic indexes to reveal how a nation or a political system is doing on psychological grounds and how this changes over time.

A second application is intervention. Once we classify the strengths and virtues, we can ask which of those can be built and how. The third application is life-span development. How do the strengths and virtues change and interact with the world over the course of life? What are the early precursors of each? What are the enabling and disabling conditions for each?

The science of positive psychology should not be difficult to create because the science of mental illness has already done most of the methodological work. We can build on the progress in mental illness and use the same kinds of operational definitions, methods of assessment, structural equations, experimental methods, interventions, and outcome testing that the science of mental illness has pioneered. These are applicable, virtually in toto, to the science of positive psychology.

What are the long-term aims of positive psychology? The first is foster-ing better prevention by buffering. The second is supplementing the available techniques for therapy by training practitioners to identify and build strengths explicitly and systematically. The third is to curtail the promiscuous victimology that pervades the social sciences. In the disease model the underlying picture of the human being is pathology and passivity. The world acts on people and pushes a response out of them. Yet the more we convince people that they are passive victims, the more we *make* them passive and helpless (Seligman, 1975). The gospel of victimology is both misleading and, paradoxically, victimizing.

The fourth aim of positive psychology involves moving psychology from the egocentric to the philanthropic. I can best illustrate this point by telling you about my teaching experience recently. I gathered 20 Penn undergraduates for a positive psychology course. Each week, we read and we wrote essays. We also did weekly assignments based on what we had discussed in class. One week we were discussing Jonathan Haidt's work on elevation (Haidt, 2000; chapter 12, this volume). Haidt began his studies of morality with the negative emotion of social disgust, a response to the base, sleazy, or subhuman actions of other people. But then he began to wonder whether there was an opposite emotion triggered by the lofty, altruistic, or superhuman actions of other people. He began collecting and analyzing stories about times people had witnessed such actions and had been moved emotionally by them. One student at the University of Virginia told a story about a time she had been coming home from volunteering at the Salvation Army, right after a heavy snowfall, when one of her fellow volunteers asked the driver to let him out soon after they had passed an old woman trying to shovel her driveway. When the young woman saw that the other volunteer had walked back to help the old woman shovel her driveway, she was flooded with feelings. When asked to describe whether these feelings made her want to do anything, the woman wrote, "I felt like jumping out of the car and hugging this guy. I felt like singing and running, or skipping and laughing. Just being active. I felt like saying nice things about people. Writing a beautiful poem or love song. Playing in the snow like a child. Telling everybody about his deed" (Haidt, 2000).

Based on such reports, my class wondered if happiness comes from the exercise of kindness as readily as it does from pleasurable activities. After a heated debate, we undertook an assignment: We were each to do one enjoyable activity and one philanthropic activity (and write about both). The results were life-changing. The "enjoyable" activity (hanging out with friends, watching a movie) paled in comparison with the effects of kindness. When our philanthropic acts were spontaneous and when they called on our strengths, the whole day went better, whereas the pleasure of the enjoy-able acts faded immediately. One junior told about her nephew telephoning for help with his third-grade arithmetic. After an hour of tutoring him, she was surprised to discover that "for the rest of the day, I could listen better, I was mellower, and people liked me a lot more than usual." One of the business students volunteered that he had come to Penn to learn how to make a lot of money as a route to happiness, but he was floored to find that he was happier helping other people.

So this is my view of the science, the applications, and the long-range aims of positive psychology. My dream is that a science of positive psychology will be developed in the next few years and with it a profession of positive psychology. Its mission will be to assess and build human strength. My dream is that psychology will come to be about the building of strength, because it is precisely in building strength that psychologists are particularly skilled. My hope is that psychologists will be called on not just to heal damaged self-esteem but also to build a sense of worth based on real abilities. My hope is that psychologists will be asked not only to repair broken marriages but also to help couples rediscover ecstasy and friendship in marriage. My hope is that psychology will not simply work on how to prevent violence in youth but also on how to build morally exemplary youth. My hope is that we will not only explicate why we distrust our leaders, but we will also ask what trustworthiness *is* in a leader and how can we build it. My hope is that we will not just repair incivility in our national life but build civility. My hope is that psychology will discover not only how to make work less boring but how to find flow and meaning in work. My hope is that psychologists will be called on not only to relieve the pain and suffering of death but to help find dignity in dying.

When I ran for APA president in 1996, people asked me why an academic who had spent his life cloistered in his laboratory would do something as difficult and as aversive as trying to lead 150,000 psychologists. Bizarre as it may sound, I believed that I had a mission, but I did not know what the mission was. I believed that if I found myself in the position of leading American psychology, I would discover my mission. And, in that role, I did. That mission was, and is, to help build positive psychology.

REFERENCES

American Psychiatric Association. (1994). *Diagnostic and statistical manual of mental disorders* (4th ed.). Washington, DC: Author.

Bornstein, M. H., Davidson, L., Keyes, C. L. M., & Moore, K. A. (Eds.). (in press). *Well-being: Positive development throughout the life course*. Mahwah, NJ: Erlbaum.

Catalano, R., Berglund, M., Ryan, J., Lonczak, H., & Hawkins, J. (2002). Positive youth development in the United States: Research findings on evaluations of positive youth development programs. *Prevention and Treatment, 5,* Retrieved

June 24, 2002, from http://www.aspe.hhs.gov/hsp/positiveyouthdev99/prg0050
015a.html

Fredrickson, B. (1998). What good are positive emotions? *Review of General Psychology*, 2, 300–319.

Haidt, J. (2000). The positive emotion of elevation. *Prevention and Treatment*, 3, Retrieved from http://journals.apa.org/prevention/volume3/pre0030003c.html

Keyes, C. L. M., & Lopez, S. J. (2002). Toward a science of mental health: Positive directions in diagnosis and interventions. In C. R. Snyder & S. J. Lopez (Eds.), *Handbook of positive psychology* (pp. 45–59). New York: Oxford University Press.

Seligman, M. (1975). *Helplessness: On depression, development, and death*. San Francisco: Freeman.

Seligman, M. (1994). *What you can change and what you can't*. New York: Knopf.

Seligman, M. E. P. (2002). *Authentic happiness*. New York: Free Press.

Seligman, M. E. P., Reivich, K., Jaycox, L., & Gillham, J. (1995). *The optimistic child*. New York: Houghton-Mifflin.

FLOURISHING

INTRODUCTION: HUMAN FLOURISHING— THE STUDY OF THAT WHICH MAKES LIFE WORTHWHILE

COREY L. M. KEYES AND JONATHAN HAIDT

"To live is the rarest thing in the world. Most people exist, that is all."—Oscar Wilde (quoted in Seldes, 1985, p. 451)

Positive psychology aims to help people live and flourish rather than merely to exist. The term "positive psychology" may seem to imply that all other psychology is in some way negative, but that implication is unintended and untrue. However, the term positive psychology contains a softer indictment—namely, that psychology has become unbalanced. In the years since World War II psychology, guided by funding agencies of the era and the rising social conscience of its practitioners, has focused on helping people and society solve serious problems. Clinical psychology has focused on mental illness; social psychology has focused on prejudice, racism, and aggression; and cognitive psychology has focused on diagnosing the errors and biases that lead to bad decisions. There are good reasons to spend more time and money on illness and problems than on health and strengths. Utilitarianism, compassion, and a concern for equality suggest that people in great pain should be helped before those who are not suffering. But there are at least two costs to focusing on illnesses, problems, and weaknesses.

The first cost is an inappropriately negative view of human nature and the human condition. We teach psychology students about the many ways the mind can go wrong and about the frightening prevalence rates of depression, child abuse, and eating disorders. We teach students that people are fundamentally selfish creatures whose occasional good deeds are accidental products of self-esteem management. Is such cynicism and pessimism really justified?

3

Positive psychology is realistic. It does not claim that human nature is all sweetness and light, but it does offer a more balanced view. Most people are doing reasonably well in life and have the capacity to thrive and flourish, even when—or especially when—confronted with challenges, setbacks, and suffering (see chapters 1 and 2, this volume). Most people have experienced powerful feelings of moral elevation and inspiration that are unconnected to any need for self-esteem (see chapter 12, this volume). Positive psychology aims to balance out the overly negative picture painted by psychology to date.

The second cost of focusing on illnesses, problems, and weaknesses is that psychology restricts its focus and forgoes the possibility of making rapid scientific progress in unexplored fields. It may be more important to understand the causes of depression than the causes of happiness, and it may be more important to understand the causes of delinquency than the causes of good citizenship. But is it *infinitely* more important? It cannot be wise for psychology to encourage all of its best young researchers to tackle illnesses, problems, and weaknesses, leaving untouched many scientifically interesting and important questions. Even if one is primarily concerned with alleviating suffering, the chapters in this volume show that a full understanding of optimism, hope, well-being, vital engagement, goals, satisfactions of work and play, and community involvement may lead to therapies and interventions that reduce psychological suffering where Prozac and psychotherapies have failed.

In short, positive psychology is a view within scientific psychology that aims to achieve a balanced and empirically grounded body of research on human nature and social relations. In particular, advocates of positive psychology maintain that more work is needed in the areas of virtues; character strengths; and the social, psychological, and biological factors that enable human beings to flourish.

IT IS TIME FOR POSITIVE PSYCHOLOGY

The story of the 20th century in the behavioral and social sciences was "two steps forward, one step back." There were many steps forward: increased life expectancy, reduced infant mortality, reduced high school dropout rates, and reduced poverty among the elderly population. Yet despite progress in many fields, other social indicators have gotten worse. Rates of depression are high in adults and rising among youth (U.S. Department of Health and Human Services, 1999). There are more effective talk and drug therapies available now for depression than ever before, yet the benefits of these treatments are short-lived or partial. In their review, Keyes and Lopez (2002) argued that decades of mental illness research have made it possible to better treat more broken down people, but it has not made it possible to prevent more people from breaking down.

Although the Gross Domestic Product increased steadily during the last half of the 20th century, the United States took several steps backward socially (see Miringoff & Miringoff, 1999). There were steady increases between 1970 and 1996 in rates of child abuse, child poverty, and adolescent suicide. During that same period, the number of people uninsured for health care increased, rates of many violent crimes increased, and real wages diminished. Fewer individuals belonged to civic organizations and volunteering declined, while the disparity between the wealthiest and poorest Americans increased. In polls, most Americans grant that something is wrong with, and missing in, life in the United States: Life has become too materialistic, morality has waned, and the sense of community and social responsibility have faded (Myers, 2000; Putnam, 2000; Schorr, 1997).

Yet people aspire to a more meaningful and fulfilling life. The percentage of high school seniors who say that "making a contribution to society" is an "extremely important" life goal has increased steadily from 18% in 1976 to 24% in 1996 (Council of Economic Advisers, 1998). In a *New York Times Magazine* survey, adults were asked what they would do with three extra hours in a day that would make them more satisfied. Almost two thirds would spend time with family and another 11% with friends (Egan, 2000). Although people cannot create a 27-hour day, they can cut back to create more time in the 24-hour day. Thus, there are an increasing number of voluntary downsizers—adults who cutback on work in terms of position, time, or pay. Schor (1998) found that downsizers are motivated by a desire to create a life that is more healthy, meaningful, and balanced, with more time for loved ones and less focus on material wealth.

It is time for mainstream psychology to catch up with the struggles of the majority of humanity that is searching for ways to make life meaningful. Almost 40 years ago, Abraham Maslow (1965) proclaimed that "psychology ought to become more positive and less negative. It should have higher ceilings, and not be afraid of the loftier possibilities of the human being" (p. 27). Maslow and others created humanistic psychology, clearly a forerunner of positive psychology in its goals and concerns, and people flocked to its call. Over time, however, too many people with nonscientific agendas joined the humanists, and after 1969 the movement was taken over by the psychotherapeutic counterculture (Taylor, 2001). The mission of making mainstream psychology more positive and less negative was never accomplished.

Psychology remains today ill-equipped to help individuals to live healthier and more meaningful lives. It has a full box of tools to work on stress, disease, and dysfunction, but preventing the worst from happening does not equal promoting the best in people. Ryff and Singer (1998) argued that psychology needs to move beyond its status as a "repair shop" if it is to become a science that assists people in their pursuit of better, healthier, more meaningful lives. Sen. Robert Kennedy issued a similar challenge to the entire nation in 1968, shortly before his assassination, with these words:

> The Gross National Product does not allow for the health of our children, the quality of their education, or the joy of their play. It does not include the beauty of our poetry or the strength of our marriages; the intelligence of our public debate or the integrity of our public officials. It measures neither our wit nor our courage; neither our wisdom nor our learning; neither our compassion nor our devotion to our country; it measures everything, in short, except *that which makes life worthwhile*. (Guthman & Allen, 1993, p. 330, emphasis added)

The purpose of this volume is to begin to study "that which makes life worthwhile," and to investigate some possible mechanisms for promoting the ranks of healthy, productive, happy, and flourishing individuals.

FLOURISHING: TOWARD A LIFE WELL-LIVED

Flourishing, for Keyes (chapter 13, this volume), exemplifies mental health. Not only are flourishing individuals free of mental illness, they also are filled with emotional vitality and they are functioning positively in the private and social realms of their lives. Far from being supermen or superwomen, flourishing individuals are truly living rather than merely existing.

Positive psychology is not self-help, but it is research that is meant to help people. Similarly, this book is not a manual on "How to Flourish," but it offers empirically grounded advice for getting more out of life. We, the editors, often felt inspired to make changes in our lives as we read these chapters and we hope that you will too. The chapters fit into four categories representing major imperatives about living a good life—Part I: Rise to life's challenges, making the most out of your setbacks and adversities; Part II: engage with and relate to other people; Part III: find fulfillment in creativity and productivity; and Part IV look beyond oneself and help others to find lasting meaning, satisfaction, and wisdom in life. The final section, Part V, describes one of positive psychology's calls to action, which is to increase the number of children and adults who are genuinely mentally healthy, or flourishing in life.

RISE TO LIFE'S CHALLENGES

Positive psychology aims to better understand how individuals can negotiate, resolve, and grow in the face of life's stressors and challenges.

Ryff and Singer's chapter 1, aptly titled "Flourishing Under Fire," reviews the large and still growing literature on human resilience, which has become a central construct in research on human development. The authors examine how individuals remain or become healthy despite risk and adversity, illustrating the relevance of resilience throughout the human life span, and they simultaneously stress the importance of integrating the biological substrate of resilience with extant paradigms that emphasize the psychological aspects of resilience.

In chapter 2 on turning points and personal growth, Wethington merges two important literatures. First, she draws on John Clausen's seminal work on psychological turning points to place individuals within the ongoing challenge of life-course transitions and changes. Second, she focuses on an important marker of human health—personal growth—which originates with Aristotle's conception of *Eudaimonia* and has been operationalized by Carol Ryff. Wethington provides us with a better understanding of how and when individuals are likely to learn important lessons about life, about themselves, and about other people as they experience psychological turning points, which are major transformations in views about the self, identity, or the meaning of life.

In chapter 3, Peterson and Chang review the large literature on optimism and its connections to human flourishing. The motivating question behind this research has been how individuals respond to adversity and setbacks as well as success and achievement. Using dispositional and cognitive (i.e., explanatory styles) conceptions of optimism and pessimism, the authors illustrate how optimism is a protective factor and how pessimism is a risk factor for physical and mental disease. However, in an important message for positive psychology, Peterson and Chang also show how culture and context may moderate the relationship of optimism and pessimism with health outcomes. They review research showing that the usual connections of optimism and pessimism with health outcomes may be inverted in collectivistic cultures, where pessimism may act as a protective factor and optimism may operate more like a risk factor.

ENGAGE AND RELATE

When John Donne said, "No man is an island," he was foreshadowing one of the major ingredients of flourishing: reaching out and engaging with others and with one's environment. The three chapters in this section work together to show how people create lives that feel rich and meaningful.

Chapters 4 by Nakamura and Czikszentmihalyi and 5 by Emmons show us that flourishing requires a kind of reaching out: the setting of goals, followed by active and energetic engagement with those goals.

Nakamura and Csikszentmihalyi tell us how people can enter a state of "vital engagement" with the tasks they undertake. They tackle the big question of meaning in life directly, asking how a sense of meaning emerges in daily life. They begin with an analysis of the psychological state of flow, a state of full absorption in an activity that challenges one's abilities and reduces one's sense of self-consciousness. Flow is deeply pleasurable, but Nakamura and Czikszentmihalyi point out that flourishing must entail more than just stringing together periods of deep pleasure. The great contribution of this chapter is to put forth a theory of flow-derived emergent meaning. Building on classic social interactionist theorists (e.g., John Dewey and G. H. Mead), they illustrate how a sense of meaning emerges over time as people experience flow in activities that link them to larger pursuits and to other people.

Emmons reviews research on the kinds of personal goals or "strivings" that people pursue and on the relationships between goal pursuit and subjective well-being (happiness). He tells us that goal pursuit is not uniformly good; the costs and benefits of striving vary with the kind of goal pursued, and he offers an intriguing taxonomy of the "big four" domains of striving. Emmons's work has important clinical applications, as can be seen in his description of his recent work with people suffering from degenerative neuro-muscular diseases. In a group of people whose objective well-being is clearly declining, the manner in which individuals set goals and strive to reach them turns out to be a major determinant of subjective well-being.

Theorists from Aristotle ("man is a social animal") through Freud ("love and work") have stressed the importance of social relationships for human happiness. But in chapter 6, Reis and Gable go further, making the valuable distinction between positive and negative psychological processes at work in close relationships. Based on a wide-ranging review, Reis and Gable argue that positive processes (based on appetitive systems in the brain) should be seen and studied as functionally independent of negative processes (based on aversive systems). Yet as in so much of psychology, researchers have focused on the negative—on conflict and on the role of relationships as buffers against stress—and assumed that the positive aspects of relationships were a result of the absence of negatives. Reis and Gable show us what a "positive psychology of relationships" would look like, a psychology that explores the active ingredients of such things as intimacy, affection, and shared fun.

FIND FULFILLMENT IN CREATIVITY AND PRODUCTIVITY

As Martin Seligman reminded us during his APA presidency, one of the original missions of psychology was to promote creativity and fulfillment.

Somewhere this mission was lost. The authors in this section seek to reclaim that mission for psychology.

Hence, this section begins with Cassandro and Simonton's chapter 7 on creativity and genius. These authors review a rich literature describing the nature, kinds, and measures of creativity and genius. Although the chapter draws on historical exemplars of creativity and genius, it challenges positive psychology to discover how these cultural goods can be nurtured in more members of successive generations. The authors show us how the products of creators have enabled flourishing for the rest of us, and how the process of creativity may also promote flourishing in the creator.

Wrzesniewski, Rozin, and Benett's chapter 8 focuses on the concept of fulfillment in daily life. The authors point out that most of our lives are taken up with work, leisure, and eating, and it is therefore here that we should think about how to get more out of each moment of our lives. The chapter then inquires into the mechanisms whereby individuals might gain such fulfillment by looking at how orientations toward work, play, and food affect what people get out of those activities. For example, Wrzesniewski and colleagues review research showing that individuals have distinct orientations toward employment: People may view work as a calling, as a career, or as a paycheck (instrumentally). Rather than argue that more people need to view work as a calling to gain more satisfaction from work, these authors suggest that a positive psychology of work should seek to better understand how contexts may be shaped to provide satisfaction for all people. Thus, rather than simply shape the person to the situation, these authors remind us that a positive psychology also should shape the situation to fit the individual.

Chapter 9 by Harter, Schmidt, and Keyes poses a central question for positive psychology: What is the utility of promoting workplace well-being? As Wrzesniewski, Rozin, and Bennett point out in the previous chapter, work takes up the largest share of an adult's waking life. The challenge for positive psychology is to show that the promotion of positive things in employees and in the workplace can add to the "bottom line" of a business. First, this chapter reviews models of employee well-being, a central component of which is employee's growth and development. Based on a meta-analysis of numerous studies, this chapter then shows that profits, productivity, employee retention, and customer satisfaction all increase as the level of workplace well-being, particularly employee personal growth, increases. In short, bottom-line outcomes are linked with the promotion of well-being in the workplace.

LOOK BEYOND ONESELF

The ancient Greeks were very concerned with the question, Why be virtuous, in cases where it is not good for you? In the dialogue, "Protagoras,"

Plato argued that people are naturally drawn to the good, once it is clear to them. The three chapters in this section support Plato's hopes. People benefit from helping others (Piliavin); as they gain in wisdom they integrate ethical concerns into their practical deliberations (Baltes and Freund); and people experience the positive emotion of elevation when they witness acts of moral beauty (Haidt).

In chapter 10 Piliavin gives us a magnificent review of a large and complicated literature: the effects of volunteering on the volunteer. American society in the 1990s experimented widely with a variety of service learning and volunteer programs for children and adolescents, as well as for elderly adults. Do such programs really work? A clear empirical answer to this question is critical, as large sums of money are spent on them. The answer Piliavin give us is an emphatic "yes," but with just the sorts of qualifiers that we need to design intelligent programs. Piliavin shows us what kinds of benefits have been studied (emotional benefits, reductions in dropout rates and antisocial activity, increased learning), and points out that different kinds of activities lead to different patterns of benefits at different ages. Most of the research so far has been correlational, and Piliavin is always cautious about extracting causal claims from such studies. However, because a few of the studies reviewed used random assignment to helping versus nonhelping conditions, Piliavin is able to guide us to the conclusion that people really can "do well by doing good."

Baltes and Freund in chapter 11 tackle one of the hardest problems in the human sciences: What is wisdom? Their article begins by summarizing the pioneering research of Baltes's group in Berlin on this question (wisdom is a metaheuristic "aimed at organizing and guiding the overall conduct of life towards excellence," but that is just a foreshadowing of their approach). They then do something completely new: They link up their research on wisdom with more recent work on the Selective Optimization with Compensation model, a model derived from life-span developmental psychology of how people pursue goals in any domain. This marriage of models gives us a comprehensive way of thinking about how people choose ends (integrating ethical and practical concerns) and the means to achieve those ends.

In chapter 12, Haidt introduces a potentially new moral emotion: elevation. Elevation is triggered by witnessing displays of compassion, courage, loyalty, or almost any other moral virtue. Elevation typically involves warm or open feelings in the chest, and it motivates people to want to rise to their own moral potential. The mere existence of elevation pushes us toward a more positive view of human nature, a view in which people are built to respond to moral beauty. Of course elevation is not a "new" emotion; it is well-known in many religious traditions and on daytime talk shows that aim to inspire their audiences. Haidt raises the question: Why then has Western emotion theory not noticed this positive moral emotion? The answer appears to be in part that psychology has spent too much time focusing on the negative emotions. Haidt ends his chapter with suggestions for a positive psychology of morality, including focusing on the positive emotions, looking to other cultures for guidance, and examining peak experiences and moral transformations.

CONCLUSION

The stated mission of the National Institute of Mental Health (NIMH) is to promote the mental health of the U.S. population. Its modus operandi, since its inception in 1946, has been the study, treatment, and prevention of mental illnesses. However, Keyes's research shows that measures of common mental illness (e.g., depression) are correlated with, but form a separate factor from, the measures he and colleagues have developed to measure and diagnose mental health. Thus, even if we could treat all known cases of mental illness and prevent the onset of any new cases, there is no reason to believe that this would result in more mentally healthy people in the population; it does result in fewer mentally unhealthy people in the population.

In addition to offering a diagnosis for mental health, chapter 13 reveals that the absence of mental health—languishing in life—is more prevalent than major depression. Languishing adults are neither mentally ill nor mentally healthy; instead, they are "running on empty," living lives of quiet despair, and their psychosocial functioning is comparable to depressed individuals. Moreover, adults who are flourishing—filled with emotional, psychological, and social well-being and free of mental illness—have better psychosocial profiles than languishing or depressed adults. To achieve the goal of widespread mental health, therefore, NIMH and psychology as a whole should think about flourishing and languishing. We must work together to study and promote "that which makes life worthwhile." That is the call to action that positive psychology issues in the first years of the 21st century.

REFERENCES

Council of Economic Advisers. (1998). *Changing America: Indicators of social and economic well-being by race and Hispanic origin*. Retrieved July 15, 2002, at http://w3.access.gpo.gov/eop/ca/pdfs/ca.pdf

Egan, J. (2000, May 7). Walking toward mindfulness. *New York Times Magazine*, 86–90.

Guthman, E. O., & Allen, C. R. (Eds.). (1993). *RFK: Collected speeches*. New York: Viking Penguin.

Keyes, C. L. M., & Lopez, S. J. (2002). Toward a science of mental health: Positive directions in diagnosis and interventions. In C. R. Snyder & S. J. Lopez (Eds.), *Handbook of positive psychology* (pp. 45–59). New York: Oxford University Press.

Maslow, A. H. (1965). A philosophy of psychology: The need for a mature science of human nature. In F. T. Severin (Ed.), *Humanistic viewpoints in psychology* (pp. 17–33). New York: McGraw-Hill.

Miringoff, M., & Miringoff, M-L. (1999). *The social health of the nation: How America is really doing*. New York: Oxford University Press.

Myers, D. G. (2000). *The American paradox: Spiritual hunger in an age of plenty*. New Haven, CT: Yale University Press.

Putnam, R. D. (2000). *Bowling alone: The collapse and revival of American community*. New York: Simon and Schuster.

Ryff, C. D., & Singer, B. (1998). The contours of positive human health. *Psychological Inquiry, 9*, 1–28.

Schor, J. B. (1998). *The overspent American: Upscaling, downshifting, and the new consumer*. New York: Basic Books.

Schorr, L. B. (1997). *Common purpose: Strengthening families and neighborhoods to rebuild America*. New York: Anchor Books.

Seldes, G. (1985). *The great thoughts*. New York: Ballantine Books.

Taylor, E. (2001). Positive psychology and humanistic psychology: A reply to Seligman. *The Journal of Humanistic Psychology, 41*, 13–29.

U.S. Department of Health and Human Services. (1999). *Mental health: A report of the Surgeon General*. Rockville, MD: Author.

I

RISE TO LIFE'S CHALLENGES

1

FLOURISHING UNDER FIRE: RESILIENCE AS A PROTOTYPE OF CHALLENGED THRIVING

CAROL D. RYFF AND BURTON SINGER

Positive human functioning is perhaps most remarkable when evident in contexts of significant life challenge and adversity. It is then, when individuals are being tested, that much becomes known about human strengths—what they are, how they come about, how they are nurtured or undermined. The growing literature on human resilience addresses this juxtaposition of being well in the face of difficulty. In this chapter, we briefly examine previous research on resilience—how the construct has been defined and measured and what have been identified as key protective factors and resources to account for such resilience. We consider these questions with a brief focus on studies of children as well as more lengthy consideration of research on adults and elderly individuals (where our own work has been conducted). Investigations of resilience are increasingly prominent in both phases of life. We then compare studies of resilience conducted at these early and later periods of the life course, giving emphasis to how the two literatures inform each other. We conclude the chapter with a discussion of targeted research priorities designed to extend and apply knowledge of positive human functioning in the face of challenge—in other words, the capacity to flourish under fire.

What follows this introduction rests on the premise that the study of flourishing (i.e., delineating positive features of the human condition) and

This research was supported by the John D. and Catherine T. MacArthur Foundation Research Network on Successful Midlife Development (Ryff), the Socioeconomic Status and Health Network (Singer), and grants from the National Institute on Aging (R01AG08979—Ryff and Essex, R01AG013613—Ryff and Singer), the National Institute of Mental Health (P50-MH61083), and National Institute of Health Center for Research Resources to the University of Wisconsin–Madison General Clinical Research Center (M01 RR03186).

the study of resilience (i.e., elaborating the capacity to prevail in the face of adversity) yield fruitful advances when joined together. Conceptions of flourishing articulate the nature of human strengths and well-being and thereby offer enriched formulations of what it means to thrive under challenge. Much of the literature on resilience has emphasized the avoidance of negative outcomes (e.g., psychological, social, emotional, or physical problems), rather than the presence of positive outcomes. Alternatively, the study of resilience brings to the literature on flourishing greater insight about how human strengths come to be, including the observation that they are sometimes forged in trial and tribulation. At the extreme end, in fact, is the proposition that particular heights of the human experience, what some call thriving, are known *only* by those who have run the gauntlet. Whether ultimate human strengths emerge from extremes of human suffering is an open and controversial question. We do not invoke the necessity that one must know pain to find the essence of what is good in life; rather, we see research on resilience as a valuable realm of balance. That is, it draws on the negative in human experience by articulating the many ways in which life can be hard, but it also emphasizes the positive in describing how some, despite (or because of) their travail, are able to love, work, play— in short, embrace life. Such a combination avoids the sometimes excessively upbeat tone that accompanies studies of well-being or the overdone darkness characterizing research on human maladies. William James (1902/1958) richly depicted this contrast long ago, with his juxtaposition of "healthy-mindedness" and "the sick soul." A leading challenge of the present era is to recognize both darkness and light as central to understanding the human condition.

RESILIENCE IN CHILDHOOD: CLASSIC STUDIES AND NEW VENUES

In reviewing the literature on childhood resilience, we first examine five types of adversity to which children have been exposed, and then consider the factors studied as possible protective influences. We also address work that conceptualizes resilience from a personality perspective. We conclude the section on childhood with consideration of needed next steps to advance the research.

Varieties of Childhood Risk

The study of resilience in childhood was launched by several classic investigations that revolved around children living under adverse conditions.

Rutter's 10-year study, for example, focused on children whose parents were diagnosed as mentally ill. The intriguing finding was that many of these children did not themselves become mentally ill or exhibit maladaptive behaviors (Rutter, 1985, 1987; Rutter, Maughan, Mortimore, & Ouston, 1979). Based on these observations, Rutter formulated resilience as the positive pole of an individual's response to stress and adversity (Rutter, 1990). *Positive* in Rutter's work frequently referred to the absence of the negative (e.g., adverse temperament, conduct disorders, affective disorders, depression) in overall functioning.

In other classic work, Garmezy and colleagues (Garmezy, 1991, 1993; Garmezy, Masten, & Tellegen, 1984) followed children from low socioeconomic status backgrounds who lived among negative family environments. Again, although some showed less competence and more disruptive profiles, others of these disadvantaged children were judged to be competent (by teachers, peers, school records) and did not display behavior problems. Studies of children of schizophrenic mothers also played a crucial role in Garmezy and Masten's formulations of childhood resilience. Many of these children thrived despite their high-risk status (Garmezy, 1974; Garmezy & Streitman, 1974; Masten, Best, & Garmezy, 1990). In these investigations, resilience was formulated as the capacity for recovery and maintaining adaptive functioning following incapacity (Garmezy, 1991) or the positive side of adaptation after extenuating circumstances (Masten, 1989).

Other pioneering research was conducted by Werner and colleagues (Werner, 1993, 1995; Werner & Smith, 1977), who followed a cohort of children born in Kauai for more than three decades, one third of whom were designated as high-risk because they were born into poverty and lived in troubled environments (parental psychopathology, family discord, poor child-rearing conditions). Of these high-risk children, one third grew up to be competent, confident, and caring adults. Werner's conception of resilience emphasized sustained competence under stress (Werner, 1995; Werner & Smith, 1992).

Protective Factors

Across these studies, there was pervasive interest in factors that could help account for positive responses to stress or adversity (Masten & Garmezy, 1985; Rutter, 1985). The aim was to show *how* children exposed to chronic poverty, parental psychopathology, parental divorce, serious care-giving deficits, or the horrors of war did not show psychological or health dysfunction. Werner (1995) referred to such factors as the mechanisms that moderate (ameliorate) a person's reaction to a stressful situation or chronic adversity so that adaptation is more successful than if protective factors were absent.

Frequent candidates to account for stress resistance in children have included temperament and personality attributes, family cohesion and warmth, and external social supports (Garmezy, 1993), as well as high IQ, problem-solving abilities, quality parenting, stable families, and high socioeconomic status (Garmezy et al., 1984). Masten's (1999) "short list" of protective factors included parenting quality, intellectual functioning, and self-perceptions (e.g., self-efficacy). Proffering an organizational framework, Werner (1995) distinguished between protective factors *within the individual* (e.g., affectionate and good-natured in infancy and early childhood; outgoing, active, autonomous, bright, and possessing positive self-concepts in middle childhood and adolescence); those *in the family* (close bonds with at least one nurturing, competent, emotionally stable parent); and those *in the community* (support and counsel from peers and elders in the community). Analytically, such protective factors have been construed as compensatory factors that have direct, independent effects on outcomes (Garmezy et al., 1984; Masten, 1989) or as interactive influences that moderate the effects of exposure to risk (Rutter, 1985, 1987; Zimmerman & Arunkumar, 1994).

Resilient Personalities

Other lines of resilience research in childhood emerged, not from the study of children growing up under adverse circumstance but from longitudinal studies of personality. The typological work of Jack Block (1971; Block & Block, 1980) described the "ego-resilients" among adolescents and young adults as those who were well-adjusted and interpersonally effective. Other personality studies (Robins, John, Caspi, Moffitt, & Stouthamer-Loeber, 1996) have adopted a typological approach to resilience. In a mixed ethnic sample of adolescent boys, those with resilient personality profiles were described as assertive, verbally expressive, energetic, personable, dependable, open-minded, smart, and self-confident. They explored implications of such characteristics for subsequent developmental problems and outcomes—those with resilient personalities were found to be successful in school, unlikely to be delinquents, and relatively free of psychopathology.

Luthar (1991) also focused on high-risk adolescents, defining risk both in terms of negative life events and sociodemographic variables (e.g., family size, ethnicity, parents' education, and occupation). The central question was why some inner-city ninth graders with high profiles of risk were able to maintain socially competent behaviors (measured by teacher ratings, grades, peer ratings). Moderator variables such as intelligence, internal locus of control, social skills, ego development, and positive life events were investigated. Ego development was found to be a compensatory factor directly related to competence, whereas locus of control and social skills emerged as interactive, moderating factors. It is important to note that this study revealed that those labeled as resilient were also significantly more depressed and anxious than competent children from low-stress backgrounds. Thus, their apparent strengths were accompanied by select areas of vulnerability.

Needed Next Steps

Recent reviews of the burgeoning literature on resilience in childhood and adolescence (Glantz & Sloboda, 1999; Luthar, Cicchetti, & Becker, 2000; Masten, 1999) underscore the need for greater operational precision and consistency in defining resilience as well as in specifying protective and vulnerability factors. The multidimensional nature of resilience—the fact that resilience in one realm does not guarantee resilient in all realms (e.g., educationally, emotionally, behaviorally)—has received increased attention, along with greater emphasis on the "ontogenetic instability" of resilience (i.e., whether high-risk individuals *maintain* consistently positive adjustment over the long term). Complexity is another recurrent theme in these reviews—the idea that resilience involves a complex interplay of multiple influences over time and that magic-bullet explanations are not likely to be found. Although personal characteristics of individuals continue to receive attention, there is growing emphasis on the important contexts surrounding children's lives (Taylor & Wang, 2000)—in the family, in the community and neighborhood, and even the surrounding cultural context. Across these reviews, resilience researchers underscore the need to *measure* risk factors, rather than infer them or assume they are present. Not all children exposed to parental psychopathology or alcoholism have experienced abusive or neglectful parenting, for example.

From the perspective of human flourishing, it is noteworthy that scholars of childhood resilience struggle with the task of delineating what constitutes positive adaptation: Should it be construed as secure attachments, development of autonomous self, emotional health, academic success, or positive relationship with peers? Further, should these constructs be integrated to create composite constructs of positive adaptation? Distinctions between adequate versus excellent functioning, between surviving and thriving are recurrently emphasized. Luthar and Cushing (1999), for example, distinguish between competence and absence of maladjustment in defining resilient outcomes. There is also growing awareness of the need to assess adjustment from multiple vantage points: parents, teachers, peers, as well as levels of academic success or performance on standardized achievement tests. Comparative referents may be important—in other words, good adjustment among those in high-risk groups may not indicate competence among those in more typical, low-risk groups.

RESILIENCE IN ADULTHOOD AND LATER LIFE

After childhood and adolescence, the literature on resilience takes two primary forms. The first deals directly with the challenges of aging and how they are successfully negotiated. The second addresses the emergent literature growth through trauma—in other words, how it is possible that positive outcomes can be products of suffering. Both of these realms are briefly summarized next, although comparatively greater emphasis is given to the challenges of aging, because this is the emphasis of our research.

Challenges of Aging

Among researchers who explicitly address the life course significance of resilience, Staudinger, Marsiske, and Baltes (1995) have distinguished between resilience as maintenance of development despite the presence of risk and resilience as recovery from trauma. They have given particular emphasis to the idea of reserve capacity, a construct from life-span developmental theory referring to an individual's potential for change, especially continued growth. Their chapter provides an extensive review of previous research in multiple aging domains (i.e., cognition, self, social transactions). Although the aging studies document positive functioning in diverse areas, they do not frequently incorporate assessments of the actual challenges or risks of aging, and few investigations include explicit measures of developmental reserve/continued growth particularly as linked with risk or threat.

Extending the childhood emphasis on resilience as a personality characteristic, Klohnen has emphasized an adult version of ego resiliency, which is defined as a "personality resource that allows individuals to modify their characteristic level and habitual mode of expression of ego-control so as to most adaptively encounter, function in, and shape their immediate and long-term environmental contexts" (1996, p. 1067). Klohnen has found strong relationships between ego resiliency and effective functioning in diverse areas of life (e.g., global adjustment, work and social adjustment, physical and psychological health).

Our program of research has emphasized the distinction between resilience as an outcome and resilience as a dynamic process (Ryff, Singer, Love, & Essex, 1998). As an outcome, we have defined resilience as the *maintenance, recovery, or improvement in mental or physical health following challenge.* Such a formulation goes beyond earlier conceptions focused on absence-of-illness indicators of resilience (e.g., *not* becoming depressed, anxious, or physically ill in the face of adversity). Mentally, we have focused on psychological well-being, which is a multidimensional model that gives emphasis to positive self-regard, quality ties to others, capacity to manage one's surrounding environment, having purpose and meaningful engagement, and continued growth and development (see Ryff, 1989; Ryff & Keyes, 1995). We also bring physical health into the definition of resilience, thereby underscoring a joint emphasis on the mind and the body in understanding optimal functioning in adulthood and later life. Positive physical health, like mental health, includes not only the absence of illness (e.g., avoidance of disease, chronic conditions, health symptoms, physical limitations) but also the presence of the positive (e.g., functional abilities, aerobic capacities, healthy behaviors—diet, exercise, sleep).

Life challenge is fundamental to our conception of resilience as a process. Thus, the model is not about lives of smooth sailing where all goes well and one manages to evade adversity but rather is about successful *engagement* with difficult events and experiences. The later years are replete with such challenge (i.e., acute health events, loss events such as retirement or widowhood, chronic stress such as caregiving, transitions such as relocation), making old age a particularly valuable period for understanding how challenges are successfully negotiated. A central feature of our studies is the tracking of these naturally occurring challenges as well as their accumulation over time. How individuals remain healthy and well in the face of cumulative challenge is a fundamental route to understanding resilience as a dynamic process.

The specific naturally occurring life challenges we have studied include normative transitions, critical and unexpected events, and chronically occurring difficulties. To illustrate the more planned and typical challenges of adult life, we have studied the experience of having and raising children (i.e., the challenges of being a parent) to assess its impact on the well-being of parents (Ryff, Lee, Essex, & Schmutte, 1994; Ryff & Seltzer, 1996). Other investigations have focused on the physical health challenges that accompany aging (Heidrich & Ryff, 1993a, 1993b, 1996) or on later life transitions (studied longitudinally), such as community relocation (Kling, Ryff, & Essex, 1997; Kling, Seltzer, & Ryff, 1997; Smider, Essex, & Ryff, 1996). Related investigations, using psychological well-being as outcome measures, have examined the challenges of caregiving (Li, Seltzer, & Greenberg, 1999; Marks, 1998), marital transitions (Marks & Lambert, 1998), career achievements (Carr, 1997), and goal pursuits (McGregor & Little, 1998).

Regarding unexpected and adverse experiences, we have also studied how growing up with an alcoholic parent (Tweed & Ryff, 1991) or having a child with Down syndrome (Van Riper, Ryff, & Pridham, 1992) influences adult psychological well-being. Drawing connection to the growing literature on social inequalities, we have examined how position in the socioeconomic hierarchies, such as persistent educational and economic disadvantage, is tied to psychological well-being (Marmot, Ryff, Bumpass, Shipley, & Marks,

1997; Ryff, Magee, Kling, & Wing, 1999). Finally, in recent work with the Wisconsin Longitudinal Study, we have examined the influence of cumulative life adversity (and advantage) on well-being (Singer & Ryff, 1999; Singer, Ryff, Carr, & Magee, 1998). This latter work goes beyond the focus on single life challenges to assessment of the impact of cumulative experience in multiple life domains.

Across these numerous investigations, empirical findings have documented that, indeed, many individuals are able to maintain, or even enhance, their well-being as they encounter various life challenges. For example, our longitudinal research on community relocation has shown that a substantial proportion of aging women sustain high levels of well-being, or actually improve, over the course of this later life transition (Ryff et al., 1998). Speaking to the question of protective resources, these studies have also clarified that those who show *gains* in multiple aspects of well-being following relocation are persons with flexible self-concepts (i.e., the capacity to change what is defined as central to one's self-definition; Kling, Ryff, et al., 1997) and effective coping strategies (e.g., problem-focused coping; Kling, Seltzer, et al., 1997). We have also documented that having psychological resources (e.g., high levels of environmental mastery or autonomy) before the move (i.e., pre-move levels of well-being) clarifies who will show positive emotional reactions shortly after the move (Smider et al., 1996).

In other aging studies, both cross-sectional and longitudinal, our work has shown that some individuals are able to maintain high levels of well-being in the face of increased chronic health conditions (Heidrich & Ryff, 1993a, 1993b, 1996). The respondents' levels of social integration (e.g., having meaningful roles and reference groups) and their effective use of social comparison processes (e.g., perceiving that one is doing well relative to others in multiple domains of life) have helped differentiate those who sustain high well-being from those who do not. These aging studies intersect with epidemiological research (e.g., Singer & Manton, 1998), which shows that rates of later life disability are, at the population level, *declining*. Our more targeted studies with smaller, frequently longitudinal samples provide clues to the kinds of psychological and social factors that possibly contribute to the maintenance of health and well-being in the later years. Alternatively, the population profiles of chronic conditions and functional capacities show trends toward better health but lack formulation and assessment of factors to account for such changes. Both agendas underscore the theme of positive health and well-being in later life.

Regarding more atypical and unexpected life challenges, such as having a child with mental retardation or growing up with an alcoholic parent (Seltzer & Ryff, 1994; Tweed & Ryff, 1991; Van Riper et al., 1992), our studies again have documented that many parents of children with disabilities do, in fact, have high well-being (at levels comparable to matched parents of nondisabled children) and that many adult children of alcoholics also show numerous psychological strengths. Still other investigations of parenting (in both the normative and nonnormative cases) have clarified *how* particular psychosocial processes (e.g., coping strategies, social comparisons, attribution processes) differentiate between parents who do, and do not, have high well-being with regard to the challenges of parenting (Kling, Seltzer, et al., 1997; Ryff et al., 1994; Ryff, Schmutte, & Lee, 1996).

Most of the findings described have explored the impact of single events or specific experiences on well-being. A key objective has also been to shift the focus to more *cumulative* profiles of life adversity and advantage (Singer et al., 1998). Such questions emerged from earlier work on career trajectories of women in science, where the accumulation of negative events was a guiding theme in explaining differential achievement patterns (Cole & Singer, 1991). These ideas were incorporated into our work with the Wisconsin Longitudinal Study (WLS), where we quantified cumulative experience in a life history framework. This research focused on a particular version of resilience—namely, the recovery of high well-being following the experience of major depression. We asked what are the life histories of such individuals who recover high levels of psychological well-being following an episode of depression? What have been their previous experiences of adversity, likely implicated in their experiences with depression, but also what have been their experiences of advantage, possibly contributing to their recovery from depression?

Our analyses of such resilient women in the WLS used person-centered life history techniques to identify multiple life pathways to midlife recovery of high well-being. Some of these individuals had experienced adverse events early in life (e.g., parental alcoholism, death of parent, limited parental income or education), but such difficult beginnings were accompanied by later experiences of advantage (e.g., upward occupational mobility, close ties to spouse). Other women experienced major adversity in adult life (e.g., unemployment, single parenting, spousal drinking, having caregiving roles), but their challenges were offset by good starting resources (e.g., high school abilities, adequate parental income and education; see Singer et al., 1998, for details of four primary pathways of histories).

Collectively, these investigations have illustrated that many midlife and aging adults are, in fact, able to maintain, or regain, their health and well-being following engagement with significant challenge, both expected (normative) and unexpected (nonnormative). These studies have used psychological well-being as a measure of flourishing in the face of such challenge, and with regard to understanding the process of resilience, have targeted various psychological and social protective factors (e.g., coping strategies, flexible self-concepts, quality relationships with others, positive comparison processes).

Growth Through Trauma: Thriving vis-à-vis Crisis

In the past decade, considerable interest has been given to the positive aftermath of life crises such as bereavement, illness, captivity, major accidents, chronic disability, abuse. This research does not have an explicit focus on aging or life-course perspectives, but rather is applied to samples of diverse ages confronting diverse challenges. The central theme, however, is that of articulating positive consequences of traumatic experience. Tedeschi and Calhoun (1995) suggested that growth after suffering can include such outcomes as new perceptions of one's self (e.g., feeling stronger and more self-assured, increased self-reliance); gains in recognizing and appreciating one's own vulnerability; change in relationships with others (e.g., closer family ties, greater appreciation of significant others, greater self-disclosure and emotional expressiveness); changed philosophy of life (e.g., taking things easier, knowing what is important, greater spirituality).

More recently, Tedeschi, Park, and Calhoun (1998) have elaborated ideas of rebirth, renewal, and bouncing back. Trauma in this framework thus becomes a possible springboard for additional growth and development. Posttraumatic growth (PTG), a term juxtaposed with posttraumatic stress disorder (PTSD), underscores the significant beneficial change that can occur in cognitive and emotional life (both having behavioral implications) following significant suffering. This realm of inquiry draws on existential philosophy, such as Frankl's logotherapy, and applies the perspectives to numerous contexts of bereavement, chronic illness and disability, HIV infection, cancer, heart attack, medical problems of children, transportation accidents, house fires, rape, and sexual abuse. Researchers in this area see PTG as related to constructs of resilience, sense of coherence, hardiness, stress inoculation, toughening, but their emphasis is on refining formulations of the types of growth that can follow crises: perceiving of oneself as survivor rather than victim; increased self-reliance and self-efficacy; heightened awareness of one's own vulnerability and mortality; improvement in ties to others—greater self-disclosure and emotional expressiveness, more compassion and capacity to give to others; clearer philosophy of life—renewed sense of priorities and appreciation of life, deeper sense of meaning and spirituality.

Personality researchers have also been drawn to ideas of growth through trauma. Aldwin and Sutton (1998) described life stress, for example, as a context for personality development in adulthood—in other words, a forum for increasing coping skills, self-esteem, self-confidence, and self-knowledge. Their work underscores the need for greater differentiation between growth and denial. Emmons, Colby, and Kaiser (1998) draw on goal perspectives to examine when losses lead to gains. They emphasize the importance of being able, in context of traumatic events, to feel pleasure when desirable events occur, to feel hopeful regarding the future, to plan and care about plans. Their research shows that goal change does not necessarily follow trauma; rather, lack of goal change was associated with recovery from loss. Moreover, those committed to spiritual and religious goals were more likely to say they had both recovered from loss and found meaning in it.

Tennen and Affleck (1998) pointed to additional personality characteristics that seem to contribute to thriving in face of adversity, such as dispositional optimism and hope, cognitive- and self-complexity, and intrinsic religiousness. Park (1998) noted that some people describe their traumatic experience as the "best thing that ever happened to me," and also suggested that optimism and hope, spirituality and religiousness, extraversion, and the appraisal and coping processes are personal characteristics relevant to understanding growth following adversity.

Carver distinguished between resilience and thriving, defining the former as a homeostatic return to earlier levels of functioning. Thriving, however, is more than recovery of homeostatic maintenance—it is being better off after the traumatic experience. The "person who experiences thriving comes to function at a continuing higher level than was the case before adverse event" (1998, p. 250). Such thriving can involve newly developed skills, confidence and sense of mastery, and strengthened personal relations. Similarly, Saakvitne, Tennen, and Affleck (1998) suggested that trauma can be transformative, leading to the reconstruction of meaning, renewal of faith, trust, hope, and connection, and redefinition of self, oneself, and sense of community.

Thus, this emergent literature on growth through trauma points to a variety of ways in which individuals' self-evaluations, their life philosophies, their ties to others, and their spirituality can be significantly changed, indeed, enhanced, in the encounter with adverse experience. Numerous personality characteristics have been identified as factors that increase the likelihood of positive sequelae in the aftermath of life crises. To date, this is an area of inquiry where the conceptual ideas sometimes outdistance scientific findings, although proposed avenues of growth through trauma are increasingly subject to empirical scrutiny.

COMPARATIVE PERSPECTIVES ON RESILIENCE IN CHILDHOOD, ADULTHOOD, AND LATER LIFE

The child and adulthood research on resilience reveals notable points of convergence as well as areas of distinctiveness. Both realms address varieties of challenge that individuals confront as they travel across the life course. In childhood, the adversities have frequently been those of growing up under conditions of extreme poverty or having a parent with severe alcoholism or psychopathology. In adulthood and aging, the difficulties have been more varied. On the one hand, they have included the losses (e.g., widowhood, functional decline), chronic stresses (e.g., caregiving), or acute events (e.g., relocation) that accompany aging. Alternatively, the adult studies have given considerable emphasis to unexpected traumas (e.g., major accidents, natural disasters, major health events, captivity, abusive experiences). Such unanticipated traumas are presumably evident in the lives of children as well, but as such, have received limited consideration in research agendas explicitly focused on childhood resilience.

Both child and adult literatures emphasize the need to assess positive outcomes in response to challenge. That is, the absence of negative effects (e.g., mental or physical illness) is viewed as insufficient to document full flourishing in the face of challenge. Child researchers have thus focused on such outcomes as secure attachments, self-development, academic success, and positive relationships with peers. In adulthood and aging, emphasis has been on multiple aspects of well-being, including positive self-regard, quality relations with others, a sense of purpose and meaning in life, continued growth and development, and the capacity to manage the surrounding environment. Positive physical health (functional capacities, good health behaviors) also received greater emphasis in the middle and later-life definitions of resilient outcomes.

How or why individuals are resilient in the face of challenge is of central interest in both literatures. That is, both realms of inquiry have formulated "protective resources" that help explain positive outcomes with respect to difficult life experiences. Childhood researchers examine a variety of protective factors including attributes within the individual child (e.g., temperament, intelligence, self-esteem, self-efficacy); close, nurturing ties to family members; as well as connections with others in the community (e.g., teachers, peers). The contexts of children's lives (e.g., family, community, neighborhood) have thus received considerable attention. The adulthood and aging literature, in contrast, gives little emphasis to contextual factors that might contribute to resilience. Apart from the emphasis on social support, which addresses the proximal social environment, limited attention is given to assessment of community or neighborhood contributions to understanding later life resilience. What receives primary attention are individual characteristics (e.g., coping strategies, personality traits, flexible self-concepts, social comparisons, optimism and hope, religion and spirituality). Some of these have been studied in childhood investigations of resilience, but others (e.g., coping strategies, optimism, spirituality) have not, and thus, offer possible avenues for future inquiry.

Finally, it is largely in the adulthood literature that researchers have emphasized ideas of growth through trauma. This realm of inquiry points to a variety of gains that can follow suffering: increased self-knowledge and self-reliance, heightened awareness of personal vulnerabilities, greater emotional expressiveness and disclosure to others, increased compassion for others, deeper levels of spirituality. These ideas and their assessment are generally missing in childhood studies of resilience, although they may have relevance for early life as well. Alternatively, the childhood research has increasingly pointed to possible "costs" that may accompany resilient profiles. That is, children of adversity may do well in certain areas (e.g., competence in school) and yet continue to suffer in certain areas of vulnerability (e.g., limited capacity to establish close ties to others). This recognition—that resilience may exact psychosocial tolls that exist side by side with the psychosocial strengths it hones—is an important insight for those attempting to understand flourishing under fire in adulthood and later life.

CONCLUSION

These comparisons point to numerous areas in which the child and adult literatures on resilience can inform and extend each other. In this final section we suggest multiple directions for future research that are pertinent to studies of resilience across the life course. It should be noted that the preceding literature review has been restricted only to those research agendas that are explicitly focused on resilience (in childhood or adulthood and aging). That is, we have made no attempt to link this body of work to other related realms, such as the enormous literature on stress and coping that sometimes gives emphasis to effective management of life stress (e.g., Folkman, 1997; Thoits, 1994). Increased interplay between these surprisingly separate domains of inquiry is in itself a fruitful future direction, but one that we do not elaborate.

We identify five venues for future inquiry next. The first two points underscore and extend observations made in earlier sections of our chapter. The three latter points are suggestions that call for substantially new directions in the study and promotion of human resilience.

First, we strongly endorse the view expressed by multiple investigators in these various literatures that it is essential to assess resilience with indicators that encompass more than the absence of illness (mental or physical). The avoidance of psychopathology, negative behavioral outcomes, or illness is no guarantee that one will also flourish and be well in multiple realms of life. This observation underscores the important interchange needed between those who study human resilience and those who study human flourishing. These largely separate realms have much to offer each other. Scholars of flourishing, such as those in this volume, push forward novel formulations (and measures) of what it means to function positively. It is critical to bring more of these components of wellness into the research on resilience, both in childhood and adulthood and later life. Alternatively, scholars of resilience remind those who would envision the positive side of the human condition that sometimes the heights of efficacy, love, and engagement in and appreciation of life are intricately woven together with some of the greatest challenges and trials that are also a part of the human journey.

Second, extant studies of resilience, from childhood through old age, have given limited attention to the stressors and challenges that constitute what individuals actually rise above. In many instances, particular life challenges (e.g., parental psychopathology, poverty, widowhood, acute health events, major accidents) are assumed to be stressful rather than including actual empirical assessments of levels of stress experienced. As those who study resilience in childhood have increasingly conveyed, it is scientifically unsound to assume that all children growing up under poverty or with a parent having mental illness are subject to extensive stress. Some are, and others are not; failure to include these assessments has contributed to the slippage that subsequently occurs in predicting childhood outcomes.

Similarly, at the other end of the life course, the growing literature on successful aging (Baltes & Baltes, 1990; Berkman et al., 1993; Bond, Cutler, & Grams, 1995; Rowe & Kahn, 1987; Schulz & Heckhausen, 1996) has delineated high levels of physical, cognitive, and personal functioning in later life and explored their correlates (sociodemographic, behavioral, physiological), but has frequently neglected how such profiles of success intersect with the *actual challenges or stresses of later life*. Without consideration of such challenges, including assessment of the actual difficulties associated with them, it is impossible to map the dynamic processes through which resilience occurs.

Third, we underscore the need to study resilience as a long-term, longitudinal process. Paradoxically, much of the early work on resilience in childhood has been conducted with longitudinal studies, but the identification of factors to account for stress resistance has been largely post-hoc (i.e., protective factors were identified after resilience has been established). Such an approach makes it difficult to determine which factors are necessary, and which may be peripheral, in explaining resilient outcomes. Prospective longitudinal studies that include a priori prediction and testing of hypothesized risk or protective factors need a much greater presence in extant literature. Extending the time frame of previous studies (i.e., tracking resilient or vulnerable children into early adulthood and midlife) would also significantly strengthen understanding of the long-term sequelae of difficult early experience that, at least in childhood, did not adversely affect development and well-being.

Later life is also an auspicious time to implement such prospective studies because this is a period in which life challenges are rapidly accumulating and individual differences in health and well-being become more pronounced. The adulthood and aging literature would, however, also benefit from richer understanding of earlier life challenges and reactions to them. That is, are individuals who show noticeable resilience in the face of later life adversity also those with strong profiles of resistance to illness (mental or physical) in dealing with earlier life stresses, including those in childhood?

Of particular importance in such life course studies is the need to track cumulative profiles of adverse experience or stress. In childhood studies, Masten (1999) has called for greater attention to the compounding and pile up of stress across time, whereas in adulthood our research has given explicit emphasis to the accumulation, both of adversity and advantage (Singer et al., 1998), in describing various pathways to resilience. We would note that careful study of individual lives frequently provides useful illustrations for how life difficulties can accumulate as well as how some have been able to escape their debilitating consequences. Our review of the life of Mark Mathabane (1986; see Singer & Ryff, 1997), who as a child suffered the atrocities of apartheid in South Africa but managed in young adulthood to rise above his horrific early experiences, provides one such case example. Higgins (1994) illustrated numerous other real-life examples of human resilience, thereby furthering understanding, at the individual level, of how life difficulties can be compounded through time and yet routes out of these difficulties are nonetheless found.

Fourth, like many others, we see the need for greater investment in multidisciplinary, integrative studies of resilience. Luthar, Cicchetti, and Becker (2000), in their recent review of childhood studies, give particular emphasis to the importance of adding biological factors, along with the psychological, social, and environmental influences that have been previously studied. Werner (1995) also noted that the majority of childhood protective factors have consisted of psychosocial factors, thereby neglecting biological insults as stressors as well as ignoring physiological factors that may constitute important protective resources. We have also called for the incorporation of biology into adult studies of resilience (Ryff et al., 1998). Specifically, we proposed possible connections between resilience and how the body responds to stress, how the immune system functions, and even how the brain reacts to various emotional stimuli.

To illustrate, we have connected social relational well-being to "allostatic load," which measures cumulative wear and tear on multiple physiological systems (see McEwen & Stellar, 1993; Seeman, Singer, McEwen, Horowitz, & Rowe, 1997). High allostatic load has been found in longitudinal studies of aging to predict incident cardiovascular disease, decline in cognitive and physical functioning, and mortality. Our question was whether cumulative social relational strengths (i.e., the positive pathway) or cumulative relational problems (i.e., the negative pathway) would be linked with allostatic load. Based on a sample of midlife adults, we found that among those on the positive pathway, a significantly lower proportion were found to have high allostatic load, compared to those on the negative pathway (Singer & Ryff, 1999).

Returning to the theme of resilience, we also asked whether the presence of good-quality social relationships (in childhood and adulthood) could afford protection against possible adverse physiological sequelae associated with persistent economic adversity. We found, as predicted, that those with cumulative profiles of economic disadvantage were more likely to have high allostatic load compared to those with persistent profiles of economic advantage. However, among those on the negative economic pathway, those who had persistently positive relational experiences were less likely to have high allostatic load than those who suffered both economic and relational adversity. That is, good-quality social relationships appeared to afford protection against the adverse biological sequelae of economic disadvantage. Our ongoing studies of resilience, involving longitudinal studies of middle- and older aged adults and a team of multidisciplinary investigators, are extending these lines of inquiry by building bridges to immune function (measured in terms of antibody response to vaccines) as well as to brain structure and function (measured in terms of hippocampal volume and cerebral activation asymmetry).

Fifth, although most earlier research on resilience has been descriptive, or more recently involved hypothesis-testing efforts to account for positive outcomes in the face of adversity, surprisingly little work in the field of resilience has been focused on intervention. This no doubt reflects the view held in many circles that not enough is currently known about how resilience comes about to embark on efforts to foster or facilitate it. To this view, we submit that active efforts to nurture positive outcomes with regard to challenge are already underway. Giovanni Fava has, for example, developed "well-being therapy" to prevent relapse among those suffering from recurrent depression (Fava, Rafanelli, Gvandi, Conti, & Bellwardo, 1998). The essence of the therapy is to give people the cognitive, emotional, and behavioral tools for having more positive, salubrious experience in their daily lives, and this is what promotes their recovery from major depression. Steve Danish (1997), in addition, directs a program among high-risk adolescents called "Going for the Goal," which is designed to teach the life skills needed to set and pursue significant life goals. Teenagers participating in this program have shown positive profiles of health behaviors and school performance. Both of these examples illustrate the potential that exists for improving the human condition by giving ever greater segments of the population (particularly those suffering from disadvantage) the resources, insight, and behaviors needed to flourish, even under fire. A key direction for the future must thus be to incorporate more of these programs into the vision and practice of public health. What we learn about those who prevail in the face of adversity provides the foundation for a new era of public education about tools for positive health promotion (Ryff & Singer, 2000).

In summary, there are numerous avenues for enriching extant research on challenged thriving. Some involve pushing forward explicit assessments of what it means to flourish (i.e., mastery, purpose, quality relationships, positive self-regard); others require more detailed evaluation of the "under fire" part—in other words, the nature and degree of adversity experienced. Long-term studies, covering wide segments of the life course, are particularly critical to understanding how life difficulties may be compounded, and for some, how life strengths may be honed in the process. Mapping the linkages between resilience as a psychosocial phenomenon and resilience as a biological process is also central to understanding the neurophysiological mechanisms that underlie the capacity to thrive in the face of adversity. Finally, the need to promote, at the level of public education and community intervention programs, the "tools" that afford resilience (e.g., positive outlooks, coping effectiveness, emotion regulation, social integration) is fundamental to promoting the greatest possible good for the largest possible segment of society.

REFERENCES

Aldwin, C. M., & Sutton, K. J. (1998). A developmental perspective on posttraumatic growth. In R. G. Tedeschi, C. L. Park, & L. G. Calhoun (Eds.), *Posttraumatic growth: Positive changes in the aftermath of crisis* (pp. 43–64). Mahwah, NJ: Erlbaum.

Baltes, P. B., & Baltes, M. M. (Eds.). (1990). *Successful aging: Perspectives from the behavioral sciences*. New York: Cambridge University Press.

Berkman L. F., Seeman, T. E., Albert, M., Blazer, D., Kahn, R., et al. (1993). High, usual and impaired functioning in community-dwelling older men and women: Findings from the MacArthur Foundation Research Network on Successful Aging. *Journal of Clinical Epidemiology, 46,* 1129–1140.

Block, J. H. (1971). *Lives through time*. Berkeley, CA: Bancroft Books.

Block, J. H., & Block, J. (1980). The role of ego-control and ego-resiliency in the organization of behavior. In W. A. Collins (Ed.), *Development of cognition, affect, and social relations: The Minnesota Symposium on Child Psychology* (Vol. 13, pp. 39–101). Hillsdale, NJ: Erlbaum.

Bond, L. A., Cutler, S. J., & Grams, A. (Eds.). (1995). *Promoting successful and productive aging*. Thousand Oaks, CA: Sage.

Carr, D. (1997). The fulfillment of career dreams at midlife: Does it matter for women's mental health? *Journal of Health and Social Behavior, 38,* 331–344.

Carver, C. S. (1998). Resilience and thriving: Issues, models, and linkages. *Journal of Social Issues, 54,* 245–266.

Cole, J. R., & Singer, B. (1991). A theory of limited differences: Explaining the productivity puzzle in science. In H. Zuckerman, J. R. Cole, & J. T. Bruer (Eds.), *The outer circle: Women in the scientific community* (pp. 277–340). New York: W. W. Norton.

Danish, S. J. (1997). Going for the goal: A life skills program for adolescents. In G. Albeee & T. Gullotta (Eds.), *Prevention works* (pp. 291–312). Newbury Park, CA: Sage.

Emmons, R. A., Colby, P. M., & Kaiser, H. A. (1998). When losses lead to gains: Personal goals and the recovery of meaning. In P. T. P. Wong & P. S. Fry (Eds.), *The human quest for meaning: A handbook of psychological research and clinical applications* (pp. 163–178). Mahwah, NJ: Erlbaum.

Fava, G. A., Rafanelli, C., Grandi, S., Conti, S., & Belluardo, P. (1998). Prevention of recurrent depression with cognitive behavioral therapy. *Archives of General Psychiatry, 55,* 816–821.

Folkman, S. (1997). Positive psychological states and coping with severe stress. *Social Science and Medicine, 45,* 1207–1221.

Garmezy, N. (1974). The study of competence in children at risk for severe psychopathology. In E. J. Anthony & C. Koupernick (Eds.), *The child in his family. Vol. 3: Children at psychiatric risk* (pp. 77–97). New York: Wiley.

Garmezy, N. (1991). Resiliency and vulnerability of adverse developmental outcomes associated with poverty. *American Behavioral Scientist, 34,* 416–430.

Garmezy, N. (1993). Vulnerability and resistance. In D. C. Funder, R. D. Parke, C. Tomlinson-Keasey, & K. Widaman (Eds.), *Studying lives through time: Personality and development* (pp. 377–398). Washington, DC: American Psychological Association.

Garmezy, N., Masten, A. S., & Tellegen, A. (1984). The study of stress and competence in children: A building block for development. *Child Development, 55,* 97–111.

Garmezy, N., & Streitman, S. (1974). Children at risk: The search for the antecedents of schizophrenia: Conceptual models and research methods. *Schizophrenia Bulletin, 8,* 14–90.

Glantz, M. D., & Sloboda, Z. (1999). Analysis and reconceptualization of resilience. In M. D. Glantz & J. L. Johnson (Eds.), *Resilience and development: Positive life adaptations* (pp. 109–128). New York: Kluwer Academic/Plenum Press.

Heidrich, S. M., & Ryff, C. D. (1993a). Physical and mental health in later life: The self-system as mediator. *Psychology and Aging, 8,* 327–338.

Heidrich, S. M., & Ryff, C. D. (1993b). The role of social comparison processes in the psychological adaptation of elderly adults. *Journal of Gerontology, 48,* P127–P136.

Heidrich, S. M., & Ryff, C. D. (1996). The self in later years of life: Changing perspectives on psychological well-being. In L. Sperry & H. Prosen (Eds.), *Aging in the twenty-first century: A developmental perspective* (pp. 73–102). New York: Garland.

Higgins, G. O. (1994). *Resilient adults: Overcoming a cruel past*. San Francisco: Jossey-Bass.

James, W. (1902/1958). *The varieties of religious experience*. New York: New American Library.

Kling, K. C., Ryff, C. D., & Essex, M. J. (1997). Adaptive changes in the self-concept during a life transition. *Personality and Social Psychology Bulletin, 23*, 989–998.

Kling, K. C., Seltzer, M. M., & Ryff, C. D. (1997). Distinctive late life challenges: Implications for coping and well-being. *Psychology and Aging, 12*, 288–295.

Klohnen, E. C. (1996). Conceptual analysis and measurement of the construct of ego-resiliency. *Journal of Personality and Social Psychology, 70*, 1067–1079.

Li, L. W., Seltzer, M. M., & Greenberg, J. S. (1999). Change in depressive symptoms among daughter caregivers: An 18-month longitudinal study. *Psychology and Aging, 14*, 206–219.

Luthar, S. S. (1991). Vulnerability and resilience: A study of high-risk adolescents. *Child Development, 62*, 600–616.

Luthar, S. S., Cicchetti, D., & Becker, B. (2000). The construct of resilience: A critical evaluation and guidelines for future work. *Child Development, 71*, 543–562.

Luthar, S. S., & Cushing, G. (1999). Measurement issues in the empirical study of resilience: An overview. In M. D. Glantz & J. L. Johnson (Eds.), *Resilience and development: Positive life adaptations* (pp. 129–160). New York: Kluwer Academic/Plenum Press.

Marks, N. F. (1998). Does it hurt to care: Caregiving, work–family conflict, and midlife well-being. *Journal of Marriage and the Family, 60*, 952–966.

Marks, N. F., & Lambert, J. D. (1998). Marital status continuity and change among young and midlife adults: Longitudinal effects on psychological well-being. *Journal of Family Issues, 19*, 652–686.

Marmot, M., Ryff, C. D., Bumpass, L. L., Shipley, M., & Marks, N. F. (1997). Social inequalities in health: Converging evidence and next questions. *Social Science and Medicine, 44*, 901–910.

Masten, A. S. (1989). Resilience in development: Implications of the study of successful adaptation for developmental psychopathology. In D. Cicchetti (Ed.), *The emergence of a discipline: Rochester Symposium on Developmental Psychopathology* (Vol. 1, pp. 261–294). Hillsdale, NJ: Erlbaum.

Masten, A. S. (1999). Resilience comes of age: Reflections on the past and outlook for the next generation of research. In M. D. Glantz & J. L. Johnson (Eds.), *Resilience and development: Positive life adaptations* (pp. 281–296). New York: Kluwer Academic/Plenum Press.

Masten, A. S., Best, K., & Garmezy, N. (1990). Resilience and development: Contributions from the study of children who overcome adversity. *Development and Psychopathology, 2*, 425–444.

Masten, A. S., & Garmezy, N. (1985). Risk, vulnerability, and protective factors in developmental psychopathology. In B. B. Lahey & A. E. Kazdin (Eds.), *Advances in clinical child psychology* (Vol. 8, pp. 1–52). New York: Plenum Press.

Mathabane, M. (1986). *Kaffir boy*. New York: Penguin Books.

McEwen, B. S., & Stellar, E. (1993). Stress and the individual. *Archives of Internal Medicine, 153,* 2093–2101.

McGregor, I., & Little, B. R. (1998). Personal projects, happiness, and meaning: On doing well and being yourself. *Journal of Personality and Social Psychology, 74,* 494–512.

Park, C. L. (1998). Implications of postraumatic growth for individuals. In R. E. Tedeschi, C. L. Park, & L. G. Calhoun (Eds.), *Posttraumatic growth: Positive changes in the aftermath of crisis* (pp. 153–178). Mahwah, NJ: Erlbaum.

Robins, R. W., John, O. P., Caspi, A., Moffitt, T. E., & Stouthamer-Loeber, M. (1996). Resilient, overcontrolled, and undercontrolled boys: Three replicable personality types. *Journal of Personality and Social Psychology, 70,* 157–171.

Rowe, J. W., & Kahn, R. L. (1987). Human aging: Usual and successful. *Science, 237,* 143–149.

Rutter, M. (1985). Resilience in the face of adversity: Protective factors and resistance to psychiatric disorder. *British Journal of Psychiatry, 147,* 598–611.

Rutter, M. (1987). Psychosocial resilience and protective mechanisms. *American Journal of Orthopsychiatry, 22,* 323–356.

Rutter, M. (1990). Psychosocial resilience and protective mechanisms. In J. Rolf, A. S. Masten, D. Cicchetti, K. H. Neuchterlein, & S. Weintraub (Eds.), *Risk and protective factors in the development of psychopathology* (pp. 181–214). New York: Cambridge University Press.

Rutter, M., Maughan, N., Mortimore, P., & Ouston, J. (1979). *Fifteen thousand hours: Secondary schools and their effects on children*. Cambridge, MA: Harvard University Press.

Ryff, C. D. (1989). Happiness is everything, or is it?: Explorations on the meaning of psychological well-being. *Journal of Personality and Social Psychology, 57,* 1069–1081.

Ryff, C. D., & Keyes, C. L. M. (1995). The structure of psychological well-being revisited. *Journal of Personality and Social Psychology, 69,* 719–727.

Ryff, C. D., Lee, Y. H., Essex, M. J., & Schmutte, P. S. (1994). My children and me: Midlife evaluations of grown children and of self. *Psychology and Aging, 9,* 195–205.

Ryff, C. D., Magee, W. J., Kling, K. C., & Wing, E. H. (1999). Forging macro-micro linkages in the study of psychological well-being. In C. D. Ryff & V. W. Marshall (Eds.), *The self and society in aging processes* (pp. 247–278). New York: Springer.

Ryff, C. D., Schmutte, P. S., & Lee, Y. H. (1996). How children turn out: Implications for parental self-evaluation. In C. D. Ryff & M. M. Seltzer (Eds.), *The parental experience in midlife* (pp. 383–422). Chicago: University of Chicago Press.

Ryff, C. D., & Seltzer, M. M. (1996). The uncharted years of midlife parenting. In C. D. Ryff & M. M. Seltzer (Eds.), *The parental experience in midlife* (pp. 3–25). Chicago: University of Chicago Press.

Ryff, C. D., & Singer, B. (2000). Interpersonal flourishing: A positive health agenda for the new millennium. *Personality and Social Psychology Review, 4,* 30–44.

Ryff, C. D., Singer, B., Love, G. D., & Essex, M. J. (1998). Resilience in adulthood and later life: Defining features and dynamic processes. In J. Lomranz (Ed.), *Handbook of aging and mental health* (pp. 69–96). New York: Springer-Verlag.

Saakvitne, K., Tennen, H., & Affleck, G. (1998). Exploring thriving in the context of clinical trauma theory: Constructivist self development theory. *Journal of Social Issues, 54,* 279–300.

Schulz, R., & Heckhausen, J. (1996). A life span model of successful aging. *American Psychologist, 51,* 702–714.

Seeman, T. E., Singer, B. H., McEwen, B. S., Horwitz, R. I., & Rowe, J. W. (1997). The price of adaptation—Allostatic load and its health consequences: MacArthur Studies of Successful Aging. *Archives of Internal Medicine, 157,* 2259–2268.

Seltzer, M. M., & Ryff, C. D. (1994). Parenting across the life-span: The normative and nonnormative cases. In D. L. Featherman, R. M. Lerner, & M. Perlmutter (Eds.), *Life-span development and behavior* (Vol. 12, pp. 1–40). Hillsdale, NJ: Erlbaum.

Singer, B., & Manton, K. G. (1998). The effects of health changes on projections of health service needs for the elderly population of the United States. *Proceedings of the National Academy of Sciences, 95,* 15618–15622.

Singer, B., & Ryff, C. D. (1997). Racial and ethnic inequalities in health: Environmental, psychosocial, and physiological pathways. In B. Devlin, S. E. Feinberg, D. Resnick, & K. Roeder (Eds.), *Intelligence, genes, and success: Scientists respond to the Bell Curve* (pp. 89–122). New York: Springer-Verlag.

Singer, B., & Ryff, C. D. (1999). Hierarchies of life histories and associated health risks. In N. E. Adler, B. S. McEwen, & M. Marmot (Eds.), Socioeconomic status and health in industrialized nations. *Annals of the New York Academy of Sciences, 896,* 96–115.

Singer, B., Ryff, C. D., Carr, D., & Magee, W. J. (1998). Life histories and mental health: A person-centered strategy. In A. Raftery (Ed.), *Sociological methodology, 1998* (pp. 1–51). Washington, DC: American Sociological Association.

Smider, N. A., Essex, M. J., & Ryff, C. D. (1996). Adaptation to community relocation: The interactive influence of psychological resources and contextual factors. *Psychology and Aging, 11,* 362–371.

Staudinger, U. M., Marsiske, M., & Baltes, P. B. (1995). Resilience and reserve capacity in later adulthood: Potentials and limits of development across the life span. In D. Cicchitti & D. J. Cohen (Eds.), *Developmental psychopathology* (Vol. 2: *Risk, Disorder, and Adaptation,* pp. 801–847). New York: Wiley.

Taylor, R. D., & Wang, M. C. (Eds.). (2000). *Resilience across contexts: Family, work, culture, and community.* Mahwah, NJ: Erlbaum.

Tedeschi, R. G., & Calhoun, L. G. (1995). *Trauma and transformation: Growing in the aftermath of suffering.* Thousand Oaks, CA: Sage.

Tedeschi, R. G., Park, C. L., & Calhoun, L. G. (Eds.). (1998). *Posttraumatic growth: Positive changes in the aftermath of crisis.* Mahwah, NJ: Erlbaum.

Tennen, H., & Affleck, G. (1998). Personality and transformation in the face of adversity. In R. G. Tedeschi, C. L. Park, & L. G. Calhoun (Eds.), *Posttraumatic growth: Positive changes in the aftermath of crisis* (pp. 65–98). Mahwah, NJ: Erlbaum.

Thoits, P. A. (1994). Stressors and problem-solving: The individual as a psychological activist. *Journal of Health and Social Behavior, 35,* 143–159.

Tweed, S., & Ryff, C. D. (1991). Adult children of alcoholics: Profiles of wellness and distress. *Journal of Studies on Alcohol, 52,* 133–141.

Van Riper, M., Ryff, C. D., & Pridham, K. (1992). Parental and family well-being in families of children with Down syndrome: A comparative study. *Research in Nursing and Health, 15,* 227–235.

Werner, E. E. (1993). Risk, resilience, and recovery: Perspectives from the Kauai Longitudinal Study. *Development and Psychopathology, 5,* 503–515.

Werner, E. E. (1995). Resilience in development. *Current Directions in Psychological Science, 4,* 81–85.

Werner, E. E., & Smith, R. S. (1977). *Kauai's children come of age.* Honolulu: University of Hawaii Press.

Werner, E. E., & Smith, R. S. (1992). *Overcoming the odds: High risk children from birth to adulthood.* Ithaca, NY: Cornell University Press.

Zimmerman, M. A., & Arunkumar, R. (1994). Resiliency research: Implications for schools and policy. *Social Policy Report (Society for Research in Child Development), 8,* 1–17.

2

TURNING POINTS AS OPPORTUNITIES FOR PSYCHOLOGICAL GROWTH

ELAINE WETHINGTON

This chapter analyzes self-reports of turning points, defined as a perceived, long–lasting redirection in the path of a person's life (Clausen, 1995; Settersten, 1999). The particular focus in this chapter is on the psychological turning point, defined as an instance when a person undergoes a major transformation in views about the self, identity, or the meaning of life (Clausen, 1993). The chapter adopts Clausen's method, using quantitative and qualitative analyses of self-report descriptions of recent situations in which people believed that they "learned new things about themselves," for the good or for the bad.

Psychological turning points may involve objective shifts in the social environment that bring about profound psychological change, such as the death of a life partner, the loss of a valued career, or the social recognition of accomplishment. They may also involve shifts in identity and meaning brought about by a more gradual process of change or through personal reflection. According to Clausen (1998), self-reported psychological turning points reflect personal judgments and appraisals of the direction and meaning of one's life, as well as the transitions or stressful events that may have triggered them. Self-reported psychological turning points can also include

The collection of the data sets used in this chapter was funded by the John D. and Catherine T. MacArthur Foundation Research Network on Successful Midlife Development (MIDMAC). The work of the author was supported by MIDMAC and NIA program project 2P50 AG11711-06, project 3 (E. Wethington, principal investigator). I appreciate the comments of Orville Gilbert Brim, Jonathan Haidt, Corey L. M. Keyes, and Karl Pillemer on previous drafts of this chapter. The Cornell University Computer-Assisted Survey Team, directed by Yasamin DiCiccio and Lisa Horn, performed the qualitative data collection. I also thank Jennifer Eng, Allison Kavey, Alexis Krulish, Melissa Trepiccione, and Ilene West for their careful research assistance in the production of this chapter.

highly personalized periods of change or decision, such as career and relationship changes (Clausen, 1998). Psychological turning points are useful to study in their own right because they offer a snapshot of how people at a particular point in time perceive psychological growth and change across their course of life and what they believe has triggered psychological change. They might also be viewed as self-perceptions of important life themes, or the "stories" that people live by. Perceived psychological turning points are clearly not the literal truth but rather a series of insights into how people make meaning of their lives through the experience of challenge and stress.

PREVIOUS STUDIES OF SELF-PERCEIVED
PSYCHOLOGICAL CHANGE ACROSS LIFE

Conceptions of human growth and development across adulthood have been dominated by a life stages or developmental stages perspective, both academically (e.g., Gould, 1978; Levinson, Darrow, Klein, Levinson, & McKee, 1978; Levinson & Levinson, 1996) and popularly (Sheehy, 1976, 1995). Psychological changes across adulthood are encouraged by confrontation and management of role transitions that are associated with collective beliefs about maturation. Successful passage through these transitions often results in acceptance of social responsibility and emotional fulfillment from meeting those responsibilities (Levinson et al., 1978). Erikson (1963) described midlife as a tension between "stagnation" and "generativity," with successful resolution indicating passage through an expected challenging stage of life.

Past research on adult life transitions and psychological growth suggests that the psychological ramifications of these transitions are dependent on both subjective interpretation (cognitive appraisal) and the individual context in which transitions take place (Thurnher, 1983). For example, McAdams and de St. Aubin (1992), in their study of generativity, suggested that men and women face dissimilar cultural demands and are subject to different social reinforcement of generative concerns early in life. For women, the transition into the parenting role is preceded by the development of generative concerns; if they are prepared, women's transitions foster no (or fewer) unexpected changes or shifts. For men, the same transition may inspire a sharper shift in concerns, which could be experienced as more psychologically significant—a turning point at which commitments and priorities are reevaluated. The impact of a life transition or event on an individual's belief system is thus dependent on the previous characteristics of that belief system. A major event or transition may invoke revelation, reevaluation, and change, or it may simply reinforce extant beliefs. The former is more likely to be remembered as a psychologically salient event (Heatherton & Nichols, 1994), because it results in "change."

This chapter uses self-reports of important psychological changes, termed psychological turning points. Clausen's (1995, 1998) definition of a turning point is used: A psychological turning point is a period or point in time when a person has undergone a major transformation in views about the self. Life events and difficulties; life transitions; and internal, subjective changes such as self-realizations or reinterpretations of past experiences may be associated with the feeling that life has reached a "turning point" (Wethington, Cooper, & Holmes, 1997). A turning point may be either positive or negative in character, or both.

Theoretical and empirical work suggest that self-report turning points are related to age-graded events and transitions, to the extent to which these events and transitions have symbolic meanings indicating maturity and normative aging (Wethington, Kessler, & Pixley, in press). This is also consistent with Clausen's (1998) observation that recollected meaning of a life transition or event would tend to change over the life course. For example, people in their middle years who are not assuming responsibility for the well-being of the next generation, either through parenting or mentoring others in work or other settings, are judged relatively harshly by others (McAdams, Hart, & Maruna, 1998). Similarly, those who feel they have accomplished too little for their years or stage in life or who have not yet reached a symbolic marker of maturity may experience a sense of loss, sadness, or disabling self-criticism. The latter is in fact one classic interpretation of the midlife psychosocial transition, the need to progress from stagnation to generativity. More popularly, this transition is one way some people understand the term "midlife crisis" (Wethington, 2000).

Although they differ in their focus, researchers agree that the experience of a turning point has both objective and subjective components (Wheaton & Gotlib, 1997). The objective components involve the aspects of change in the environment such as an event or series of events that bring about the need to adapt or change. The long tradition of research on life events, chronic difficulties, and psychological health provides a way of predicting which life events might produce the potential for a major change in the way a person views his or her character and personality. Previous research has found that self-reported stress is associated with perception of stress-related growth (Park, Cohen, & Murch, 1996; Schaefer & Moos, 1992). Previous research has also found that exposure to stress is also associated with positive action to solve the problem (Thoits, 1994). For example, coping with psychological impact of loss, such as widowhood, may be resolved by replacing the lost partner or by relying on other close relationships (e.g., Umberson, Wortman, & Kessler, 1992). Depending on the severity of the loss and the difficulties in finding appropriate compensation, a loss could be associated with eventually perceiving psychological growth—a psychological turning point. Several groups of researchers (e.g., Brown & Harris, 1978) have produced extensive documentation regarding the types of specific psychological consequences posed by life events and chronic difficulties with different types of objective characteristics. Namely, the more objectively and psychologically challenging the stressor, the more likely subsequent psychological change or reaction, both negative (e.g. Brown & Harris, 1978) and positive (Aldwin, Sutton, & Lachman, 1996).

The focus on stressful life events, however, is a less than perfect fit to the study of psychological turning points. The occurrence of a major change in the view of one's own character does not require that the provoking situation involve negative events, emotions, or long-term consequences. Research on life events has long focused on the negative aspects of events, following findings in the 1970s that suggested that positive events are not apt to have long-lasting negative impacts on well-being (e.g., Turner & Wheaton, 1995).

Psychological turning points, however, need not be negative. In fact, Clausen (1998) found that many of the most enduring turning points were triggered by positive events. The long-lasting positive changes were not necessarily classifiable as happiness. The changes are better classified as involving self-perceived psychological growth and change, such as the recognition of personal growth, satisfaction in maturity, concern for others, and continued emotional stability (Aldwin et al., 1996; Park et al., 1996). Such feelings may be consequences of mastering life challenges or meeting developmental milestones that carry social significance. (Recent research also suggests that the accumulation of positive changes may also perturb well-being; Keyes, 2000.)

Based on the previous literature on psychological turning points, this chapter poses several hypotheses regarding the distribution and experience of self-reported psychological turning points among adults. First, events and situations symbolizing appropriate enactment of important social roles will be associated with reporting psychological turning points involving changes in views of the self (Clausen, 1995). This hypothesis suggests that psychological turning points will be associated with characteristics of major life roles that define success in adulthood, work, marriage, parenting, and family. Second, reporting a psychological turning point will be related to personality characteristics that influence reactions to life stressors and to beliefs that affect how people appraise and cope with challenging events and situations (Thurnher, 1983). These characteristics and beliefs include level of insight into the self, the capacity to reflect on and to make sense of changes, learning from experience, self-directedness, openness to experience, and negative affect. Successful coping may be perceived as a kind of psychological growth. Third, psychological turning points, both positive and negative, will be related to stressors and environmental challenges.

QUANTITATIVE DATA AND METHODS

The quantitative analyses are conducted on data from 3,032 participants in the MacArthur Foundation National Study of Mildife in the United States (MIDUS). These were respondents in a national sample generated by random-digit dialing selection procedures. The exact response rate for MIDUS cannot be computed because only about half of the people contacted were eligible for the interview, and only eligible participants were included in calculating the response rate. The estimate, however, is 70% for the telephone interview and 86.8% for completion of a subsequent mail questionnaire among telephone respondents, yielding an overall response rate of 60.8% (.70 × .868). For greater detail on the MIDUS sample and response rate see Mroczek and Kolarz (1998).

A series of weights that adjusted for differences in (a) the probability of selection and (b) differential nonresponse by socioeconomic status, race, age, gender, and other factors adjusts for differences between the MIDUS sample and the adult U.S. population. Because the MIDUS data used in this chapter are derived from the mail questionnaires, all analyses use weighted data.

Psychological Turning Points

In the questionnaire portion of the MIDUS study, respondents were asked seven questions about the occurrence of turning points in the past 12 months. The study analyzes two of these questions, which asked about psychological turning points involving learning (a) new and upsetting things about the self and (b) new and good things about the self. The concept of turning point was defined in an introduction to the question sequence:

> The following questions are about what we call "psychological turning points." Psychological turning points are major changes in the ways that people feel or think about an important part of their lives, such as work, family, and beliefs about themselves and about the world. Turning points involve people changing their feelings about how important or meaningful some aspect of life is or how much commitment they give it.

The two questions about turning points involving changes in oneself are included in the extract that follows:

Sometimes things happen that force people to learn upsetting things about themselves. This can lead to a big change in your feelings about who you are, what you stand for, and what your life is all about. Did you have a major psychological turning point like this in the past 12 months? (PROBES: Briefly, what did you learn? What impact has learning this had on you?)

What about the opposite situation: discovering important good things about yourself that changed your view of who you are, what you stand for, or how you should lead your life.

(PROBES: Briefly, what did you learn? What impact has learning this had on you?)

If respondents checked "yes" to the turning point questions, they were asked to write what they had learned and what impact it had on them. The questions about turning points were developed in three small-scale pilot studies exploring different ways of describing this concept for participants (Wethington et al., 1997). There was a high prevalence of reported turning points in the MIDUS sample (49% reported at least one of the seven possible psychological turning points in the past 12 months). This indicates that most of the psychological turning points reported in the MIDUS study were what Clausen (1998) would classify as "little" turning points, rather than profound redirections in the course of life that changed its trajectory irrevocably.

Chronic Difficulties and Life Events

Chronic difficulties and events are hypothesized to trigger, at least in some cases, a psychological turning point. The self-administered portion of the MIDUS instrument assessed chronic stress in multiple domains of adult life. For psychological turning points, reports of chronic stress in the important domains of life, marriage, work, and parenting may be related to reports of a recent turning point. These three domains are the major life roles associated with judging the success of adult life and gauging its accomplishments. Five measures of chronic stress are used in the MIDUS analyses: marital problems, spouse adjustment problems (alcohol and substance abuse, financial problems, problems at school or work, difficulty finding or keeping a job, legal problems, and difficulty getting along with people), job chronic stress, control at work, and children's health and adjustment problems.

Personality and Beliefs

Six measures are used to evaluate personality, coping, and affect in the MIDUS analyses: trait (a) neuroticism, (b) openness to experience,

(c) insight, (d) reappraisal, (e) self-direction, and (f) depression episode in the past 12 months (a dummy variable). High scores on neuroticism and having a history of depression may indicate higher levels of emotional reactivity in response to stress. High scores on openness to experience may tap a willingness or openness to learn, even under adverse circumstances; high scores on insight may indicate a greater reliance on making meaning from past experiences. Reappraisal reflects another set of beliefs about coping with stress, positive and flexible reappraisal, as well as a belief that one can learn from stressful experiences. A high score on self-direction indicates a tendency for independence, self-directedness, and planning. All may be associated with the tendency to report a psychological turning point, independently of exposure to stress.

Qualitative Data and Methods

The source of narratives for the qualitative analyses was the Psychological Experiences Study (PTP), an intensive study of 724 of the original respondents from the MIDUS sample. The PTP study took place three years after the MIDUS survey, and it was administered by telephone, with a random selection of respondents from the 3,032 original participants. The study repeated the psychological turning point questions from the MIDUS study and asked respondents to report whether they had been experienced over the past five years (rather than 12 months, as in the MIDUS study). The PTP study provides rich data on the content of psychological turning points, because responses were extensively probed in the personal interview. The initial probes were, "In what year did that happen? (In what month?)" "Briefly, what happened?" "What impact did this have on you?" Interviewers were trained to probe tactfully for concrete information if the respondent was vague about details in response to the initial probes.

The turning point narratives were coded for their themes. All turning points were double-coded and discrepancies resolved by a third coder. The first theme for coding was the cause to which people attributed their psychological turning points. The second classification theme was the self-reported impact of the situation described as a turning point. The themes emerged as the data were coded; no a priori theme was imposed.

It is important to note that all of the data on turning points was collected retrospectively, and thus should be interpreted cautiously. Participants were not reporting turning points as they occurred but as they currently reconstructed them based on subsequent events. The narratives thus are not to be taken as literal truth but as stories about changes in oneself and how they came about.

The analyses of the quantitative data addressed two important theoretical questions regarding psychological turning points. First, how are psychological turning points distributed by age and by gender? Second, are psychological turning points related to difficulties associated with important social roles?

The Distribution of Psychological Turning Points by Age and Gender

Women reported significantly more turning points involving changes in views about themselves over the past 12 months (MIDUS) and in the past five years (PTP; see Table 2.1). Women were significantly more likely to report discovering something upsetting about themselves or finding out something good about themselves. Among men and women who learned something upsetting about themselves, 49% also said they learned something good about themselves.

Table 2.1 presents the proportion of men and women who learned something upsetting or something good about themselves, by five age groups, in both the MIDUS and the PTP studies. Overall, younger people between

TABLE 2.1
Reports of Psychological Turning Points, by Age and Gender
(Percentages)

MIDUS (12-month recall)				
	Learning something upsetting about self		Learning something good about self	
	Men	Women	Men	Women
N	1318	1715	1316	1714
Age 25–34	8.4	16.9	10.9	22.5
Age 35–44	10.7	17.8	9.5	21.2
Age 45–54	10.2	17.0	10.2	19.3
Age 55–64	6.1	8.4	7.3	10.1
Age 65–74	8.4	10.3	5.8	12.8
PTP (5-year recall)				
	Men	Women	Men	Women
N	356	366	356	366
Age 25–34	20.0	43.9	47.6	65.9
Age 35–44	18.9	45.9	34.7	52.5
Age 45–54	26.9	31.6	31.2	43.0
Age 55–64	15.6	31.3	22.2	43.8
Age 65–78	21.9	22.9	28.1	38.3

the ages of 25 and 54 were more likely than people aged 55 and older to have learned something upsetting about themselves and something good about themselves.

Turning Points and Role-Related Chronic Difficulties and Events

Events and chronic difficulties associated with important social roles were hypothesized to be associated with positive psychological turning points. An important caution is that the data are cross-sectional, and causal priority cannot be assessed. Overall, this hypothesis is confirmed, although the relationships between stressors and reporting a psychological turning point are very modest. Table 2.2 presents regression analyses assessing the relationship of chronic difficulties and events in important life roles, controlled for demographic factors, personality, and beliefs about coping with stress.

A consistent finding across all three analyses is that reporting stressful chronic difficulties or life events in different life roles related to reporting both negative and positive psychological turning points. This relationship is estimated as controlling for factors that might partially account for the relationship between stressors and reporting a turning point, age, being

TABLE 2.2
Regression of Psychological Turning Points on Demographic Indicators, Personality, and Stressful Events and Difficulties for Married, Working Respondents With Children (MIDUS, N = 2026)

Variable	Learning something upsetting about self			Learning something good about self		
	B	$SE (B)$	$Beta$	B	$SE (B)$	$Beta$
Age (years)	-.00	.00	-.00	-.00	.00	-.07[a]
Completed college	.02	.01	.03	.07	.02	.09[a]
Female	.06	.01	.09[a]	.09	.02	.13[a]
Depression episode in last 12 months	.08	.02	.08[a]	.04	.02	.04[b]
Neuroticism	.03	.01	.07[c]	.01	.01	.02
Openness	.02	.02	.03	.02	.02	.02
Insight	.05	.01	.09[a]	.05	.01	.09[a]
Reappraisal	.01	.01	.02	.02	.01	.03
Self-direction	-.04	.01	-.09[a]	-.02	.01	-.03
Spouse adjustment problems	.01	.01	.03	-.01	.01	-.01
Serious marital problems	.06	.01	.14[a]	.05	.01	.11[a]
Job stress	.03	.01	.12[a]	.02	.01	.07[a]
Control at work	.02	.01	.03	.02	.01	.05[c]
Children's problems	.01	.01	.03	.01	.00	.07[a]

[a]p <.01.   [b]p <.10.   [c]p <.05.
Note. R^2 = .11, R^2 (adjusted) = .10 for learning something upsetting about self. R^2 = .09, R^2 (adjusted) = .08 for learning something good about self.

female, education, negative affect, personality, and beliefs about coping with stress. Conventional theory and research on life events and psychological distress are sufficient to explain why negative events are correlated to reporting negative psychological turning points. It is not so obvious, however, why negative events and difficulties are related to reporting *positive* psychological turning points. The following qualitative analysis of the narrative reports considers this finding in more depth.

Qualitative Findings: Reported Causes of Psychological Turning Points

Respondents attributed their psychological turning points to a variety of causes (see Table 2.3). The majority of respondents connected turning points to concrete changes in the environment, either major negative events or long-lasting chronic difficulties. Only a minority of respondents (fewer than 1 in 10) reported that they found out something upsetting about themselves through reflection, meditation, therapy, or prayer. Nearly 75% of respondents attributed turning points to objective situations that had raised the level of challenge in their lives or revealed previously unnoticed character flaws.

A number of respondents (28.8% of men, 27.2% of women) reported that health problems led them to find out something upsetting about them-

TABLE 2.3
Self-Reported Causes of Psychological Turning Points, by Gender
(PTP, Percentages)

	Learning something upsetting about self		Learning something good about self	
	Men	Women	Men	Women
Reflection, therapy, or religious experience	10.2	4.0	10.3	13.3
Health problems, fitness, health habits	28.8	27.2	5.7	9.1
Parenthood, parenting, and generational relationships	13.6	5.6	19.5	9.1
Marital, partner, and sexual relationships	8.5	17.6	2.3	15.8
Work and career	22.0	8.8	29.9	20.0
Legal and financial	3.4	2.4	3.4	1.2
Education and training	0.0	0.0	2.3	2.4
Illnesses and deaths of others	5.1	11.2	8.0	13.9
Other[a] situations exposing personality and character flaws	5.1	11.2	10.3	9.7
Achievements	0.0	0.0	4.6	2.4
"Aging"	3.4	2.4	3.4	3.0

[a]Specific cause not disclosed by respondent (may be objective situation or reflection/therapy/religious experience).

selves. The attribution to health problems might seem at first glance to be an inappropriate response. Many of the respondents who reported health problems described health problems as threats to their ability to manage their lives or to their views of themselves as disciplined people (see following section for a more detailed consideration of this issue).

As hypothesized, many respondents attributed learning something up-setting about themselves to stresses and challenges emanating from work, marriage, parenting, and family relationships. No respondents attributed learning something upsetting to personal achievements (although these were associated with learning good things about themselves).

As noted in the description of quantitative findings, many respondents reported both psychological turning points, learning both upsetting and good things about themselves. An examination of the qualitative responses of participants who reported both types of turning points revealed that 45% described the same provoking situation in response to the two questions. Almost half of respondents who learned both good and bad things about themselves were prompted to do so from a single situation or event.

Those participants who reported only a positive psychological turning point (learning something good about themselves) were more likely to attribute the cause of the turning point to a positive event, even a rela-tively minor one. These positive or minor events were described as having symbolic value in their lives, most particularly taking on additional roles and social responsibilities. These included getting married, finishing school, having a child, adopting a child, and starting a new business. Other respon-dents reported learning something good about themselves from experiencing the appreciation of others, at work, from their families, or from social groups and public institutions. Another type of attribution was succeeding in challenging situations, such as managing the care of an elderly parent or accomplishing difficult tasks at work. Several respondents reported learn-ing new things about themselves from mastering new tasks, like learning how to use a computer for the first time in their lives. Finally, some respon-dents reported that they learned good things about themselves through praying, meditating, fasting, or deep religious experiences.

Self-Reported Impacts of Psychological Turning Points

Turning points are often described as life-changing and transformative. Table 2.4 summarizes the types of impact reported. A possible total of two types of impact were coded for each respondent. Two findings stand out. First, learning something new about oneself has a number of outcomes that are negative and positive. Second, it is notable that the majority of respondents reported not only negative impacts but also positive impacts from the situations they associated with learning something upsetting about themselves. In fact, the majority of those who learned something upsetting about themselves went on to describe the positive impact of these lessons.

There are two predominant themes in the reports of negative psychological impacts. One of the themes was the unexpected nature of depression and its impact on self-worth. One respondent offered, "I always thought that depression was all in your head, but I found out it is something you cannot control." Another said, "The sadness was the worst. It was overwhelming. I still don't see the end." Almost all respondents who reported depression as the predominant negative impact also described exceptionally severe events and changes or cascades of disasters as triggering the turning point. These events probably meet the criteria of severity associated with onset of depression (Brown & Harris, 1978). These respondents (and others who were not depressed) also frequently indicated that their lives were out of control or that their efforts at coping had failed. Others questioned their self-worth. One participant, contemplating continued unemployment, remarked, "For the first time in my life, failure is a part of my vocabulary."

The majority who described negative impacts also went on to describe how the same situations had had positive impacts, even when the situation was very stressful. These impacts are best described as lessons learned rather

TABLE 2.4
Self-Reported Impacts of Learning Upsetting Thing About Self, by Gender
(PTP, Percentages[a])

	Learning something upsetting about self		Learning something good about self	
	Men	Women	Men	Women
Depression	19	15	—	—
Questioning personal values and beliefs	5	2	—	—
Failed coping	4	10	—	—
Questioned self-worth	5	12	—	—
Life out of control	19	15	—	—
Long-term positive change	0	4	8	3
Withdrew from situation or reduced commitment	15	13	8	7
Learned what was important in life	28	19	17	21
Mastered the problem	4	4	8	4
Mastered the self	9	16	13	4
Gained more confidence	3	2	32	42
Learned can withstand stress	1	7	5	20
Learned new things about self, others, or situation	17	6	28	24
Compensated for loss	4	7	13	7
Renewed or found religious faith	1	7	1	5

[a]Percentages sum to more than 100% in columns because up to two impacts were coded per respondent.

than positive reappraisals of the situations to which the turning points are attributed (e.g., Aldwin et al., 1996). The majority of narratives about positive impact were reports of successful coping with the situation that caused the psychological turning point or plans for avoiding such problems in the future. The self-reported positive impacts group into several themes.

A frequently mentioned theme is learning what is important in life. "It's really sad that it takes a major event to make you realize things, but I guess that's the way the human mind behaves." After describing a job loss and career change that led to losing most of the family savings, one respondent reported learning, "It's not money that makes life good." After tending her mother through her last illness, a woman reported that despite her ambivalent reaction of deep sadness and welcome relief, the help she received from her sisters "made me realize the value of family."

Related themes of response are mastering the problem and withdrawing from the situation. Some were resolutions to plan better in the future. For example, one young woman diagnosed with a set of chronic diseases said, "I realized I need to make some dramatic changes in my life to stay healthy. I've started a regular regimen of doctor visits, [I control] my cholesterol and diabetes."

Still others report that the experience of stress itself had positive impacts on them. Specifically, they felt more confident or hardened, even if they could not master or change the situation they believe provoked the turning point. Almost every participant who reported this positive impact from a stressful situation said, "I felt stronger for it." Other frequent refrains were, "Now I know what I can take" and "I know that I could handle something like that again without breaking."

Some themes appear to be especially connected to different types of situations (although the numbers in each category are very small and should be interpreted with caution). Taking steps to maintain health in the wake of health problems was often described as "improving my character." Other respondents who reported health problems, primarily those with fatal diseases and shortened futures, frequently reported that they had "finally learned that family is the most important thing in life" and that they had "wasted their precious lives and time."

When learning upsetting things about themselves, participants tended to phrase the psychological impact as a lesson (see also Aldwin et al., 1996). When learning good things about themselves, respondents overwhelmingly reported becoming more confident or developing higher self-esteem. This reaction was reported not only by respondents who mastered difficult new tasks, such as the computer, but also for some of those who experienced negative events, for example, "As a widow, you begin to learn your own strengths. Strengths you didn't even know you had. It has given me confidence." Similarly, many respondents report that learning something good about themselves has made them more aware, more focused, and more able to meet challenge in the future.

Another major theme in reported positive impact is attaining and fulfilling goals. The goals people reported attained are varied, but include love, stronger relationships, public recognition, better health, stronger mental health, and self-respect (Schaefer & Moos, 1992). The narratives are particularly poignant when the triggering situation involves coming to terms with the end of life. One dying man reported, "I have learned to be sharing and open in my relationships. I have finally found peace."

CONCLUSION

Does tragedy only reap sorrow? People who report having experienced psychological turning points, even those that involved extremely stressful situations, also reported the experience of positive psychological growth. The major finding of these analyses is that perceptions of growth and strength are often born out of suffering and setbacks, as well as accomplishments and achievements.

This study has found support for its three initial hypotheses. First, events and situations symbolizing appropriate enactment of adult social roles are associated with psychological turning points. The quantitative analyses demonstrate that reports of both negative and positive psychological turning points are associated with expected and unexpected changes in major life roles: Marital stress, problems involving children, and chronic job stress are associated with reporting both negative and psychological turning points. Qualitative analyses revealed that major changes or disturbances in these important social roles, such as job loss, divorce, the illness of a child, and the diagnosis of fatal illness can be triggers of negative psychological turning points. Moreover, successes and recognition in these roles were frequently nominated as causes of positive psychological turning points.

Second, reports of having undergone a psychological turning point were modestly associated with personality characteristics, recent psychological disturbance (depression episode in the past 12 months), and beliefs about coping with stressful situations. Having a history of depression and trait neuroticism are associated with reporting both negative and positive psychological turning points. Those who report higher scores on insight as a coping strategy are also somewhat more likely to report both negative and positive psychological turning points. Because the quantitative data are cross-sectional, the analyses do not establish a causal priority in the association. It is just as likely that experiencing a psychological turning point may affect one's beliefs about coping with stress, as previous beliefs about coping with stress have affected the probability of reporting a psychological turning point. For example, it is likely that people with more insight are simply more likely to report a psychological turning point in an interview situation. However, analyses of qualitative data show, three years after the personality characteristics and beliefs about coping were assessed, that people frequently mention new insight as a positive psychological consequence of undergoing the events and difficulties that they report triggered the psychological turning point.

Third, both positive and negative psychological turning points were associated with stressors and challenges. Chronic stressors in marriage, at work, and with parenting were consistently predictive of reporting both negative and positive psychological turning points. The qualitative data confirm this interpretation for positive as well as negative psychological turning points.

The findings of this chapter, although preliminary and limited by the cross-sectional design of the study, have implications for studies of stress as well as for studies of psychological growth across the life span. The analyses of the qualitative data on psychological turning points raise several issues. When people reported the negative psychological impacts of learning upsetting things about themselves, they described depression, failed coping, and devaluation of the self. When they described positive impacts of negative psychological turning points, they reported how they coped successfully with the consequences of the events or difficulties that caused the turning point. Many of the responses echo items from typical coping inventories of coping behavior and coping style. People may report experiencing positive psychological growth because they believe they coped well with exceptionally challenging situations (see also Schaefer & Moos, 1992). They attribute success to solving the problem, to taking steps to avoid similar problems in the future, and to acquiring new knowledge and self-knowledge. Studies of coping with life challenges tend to focus on the management of depression as an outcome. This chapter suggests that studies of coping might gain new insights by shifting the focus to concrete outcomes, such as goal attainment, compensation for loss, and exiting the situation (see also Thoits, 1994). Stress research might also gain from investigation of the attainment of positive psychological health (see also Keyes, 2000).

The qualitative data suggest that reports of positive turning points are associated with mastering difficult situations. Longitudinal studies of responses to stress, particularly those that use a life span or life course perspective on the consequences of exposure to stress, might also benefit by incorporating outcomes from research on positive mental health (e.g., Keyes, 2000). Self-generated effort can reduce the negative effects of life difficulties (Thoits, 1994). Positive events may reverse the negative effects of earlier ones.

REFERENCES

Aldwin, C. M., Sutton, K. J., & Lachman, M. (1996). The development of coping resources in adulthood. *Journal of Personality, 64,* 837–871.

Brown, G. W., & Harris, T. O. (1978). *Social origins of depression: A study of psychiatric disorder in women.* New York: Free Press.

Clausen, J. A. (1993). *American lives: Looking back at the children of the Great Depression.* New York: The Free Press.

Clausen, J. A. (1995). Gender, contexts, and turning points in adults' lives. In P. Moen, G. H. Elder, & K. Luscher (Eds.), *Examining lives in context: Perspectives on the ecology of human development* (pp. 365–389). Washington, DC: American Psychological Association.

Clausen, J. A. (1998). Life reviews and life stories. In J. Z. Giele & G. H. Elder (Eds.), *Methods of life course research: Qualitative and quantitative approaches* (pp. 189–212). Thousand Oaks, CA: Sage.

Erikson, E. H. (1963). *Childhood and society.* New York: Norton.

Gould, R. (1978). *Transformations: Growth and change in adult life.* New York: Simon and Schuster.

Heatherton, T., & Nichols, P. A. (1994). Personal accounts of successful versus failed attempts at life change. *Personality and Social Psychology Bulletin, 20,* 664–675.

Keyes, C. L. M. (2000). Subjective change and its consequences for emotional well-being. *Motivation and Emotion, 24,* 67–84.

Levinson, D. J., Darrow, C. N., Klein, E. B., Levinson, M. H., & McKee, B. (1978). *The seasons of a man's life.* New York: Knopf.

Levinson, D. J., & Levinson, J. D. (1996). *The seasons of a woman's life.* New York: Knopf.

McAdams, D. P., & de St. Aubin, E. (1992). A theory of generativity and its assessment through self-report, behavioral acts, and narrative themes in autobiography. *Journal of Personality and Social Psychology, 62,* 1003–1015.

McAdams, D. P., Hart, H. M., & Maruna, S. (1998). The anatomy of generativity. In D. P. McAdams & E. de St. Aubin (Eds.), *Generativity and adult development: How and why we care for the next generation* (pp. 7–44). Washington, DC: American Psychological Association.

Mroczek, D. K., & Kolarz, C. (1998). The effects of age on positive and negative affect: A developmental perspective on happiness. *Journal of Personality and Social Psychology, 75,* 1333–1349.

Park, C. L., Cohen, L. H., & Murch, R. L. (1996). Assessment and prediction of stress-related growth. *Journal of Personality, 64,* 71–105.

Schaefer, J. A., & Moos, R. H. (1992). Life crises and personal growth. In B. N. Carpenter (Ed.), *Personal coping: Theory, research, and application* (pp. 149–170). Westport, CT: Praeger.

Settersten, R. A. (1999). *Lives in time and place: The problems and promises of developmental science*. Amityville, NY: Baywood.

Sheehy, G. (1976). *Passages: Predictable crises of adult life*. New York: Dutton.

Sheehy, G. (1995). *New passages: Mapping your life across time*. New York: Random House.

Thoits, P. A. (1994). Stressors and problem-solving: The individual as psychological activist. *Journal of Health of Social Behavior, 35*, 143–160.

Thurnher, M. (1983). Turning points and developmental change: Subjective and "objective" assessments. *American Journal of Orthopsychiatry, 53*, 52–60.

Turner, R. J., & Wheaton, B. (1995). Checklist measurement of stressful life events. In S. Cohen, R. C. Kessler, & L. U. Gordon (Eds.), *Measuring stress: A guide for health and social scientists* (pp. 29–58). New York: Oxford University Press.

Umberson, D., Wortman, C. B., & Kessler, R. C. (1992). Widowhood and depression: Explaining long-term gender differences in vulnerability. *Journal of Health and Social Behavior, 33*, 10–24.

Wethington, E. (2000). Expecting stress: Americans and the "midlife crisis." *Motivation and Emotion, 24*, 85–103.

Wethington, E., Cooper, H., & Holmes, C. S. (1997). Turning points in midlife. In I. H. Gotlib & B. Wheaton (Eds.), *Stress and adversity across the life course: Trajectories and turning points* (pp. 215–231). New York: Cambridge University Press.

Wethington, E., Kessler, R. C., & Pixley, J. E. (in press). Turning points in adulthood. In C. Ryff, R. C. Kessler, & O. G. Brim (Eds.), *Midlife in the United States*. Chicago: University of Chicago Press.

Wheaton, B., & Gotlib, I. H. (1997). Trajectories and turning points over the life course: Concepts and themes. In I. H. Gotlib & B. Wheaton (Eds.), *Stress and adversity across the life course: Trajectories and turning points* (pp. 1–25). New York: Cambridge University Press.

3

OPTIMISM AND FLOURISHING

CHRISTOPHER PETERSON AND EDWARD C. CHANG

Positive psychology is a rapidly emerging initiative within the social sciences, as evidenced by this book and other recent volumes devoted to positive psychology (e.g., Chang, 2001b; Gillham, 2000; Snyder & Lopez, 2002). To paraphrase Seligman (1998), positive psychology entails a focus on human strength as well as weakness, an interest in resilience as well as vulnerability, and a concern with cultivating wellness as well as remediating pathology. Positive psychologists seem to agree that optimism is an important construct to be included in this new approach to psychology (Peterson, 2000; Peterson & Steen, 2002).

As optimism researchers, we are pleased to see optimism featured in what seems to be a long-needed antidote to psychology's focus on what goes wrong with people. But we are also aware of some questions that need to be considered for optimism to thrive as part of this new psychology of flourishing. Perhaps the most general question to be raised concerns the type of optimism most pertinent to flourishing. Optimism and pessimism are both complex concepts, and research to date usually renders them in simplistic fashion.

In this contribution, we discuss optimism as studied within contemporary psychology, and we do so in the context of issues that might profitably be raised about the meaning of these concepts. Although empirical research into optimism has yielded a number of interesting and reliable findings, we believe that the best is yet to come, so long as optimism and pessimism are approached with sufficient conceptual and methodological sophistication. We begin by discussing the meanings of optimism and pessimism, focusing on distinctions that might be made within these constructs but rarely are. We illustrate the power of these distinctions in two ways: (a) by discussing how researchers might look more closely at data in light of them and (b) by summarizing research on the cultural context of optimism that makes most sense in terms of these distinctions.

IN THE BEGINNING: MEANINGS OF OPTIMISM AND PESSIMISM

The term *optimism* is a relatively recent arrival on the historical scene, as is its cousin *pessimism* (Sicinski, 1972). In the 1700s, Leibniz characterized optimism as a mode of thinking, and Voltaire popularized the term in his 1759 novel *Candide*, which was highly critical of the shallowness of an optimistic perspective. Interesting to us, pessimism appeared fully a century later, when it was independently introduced by Schopenhauer and Coleridge.

At least in their original forms, optimism and pessimism were not symmetric. Optimism as discussed by Leibniz was cognitive in its emphasis, reflecting a reasoned judgment that good would predominate over evil, even if goodness were associated with suffering. In contrast, pessimism as discussed by Schopenhauer had an emotional referent: The pessimistic individual was one for whom suffering would outweigh happiness. Note therefore that someone can be optimistic in the cognitive Leibniz sense yet pessimistic in the emotional Schopenhauer sense.

Does it really matter to the contemporary world how Leibniz and Schopenhauer originally defined optimism and pessimism? We think it does because these philosophers introduced complexities that survive in everyday connotations of optimism and pessimism, even if they are neglected by researchers. An optimistic person, as described by Leibniz, is one who has arrived at a *reasoned* conclusion that eventually good will outweigh bad. Optimism is not accepted on blind faith; it is not happiness or even contentment; it is not freedom from setbacks and disappointments. Indeed, Voltaire's Candide is not a good example of optimism so defined.

Some of the ostensible puzzles of optimism and pessimism research can be resolved if we approach these constructs as complex and occasionally independent of one another. If we want to cultivate well-being, we need to be clear just how we wish to define the good life. In some cases, optimism as a cognitive perspective should be encouraged even though pessimism as an emotional mode is validated and left intact.

OPTIMISM AND PESSIMISM IN TODAY'S PSYCHOLOGY

Peterson (2000) reviewed some of the contemporary work on optimism, noting that most discussions of optimism take one of two forms. In the first, optimism is posited as an inherent part of human nature, either to be praised or decried. Enemies of optimism, as it were, included such writers as Sophocles, Nietzsche, and Freud, whereas its proponents included such individuals as Socrates, de Condorcet, Maslow, and Rogers. This first tack on optimism was thoroughly reviewed by Tiger (1979).

The second approach to optimism approaches it as an individual difference: a characteristic that people possess to varying degrees. These two approaches can be compatible. Our human nature provides a baseline optimism, of which individuals show more versus less, and our experiences influence the degree to which we are optimistic or pessimistic. In this chapter, we focus on this second tradition of optimism and pessimism as individual differences, but we return in our conclusion to comment on the first tradition of optimism and pessimism as human nature and the relationship they have to well-being and the "good life."

At present, the well-known approaches to optimism and pessimism as individual differences include lines of research into (a) dispositional optimism and (b) explanatory style undertaken. Neither of these research traditions makes the sorts of distinctions suggested by our brief historical review, and furthermore, there have been few attempts to examine critically points of convergence and divergence between dispositional optimism and explanatory style. These are different yet related constructs, and one of our purposes is to compare and contrast them. To be sure, there have been some previous attempts to do so, but these have tended to be partisan endeavors, typically written by someone with a clear allegiance to only one of these cognates of optimism and thus a desire to dismiss or subsume the other.

We briefly survey these popular approaches to optimism as an individual difference variable. It is no coincidence that each has an associated self-report questionnaire measure that lends itself to efficient research. The correlates of each version of optimism have therefore been extensively investigated. Research seems to show that optimism, however measured, is linked to desirable characteristics—happiness, perseverance, achievement, and health—although a close reading of the actual studies often leads to the more exact conclusion that pessimism is associated with undesirable characteristics.

In any event, what is less clear is why these correlations occur (Peterson & Steen, 2002). Optimism and pessimism research to date has looked more at correlations with distant adaptational outcomes than at the mechanisms that lead to these outcomes. Researchers have promiscuously moved from one outcome measure to another to still another. This restlessness has doubtlessly kept alive interest in optimism and pessimism, but it has precluded a full understanding of the phenomena.

Especially as optimism researchers join the positive psychology movement, greater attention to mechanisms is needed. We can expect that numerous mechanisms can lead from optimism and pessimism to outcomes and also that the particular mix of mechanisms will depend on the outcome of interest (Peterson & Bossio, 1991). Complicating any specification of the process by which effects are produced is the fact that the same construct—for example, mood—may be a mechanism in one case but an outcome in another.

Likely mechanisms are to be found on a variety of levels, starting with biology. Emotional mechanisms also deserve attention, given the extensive research literature showing a link between pessimism and depression (Sweeney, Anderson, & Bailey, 1986). There are probably several cognitive pathways linking optimism and pessimism to outcomes. Expectations and attributions are not isolated beliefs but rather parts of a complex knowledge system that can influence well-being in numerous ways. Yet another explanation of why optimistic thinking is related to outcomes entails a social pathway. Pessimistic people are often socially isolated (Anderson & Arnault, 1985), and social isolation predicts poor adaptation in a wide variety of realms (Cohen & Syme, 1985). Conversely, optimistic people may reap the benefits of rich social networks and appropriate social support.

As we see it, the most typical and robust mechanism linking optimism and outcomes entails behavior. We speculate that optimistic individuals may be more likely than pessimistic individuals to enter settings in which good things can and do happen. The more general point is that positive psychologists should not look just within the person but also at the person's setting, including his or her culture. Optimism may influence not only the settings that people choose but also what they do in these settings. Just as important, settings differ in the degree to which they allow positive characteristics to develop and be deployed. Positive psychology should not decontextualize the strengths and abilities that make possible the good life; congratulating the winner should be no more a part of psychology than blaming the victim (cf. Ryan, 1978).

Dispositional Optimism

Scheier and Carver (1992) have studied extensively a personality variable they identify as *dispositional optimism:* the global expectation that good things will be plentiful in the future and bad things scarce. Scheier and Carver's overriding perspective is in terms of how people pursue goals, defined as desirable values. To Scheier and Carver, virtually all realms of human activity can be cast in goal terms, and people's behavior entails the identification and adoption of goals and the regulation of actions with respect to these goals. The authors therefore refer to their approach as a self-regulatory model (Carver & Scheier, 1981).

Optimism enters into self-regulation when people ask themselves about impediments to the achievement of the goals they have adopted. In the face of difficulties, do people nonetheless believe that goals will be achieved? If so, they are optimistic; if not, they are pessimistic. Optimism leads to continued efforts to attain the goal, whereas pessimism leads to passivity.

Scheier and Carver (1985) measure optimism (versus pessimism) with a brief self-report questionnaire called the Life Orientation Test (LOT). Representative items, with which respondents agree or disagree, include,

1. In uncertain times, I usually expect the best.
2. If something can go wrong for me it will. [reverse-scored]

Positive expectations are usually combined with reverse-scored negative expectations, and the resulting measure is investigated with respect to psychological and physical well-being. More recently, Scheier, Carver, and Bridges (1994) have introduced the revised Life Orientation Test (LOT-R), which is believed to be a better measure of dispositional optimism. Whether based on the LOT or the LOT-R, results show that dispositional optimism is linked to desirable outcomes and in particular to active and effective coping (e.g., Carver et al., 1993; Scheier & Carver, 1987; Scheier et al., 1989; Strack, Carver, & Blaney, 1987). However, some studies have found that it may be the decreased use of passive and ineffective coping efforts rather than the increased use of active coping efforts that distinguishes individuals who are dispositionally optimistic from those who are dispositionally pessimistic (Chang, 1998).

The optimism items of the LOT negatively correlate with the pessimism items but not so highly that the LOT or LOT-R are unidimensional (e.g., Chang, D'Zurilla, & Maydeu-Olivares, 1994; Marshall, Wortman, Kusulas, Hervig, & Vickers, 1992; Robinson-Whelen, Kim, MacCallum, & Kiecolt-Glaser, 1997). Furthermore, optimism and pessimism so measured have somewhat different correlates. We discuss some of the relevant studies later in this chapter, but for the time being, let us comment that the occasional independence of optimism and pessimism is more than a methodological nuisance. In substantive terms, some people can be said to have hedonically rich expectations, whereas other people have muted expectations. At the extremes of this dimension, we may find *DSM-IV* personality disorders— for example, borderline personality disorder in the case of extreme expectations and obsessive–compulsive personality in the case of minimal expectations manifesting as anhedonia (American Psychiatric Association, 1994). Be that as it may, it seems prudent for researchers to distinguish optimism and pessimism when using the LOT. It may well be that the independence of optimism and pessimism is related to the separate brain systems apparently responsible for positive versus negative affectivity (R. Davidson, 1984).

Explanatory Style

Seligman and his colleagues have approached optimism in terms of an individual's characteristic explanatory style—how he or she explains the causes of bad events (Buchanan & Seligman, 1995). Those who explain bad events in a circumscribed way, with external, unstable, and specific causes, are described as optimistic, whereas those who favor internal, stable, and global causes are described as pessimistic.

The notion of explanatory style emerged from the attributional reformulation of the learned helplessness model (Abramson, Seligman, & Teasdale, 1978). Briefly, the original helplessness model proposed that following experience with uncontrollable aversive events, animals and people become helpless–passive and unresponsive—presumably because they have "learned" that there is no contingency between actions and outcomes (Maier & Seligman, 1976). This learning is represented cognitively as a generalized expectancy that future outcomes will be unrelated to outcomes. It is this generalized expectation of response–outcome independence that produces later helplessness.

Explanatory style was added to the helplessness model to better account for the boundary conditions of human helplessness following uncontrollability. When is helplessness general, and when is it circumscribed? People who encounter a bad event ask "why?" Their causal attribution determines how they respond to the event. If it is a stable (long-lasting) cause, helplessness is thought to be chronic. If it is a pervasive (global) cause, helplessness is thought to be widespread. If it is an internal cause, self-esteem is thought to suffer.

People have a habitual way of explaining bad events—an explanatory style—and this explanatory style is posited as a distal influence on helplessness following adversity (Peterson & Seligman, 1984). Explanatory style is typically measured with a self-report questionnaire called the Attributional Style Questionnaire (ASQ) that presents respondents with hypothetical events involving themselves and asks them to provide "the one major cause" of each event if it were to happen to them (Peterson et al., 1982). They then rate these provided causes along dimensions of internality, stability, and globality. Ratings are combined by averaging within dimensions, separately for good events and for bad events.

In some versions of the ASQ, respondents make attributions for bad events and good events. Explanatory style based on bad events is usually independent of explanatory style for good events, which points again to the potential importance of distinguishing pessimism and optimism. Explanatory style based on bad events usually has more robust correlates than explanatory style based on good events, although correlations are typically in the opposite directions (Peterson, 1991). However, researchers have not usually looked for domains in which explanatory style for good events should be especially pertinent. A start in this direction was made by Abramson, Metalsky, and Alloy (1989), who speculated that "good" explanatory style is pertinent to the savoring of good events and may thus be related to recovery from depression. "Bad" explanatory style, emphasized by the reformulated helplessness theory, predicts the onset of depression. But this interesting possibility has not been systematically explored.

A second way of measuring explanatory style is with a content analysis procedure—the CAVE (an acronym for Content Analysis of Verbatim Explanations)—that allows written or spoken material to be scored for naturally occurring causal explanations (Peterson, Schulman, Castellon, & Seligman, 1992). Researchers identify explanations for bad events, "extract" them, and present them to judges who rate them along the scales of the ASQ. The CAVE technique makes possible longitudinal studies after the fact, so long as spoken or written material can be located from early in the lives of individuals for whom long-term outcomes of interest are known.

Remember that the generalized expectation of response–outcome independence is hypothesized as the proximal cause of helplessness, even though research in this tradition has rarely looked at this mediating variable. Rather, researchers measure explanatory style and correlate it with outcomes thought to revolve around helplessness: depression; illness; and failure in academic, athletic, and vocational realms. Results are usually as expected: A pessimistic explanatory style correlates with poor adaptation in a variety of domains.

As explanatory style research has progressed and theory has been modified, the internality dimension has become of less interest. It has more inconsistent correlates than stability or globality, it is less reliably assessed, and there are theoretical grounds for doubting that it has a direct impact on expectations per se (Peterson, 1991). Indeed, internality may well conflate self-blame and self-efficacy, which would explain why it fares poorly in empirical tests. In a modification of the helplessness reformulation, Abramson et al. (1989) emphasized only stability and globality.

The most important recent chapter in helplessness research was the reframing of explanatory style by Seligman (1991) in his book *Learned Optimism*, in which he described how his lifelong interest in what can go wrong with people changed into an interest in what can go right (Seligman, 1975). Research on helplessness was flipped into an interest in what Seligman called optimism, although he could have called it mastery, effectance, or control. His terminology is justified by the central concern in helplessness theory with expectations, but it is worth emphasizing yet again that these expectations tend not to be explicitly studied and also that these expectations are not about the likelihood of good events but rather about the contingency between events, good and bad, and responses.

COMPARISONS AND CONTRASTS: WHICH DISTINCTIONS DESERVE ATTENTION?

On one level, the Scheier and Carver approach is congruent with the Seligman approach. LOT/LOT-R correlates and ASQ/CAVE correlates are strikingly similar. Optimism measured in these ways correlates with good mood and absence of depression, good health, achievement, and active coping. Some of the relevant studies have had longitudinal designs that controlled for baseline levels of the outcomes of interest; optimism predicts well-being above and beyond these baselines. Measures of dispositional optimism and explanatory style tend to converge when they are—rarely—examined together in the same study (e.g., Hjelle, Busch, & Warren, 1996; Hull & Mendolia, 1991; Peterson & Vaidya, 2001).

However, a closer look reveals some critical differences between dispositional optimism and explanatory style. As we have already described, the LOT is a straightforward measure of expectation about the occurrence of events. An optimistic expectation leads to the belief that goals will be achieved, although it is neutral with respect to how this will happen. In contrast, ASQ measures perceived causality, so it is influenced in addition by people's beliefs about how goals are realized. Said another way, optimistic explanatory style is more entwined with agency than is dispositional optimism, and this distinction seems an important one for researchers and theorists to keep in mind.

Both approaches either ignore whether optimism or pessimism might be warranted by the objective situation or assume that their reality basis does not matter. Perhaps this is why many researchers approach optimism and pessimism in broad cross-situational terms.[1] In any event, we think the veracity of optimism and pessimism is too important to overlook. Sometimes causal explanations or expectations are well-grounded in reality; they are accurate given the individual's setting and his or her resources. This type of optimism is likely to be linked to desirable outcomes, although a researcher must be sure that the optimistic beliefs add something to prediction of these outcomes above and beyond the reality on which the beliefs are based. Otherwise, results are trivial. So, a wealthy individual may believe that she can pay all of her bills every month, but it is her bank account that makes this

---

[1]There exists a small research tradition based on the premise that optimistic and pessimistic expectancies or attributions may involve situation-, goal-, or content-specific dimensions or concomitants. More than half a century ago, Sanford, Conrad, and Franck (1946) considered the value of assessing for expectancies regarding the consequences of war. More recently, researchers have looked at optimism associated with academic performance (Peterson & Barrett, 1987; Prola & Stern, 1984), love relationships (Carnelley & Janoff-Bulman, 1992), AIDS (Taylor et al., 1992), and even with seeing the dentist (Wardle, 1984). The problem with this research is that it tends not to include measures of domain-irrelevant optimism, which means that the premise of situational specificity is never tested.

possible and not her optimism per se. Such possibilities are why longitudinal designs controlling for baseline levels of the outcomes of interest are more compelling than simple cross-sectional demonstrations of a link between optimism and an apparent outcome.

Sometimes causal explanations or expectations are objectively unrealistic, in which case positive thinking not only pays no dividends but may have considerable costs. For example, a recent study found that the positive associations between negative life events and depressive and physical symptoms were exacerbated by high dispositional optimism (Chang & Sanna, in press). That is, dispositionally optimistic individuals who experienced the greatest accumulation of negative life events over a one-year period (implying that their optimism was unwarranted) reported the highest levels of depressive and physical symptoms. It is interesting to note that another study found a very different set of findings when appraised stress, rather than negative life events, was examined. Chang (in press) showed that the positive associations between appraised stress and depressive and psychological symptoms were significantly more exacerbated for dispositional pessimists than for dispositional optimists. These finding were consistent across a sample of younger adults and older adults. Given that subjective (e.g., stress appraisal) and objective indexes of stress (e.g., negative life events) have been found to make independent contributions to adjustment (e.g., Cohen, Tyrrell, & Smith, 1993), these contrasting findings for dispositional optimism and pessimism indicate that there may be costs and benefits associated with both of these states (Tennen & Affleck, 1987).

For another example, consider a robust finding documented in the epidemiology literature. Research participants are asked to provide a percentage estimate of the likelihood, compared to peers, that they will someday contract an illness or experience some trauma. People consistently and strikingly underestimate their risks: The average individual sees him- or herself as below average in risk for a variety of maladies, which of course cannot be. This phenomenon is identified as an optimistic bias (Weinstein, 1989), and it is decried because it may lead people to neglect the basics of health promotion and maintenance. For example, people who believe that they are below risk for contracting HIV may behave exactly in ways that increase their risk (Kok, Ho, Heng, & Ong, 1990). Compared to their separate effects, the combination of an optimistic bias and dispositional optimism may result in even more health-compromising outcomes. For example, K. Davidson and Prkachin (1997) found that adults who expressed both high dispositional optimism and a high optimistic bias tended to display the greatest decrease in exercise over a six-week period relative to others who differed from them on these two dimensions.

For yet another example, "John Henryism" is a personality characteristic reflecting the degree to which someone believes that important life outcomes can be controlled if enough effort is exerted. Among African American males of low socioeconomic status who lack the resources to make their belief in control a reality, John Henryism is linked to elevated blood pressure and presumably to all of the negative cardiac outcomes that result from hypertension (James, Hartnett, & Kalsbeek, 1983). Along these lines, the Type A coronary-prone behavior pattern seems to involve exaggerated beliefs about what the individual can make happen, and this style again has been linked to cardiac morbidity and mortality (Friedman & Rosenman, 1974). One can also argue that such problematic styles as hostility, perfectionism, and procrastination entail erroneous expectations (Peterson, 1999).

In a third case, optimism is neither realistic nor unrealistic but rather indeterminate. A person's circumstances do not guarantee a given outcome, and they do not preclude it. Beliefs thus can translate themselves into outcomes via self-fulfilling prophecies. These types of optimism and pessimism are usually of most interest to researchers, who assign to these beliefs a causal role and thus try to study situations in which optimism and pessimism matter above and beyond reality. There is nothing wrong with this strategy of investigation, and the necessary qualifications are well-understood by researchers. But we must be aware that when the members of the general public hear about a given finding (e.g., "optimism is associated with a long and productive life"), they may not be aware of the necessary qualification, usually because we as researchers do not stress the qualifications ourselves. Optimism in a war zone or during a famine probably has little effect on outcomes that are beyond the influence of an individual person's beliefs. Optimism on one's death bed may bring contentment, but it will not reverse an insidious disease process or prolong life.

Taken together, these ideas about optimism and pessimism as individual differences—both the established theories as well as the qualifications just made—suggest a family of features that should all be taken seriously. A composite account of optimism and pessimism should (a) distinguish positive expectations from negative expectations; (b) acknowledge the person's sense of agency (or not) with respect to the outcomes that are the subject of expectancies; (c) allow for the possibility that these beliefs may be accurate, inaccurate, or indeterminate; and (d) specify whether optimism and pessimism are rendered in mainly cognitive terms or mainly emotional terms. Consider what it means to take seriously these different features. Optimism and pessimism are complex constructs, and it makes no sense to speak of the former as always desirable and the latter as always undesirable. Nonetheless, optimism researchers often generalize glibly across features that matter.

For example, dispositional optimism is a positive expectation with a cognitive flavor; it collapses across agency and across reality basis. Look at the disparate phenomena that are thereby subsumed. Complicating additional research into dispositional optimism is that the typical way of scoring this individual difference from the LOT or LOT-R is to juxtapose it with dispositional pessimism (a negative expectation again with a cognitive flavor collapsed across agency and reality bases). Are the possible examples of dispositional optimism meaningful opposites of the possible examples of dispositional pessimism?

In contrast, explanatory style is a negative expectation (given that explanatory style is usually scored from attributions about negative events) with a cognitive flavor and an assumption of agency. What about its reality basis? If we add in the assumptions of the learned helplessness model from which explanatory style sprung, then we might assert that there is a (past) reality basis, but typical research does not look at this (Peterson, Maier, & Seligman, 1993); perhaps it is best to say that like dispositional optimism the explanatory style construct does not make this distinction. Regardless, when we start to investigate what explanatory style does and does not capture, we again see oversimplifications.

For example, a recent study has linked pessimistic explanatory style to increased mortality as a result of accidental trauma (Peterson, Seligman, Yurko, Martin, & Friedman, 1998). On the face of it, this finding may reflect helplessness on the part of pessimists: They are poor problem solvers and do not do a good job removing themselves from harm's way. But follow-up studies have suggested a different interpretation: Those with a pessimistic explanatory style lead a more risky life and may actually prefer potentially dangerous settings (Peterson et al., 2001). What this might mean is not yet clear, but "pessimists" are not acting in helpless fashion—just in a foolish fashion. Inasmuch as other studies show that pessimistic explanatory style indeed predicts helpless behavior in some circumstances (Alloy, Peterson, Abramson, & Seligman, 1984), we must conclude that this form of pessimism indexes different ways of behaving, some well-described by the learned helplessness model and others not.

A close look at which features of optimism or pessimism are tapped by a given operationalization suggest the mechanisms that lead from these psychological states to various outcomes of interest. To continue the example under discussion, if the key feature of a pessimistic explanatory style is diminished agency, then we would expect that pessimistic individuals would respond to unpleasant circumstances by seeking "external" solutions, like putting themselves in situations that promise to distract them. This is exactly what we have found in our research, along with an interesting twist along the lines of gender: Women with a pessimistic explanatory style report that they respond to bad moods by eating, whereas their male counterparts report that they respond to bad moods by doing something dangerous or reckless (Peterson et al., 2001).

WHAT DO THE DATA SHOW?

Most of us casually treat optimism and pessimism as simple opposites. Indeed, we often measure these constructs with the same scale, anchored at one end with optimism and at the other with pessimism. Literally hundreds of studies using a variety of operationalizations and designs show that when people are placed along a continuum from pessimistic to optimistic and examined with respect to some measure of adaptation, "optimism" seems to be correlated with good outcomes and "pessimism" with bad outcomes. The conclusion follows from these findings that optimism accompanies flourishing, whether our focus is on good mood and morale; on perseverance and active problem solving; on social connectedness; on academic, military, political, and vocational success; or on good health, longevity, recovery from illness, and freedom from trauma (Peterson, 2000). These data have been the subject of numerous reviews, and we therefore do not enumerate the relevant studies.

What we do instead is to direct the reader's attention to Figure 3.1. The x-axis of the graph represents an pessimism–optimism continuum, and the y-axis represents any and all outcome measures of interest. Both axes have identified midpoints. For the x-axis, the midpoint corresponds to the individual who is neither pessimistic nor optimistic—the average Joe or Josephine. For the y-axis, the midpoint is average, typical, or unremarkable functioning with respect to the measured outcome: mood, health, achievement, and so on. A family of hypothetical lines is shown, all of which would be described by the positive correlation coefficients consistent with the typical interpretation of the optimism-flourishing literature. The important point is that each line suggests a different conclusion about the relationship of optimism and pessimism to well-being.

Suppose the outcome measure reflects only degrees of good functioning. Then it is only possible to have lines *a*, *b*, or *c*. The only literally straight line among these is *b*, which shows that pessimism has a cost and that optimism has a benefit. Line *a* in contrast shows that pessimism has a cost but that optimism has no particular benefit; it captures what has been dubbed the power of nonnegative thinking. Line *c* shows that pessimism has no cost but that optimism has a benefit. The remaining lines can be analogously interpreted.

Nearly all optimism research looks at the overall relationship among variables without examining the full distribution of data that make up the relationship. Although imprecise measurement would often preclude definitive distinctions among the literally straight lines and the others, we are aware of no published studies that have even made the attempt. We think that researchers should scrutinize their data as closely possible. If it were established that optimism per se confers no particular advantage beyond

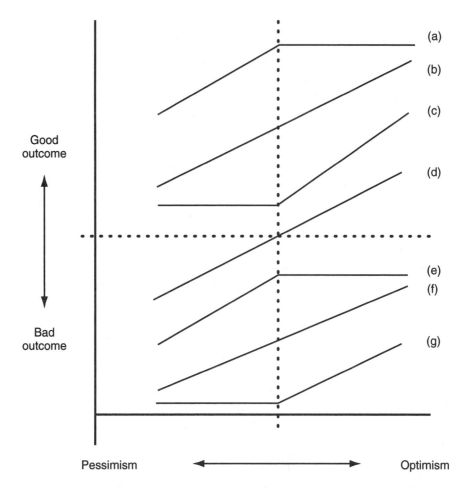

Figure 3.1. What do the data show? Possible forms of a correlation between optimism/pessimism and outcome measures.

the absence of pessimism, we would have an intriguing view of human nature reminiscent of humanistic psychology of the 1960s: People function well unless they have a reason not to do so. Conversely, if pessimism per se does not compromise how people function, we should leave these beliefs alone in therapeutic or preventive interventions. And so on.

Another criticism of not looking closely at what the data show is that researchers may study lines *e*, *f*, or *g*, and then discuss the results as if the data reflected lines *a*, *b*, or *c*. For example, if we find that pessimistic individuals are depressed and physically ill (e.g., Peterson & Seligman, 1984; Peterson, Seligman, & Vaillant, 1988), we glibly render this result as showing that optimistic people are happy and healthy, even if our outcomes measures did not "allow" people to manifest happiness or health (e.g., Peterson & Bossio, 1991).

There is more to happiness than the absence of depression (Myers & Diener, 1995), and there is more to health than the absence of illness (Seeman, 1989). But somehow this obvious point can be ignored when optimism researchers interpret their findings. So long as outcome measures reflect only degrees of pathology, no conclusions can be drawn about flourishing. This is an important lesson for positive psychologists of all stripes. It is not enough to study "positive" predictors like optimism or wisdom or courage or future-mindedness; one must also study "positive" outcomes. For example, according to Ryff's (1989; also, Ryff & Keyes, 1995) conceptualization of subjective well-being, positive psychological adjustment in adults can be viewed as reflecting several relatively distinct and important dimensions (autonomy, environmental mastery, personal growth, positive relations with others, purpose in life, and self-acceptance; see also chapter 13, this volume).

An example of the interesting results that can come from a full range of outcome measures is research into defensive pessimism by Norem and Cantor (1986). Some students cope with anxiety about pending exams by expressing negative expectations. This process harnesses their anxiety, which might otherwise interfere with their performance. They actually do better on the exam than individuals who are not allowed to indulge their pessimism. The only way that this finding was possible was by using an outcome measure that allowed a full range of possibilities, from bad to good. These data also show that pessimism is not always dysfunctional: Its role depends on the context.

THE CULTURAL CONTEXT OF OPTIMISM AND PESSIMISM

Let us move to a discussion of the cultural context of optimism and pessimism, where studies to date show that the distinctions so far made matter (e.g., Anderson, 1999; Crittendon, 1996; Domino & Lin, 1993; Heine & Lehman, 1995; Kuroda & Suzuki, 1991; Lee, Hallahan, & Herzog, 1996; Oettingen, 1995; Schutte, Valerio, & Carrillo, 1996). One question is whether cultures vary in their overall optimism and pessimism. In keeping with our argument, we can ask more specifically if cultures differ in the types of optimism that are common. This question then leads to additional questions about the relationship of optimism and pessimism to different outcomes. Do these relationships vary by culture? Are the mechanisms linking optimism and pessimism to outcomes a function of culture?

Remember the features of optimism that we introduced. Might cultures differ in their endorsement of these features? In the contemporary United

States, for example, feeling good is very important to people, and we should expect to see a relentless accent on the positive (Heine, Lehman, Markus, & Kitayama, 1999). In contrast, traditional Muslim cultures value sobriety and solemnity. This does not mean that clinical depression is a goal people seek, but it does suggest that positive expectations do not run amok. "Be your own best friend" is an unlikely bumper sticker slogan to see in Saudi Arabia, for example.

Cultures clearly differ in their emphasis on individual agency (Markus & Kitayama, 1991), and again the contemporary United States would seem to fall far out on this continuum (Peterson et al., 1993). In the United States, the most important goals we have as a people include individual choices, individual rights, and individual fulfillment (Peterson, 2000). Americans are greatly occupied with what they can and cannot accomplish in their everyday lives, and in particular with what they can acquire. These expectations tend to be decontextualized, unqualified by a consideration of the social, economic, and historical factors that can shape outcomes (Wallach & Wallach, 1983). In the United States, all things are possible to the right-thinking individual, and this sort of positive thinking is a tradition that dates back hundreds of years (Meyer, 1988).

Other cultures emphasize individual agency less but other aspects of optimism more. Indeed, optimism need not be attached just to individual agency. Collective agency—collective optimism, if you will—is an important value for cultures that emphasize the collectivity over the individual (Zaccaro, Blair, Peterson, & Zazanis, 1995). So Western cultures have been described as being individualistic (Markus & Kitayama, 1991; Triandis, 1995). In such cultures, individuals are expected to seek independence from others by attending to the self (Greenwald, 1980). As a result, individuals from such cultures grow to develop a sense of the self largely independent of others. In cultures where the independent self is predominant, we find a self-enhancing bias involving overly positive views of the self, illusions of control, and unrealistic optimism (e.g., Taylor & Brown, 1988).

In contrast, the focus in Eastern cultures traditionally has been on a view of the individual who maintains a fundamental relatedness with others (Markus & Kitayama, 1991). Attending to others, harmonious interdependence with them, and fitting in not only are valued but are often expected, which results in an interdependent view of the self (Weisz, Rothbaum, & Blackburn, 1984; Yee, 1992). Within collectivist culture, the resulting bias appears to be toward self-effacement: the tendency to see oneself as being more typical or average than others (Heine & Lehman, 1995).

Insofar as research has linked optimism to self-enhancing biases and pessimism to self-effacing biases, one should find cultural differences in optimism and pessimism. Yet only a few studies have looked at this issue empirically (Chang, 2001a). We now review some key findings obtained in two recent studies of cultural differences in the features of optimism and pessimism.

Optimism and Pessimism Among Asians and Non-Asians

In a recent study, Lee and Seligman (1997) assessed the explanatory style for both bad events and good events of three college student groups: mainland Chinese, Chinese Americans, and European Americans. With respect to explanatory style for good events, both Chinese Americans and European American students had elevated scores relative to mainland Chinese students. Thus, Chinese Americans appeared to be just as optimistic as European Americans, whereas mainland Chinese were less optimistic than the two American groups. In contrast, both mainland Chinese and Chinese Americans had elevated scores for explanatory style for bad events compared to European Americans. So Chinese Americans appeared to be as pessimistic as mainland Chinese, whereas European Americans were less pessimistic than both Asian groups.

These findings raise some possibilities for future investigation. For example, that pessimistic explanatory style based on bad events was elevated for both Asian groups raises the possibility that this sort of pessimism might be a sensibility of Asians less likely to change with acculturation. Said another way, what has *not* changed for Chinese who have immigrated to the United States? Kao, Nagata, and Peterson's (1997) research provides one answer: A pessimistic explanatory style (based on bad events) was linked among a group of Asian American college students to a style of family upbringing that emphasized submissiveness and deemphasized dominance.

In a different study, Chang (1996) examined dispositional optimism and pessimism in Asian American and European Americans college students. All participants completed measures at two points in time. At Time 1, participants completed a version of the LOT separately scored for optimism and pessimism (Chang, Maydeu-Olivares, & D'Zurilla, 1997). At Time 2, approximately a month and a half later, participants completed measures of depressive symptoms and physical symptoms.

As Lazarus and Folkman (1984) argued, links between individual differences variables like optimism and adjustment are likely to be mediated by styles of coping. Hence, a measure of coping strategies that assessed engaged coping (i.e., problem solving, cognitive restructuring, expressing emotion, and seeking social support) and disengaged coping (i.e., problem avoidance, wishful thinking, self-criticism, and social withdrawal) was also included in the study at Time 1.

Several questions were addressed. First, do Asian Americans and European Americans differ on optimism or pessimism as measured by the LOT?

Like Lee and Seligman (1997), Chang (1996) found that the two groups did not differ with respect to optimism. However, the Asian Americans were more pessimistic than the European Americans.

Second, do optimism or pessimism differentially predict adjustment among Asian Americans and European Americans? To address this question, Chang (1996) conducted a series of regression analyses to identify predictors of each adjustment measure for each ethnic group. In addition to separate optimism and pessimism scores, scores on each of the coping strategies (as well as age and sex) were also included. Results of these analyses indicated that there were indeed different predictors of adjustment in the two groups. Among Asian Americans, low scores on optimism predicted psychological and physical adjustment, whereas among European Americans, high scores on pessimism predicted psychological adjustment.

Third, are there differences in the pattern of associations among the study variables between Asian Americans and European Americans? Chang (1996) found that the pattern of correlations between the various study measures for Asian Americans was different from the one found for European Americans. Most striking was the difference in the direction of the associations between pessimism and two of the engagement coping strategies (problem solving and expressing emotions) for Asian Americans compared to European Americans. Specifically, pessimism was negatively associated with use of problem solving and expressing emotions for European Americans. In contrast, pessimism was found to be associated positively with use of these coping strategies for Asian Americans. So, increased active coping among Asian Americans was predicted by high pessimism scores, where decreased active coping among European Americans was predicted by high pessimism scores.

Asians as Defensive Pessimists?

Is the complex pessimism of Asians a problem, or might it be beneficial in the cultural context in which it occurs? One possibility might be that pessimism helps Asians achieve positive consequences. As Norem and Cantor (1986) and Aspinwall and Brunhart (1996) argued, optimism and pessimism are not simply what people *have* because they are optimists or pessimists but rather a reflection of what people *do* (e.g., using a particular way of thinking about certain things) in relation to a specific goal. Hence, Asian Americans also might use their pessimism as a strategy to think about potential negative consequences as a means to motivate themselves toward proactive behavior (e.g., problem solving) while at the same time preserving social harmony through the expression of modesty (e.g., not setting themselves apart from their peers). Insofar as the link between pessimism and problem solving does result in more positive rather than negative consequences, this can help explain why elevated pessimism is maintained among Asians. As emphasized earlier, greater research attention to mechanisms can help make sense of why culture seems to matter.

CONCLUSION

We have covered a number of topics in this chapter, from the philosophical origins of the notions of optimism and pessimism to empirical studies of these psychological characteristics among different ethnic groups. The general theme that runs through what we have written is the idea that distinctions matter. Optimism and pessimism are not simple opposites, and findings with respect to the one construct cannot be flipped into conclusions about the other. Furthermore, within the constructs of optimism and pessimism, there are potentially important features that should be taken into account. Most research, including our own, has not grappled fully with these distinctions, but we urge strongly that future research take them seriously, especially as cross-cultural studies of optimism and pessimism are beginning in earnest.

Western investigators are translating the LOT and the ASQ and going forth to measure the optimism and pessimism of the world. Interesting findings will no doubt result, but we suspect that these might be even more interesting if researchers do not expect optimism and pessimism to work the same way in all cultures. Different cultures will emphasize different features of these psychological states, and they will likely bear different relationships to different outcomes. In that regard, it is worth briefly returning to our earlier comments on the importance of assessing expectancies with respect to positive outcomes. It is critical for researchers to consider what are appropriate and inappropriate positive and negative outcomes. For example, although many of the dimensions of subjective well-being (e.g., autonomy, personal growth, and self-acceptance) identified by Ryff and her colleagues are likely to appear as meaningful indexes of adjustment for most Westerners, it remains to be seen whether they are useful and meaningful for most Easterners.

We do not doubt that some form of optimism or the absence of some form of pessimism is linked to the good life around the world, but just which forms will probably vary. If we wish to encourage well-being and help people flourish, we need more than a one-size-fits-all optimism-boosting program. Remember Chang's (1996) finding that lack of optimism—not the presence of pessimism—predicted subsequent depressive symptoms in Asian Americans. Accordingly, a culture-specific intervention consistent with Beck's (1976) cognitive framework might focus distinctly on increasing optimistic thoughts in distressed Asian American clients rather than on decreasing their pessimistic thoughts. As noted by Chang (1996), "By decreasing pessimism in Asian Americans, one could conceivably take away a major source of motivation that is related to adaptive and engaged coping behaviors such as problem solving" (p. 121). Hence, it may be particularly valuable to use interventions that focus on increasing this client group's level of optimism, whereas for European Americans, it may be more valuable to use interventions that focus on decreasing their level of pessimism.

Furthermore, findings from Chang's (1996) study also suggest the need for examining the clinical significance of various *combinations* of high and low optimism and pessimism within individuals. Because Asians and Asian Americans may "normally" express elevated levels of pessimism (Chang, 1996; Lee & Seligman, 1997), it would be important to distinguish subgroups who do and do not express a concomitant level of optimism. For example, Asian Americans who express high levels of pessimism relative to European Americans, but little optimism, may be particularly vulnerable to psychological and physical problems. In contrast, it may be that some Asians, despite high expectations of negative outcomes, express a "balance" of negative and positive thoughts that functions adaptively for them. Because most of the conceptual models and measures of optimism and pessimism have been based on studies of Westerners (e.g., European Americans), it may be useful to develop models of optimism and pessimism that are derived from an understanding of other cultural groups.

Optimism is predicated on evaluation—on given affects and emotions, as it were—and these, of course, vary dramatically across cultures. Because of the simplicity of the LOT and the ASQ, researchers may be tempted simply to translate these measures and administer them. This would be a mistake if we want to understand the many faces of flourishing. Future research, as we see it, should approach optimism and pessimism as nuanced and culturally shaped.

Another important strategy for future research is to take a developmental approach. What are the origins of optimism and pessimism in different cultures? Are they differentially socialized? Studies like this might answer a normative question of interest to positive psychology: Is the typical person an optimist, a pessimist, or expectationally neutral? Does something unusual in the course of development need to occur to impart to someone an optimistic world view? Is optimism simply the developmental default, deep-wired into human beings by evolution (Tiger, 1979)? Or is pessimism the default? Or perhaps the child is a blank slate, equally able to become an optimist or a pessimist, depending on the idiosyncratic influences to which he or she is exposed throughout life? Is optimism linked to flourishing among children as it appears to be among adults?

Aristotle thought that youth lacked the life experience to decide for themselves how to pursue the good life. Indeed, he believed that only elders who had lived a full life could accurately appraise whether or not they had lived a good life. As if contemporary researchers have conspired to agree with Aristotle centuries ago, the extant literature on optimism, however conceptualized, has focused largely on adults (Fischer & Leitenberg 1986). However, some preliminary findings show that children can learn to be less pessimistic and to solve their problems more effectively; these skills promote greater resilience (Gilham, Reivich, Jaycox, & Seligman, 1995). The cultivation of resilience among children may well provide a route to the good life among adults, and we call for its further study.

REFERENCES

Abramson, L. Y., Metalsky, G. I., & Alloy, L. B. (1989). Hopelessness depression: A theory-based subtype of depression. *Psychological Review, 96,* 358–372.

Abramson, L. Y., Seligman, M. E. P., & Teasdale, J. D. (1978). Learned helplessness in humans: Critique and reformulation. *Journal of Abnormal Psychology, 87,* 49–74.

Alloy, L. B., Peterson, C., Abramson, L. Y., & Seligman, M. E. P. (1984). Attributional style and generality of learned helplessness. *Journal of Personality and Social Psychology, 46,* 681–687.

American Psychiatric Association. (1994). *Diagnostic and statistical manual of mental disorders* (4th ed.). Washington, DC: Author.

Anderson, C. A. (1999). Attributional style, depression, and loneliness: A cross-cultural comparison of American and Chinese students. *Personality and Social Psychology Bulletin, 25,* 482–499.

Anderson, C. A., & Arnault, L. H. (1985). Attributional style and everyday problems in living: Depression, loneliness, and shyness. *Social Cognition, 3,* 16–35.

Aspinwall, L. G., & Brunhart, S. M. (1996). Distinguishing optimism from denial: Optimistic beliefs predict attention to health threats. *Personality and Social Psychology Bulletin, 22,* 993–1003.

Beck, A. T. (1976). *Cognitive therapy and the emotional disorders.* New York: International Universities Press.

Buchanan, G. M., & Seligman, M. E. P. (Eds.). (1995). *Explanatory style.* Hillsdale, NJ: Erlbaum.

Carnelley, K. B., & Janoff-Bulman, R. (1992). Optimism about love relationships: General vs. specific lessons from one's personal experiences. *Journal of Social and Personal Relationships, 9,* 5–20.

Carver, C. S., Pozo, C., Harris, S. D., Noriega, V., Scheier, M. F., et al. (1993). How coping mediates the effect of optimism on distress: A study of women with early stage breast cancer. *Journal of Personality and Social Psychology, 65,* 375–390.

Carver, C. S., & Scheier, M. F. (1981). *Attention and self-regulation: A control-theory approach to human behavior*. New York: Springer-Verlag.

Chang, E. C. (1996). Cultural differences in optimism, pessimism, and coping: Predictors of subsequent adjustment in Asian American and Caucasian American college students. *Journal of Counseling Psychology, 43,* 113–123.

Chang, E. C. (1998). Dispositional optimism and primary and secondary appraisal of a stressor: Controlling for confounding influences and relations to coping and psychological and physical adjustment. *Journal of Personality and Social Psychology, 74,* 1109–1120.

Chang, E. C. (2001a). Cultural influences on optimism and pessimism: Differences in Western and Eastern construals of the self. In E. C. Chang (Ed.), *Optimism and pessimism: Implications for theory, research, and practice* (pp. 257–280). Washington, DC: American Psychological Association.

Chang, E. C. (Ed.). (2001b). *Optimism and pessimism: Implications for theory, research, and practice*. Washington, DC: American Psychological Association.

Chang, E. C. (in press). Optimism-pessimism and stress appraisal: Testing a cognitive interactive model of psychological adjustment in adults. *Cognitive Therapy and Research*.

Chang, E. C., D'Zurilla, T. J., & Maydeu-Olivares, A. (1994). Assessing the dimensionality of optimism and pessimism using a multimeasure approach. *Cognitive Therapy and Research, 18,* 143–160.

Chang, E. C., Maydeu-Olivares, A., & D'Zurilla, T. J. (1997). Optimism and pessimism as partially independent constructs: Relations to positive and negative affectivity and psychological well-being. *Personality and Individual Differences, 23,* 433–440.

Chang, E. C., & Sanna, L. J. (in press). Optimism, accumulated life stress, and psychological and physical adjustment: Is it always adaptive to expect the best? *Journal of Social and Clinical Psychology*.

Cohen, S., & Syme, S. L. (1985). *Social support and health*. Orlando, FL: Academic Press.

Cohen, S., Tyrrell, D. A. J., & Smith, A. P. (1993). Negative life events, perceived stress, negative affect, and susceptibility to the common cold. *Journal of Personality and Social Psychology, 64,* 131–140.

Crittendon, K. S. (1996). Causal attribution processes among the Chinese. In M. H. Bond (Ed.), *The handbook of Chinese psychology* (pp. 263–279). Hong Kong: Oxford University Press.

Davidson, K., & Prkachin, K. (1997). Optimism and unrealistic optimism have an interacting impact on health-promoting behavior and knowledge changes. *Personality and Social Psychology Bulletin, 23,* 617–625.

Davidson, R. J. (1984). Affect, cognition, and hemispheric specialization. In C. E. Izard, J. Kagan, & R. B. Zajonc (Eds.), *Emotions, cognition, and behavior* (pp. 320–365). New York: Cambridge University Press.

Domino, G., & Lin, W. (1993). Cancer metaphors: Taiwan and the United States. *International Journal of Psychology, 28,* 45–56.

Fischer, M., & Leitenberg, H. (1986). Optimism and pessimism in elementary school-aged children. *Child Development, 57,* 241–248.

Friedman, M., & Rosenman, R. (1974). *Type A behavior and your heart.* New York: Knopf.

Gillham, J. (Ed.). (2000). *The science of optimism and hope: Research essays in honor of Martin E. P. Seligman.* Radnor, PA: Templeton Foundation Press.

Gillham, J., Reivich, K. J., Jaycox, L. H., & Seligman, M. E. P. (1995). Prevention of depressive symptoms in school-children: Two-year follow-up. *Psychological Science, 6,* 343–351.

Greenwald, A. G. (1980). The totalitarian ego: Fabrication and revision of personal history. *American Psychologist, 35,* 603–618.

Heine, S. J., & Lehman, D. R. (1995). Cultural variation in unrealistic optimism: Does the West feel more vulnerable than the East? *Journal of Personality and Social Psychology; 68,* 595–607.

Heine, S. H., Lehman, D. R., Markus, H. R., & Kitayama, S. (1999). Is there a universal need for positive self-regard? *Psychological Review, 106,* 766–794.

Hjelle, L. A., Busch, E. A., & Warren, J. E. (1996). Explanatory style, dispositional optimism, and reported parental behavior. *Journal of Genetic Psychology, 157,* 489–499.

Hull, J. G., & Mendolia, M. (1991). Modeling the relations of attributional style, expectancies, and depression. *Journal of Personality and Social Psychology, 61,* 85–97.

James, S. A., Hartnett, S. A., & Kalsbeek, W. D. (1983). John Henryism and blood pressure differences among black men. *Journal of Behavioral Medicine, 6,* 259–278.

Kao, E. M., Nagata, D. K., & Peterson, C. (1997). Explanatory style, family expressiveness, and self-esteem among Asian American and European American college students. *Journal of Social Psychology, 137,* 435–444.

Kok, L. P., Ho, M. L., Heng, B. H., & Ong, Y. W. (1990). A psychosocial study of high risk subjects for AIDS. *Singapore Medical Journal, 31,* 573–582.

Kuroda, Y., & Suzuki, T. (1991). A comparative analysis of the Arab culture: Arabic, English and Japanese languages and values. *Behaviormetrika, 30,* 35–53.

Lazarus, R. S., & Folkman, S. (1984). *Stress, appraisal, and coping.* New York: Springer.

Lee, F., Hallahan, M., & Herzog, T. (1996). Explaining real-life events: How culture and domain shape attributions. *Personality and Social Psychology Bulletin, 22,* 732–741.

Lee, Y.-T., & Seligman, M. E. P. (1997). Are Americans more optimistic than the Chinese? *Personality and Social Psychology Bulletin, 23,* 32–40.

Maier, S. F., & Seligman, M. E. P. (1976). Learned helplessness: Theory and evidence. *Journal of Experimental Psychology: General, 105,* 3–46.

Markus, H. R., & Kitayama, S. (1991). Culture and the self: Implications for cognition, emotion, and motivation. *Psychological Review, 98,* 224–253.

Marshall, G. N., Wortman, C. B., Kusulas, J. W., Hervig, L. K., & Vickers, R. R. (1992). Distinguishing optimism from pessimism: Relations to fundamental dimensions of mood and personality. *Journal of Personality and Social Psychology, 62,* 1067–1074.

Meyer, D. (1988). *The positive thinkers: Popular religious psychology from Mary Baker Eddy to Norman Vincent Peale and Ronald Reagan* (Rev. ed.). Middletown, CT: Wesleyan University Press.

Myers, D. G., & Diener, E. (1995). Who is happy? *Psychological Science, 6,* 10–19.

Norem, J. K., & Cantor, N. (1986). Defensive pessimism: Harnessing anxiety as motivation. *Journal of Personality and Social Psychology, 51,* 1208–1217.

Oettingen, G. (1995). Explanatory style in the context of culture. In G. M. Buchanan & M. E. P. Seligman (Eds.), *Explanatory style* (pp. 209–224). Hillsdale, NJ: Erlbaum.

Peterson, C. (1991). Meaning and measurement of explanatory style. *Psychological Inquiry, 2,* 1–10.

Peterson, C. (1999). Personal control and well-being. In D. Kahneman, E. Diener, & N. Schwarz (Eds.), *Well-being: The foundations of hedonic psychology* (pp. 288–301). New York: Russell Sage.

Peterson, C. (2000). The future of optimism. *American Psychologist, 55,* 44–55.

Peterson, C., & Barrett, L. C. (1987). Explanatory style and academic performance among university freshmen. *Journal of Personality and Social Psychology, 53,* 603–607.

Peterson, C., Bishop, M. P., Fletcher, C. W., Kaplan, M. R., Yesko, E. S., et al. (2001). Explanatory style as a risk factor for traumatic mishaps. *Cognitive Therapy and Research, 25,* 633–649.

Peterson, C., & Bossio, L. M. (1991). *Health and optimism.* New York: Free Press.

Peterson, C., Maier, S. F., & Seligman, M. E. P. (1993). *Learned helplessness: A theory for the age of personal control.* New York: Oxford University Press.

Peterson, C., Schulman, P., Castellon, C., & Seligman, M. E. P. (1992). CAVE: Content analysis of verbatim explanations. In C. P. Smith (Ed.), *Motivation and personality: Handbook of thematic content analysis* (pp. 383–392). New York: Cambridge University Press.

Peterson, C., & Seligman, M. E. P. (1984). Causal explanations as a risk factor for depression: Theory and evidence. *Psychological Review, 91,* 347–374.

Peterson, C., Seligman, M. E. P., & Vaillant, G. E. (1988). Pessimistic explanatory style is a risk factor for physical illness: A thirty-five year longitudinal study. *Journal of Personality and Social Psychology, 55,* 23–27.

Peterson, C., Seligman, M. E. P., Yurko, K. H., Martin, L. R., & Friedman, H. S. (1998). Catastrophizing and untimely death. *Psychological Science, 9,* 49–52.

Peterson, C., Semmel, A., von Baeyer, C., Abramson, L. Y., Metalsky, G. I., et al. (1982). The Attributional Style Questionnaire. *Cognitive Therapy and Research, 6*, 287–299.

Peterson, C., & Steen, T. A. (2002). Optimistic explanatory style. In C. R. Snyder (Ed.), *Handbook of positive psychology* (pp. 244–256). New York: Oxford University Press.

Peterson, C., & Vaidya, R. S. (2001) . Explanatory style, expectations, and depressive symptoms. *Personality and Individual Differences, 31*, 1217–1223.

Prola, M., & Stern, D. (1984). Optimism about college life and academic performance in college. *Psychological Reports, 55*, 347–350.

Robinson-Whelen, S., Kim, C., MacCallum, R. C., & Kiecolt-Glaser, J. K. (1997). Distinguishing optimism from pessimism in older adults: Is it important to be optimistic or not be pessimistic? *Journal of Personality and Social Psychology, 73*, 1345–1353.

Ryan, W. (1978). *Blaming the victim* (Rev. ed.). New York: Random House.

Ryff, C. D. (1989). Happiness is everything, or is it? Explorations on the meaning of psychological well-being. *Journal of Personality and Social Psychology, 57*, 1069–1081.

Ryff, C. D., & Keyes, C. L. M. (1995). The structure of psychological well-being revisited. *Journal of Personality and Social Psychology, 69*, 719–727.

Sanford, R. N., Conrad, H. S., & Franck, K. (1946). Psychological determinants of optimism regarding consequences of the war. *Journal of Psychology, 22*, 207–235

Scheier, M. F., & Carver, C. S. (1985). Optimism, coping, and health: Assessment and implications of generalized outcome expectancies. *Health Psychology, 4*, 219–247.

Scheier, M. F., & Carver, C. S. (1987). Dispositional optimism and physical well-being: The influence of generalized outcome expectancies on health. *Journal of Personality, 55*, 169–210.

Scheier, M. F., & Carver, C. S. (1992). Effects of optimism on psychological and physical well-being: Theoretical overview and empirical update. *Cognitive Therapy and Research, 16*, 201–228.

Scheier, M. F., Carver, C. S., & Bridges, M. W. (1994). Distinguishing optimism from neuroticism (and trait anxiety, self–mastery, and self-esteem): A reevaluation of the Life Orientation Test. *Journal of Personality and Social Psychology, 67*, 1063–1078.

Scheier, M. F., Matthews, K. A., Owen, J. F., Magovern, G. J., Lefebvre, R. C., et al. (1989). Dispositional optimism and recovery from coronary artery bypass surgery: The beneficial effects on physical and psychological well-being. *Journal of Personality and Social Psychology, 57*, 1024–1040.

Schutte, J. W., Valerio, J. K., & Carrillo, V. (1996). Optimism and socioeconomic status: A cross-cultural study. *Social Behavior and Personality, 24*, 9–18.

Seeman, J. (1989). Toward a model of positive health. *American Psychologist, 44*, 1099–1109.

Seligman, M. E. P. (1975). *Helplessness: On depression, development, and death*. San Francisco: Freeman.

Seligman, M. E. P. (1991). *Learned optimism*. New York: Knopf.

Seligman, M. E. P. (1998). Positive social science. *APA Monitor, 29*(4), 2, 5.

Sicinski, A. (1972). Optimism versus pessimism (Tentative concepts and their consequences for future research). *The Polish Sociological Bulletin, 25–26,* 47–62.

Snyder, C. R., & Lopez, S. J. (Eds.). (2002). *The handbook of positive psychology*. New York: Oxford University Press.

Strack, S., Carver, C. S., & Blaney, P. H. (1987). Predicting successful completion of an aftercare program following treatment for alcoholism: The role of dispositional optimism. *Journal of Personality and Social Psychology, 53,* 579–584.

Sweeney, P. D., Anderson, K., & Bailey, S. (1986). Attributional style in depression: A meta-analytic review. *Journal of Personality and Social Psychology, 50,* 974–991.

Taylor, S. E., & Brown, J. D. (1988). Illusion and well-being: A social psychological perspective on mental health. *Psychological Bulletin, 103,* 193–210.

Taylor, S. E., Kemeny, M. E., Aspinwall, L. G., Schneider, S. G., Rodriguez, R., et al. (1992). Optimism, coping, psychological distress, and high-risk sexual behavior among men at risk for acquired immunodeficiency syndrome (AIDS). *Journal of Personality and Social Psychology, 63,* 460–473.

Tennen, H., & Affleck, G. (1987). The costs and benefits of optimistic explanations and dispositional optimism. *Journal of Personality, 55,* 376–393.

Tiger, L. (1979). *Optimism: The biology of hope*. New York: Simon & Schuster.

Triandis, H. C. (1995). *Individualism and collectivism*. San Francisco: Westview Press.

Wallach, M. A., & Wallach, L. (1983). *Psychology's sanction for selfishness: The error of egoism in theory and therapy*. San Francisco: Freeman.

Wardle, J. (1984). Dental pessimism: Negative cognitions in fearful dental patients. *Behaviour Research and Therapy, 22,* 553–556.

Weinstein, N. D. (1989). Optimistic biases about personal risks. *Science, 246,* 1232–1233.

Weisz, J. R., Rothbaum, R. M., & Blackburn, T. C. (1984). Standing out and standing in: The psychology of control in America and Japan. *American Psychologist, 39,* 955–969.

Yee, A. H. (1992). Asians as stereotypes and students: Misperceptions that persist. *Educational Psychology Review, 4,* 95–132.

Zaccaro, S. J., Blair, V., Peterson, C., & Zazanis, M. (1995). Collective efficacy. In J. E. Maddux (Ed.), *Self-efficacy, adaptation, and adjustment: Theory, research, and application* (pp. 305–328). New York: Plenum Press.

II

ENGAGE AND RELATE

4

THE CONSTRUCTION OF MEANING THROUGH VITAL ENGAGEMENT

JEANNE NAKAMURA AND MIHALY CSIKSZENTMIHALYI

Some people go through life as if dragged against their will: Nothing in the world is interesting, nothing they do is meaningful. Other individuals relish almost every moment of their lives and find it permeated with meaning. What accounts for the difference? In this chapter we suggest that one important way people find meaning in their lives is by becoming deeply involved in activities that afford them scope. Even apparently trivial activities become meaningful over time if done with care and concentration. And many cultural domains—such as the arts, literature, and scientific research—allow persons to build meaningful lives by providing almost unlimited opportunities for engagement.

Finding meaning and enjoyment in one's relationship with the world constitutes the notion of flourishing explored in this chapter (cf. Csikszentmihalyi & Rathunde, 1998; Emmons, 1999). Elsewhere, we have described participation in an enduring relationship that is at once enjoyed and meaningful as *vital engagement* (Nakamura, 1995, 1996). We will examine this optimal developmental outcome in a context that places it in bold relief: the creative work of scientists and artists. Although we will focus on long-term creators and their relationship to science or art, a person can be vitally engaged in any relationship with the world, one of work or love, play or service, no matter how humble.

We develop the concept of vital engagement in two stages. The lion's share of the chapter will be devoted to the phenomenon of enjoyable interaction with the environment—in particular, the body of theory and research on the flow state. The next section will focus on how people achieve meaningful relationships with the environment. Rather than review

The Creativity in Later Life Project was generously supported by the Spencer Foundation.

the growing literature on meaning and on the meaning of life (see chapter 5, this volume), we specifically consider how an enjoyed relationship acquires meaning. First, however, we present the perspective from which we approach vital engagement and describe the phenomenon in more detail.

EXPERIENCE AND VITAL ENGAGEMENT

The fullness of a person's participation in the world has been granted central importance in human development by some psychologists through the years (e.g., Allport, 1937; Buhler & Massarik, 1968). Recently, this view of positive functioning has been extended to the end of the life course by the MacArthur Study on Aging in America. Whereas growing old was associated with social disengagement by early researchers (Cumming & Henry, 1961), continued active engagement with life emerged as a key aspect of successful aging in the MacArthur Study (Rowe & Kahn, 1998). We share Rowe and Kahn's focus on the person's connection to the world, though we think of vital engagement as a general way of being related to the world, possible in innumerable activities, whereas they focus on "love and work"; and we train our attention on the quality of the experienced relationship whereas their scope is broader, addressing the sheer number of older people's social ties and the sheer fact of continued productivity.

Indeed, what most distinguishes the notion of vital engagement from related concepts in the study of lives is attention to the experiential. We focus on the relationship between a person and the environment (*experience* in the sense of Dewey, 1958, 1963) and on the subjective phenomenology of this transaction (*subjective experience* in Csikszentmihalyi's [1975/2000] sense; see also Inghilleri, 1999). The pragmatist tradition within philosophical psychology is the clearest predecessor of the perspective taken, including the view of optimal functioning and the more general model of experience, attentional processes, and the self (Dewey, 1913, 1958, 1963; James, 1890/ 1981; Mead, 1934).

From this perspective, people are capable of actively forming goals, investing their attention selectively, and constructing the meaning of their experience. As noted elsewhere (Csikszentmihalyi & Rathunde, 1998), others have developed this notion of people as active shapers as well as products of their own experience (for an influential treatment, see Lerner & Busch-Rossnagel, 1981; for a recent summary, see Brandstadter, 1998). At the same time, humans are socioculturally and historically situated actors whose experience is constituted jointly by environment and person. A person's goals influence transactions with the environment—but only through transactions with the environment will a self be realized. This interactionism (cf. Magnusson & Stattin, 1998) is counterposed to mechanistic psychologies that depict passive actors moved by forces outside their control but also to those humanistic and other psychologies that imply the possibility of subjective experience and initiative unshaped by culture or history.

The sociocultural system supplies the taken-for-granted structures of people's experience (Berger & Luckmann, 1966). As consciously encountered by an individual, it is in addition both (a) a source of demands and constraints on the pursuit of needs and desires; and, on the other hand, (b) a source of resources, action opportunities, and affordances (Brandstadter, 1998). The former is a long-standing focus of psychologists, who have studied accommodation, defense, and resistance to externally imposed demands and constraints. This chapter addresses the latter, less studied role of sociocultural systems (in this case, art and science) as spheres that provide media for positive experience and self-realization. The arts and sciences encompass both a cultural domain—or body of knowledge, practices, and tools—and an associated social field—or community of practice (Csikszentmihalyi, 1996). We will consider how creative artists and scientists exploit the opportunities for vital engagement that these spheres afford.

In the course of daily life, people encounter a vast amount of information. Information appears in consciousness through the selective investment of attention. People's *subjective experience*, the content of consciousness from moment to moment, is thus determined by their decisions about the allocation of limited attention. As William James observed years ago, with perhaps a touch of exaggeration: "My *experience is what I agree to attend to*. Only those items which I *notice* shape my mind" (cited in Csikszentmihalyi, 1978, p. 339). The attention of highly successful scientists, for example, is drawn constantly to their work; the eminent chemist Linus Pauling liked to say, "I don't think that I'm smarter than a lot of other people working in science, but perhaps I think more about the problems" (Creativity in Later Life Project, 1990a, p. 16). Attention may be divided or undivided (Csikszentmihalyi, Rathunde, & Whalen, 1993; Dewey, 1913); indifferent or caring (Dewey, 1958). The quality of the attention paid to the world affects the nature of people's interactions and the quality of their subjective experience. Pauling gave his attention to scientific problems enthusiastically; his work "was not compulsive or burdensome, but engrossing and enjoyable" (Goertzel & Goertzel, 1995, p. 82).

Information, the medium of exchange between person and environment, is also the material out of which the self is formed. The self emerges when consciousness becomes aware of itself as information about the body, subjective states, and the personal past and future. Mead (1934) distinguished between two aspects of the self. The sum of one's conscious processes make up the "I," or knower; the "me," or the known, is defined by the information about oneself that enters awareness when attention is turned on oneself. The distinction is helpful in conceptualizing vital engagement.

Vital Engagement

The concept of vital engagement is meant to capture a certain way of being related to the world—one of engagement or felt connection to the object or other that is experienced as vital in two senses. These are the relationship's felt significance or meaningfulness to the self (Mead's *me*) and the vitality experienced when interaction with the object is going well for the individual (Mead's *I*). A polar opposite relationally is alienation, which implies an active separation or estrangement between self and object rather than connection and belonging.

A single life yields instances of both engagement and alienation. One social scientist who had been deeply engaged in his work for many decades recalled quickly becoming "very interested and involved" in it. He also recalled his estrangement in an earlier line of work that had thwarted his desire to do something that would "live beyond" him and be absorbing:

> I decided I would have to stop being a chemist, because of the fact that I wanted something that after five o'clock I would continue to think about. And that I just *wouldn't stop* thinking about. But with chemistry, it didn't—it was not that intrinsically involving. (Creativity in Later Life Project, 1990b, p. 4)

The concept of vital engagement is informed by the work of John Dewey (1913, 1958, 1963), in particular his conceptions of interest and artistic–aesthetic experience. Dewey's (1958) model for optimal functioning was artistic–aesthetic experience: transactions between person and environment that fully absorb the individual. He maintained that any experience—repairing a car, gardening, cooking—has artistic–aesthetic quality if characterized by "active and alert commerce with the world; at its height [this] signifies complete interpenetration of self and the world of objects and events" (p. 19). Turning to the notion of shaping experience through the selective investment of attention, interest relates the person to a particular sphere. In it, the self becomes "engaged, engrossed, or entirely taken up with some activity because of its recognized worth" (Dewey, 1913, p. 17).

In vital engagement, the relationship to the world is characterized by completeness of involvement or participation and marked by intensity. There is a strong felt connection between self and object; a writer is "swept away" by a project, a scientist is "mesmerized by the stars." The relationship has subjective meaning; work is a "calling." The object—whether it is a cultural domain like poetry or a person, group, institution, political cause, or something else—is experienced as significant and worthy of attention. Likewise, it is valued aspects of the self that are absorbed or invested in the relationship and realized or expressed through it—a poet's gift, a scientist's iconoclasm, a journalist's belief in democracy.

The relationship to the world provides experiential rewards in the here and now; it is distinguished by experiences of enjoyment and absorption. Attention is experienced as willingly invested rather than coerced. At the same time, the relationship is characterized by duration—that is, the cathexis of attention and energy has endured over a period of time rather than being a transient state. We will define *vital engagement* in this chapter as a relationship to the world that is characterized both by experiences of flow (enjoyed absorption) and by meaning (subjective significance). Illustrations will be drawn from interviews conducted with artists and scientists who are still actively working late in life. Subjective, life-historical recollections have recognized limitations as data about the way that experience unfolds. We accept these limitations in the service of initiating discussion of these phenomena but advocate future research using complementary data.

Interest

In developmental psychology, the study of early interest as it relates to learning and development (Oppenheimer & Valsiner, 1991; Renninger, Hidi, & Krapp, 1992) has generated a relational concept closely akin to the notion of vital engagement. Influenced in part by Dewey, several contemporary researchers define interest as a long-term, historied relationship between a person and an object of interest (Krapp & Fink, 1992; Prenzel, 1992). The specificity of object differentiates the interest relationship from general dispositions, such as intrinsic motivational orientation (Schiefele, 1992). The concept is interactionist, locating interest in the relationship *between* the person and object (Rathunde, 1995). In contrast, two other constructs—the notions of trait interest (e.g., vocational preferences) and interestingness (i.e., the predictably engaging object)—emphasize either the person *or* the object (Krapp, Hidi, & Renninger, 1992; Prenzel, 1992). Prenzel (1992) identified the following characteristics of interest relationships: (a) relevant skills and the internal representation of the object are complex, (b) positive emotions attach to the object and to interaction with it, (c) person–object interaction is intrinsically motivated, and (d) the object is valued.

The concept of interest as defined by some contemporary interest researchers is thus closely related to the notion of vital engagement, in focusing on the relationship between the person and object, presuming duration and intrinsic motivation, and stressing value or importance as well as enjoyment. On the other hand, even these researchers describe the *object* as valued while giving less attention to the notion that valued aspects of the *self* find realization within the relationship. Much of the latter attention has focused on learning, or the individual's development of domain knowledge. Relatedly, the notion of interest is heavily associated with a particular subset of activities (e.g., hobbies, intellectual pursuits), whereas we wish to denote intense relationship to any focus of attention, from work in a calling, to human relationships, to civic or political engagement. Finally, although some interest researchers, drawing on Mead and Vygotsky, recognize the culturally and socially constructed nature of the interest objects that they study, these objects nevertheless have tended to be conceptualized ahistorically; the object's own processes of change have received relatively little attention. In the arts and sciences, in contrast, historical changes in the fertility of a domain, paradigm shifts, and fluctuations in a domain's impact on the wider society all prominently influence creators' vital engagement over the life course.

The differences noted may have their roots in the interest literature's focus on childhood and on the formation of interest. Most contemporary interest researchers share a concern with educational settings; they focus on the first decades of life and the role of others early in the learning process. In childhood, interests are less reflectively based on values (Krapp & Fink, 1992), tied to remote ends (Fink, 1991), or invested with elaborated meanings. Whereas it is manifest that the adult creator's relationship to art or science is critically shaped by conditions and changes in the domain, this is less true of children's interests. Balancing the focus of the contemporary interest literature, the examples in this chapter are drawn from the lives of artists and scientists in the second half of life (cf. Rathunde, 1995).

FLOW: THE SUBJECTIVE EXPERIENCE OF FULL INVOLVEMENT

We turn next to the nature of the enjoyment that characterizes vital engagement. Although in everyday usage *enjoyment* may connote pleasure or contentment, when Csikszentmihalyi and his colleagues (1975/2000) studied people engaged in enjoyable interaction with the environment— activities engaged in for their experiential rewards—they found that the subjective experience of enjoyment is one of full involvement. Subsequent work (Csikszentmihalyi, 1990, 1997; Csikszentmihalyi & Csikszentmihalyi, 1988) has explored further the nature and conditions of the subjective experience of joyful involvement.

When one is completely absorbed in interaction with the world, experience unfolds organically and it is possible to enter a state of flow (Csikszentmihalyi, 1975/2000). The flow state has the following characteristics: intense and focused concentration on the here and now; a loss of self-consciousness as action and awareness merge; a sense that one will be able to handle the situation because one knows how to respond to whatever will happen next; a sense that time has passed more quickly or slowly than normal; and an experience of the activity as rewarding in and of itself, regardless of the outcome.

Parameters of experience that foster the flow state have been identified: clarity about one's immediate goals, throughout the interaction; continuous and unambiguous feedback about the progress that one is making as the activity unfolds; and finally, perceived opportunities for action that stretch one's existing capacities. In flow, people thus feel that their capacities are being fully used (de Charms, 1968; Deci, 1975; White, 1959). Entering flow depends on establishing a balance between perceived capacities and perceived challenges; remaining in flow depends on maintaining this balance (Berlyne, 1960; Hunt, 1965). If one begins to feel that the challenges of the situation exceed one's skills, the focus of attention in the here and now gets disrupted; one becomes worried, then anxious. If one begins to feel that one's skills exceed the opportunities for action offered by the situation, attention drifts; one first relaxes and then grows bored. The shift toward an aversive experiential state constitutes information about one's relationship to the environment, offering a cue to adjust one's level of skill or challenge.

One sphere in which flow has been described is creative work in the arts and sciences (Csikszentmihalyi, 1996). An extended account from one of the creators interviewed in the Creativity in Later Life study makes the nature of the flow state in vital engagement more concrete. For long-term artists and scientists, a central component of the life structure is their relationship to the cultural domain that they find absorbing. They describe not isolated flow experiences, but a *flow activity*[1] (Csikszentmihalyi, 1975/ 2000, 1990) with which they have become heavily identified and to which they have sustained a long commitment.

Mark Strand, a Pulitzer prize recipient and former poet laureate of the United States, has suggested that he writes poetry because "it amuses me, and I seem focused when I'm writing"; in other words, the activity holds experiential rewards. In his account of the phenomenology of the writing process when he is feeling "focused," some of the details are particular to the domain of literature, but the contours of his subjective experience are easily recognized as those of the flow state. He has described the intense concentration on the immediate interaction, the loss of temporal awareness and self-consciousness, and the merging of action and awareness that he experiences. Fully engaged with the emerging poem and immersed in the

---

[1] An activity whose structural characteristics (e.g., clear goals, immediate feedback, a complex system of challenges) make flow experiences likely.

medium of language, he must permit the process of meaning making to unfold moment by moment if he is to stay in flow, rather than allowing excited anticipation of the end-product to pull his attention out of the present. When the poet is "completely absorbed in a poem," he experiences a sense of control over the creative process:

> You're right in the work, you lose your sense of time, you're completely enraptured, you're completely caught up in what you're doing . . . it's not that you're swayed by the possibilities you see in this work, although that's a little of it; if that becomes too powerful then you get up, because the excitement is too great. You can't continue to work, or continue to see the end of the work, because you're jumping ahead of yourself all the time. The idea is to be so—so saturated with it that there's no future or past, it's just an extended present in which you're making meaning. And dismantling meaning, and remaking it. . . . With undue regard for the words you're using. It's meaning carried to a high order. It's not just essential communication, daily communication; it's a total communication. . . . When you're working on something and you're working well, you have the feeling that there's no other way of saying what you're saying. (Creativity in Later Life Project, 1991, p. 5)

Vitally engaged scientists similarly indicate that they become completely caught up in their work when it is going well, and enjoy the process of discovery or the unraveling of a challenging problem. Physicist Victor Weisskopf (1991) captured the subjective experience, calling the pleasure of doing research the "joy of insight."

Flow in Work and Love, Play and Duty

A given individual can find flow in virtually any interaction, even the most trivial, depending on the skills that are brought to it and the challenges that can be identified in it (Csikszentmihalyi, 1996). To date, the largest body of flow research has focused on what can broadly be characterized as forms of play. Though other considerations like health and fitness and fame and fortune might motivate participation in "play" pursuits, a key motive is just the sheer enjoyment of the activity. In a series of studies, flow has been reported by people at play, including rock climbers, chess players, basketball players, social dancers (Csikszentmihalyi, 1975/2000), and elite athletes across diverse sports (Jackson, 1992, 1995).

Another set of studies has explored the experience of flow in artistic activities; for example, in the performance of music (Csikszentmihalyi & Rich, 1997; Elliott, 1995), in viewing works of visual art (Csikszentmihalyi & Robinson, 1990), or when writing poetry and fiction (Perry, 1999). Involvement in religious practices has been studied from the perspective of flow with reference to rituals (Turner, 1974) and Confucianism (Eno, 1990).

The role of flow in the evolution of world religions has also been analyzed (Inghilleri, 1999; Massimini & Delle Fave, 1991).

Flow occurs in social interactions, though research on this topic is more limited. It occurs, in particular, within exchanges such as business transactions (Lipman-Blumen, 1999) and the coordinated activity of team sports (Jackson & Csikszentmihalyi, 1999). In unstructured social situations, participants' positive affect is not usually accompanied by intense concentration; nevertheless, flow can occur in informal interaction and in conversation (Csikszentmihalyi, 1990, 1996; Csikszentmihalyi & Larson, 1984). Enjoyed absorption is clearly experienced in activists' sustained pursuit of social change (Colby & Damon, 1992), however grueling that work may be. Finally, in paid work, the conditions for entering flow very often are present—even though, for many people, enjoyment is undermined by powerful negative stereotypes about work (Csikszentmihalyi, 1996; LeFevre, 1988).

The key finding is that the phenomenology of enjoyment is the same across all the different kinds of activity that for some people at some times prove deeply involving. The intense absorption feels the same, whether found in work or play, love or duty.

Measuring Flow

Given the importance of flow to the quality of life—and also to development, as will be discussed shortly—the question of measurement becomes central. It is an inherently challenging task because attending to one's subjective state to describe it disrupts the merging of action and attention that characterizes being in flow. Researchers have used a variety of measures to identify, characterize, and quantify the subjective experience of flow in daily life. These measures include (a) qualitative interviews that probe the nature and conditions of the flow experience, (b) paper-and-pencil measures that address the frequency of flow or its component dimensions in people's lives, and (c) real-life, real-time measures of the nature and everyday contexts of flow experience that use the Experience Sampling Method or ESM (Csikszentmihalyi & Larson, 1987). In ESM studies, participants carry a paging device. When signaled, they record their activities, thoughts, and subjective states at the time. ESM research is more resource-intensive than other approaches to the study of flow. Nevertheless, data about the daily experience of families, adolescents, and working parents, including longitudinal data, have been collected.

Large-scale data collection concerning the frequency of flow is a possibility as a component in evaluation of the population's optimal psychological functioning. Recently, the U.S. Bureau of the Census has shown interest in using the ESM to gather data about Americans' subjective experience, including flow, on a large scale. Already, at the other end of the spectrum in terms of measures, a single item has been included on a Gallup poll (D. Clinton, personal communication, 1998) and on a German national survey (Noelle-Neumann, 1995) to gauge the frequency of flow experiences in a broad cross-section of each population. Both polls asked how often the respondents experience involvement so intense that they lose track of time. The results of the two polls were similar. Although about one fifth of those surveyed (16% of Americans, 23% of Germans) reported having the experience described on a daily basis, more than one third in each poll indicated that they rarely or never experience involvement so intense that they lose track of time (42% of Americans, 35% of Germans). The proportions of people reporting that they do not experience flow raise questions about intervention. Several successful interventions informed by the flow model have been undertaken (Inghilleri, 1999; Massimini & Delle Fave, 2000). It bears noting that these interventions have focused on identifying and cultivating interests and activities that provide enjoyment rather than directly targeting the quality of experience itself.

Flow, Emergent Motivation, and Development

As already described, when one is in flow, the quality of subjective experience influences what one seeks to do next. Subjective states provide feedback about the changing relationship to the environment. Anxiety and boredom are attended to as negative feedback and flow as positive feedback; one continuously adjusts the ongoing relationship with the environment to find the optimal balance point between one's capacities for action and the perceived opportunities for action. What happens at any given moment is responsive to what happened the moment before within the relationship, rather than being dictated by some drive ascribed to the person or some directive ascribed to the environment. In a flow activity, motivation is emergent in the sense that proximal goals arise out of the interaction between person and object (Csikszentmihalyi, 1985; Csikszentmihalyi & Nakamura, 1999).

Because the subjective state is intrinsically rewarding, people seek to reproduce flow experiences. As they master challenges in an activity, however, they develop greater levels of skill, and the activity ceases to be as involving as before; they must identify increasingly complex challenges if they are to continue experiencing flow. Experiential goals thus introduce a principle of selection into psychological functioning that fosters growth. The optimal level of challenge stretches a person's existing capacities (e.g., Vygotsky, 1978); staying in flow results in a more complex set of skills. Because the dynamics of flow align optimal subjective experience with the stretching of capacities, to find flow in what one is doing—to be caught up in an activity from moment to moment for its own sake—is to *grow* (Csikszentmihalyi, 1990; Massimini & Delle Fave, 2000; cf. the Aristotelian notion of happiness as the realization of one's potentialities).

Emergent motivation has a second sense as well. Wholly new relationships and long-term goals may emerge as a result of positive subjective experience. People take note of their present experience and compare their subjective state to alternatives based on experiences in the past. If the present experience is more positive, then maintaining it becomes the goal; if it is less positive, then the goal becomes changing subjective experience in favor of one of the alternatives (Csikszentmihalyi & Nakamura, 1999). An experience may be positive in and of itself or because it solves a problem that was attended by negative experiential states. An unfamiliar or previously unengaging activity can become intrinsically motivating if a person happens to find flow in it (cf. functional autonomy of motives). The motivation to persist in or return to the new activity is emergent, arising out of the interaction itself. In this way, the experience of flow fosters the expansion of an individual's set of enjoyed pursuits, as distinct from the growth of capacities within an existing involvement. This expansion of a person's resources for enjoyment may occur because of chance encounters or because institutions or other people (e.g., parents, educators, peers) expose the individual to new experiences. Most reliably, however, it occurs through a person's own active exploration of the world.

It was intrinsic enjoyment that Nobel Laureate Pauling responded to, in moving toward chemistry as a hobby and, subsequently, a career. Looking back, Pauling explained, "I don't think that I ever sat down and asked myself, 'Now what am I going to do in life?' I just went ahead doing what I liked to do" (Creativity in Late Life Project, 1990a, p. 8). His direction in life was emergent: It took form out of the matrix of his experience, guided by discovery of what he enjoyed doing. Pauling's case illustrates how a new encounter, more positive than previous positive experiences, can give rise to a new goal. A life structure may form around flow activities discovered in this manner. Pauling recalled,

> First I liked to read. And I read many books. . . . When I was eleven, I began collecting insects and reading books in entomology. When I was twelve, I made an effort to collect minerals. . . . I read books on mineralogy, and copied tables of properties, hardness and color and streak and other properties of the minerals, out of the books. And then when I was thirteen I became interested in chemistry. (Creativity in Later Life Project, 1990a, p. 8)

Of his continued engagement with science at age 89, more than seventy years later, he observed,

The question "[What currently is the] most important thing that I feel I *have* to do?" doesn't seem to me to be quite the right question. It might be: "What are the things that I do?" I work on problems in pure science, just to please me, by giving me the pleasure of thinking that I've solved a problem, or sometimes to satisfy my curiosity. (Creativity in Later Life Project, 1990a, p. 14)

THE EXPERIENCE OF MEANING

We have described the experience of intense involvement, or flow. The reader might at this point be of two minds—on the one hand convinced that experiencing whole-hearted involvement in the present is surely preferable to being bored or anxious, but on the other hand thinking that *flourishing* entails something beyond moments of enjoyment, in particular, a sense that one's pursuits serve a larger purpose or otherwise hold vital meaning. Indeed, at the outset of this chapter, we proposed that the optimal outcome of human development is a life characterized by the conjunction of enjoyment and meaning in one's endeavors. An experience that draws a person into participation in the world yet holds little subjective significance may be absorbing—but not vitally engaging. Involving activities are vitally engaging to the extent that they hold meaning for the individual.

The flow model insists neither that challenges nor skills must be strongly valued for an experience to be involving. It is the level of perceived challenge in relation to the person's level of skill, or capacities for action, that is an essential condition for flow and not the qualitative dimension, its perceived significance. A person in a barren waiting room may escape tedium by picking up and becoming briefly absorbed in a crossword puzzle that proves neither too easy nor too hard. Concentration may be high and the interaction enjoyed as long as it lasts, yet the activity may hold scant importance for the person. Its interruption is of little consequence. We suggest that there must be a germ of subjective importance in even a brief flow experience. However, it is possible for the individual to find minimal subjective importance in the aspects of the self that are realized in this brief encounter, or in the aspects of the world that the activity incorporates.

The rest of this chapter will explore the relationship between enjoyment and felt meaning, taking up the expansive topic of meaning specifically at its point of contact with flow theory. The question is how enjoyable experiences become subjectively meaningful or significant as well—that is, how flow leads to vital engagement. The answer proposed is that meaning can grow out of flow in the context of a sustained relationship with an object. We view long-term engagement with art or science as a model for vital engagement in other spheres of life.

Meaning

Rather than undertaking a review of the existing theory and research on meaning, we merely wish to recognize the existing landscape into which the phenomenon of vital engagement fits. Meaning, in particular the sense that life has meaning, was a central interest of mid-twentieth-century existential and humanistic psychology but held little interest within the behaviorist and cognitivist paradigms that prevailed. Since the 1980s, though, it has become the focus of renewed attention within psychology (Baumeister, 1991; Emmons, 1999; Wong & Fry, 1999). The desire for meaning is viewed as a basic human motivation. A sense that life has meaning is associated with well-being and is seen as necessary for long-term happiness. The sources of meaning in most people's lives (e.g., relationships, life goals, religious participation), the ways in which meaning is structured (e.g., through goal hierarchies), and the functions served by meaning all have received research attention.

Meaning can be distinguished on the basis of its *origins*, including enculturation, the push of confronted problems, and the pull of enjoyment. Much that is meaningful is taken for granted, woven early into experience, and as likely to be unarticulated as articulated (Berger & Luckmann, 1966); this is meaning that a person is "born into" by virtue of family, culture, and history. Alternatively, meaning may be actively formulated in response to a problem encountered during the course of a life; the resulting crisis of meaning "pushes" a person to create new goals or understandings. Dewey and many others (e.g., Csikszentmihalyi & Beattie, 1979) have ascribed a critical constructive role in human experience to the problems that are inevitably thrown up by life, triggering a person's reflection. Current studies of trauma and coping investigate how adverse experience is made sense of or becomes a source of meaning and how a person sustains a sense of meaning in the face of negative events (Cohler, 1991; Emmons, 1999). Finally, a "pull" model of the origin of meaning contrasts with both the enculturation and the "push" models. As a person is drawn onward by enjoyable interaction with an object, the meaning of the relationship gradually deepens. In this discussion of vital engagement, the focus will be on meaning that is rooted specifically in positive experience rather than in negative experience or early experience in general.

This *emergent meaning* merits investigation because it has been comparatively neglected and because it helps illuminate one route to vital engagement, the path that leads through experiences of flow. In focusing on long-term artists and scientists, we consider not isolated flow experiences but instead individuals who establish and sustain an intense relationship to a flow activity. They illustrate how a sense of meaning emerges out of an extended relationship with an object (including symbolic domains such as physics or poetry) if transactions with the object are characterized by enjoyable absorption. People develop a felt sense of the positive significance of their relationship with the object, and this felt meaning deepens over time.

The Coincidence of Enjoyment and Meaning

Wrzesniewski, McCauley, Rozin, and Schwartz's (1997) study of people's relationship to their work provides data about the significance of enjoying meaningful participation in the world. Adults in a variety of occupations were able to say readily whether they experienced their work as a job, emphasizing its financial rewards; a career, emphasizing its opportunities for advancement; or a calling, emphasizing "enjoyment of fulfilling, socially useful work" (p. 21). When work is experienced as a calling, it exhibits the coincidence of positive subjective experience and meaningfulness that defines vital engagement. Individuals who view their work as a calling report both higher work satisfaction and higher satisfaction with life in general than those who view their work as a job or career.

There is anecdotal evidence that it may be difficult to sustain prolonged involvement in an endeavor that is experienced as significant if a person does not find enjoyment within the activity itself. If involvement is sustained anyway, subjective well-being may suffer. Colby and Damon (1992) described social activists as "joyfully absorbed" in their ongoing interactions with the world. These individuals experienced flow particularly in relating to others. The quality of subjective experience appeared to be secondary to the activists' profound commitment to valued ends and their sense that the work was worthwhile. At the same time, the few individuals who were struggling with burnout clearly deemed their work important while being unable to find enjoyment in the activity itself. In the same vein, the accounts of a small number of individuals who left medical careers (Ebaugh, 1988) suggest that the perceived significance of the activity was insufficient to make the occupation satisfying when the work process itself was not enjoyable.

There is evidence of a reverse pattern as well—that is, it may be difficult to commit oneself to an enjoyed activity if one cannot see the activity as important in a larger sense. The data come from a longitudinal study of talented adolescents using the ESM (Csikszentmihalyi et al., 1993). Teenagers still committed to involvement in their talent area were more likely than their less committed peers to have found the activity both absorbing and important earlier in high school. Of particular significance, neither pattern of incomplete engagement boded well for teenagers' continued commitment. The domains of science and art carried different risks. Teenagers withdrawing from math or science had been more likely than their still committed peers to experience the activities as important but stressful or boring. On the other hand, teenagers in the process of withdrawing from the arts had been more likely than still committed peers to find the arts absorbing but lacking in long-term importance. Enjoyment without a sense of purpose or larger meaning did not foster commitment.

Emergent Meaning and the Creator's Enduring Relationship to a Domain and Field

There appears to be a form of subjective meaning that is intimately associated with involvement in a pursuit such as art or science when that involvement is a source of flow for the individual. This form of meaning appears to be an outgrowth of long-term, absorbing participation in a domain.

How does an activity that occasions flow come to be experienced as meaningful as well as absorbing? Just as goals can be emergent, arising out of the evolving interaction with the domain, so the felt sense of an endeavor's meaningfulness can be emergent, formed and deepened through experience as an individual interacts with the domain and with the associated community of practice or social field. Alternatively, as mentioned, information that an endeavor matters can be "presented" from outside the person, rather than experientially "discovered" (Csikszentmihalyi, 1985).

Talent plus enjoyment are not inevitably associated with a sense that an activity is important enough to warrant continued commitment (Csikszentmihalyi et al., 1993). What one can accomplish in a domain must be valued by the actor if it is to be vitally engaging. It is possible for an individual to see no future for him- or herself in an activity or to devalue the endeavor or the opportunities for action that the activity presents. This valuing is part of the information in consciousness that shapes a person's encounters with the domain. To say that meaning *emerges* is to say that interactions with the domain transform this information in consciousness.

Every flow experience has the potential for meaningfulness. Even a brief exercise of one's capacities holds a seed of subjective significance because it fully absorbs the self. However, felt meaning that is enduring arises when participation continues over time in an endeavor that stretches the person's capacities and is enjoyably absorbing.

In its most natural form, the relationship to the domain begins in attraction to the object (Renninger & Leckrone, 1991). A sense of the object's significance takes shape and matures concurrent with the development of a capacity to find flow in the domain. An example is the development of Pauling's interest in science. He was "entranced by chemical phenomena" (Pauling, 1970, p. 282) and by the enjoyment of solving individual problems. As he immersed himself in the problems of chemistry, he also came to see and value the prospect of constructing a deep and comprehensive understanding of the physical world:

I became interested in chemistry. I was very excited when I realized that chemists could convert certain substances into other substances with quite different properties, and that this was essentially the basis of chemistry. . . . ever since then, I have spent much of my time trying better to understand chemistry. And this means really to understand the world—the nature of the universe. (Creativity in Later Life Project, 1990a, pp. 8–9)

When a person begins to perform within the rules of a symbolic domain, meaning begins to accrue from several sources: an identification with the domain, its history, traditions, and goals; a feeling of solidarity with the field and its practitioners; a self-image arising from one's own practice—from the peculiar style of one's work. Thus, with time, the sheer practice of one's calling generates layers of important meaning. Engagement in an artistic or scientific pursuit—or any other calling—begins to tie practitioners into a network of enterprises that connects them with the past and the future and locates them within an evolving human project—thus creating its own meaning. Consider, for example, some of the ways meaning develops through the lifelong creator's interactions with the field or community of practice.

The Field as a Source of Meaning

The felt significance of an enjoyed relationship to a domain develops in part through one's membership in a community of practice and interactions with other members of the community. If the state of the field is negative, interactions can render members' relationship to the domain less meaningful as well as corrode the quality of their experience. Insofar as the community or interactions with its members are positive, however, they can foster and deepen the meaning of the relationship to the domain.

The social context of artistic or scientific activity changes across the course of a career (for a review, see Mockros & Csikszentmihalyi, 2000). Three key formative influences on the individual's relationship to the domain are teachers, peers, and students. At the outset of a career, teachers can play a critical role in conveying the meaningfulness of a life in science or art to students who already *enjoy* the activity. In Bloom (1985) and colleagues' study of the development of talent, many young adult sculptors and mathematicians recalled that the most decisive factor in forming a commitment to a career was close contact with a teacher who was a working professional and modeled participation in the discipline as a vitally engaging way of life.

Peers, as coparticipants, can affirm, strengthen, and enrich at any point in life the emergent meaning of the relationship to the domain. One scientist in his 60s stressed the important role played by colleagues beginning when his interest in science was first sparked in childhood and continuing through a series of collaborations down to the present. By sharing his enthusiasm, the first of many "best friends" or "buddies" played a key role in the formation of his sense that science would be an exciting and important domain to engage: "Pretty soon we were hunting butterflies together and after that we were fantasizing about expeditions and careers, and competing to see who could collect the most different kinds of butterflies" (p. 7). Together they went to the zoo and the natural history museum, "enthralled by the grandeur"; they tackled an advanced textbook, and were "awestruck" by its mysteries (Creativity in Later Life Project, 1994a).

The relationship to students or apprentices can play a major role in the continued enrichment of work's meaningfulness during a scientist's late career. A female scientist in her 60s placed great importance on her relationships with students, professing a strong sense that currently they connect her to the moving frontier of knowledge and carry her influence into the future. As she put it, "It keeps you part of the ongoing stream, even as you get older" (Creativity in Later Life Project, 1994b, p. 16). The meaning of her current work is substantially deepened by its embedding within a longer time frame than that of her own career.

Finally, even brief interactions and relationships that are symbolically mediated can enrich the relationship to the domain by providing a sense of community or fellowship that is coextensive with the domain's reach across time and place. As a writer in his 60s noted, after first enthusiastically enumerating the experiential rewards of writing:

> There are many, many nice things about it. . . . one can be a writer almost anywhere, at any place, any time. And that's nice. It makes for a nice fellowship, too. And the final thing that I just thought of, is a beautiful aspect of writing. And that is that you belong to human culture for, say, from Homer on. You're part of a great fellowship of human expression. There are works of high art in all these cultures that go back all these years. And there's something very beautiful about that. (Creativity in Later Life Project, 1994c, p. 9)

How does this wider sense of community emerge through lived experience? In this case, the writer's awareness of a global fellowship was sharpened through interactions with members of the extended community of writers. The writer recounted the moving experience of meeting native Africans in the remotest parts of the continent who were eager to share with him whole novels that they had inscribed in flimsy dimestore notebooks.

These examples could be multiplied endlessly. They suggest some of the ways in which a person's relationship to a domain forms and evolves within a community of practice. Of chief relevance, they illustrate how the person's relationship to this community of practice, and interactions with specific members of it, can help create and sustain an emergent sense of the enterprise's significance. This connection to a community of practice is only one of the ways in which the gradual accumulation of connections tends to lead to a more complexly meaningful relationship to the world.

CONCLUSION

Vital engagement, a sustained self–object relationship that is both enjoyed and meaningful, is one feature of optimal development. Enjoyment, or flow, is found through the tackling of opportunities for action that challenge a person's existing skills. The resulting state of focused involvement is the same, regardless of the activity in which it is found. When the relationship is felt to be meaningful as well as absorbing, the person becomes vitally engaged. Often, extended engagement with a flow activity like science or art begins in a felt conviction that the object of attention is inherently important. In these cases, the enjoyment of the relationship and its meaning may increase together. In other cases, scientific or artistic endeavors are at first undertaken for the sake of their experiential rewards alone. Flow may provide a route to meaning, in that a flow activity's subjective significance will grow richer over the course of a creator's extended engagement with it.

In this chapter, the focus has been on meaning-making activities—art and science—but it need not have been. Vital engagement is possible not only in mature creative work and interests like hobbies and sports, but in a whole variety of activities—raising children, fostering another's learning, performing one's craft well, serving as custodian of an institution. In an engaged life, the conjunction of enjoyment and subjective meaning characterizes vocation, social relationships, participation in the community—a person's central relationships with the world.

REFERENCES

Allport, G. (1937). *Pattern and growth in personality*. New York: Holt, Rinehart and Winston.

Baumeister, R. (1991). *Meanings of life*. New York: Guilford Press.

Berger, P. L., & Luckmann, T. (1966). *The social construction of reality*. Garden City, NY: Doubleday.

Berlyne, D. (1960). *Conflict, arousal, and curiosity*. New York: McGraw-Hill.

Bloom, B. (Ed.). (1985). *Developing talent in young people*. New York: Ballantine Books.

Brandstadter, J. (1998). Action perspectives in human development. In R. M. Lerner (Ed.), *Handbook of child psychology* (Vol. 1, pp. 807–863). New York: Wiley.

Buhler, C., & Massarik, F. (Eds.). (1968). *The course of human life*. New York: Springer.

Cohler, B. J. (1991). The life story and the study of resilience and response to adversity. *Journal of Narrative and Life History, 1*, 169–200.

Colby, A., & Damon, W. (1992). *Some do care*. New York: Free Press.

Creativity in Later Life Project. (1990a). Unpublished data.

Creativity in Later Life Project. (1990b). Unpublished data.

Creativity in Later Life Project. (1991). Unpublished data.

Creativity in Later Life Project. (1994a). Unpublished data.

Creativity in Later Life Project. (1994b). Unpublished data.

Creativity in Later Life Project. (1994c). Unpublished data.

Csikszentmihalyi, M. (1978). Attention and the holistic approach to behavior. In K. S. Pope & J. L. Singer (Eds.), *The stream of consciousness* (pp. 335–358). New York: Plenum Press.

Csikszentmihalyi, M. (1985). Emergent motivation and the evolution of the self. *Advances in Motivation and Achievement, 4*, 93–119.

Csikszentmihalyi, M. (1990). *Flow*. New York: Harper & Row.

Csikszentmihalyi, M. (1996). *Creativity*. New York: HarperCollins.

Csikszentmihalyi, M. (1997). *Finding flow*. New York: Basic Books.

Csikszentmihalyi, M. (2000). *Beyond boredom and anxiety*. San Francisco: Jossey-Bass. (Original published 1975)

Csikszentmihalyi, M., & Beattie, O. (1979). Life themes: A theoretical and empirical exploration of their origins and effects. *Journal of Humanistic Psychology, 19*, 45–63.

Csikszentmihalyi, M., & Csikszentmihalyi, I. (Eds.). (1988). *Optimal experience*. Cambridge: Cambridge University Press.

Csikszentmihalyi, M., & Larson, R. (1984). *Being adolescent*. New York: Basic Books.

Csikszentmihalyi, M., & Larson, R. (1987). Validity and reliability of experience-sampling method. *Journal of Nervous and Mental Disease, 175*, 526–536.

Csikszentmihalyi, M., & Nakamura, J. (1999). Emerging goals and the self-regulation of behavior. In R. S. Wyer (Ed.), *Advances in social cognition: Vol. 12. Perspectives on behavioral self-regulation* (pp. 107–118). Mahwah, NJ: Erlbaum.

Csikszentmihalyi, M., & Rathunde, K. (1998). The development of the person: An experiential perspective on the ontogenesis of psychological complexity. In R. M. Lerner (Ed.), *Handbook of child psychology* (pp. 635–685). New York: Wiley.

Csikszentmihalyi, M., Rathunde, K., & Whalen, S. (1993). *Talented teenagers*. Cambridge: Cambridge University Press.

Csikszentmihalyi, M., & Rich, G. (1997). Musical improvisation: A systems approach. In R. K. Sawyer (Ed.), *Creativity in performance* (pp. 43–66). Greenwich, CT: Ablex.

Csikszentmihalyi, M., & Robinson, R. (1990). *The art of seeing*. Malibu, CA: Getty Trust.

Cumming, E., & Henry, W. (1961). *Growing old: The process of disengagement*. New York: Basic.

de Charms, R. (1968). *Personal causation*. New York: Academic Press.

Deci, E. (1975). *Intrinsic motivation*. New York: Plenum Press.

Dewey, J. (1913). *Interest and effort in education*. Cambridge, MA: Riverside Press.

Dewey, J. (1958). *Art as experience*. New York: Capricorn Books.

Dewey, J. (1963). *Experience and education*. New York: Collier.

Ebaugh, H. R. F. (1988). *Becoming an ex*. Chicago: University of Chicago Press.

Elliott, D. J. (1995). *Music matters*. New York: Oxford University Press.

Emmons, R. A. (1999). *The psychology of ultimate concerns*. New York: Guilford Press.

Eno, R. (1990). *The Confucian creation of heaven*. New York: SUNY Press.

Fink, B. (1991). Interest development as structural change in person–object relationships. In L. Oppenheimer & J. Valsiner (Eds.), *The origins of action: Interdisciplinary and international perspectives* (pp. 175–204). New York: Springer.

Goertzel, T., & Goertzel, B. (1995). *Linus Pauling: A life in science and politics*. New York: Basic Books.

Hunt, J. (1965). Intrinsic motivation and its role in development. *Nebraska Symposium on Motivation, 12*, 189–282.

Inghilleri, P. (1999). *From subjective experience to cultural change*. New York: Cambridge University Press.

Jackson, S. (1992). Athletes in flow: A qualitative investigation of flow states in elite figure skaters. *Journal of Applied Sport Psychology, 4*, 161–180.

Jackson, S. (1995). Factors influencing the occurrence of flow in elite athletes. *Journal of Applied Sport Psychology, 7*, 135–163.

Jackson, S., & Csikszentmihalyi, M. (1999). *Flow in sport: The keys to optimal experiences and performances*. Urbana, IL: Human Kinetics.

James, W. (1981). *The principles of psychology*. Cambridge, MA: Harvard University Press. (Originally published 1890)

Krapp, A., & Fink, B. (1992). The development and function of interests during the critical transition from home to preschool. In K. A. Renninger, S. Hidi, & A. Krapp (Eds.), *The role of interest in learning and development* (pp. 397–429). Hillsdale, NJ: Erlbaum.

Krapp, A., Hidi, S., & Renninger, K (1992). Interest, learning, and development. In K. A. Renninger, S. Hidi, & A. Krapp (Eds.), *The role of interest in learning and development* (pp. 3–25). Hillsdale, NJ: Erlbaum.

LeFevre, J. (1988). Flow and the quality of experience during work and leisure. In M. Csikszentmihalyi & I. Csikszentmihalyi (Eds.), *Optimal experience* (pp. 307–318). Cambridge: Cambridge University Press.

Lerner, R. M., & Busch-Rossnagel, N. (Eds.). (1981). *Individuals as producers of their development*. New York: Academic Press.

Lipman-Blumen, J. (1999). *Hot groups*. New York: Oxford University Press.

Magnusson, D., & Stattin, H. (1998). Person-context interaction theories. In R. M. Lerner (Ed.), *Handbook of child psychology* (Vol. 1, pp. 685–759). New York: Wiley.

Massimini, F., & Delle Fave, A. (1991). Religion and cultural evolution. *Zygon, 16*(1), 27–48.

Massimini, F., & Delle Fave, A. (2000). Individual development in a bio-cultural perspective. *American Psychologist, 55*, 24–33.

Mead, G. H. (1934). *Mind, self and society*. Chicago: University of Chicago Press.

Mockros, C., & Csikszentmihalyi, M. (2000). The social construction of creative lives. In A. Montuori & R. Purser (Eds.), *Social creativity* (Vol. 1, pp. 175–218). Creskill, NJ: Hampton Press.

Nakamura, J. (1995, May). *The presence and absence of unifying themes in creative lives*. Paper presented at the Wallace National Research Symposium on Talent Development, Iowa City, IA.

Nakamura, J. (1996, Nov.). *Writers' narratives of engagement in later life*. Poster presented at the annual meeting of the Gerontological Society of America, Washington, DC.

Noelle-Neumann, E. (1995). *AWA spring survey*. Allensbach am Bodensee, Germany: Allensbach Institut für Demoskopie.

Oppenheimer, L., & Valsiner, J. (Eds.). (1991). *The origins of action: Interdisciplinary and international perspectives*. New York: Springer.

Pauling, L. (1970). Fifty years of progress in structural chemistry and molecular biology. In G. Holton (Ed.), *The twentieth-century sciences: Studies in the biography of ideas* (pp. 281–307). New York: Norton.

Perry, S. (1999). *Writing in flow: Keys to enhanced creativity*. Cincinnati, OH: Writers' Digest Books.

Prenzel, M. (1992). The selective persistence of interest. In K. A. Renninger, S. Hidi, & A. Krapp (Eds.), *The role of interest in learning and development* (pp. 71–98). Hillsdale, NJ: Erlbaum.

Rathunde, K. (1995). Wisdom and abiding interest: Interviews with three noted historians in later life. *Journal of Adult Development, 2*, 159–172.

Renninger, K., Hidi, S., & Krapp, A. (Eds.). (1992). *The role of interest in learning and development*. Hillsdale, NJ: Erlbaum.

Renninger, K., & Leckrone, T. (1991). Continuity in young children's actions: A consideration of interest and temperament. In L. Oppenheimer & J. Valsiner (Eds.), *The origins of action: Interdisciplinary and international perspectives* (pp. 205–238). New York: Springer.

Rowe, J. W., & Kahn, R. L. (1998). *Successful aging*. New York: Pantheon.

Schiefele, U. (1992). Topic interest and levels of text comprehension. In K. A. Renninger, S. Hidi, & A. Krapp (Eds.), *The role of interest in learning and development* (pp. 151–182). Hillsdale, NJ: Erlbaum.

Turner, V. (1974). Liminal to liminoid in play, flow, and ritual: An essay in comparative symbology. *Rice University Studies, 60, 3,* 53–92.

Vygotsky, L. (1978). *Mind in society.* Cambridge, MA: Harvard University Press.

Weisskopf, V. (1991) *The joy of insight.* New York: Basic Books.

White, R. (1959). Motivation reconsidered: The concept of competence. *Psychological Review, 66,* 297–333.

Wong, P. T. P., & Fry, P. S. (Eds.). (1999). *The human quest for meaning: A handbook of psychological research and clinical applications.* Mahwah, NJ: Erlbaum.

Wrzesniewski, A., McCauley, C., Rozin, P., & Schwartz, B. (1997). Jobs, careers, and callings: People's relations to their work. *Journal of Research in Personality, 31,* 21–33.

5

PERSONAL GOALS, LIFE MEANING, AND VIRTUE: WELLSPRINGS OF A POSITIVE LIFE

ROBERT A. EMMONS

Nothing is so insufferable to man as to be completely at rest, without passions, without business, without diversion, without effort. Then he feels his nothingness, his forlornness, his insufficiency, his weakness, his emptiness. (Pascal, *The Pensees*, 1660/1950, p. 57).

As far as we know humans are the only meaning-seeking species on the planet. Meaning-making is an activity that is distinctly human, a function of how the human brain is organized. The many ways in which humans conceptualize, create, and search for meaning has become a recent focus of behavioral science research on quality of life and subjective well-being. This chapter will review the recent literature on meaning-making in the context of personal goals and life purpose. My intention will be to document how meaningful living, expressed as the pursuit of personally significant goals, contributes to positive experience and to a positive life.

THE CENTRALITY OF GOALS IN HUMAN FUNCTIONING

Since the mid-1980s, considerable progress has been made in understanding how goals contribute to long-term levels of well-being. Goals have been identified as key integrative and analytic units in the study of human

Preparation of this chapter was supported by a grant from the John Templeton Foundation. I would like to express my gratitude to Corey Lee Keyes and Jon Haidt for the helpful comments on an earlier draft of this chapter.

motivation (see Austin & Vancouver, 1996; Karoly, 1999, for reviews). The driving concern has been to understand how personal goals are related to long-term levels of happiness and life satisfaction and how ultimately to use this knowledge in a way that might optimize human well-being. How do goals contribute to living the positive life? Of all of the goals that people strive for, which really matter? Which goals most provide a sense of meaning and purpose? Which goals are worth living for and possibly worth dying for?

Goal attainment is a major benchmark for the experience of well-being. When asked what makes for a happy, fulfilling, and meaningful life, people spontaneously discuss their life goals, wishes, and dreams for the future. For many people, of course, the primary goal in life *is* to be happy. Yet research indicates that happiness is most often a by-product of participating in worthwhile projects and activities that do not have as their primary focus the attainment of happiness. Whether they focus primarily on basic research or intervention, psychologists also see goal-striving as vital to "the good life." Psychological well-being has been defined as "the self-evaluated level of the person's competence and the self, weighted in terms of the person's hierarchy of goals" (Lawton, 1996, p. 328). Frisch (1998) defined happiness as "the extent to which important goals, needs, and wishes have been fulfilled" (p. 35). Along with researchers, therapists are increasingly advocating a motivational analysis of life trajectories. For example, quality of life therapy (Frisch, 1998) advocates the importance of revising goals, standards, and priorities as a strategy for boosting life happiness and satisfaction. Similarly, the development of goals that allow for a greater sense of purpose of life is one of the cornerstones of well-being therapy (Fava, 1999), meaning-centered counseling (Wong, 1998), and goal-focused group psychotherapy (Klausner et al., 1998).

People spend significant amounts of their daily lives reflecting on, deciding between, and pursuing personally important and meaningful goals, goals that lend order and structure to these lives. Without goals, life would lack structure and purpose. Goals, according to Klinger (1998), serve as "the linchpin of psychological organization" (p. 44). As internal representations of desired outcomes, they determine the contents of consciousness. Most thoughts and accompanying emotional states are determined by goals. Klinger (1998) has demonstrated that our preoccupations and the emotions we feel are tied to the nature of our goals and the status of these pursuits. Further, because quality of life is determined by the contents of consciousness (Csiskszentmihalyi, 1990), goal striving should be at the forefront of a science of positive psychology. Goals are the concretized expression of future orientation and life purpose, and provide a convenient and powerful metric for examining these vital elements of a positive life. Examples of personal goals are shown in Exhibit 5.1.

EXHIBIT 5.1
Examples of Personal Strivings

"Avoid letting anything upset me."
"Work toward higher athletic capabilities."
"Meet new people through my present friends."
"Promote happiness and hope to others."
"Accept others as they are."
"Be myself and not do things to please others."
"Not eat between meals to lose weight."
"Not be a materialistic person."
"Appear intelligent to others."
"Always be thankful, no matter what the circumstances."
"Reciprocate kindnesses."
"Keep my beagles happy and healthy."
"Do what is pleasing to God."

GOALS AND LIFE MEANING

Goals are essential components of a person's experience of his or her life as meaningful and contribute to the process by which people construe their lives as meaningful or worthwhile. For example, a generative goal to "teach my son to make a difference in his community" lends meaning and direction to the role of parenthood. The goals construct has given form and substance to the amorphous concept of "meaning in life" that humanistic psychology has long understood as a key element of human functioning. Some have argued that the construct of "meaning" *has no meaning* outside of a person's goals and purposes—that is, what a person is trying to do. Goals are signals that orient a person to what is valuable, meaningful, and purposeful. This is not to say, however, that all goals provide meaning or even contribute to a sense of meaning. Many goals are trivial or shallow and, although necessary for daily functioning, have little capacity to contribute to a sense that life is meaningful. Psychologists are beginning to warm to the concept of personal meaning (Wong & Fry, 1998) and are gradually recognizing that despite its somewhat vague and boundless nature, the topic can be seriously and fruitfully investigated (Debats, 1996; Ryff, 1989; Wong & Fry, 1998). The scientific and clinical relevance of the personal meaning construct has been demonstrated in the adjustment literature, in which indicators of meaningfulness (e.g., purpose in life, a sense of coherence) predict positive functioning (French & Joseph, 1999; Robak & Griffin, 2000), whereas indicators of meaninglessness (e.g., anomie, alienation) are regularly associated with psychological distress and pathology (Baumeister, 1991; Keyes, 1998; Seeman, 1991).

Recent empirical research has demonstrated that a strong sense of meaning is associated with life satisfaction and happiness, and a lack of meaning is predictive of depression and disengagement (Reker & Wong, 1988; Wong & Fry, 1998). Meaning is conceptualized in most research as a relatively independent component of well-being, and researchers have recently advocated including it in conceptual models of well-being, quality of life, and personal growth (Compton, Smith, Cornish, & Qualls, 1996; Ryff & Keyes, 1995).

Consensus is emerging on what can be considered to be a taxonomy of meaning. Table 5.1 shows the major categories of life meaning that have emerged across three different research programs on personal meaning. What is impressive is that these studies have used diverse methodologies (including rating scales, surveys, and interviews) in heterogeneous populations. The four life meaning categories of achievements/work, relationships/intimacy, religion/spirituality, and self-transcendence/generativity appear to encompass most of the domains in which people strive for a sense of meaning. Achievement/work includes being committed to one's work, believing in its worth, and liking challenge. Relationships/intimacy includes relating well to others, trusting others, and being altruistic and helpful. Religion/ spirituality includes having a personal relationship with God, believing in an afterlife, and contributing to a faith community. Transcendence/ generativity encompasses contributing to society, leaving a legacy, and transcending self-interests. What makes this finding of the robustness of these meaning factors especially impressive is that these studies have used diverse methodologies (including rating scales, surveys, and interviews) in heterogeneous populations. For example, the personal strivings methodology (Emmons, 1999) uses a semiprojective sentence-completion task; the Personal Meaning Profile developed by Wong (1998) resembles Q-sort items; and Ebersole (1998) used narrative methodology to ask people to write about the central personal meaning in their life.

The science of personality has converged on a Big 5 (openness, conscientiousness, extraversion, agreeableness, and neuroticism) taxonomy of personality traits (John & Srivastava, 1999); perhaps the personal meaning literature will eventually embrace a "Big 4" taxonomy of personal meaning dimensions (WIST; work, intimacy, spirituality, and transcendence). Such

TABLE 5.1
A Consensual Taxonomy of Life Meaning

Ebersole (1998)	Emmons (1999)	Wong (1998)
Life narratives	Personal strivings	Personal meaning profile
Life work	Achievement	Achievement
Relationships	Intimacy	Relationship
Religious beliefs	Religion/spirituality	Religion
Service	Generativity	Self-transcendence

convergence is likely to yield assessment and intervention dividends. For example, assessment instruments designed to measure life meaning must capture, at a minimum, the WIST categories of meaningful experience. Clinicians might routinely assess a client's level of satisfaction with WIST, design interventions to assist clients in developing sources of fulfillment within these broad life domains, and offer motivational restructuring emphasizing these domains when lives are lacking in meaningful pursuits.

Beyond identifying these motivational clusters, more specific questions can be asked. Are there certain types of goals that are consistently linked with happiness? Does the way in which people strive for their goals—for example by framing the goal in abstract or concrete terms or using approach versus avoidance language—affect the experience of subjective well-being (SWB)? Do the goals need to be integrated into a more or less coherent package where conflict is minimized for maximal positive well-being? What advice could be given to persons so that they might extract more pleasure from their goal pursuits? These are questions toward which the remainder of the chapter is directed.

SUBJECTIVE WELL-BEING AND THE POSITIVE LIFE

Before examining the contribution that goals make to the positive life, we must first consider how the positive life has been measured in goals research. In a series of articles and columns initiating the science of "positive psychology," Seligman (1998, 1999; Seligman & Csikszentmihalyi, 2000) has begun to sketch the scaffold of a comprehensive taxonomy of human strength and civic virtues. Three broad domains, or "pillars," are (a) positive subjective experience, (b) positive personal and interpersonal traits, and (c) positive institutions and communities. Positive subjective experiences include the intrapsychic states of happiness and life satisfaction, flow, contentment, optimism, and hope. SWB is generally defined as an individual's cognitive evaluation of life, the presence of positive or pleasant emotions, and the absence of negative or unpleasant emotions (Oishi, Deiner, Suh, & Lucas, 1999). Pleasant emotions include happiness, joy, contentment, and elation; unpleasant emotions include sadness, anxiety, depression, and anger (Diener, Suh, Lucas, & Smith, 1999). The cognitive component of SWB, life satisfaction, is measured most commonly through the Satisfaction With Life Scale (SWLS; Diener, Emmons, Larsen, & Griffin, 1985), a brief but highly reliable global evaluation of one's life as a whole. Widely used in both clinical and nonclinical samples, evidence for the reliability and validity of the SWLS is available in Pavot and Diener (1993). Various other trait-like indexes of positive well-being, including measures of vitality, self-actualization, self-esteem, and openness to experience, have been used in goals research (e.g., Kasser & Ryan, 1993, 1996).

GOAL CONTENT: THE "WHAT" OF GOAL STRIVING

When it comes to contributing to the good life, experience, common sense, and research tell us that not all goals are created equally. People strive for diverse ends in their goal pursuits, and not all ends are equally likely to contribute to well-being. In a systematic review of the literature on personality and well-being, DeNeve and Cooper (1998) speculate that personality traits determine the types of goals toward which individuals strive, with goal-striving having a more direct link to SWB than do personality traits. Coding personal goals into broad, thematic clusters enables the examination of the relationship between the ends that people strive for and their well-being independently of outcome or other goal-striving processes. We have developed a coding system for classifying personal strivings into 12 thematic content categories (Emmons, 1999, app. B). Three types of goal strivings consistently relate to SWB: intimacy, generativity, and spirituality. These three goal types correspond to three of the four major categories of personal meaning from Table 5.1. Definitions and examples of each of these categories of goal striving are shown in Exhibit 5.2.

EXHIBIT 5.2
Goal Themes Associated With Well-Being

Intimacy

Goals that express a desire for close, reciprocal relationships. (E.g., "Help my friends and let them know I care," "Accept others as they are," "Try to be a good listener.")

Spirituality

Goals that are oriented to transcending the self. (E.g., "Deepen my relationship with God," "Learn to tune into higher power throughout the day," "Appreciate God's creations.")

Generativity

A commitment and concern for future generations. (E.g., "Be a good role model for my siblings," "Feel useful to society," "Do volunteer work that enhances educational opportunities for children.")

Power

Goals that express a desire to influence and affect others. (E.g., "Force men to be intimate," "Be the best when with a group of people," "Get others to see my point of view.")

In both community and college student samples, we have found that the presence of intimacy strivings, generativity strivings, and spiritual strivings within a person's goal hierarchy predict greater SWB, particularly higher positive affect. Conversely, power strivings tend to be associated with lower levels of SWB (Emmons, 1991), especially with higher levels of negative affect. In each case, we examine the proportion of striving in that category relative to the total number of strivings generated. This provides a rough index of the centrality of each motivational theme within the person's overall goal hierarchy. Power and intimacy strivings reflect the broader motivational orientations of agency and communion. Intimacy strivings reflect a concern for establishing deep and mutually gratifying relationships, whereas power strivings reflect a desire to influence others and have impact on them. The ability to engage in close intimate relationships based on trust and affection is the hallmark of psychosocial maturity and a key component to psychological growth (Ryff, 1989). Empirical research has documented the powerful effect of attachments on health and well-being (see Myers, 2000, for a review). On the other hand, persons who are primarily power-oriented and who possess many agentic strivings—to impress or control others—appear to be at risk for lower well-being and poorer physical health. In a recent study examining social motives and distress in gay men differing in HIV status, power strivings were positively related to distress scores (a composite of anxiety and depression) in HIV-positive men (Igreja, Zuroff, Koestner, & Saltaris, 2000). The authors of this study suggest that the ability to control and influence others is highly threatened by their physical state, and this leads to increased distress. Conversely, intimacy strivings were found to buffer HIV-positive individuals against distress by increasing the perceived availability of social support. Individuals high in power strivings may also be committing their lives primarily to obtaining extrinsic sources of satisfaction such as materialistic goals that fail to meet the basic needs for relatedness and autonomy (Ryan & Deci, 2000).

Generativity strivings, defined as those strivings that involve creating, giving of oneself to others, and having an influence on future generations (McAdams & de St. Aubin, 1992) also seem to result in higher levels of life satisfaction and positive affect (Ackerman, Zuroff, & Moskowitz, 2000). Generativity is a concern for guiding and promoting the next generation through parenting, as well as through teaching, mentoring, counseling, leadership, and generating products that will survive the self and contribute positively to the next generation. Generativity is manifested both privately and publicly as an inner desire whose realization may promote healthy development and psychological and physical well-being. From a societal perspective, generativity is a valuable resource that "may undergird social institutions, encourage citizen's contributions and commitments to the public good, motivate efforts to sustain continuity from one generation to the next, and initiate social change" (McAdams & de St. Aubin, 1998, p. 3). Although generativity is a concern for promoting the well-being of later generations, there is an immediate positive impact on the promoter's *own* well-being. In a stratified sample of young, mid-life, and older adults, McAdams, de St. Aubin, and Logan (1993) found that generative concern was related to both greater reported happiness and life satisfaction; and Keyes and Ryff (1998) found that higher levels of generative motives, behaviors, and traits each contributed to heightened levels of psychological and social well-being in a nationally representative sample. Although mid-life adults in their study showed the highest levels of generativity, there was no age-cohort effect for generativity on happiness and satisfaction, suggesting that its tie to well-being is not age-specific. Generative concerns most likely contribute to well-being by fostering behaviors and commitments that create and sustain positive interpersonal and transgenerational relationships (Ackerman et al., 2000).

Spiritual strivings refer to goals that are oriented around the sacred. They are those personal goals that are concerned with ultimate purpose, ethics, commitment to a higher power, and a seeking of the divine in daily experience. This conception of spirituality is consistent with a number of theorists who, while acknowledging the diversity of meaning, affirm as a common core meaning of spirituality/religion that of the recognition of a transcendent, meta-empirical dimension of reality and the desire to establish a relationship with that reality. The scientific study of spirituality, long taboo in the behavioral sciences, is beginning to open up new vistas for understanding personal meaning, goal-striving, and subjective well-being. Given the prevalence of religion in society, it would be surprising if spiritual and religious concerns did not find expression in one form or another through personal goals. In our research, people differ in their tendency to attribute spiritual significance to their strivings, with percentages of spiritual strivings ranging from zero to nearly 50%, depending on the nature of the sample studied. College males have the lowest level of avowed spiritual strivings, whereas elderly, church-going females tend to have the highest levels. Spiritual strivings are related to higher levels of SWB, especially to greater positive affect and to both marital and overall life satisfaction (Emmons, Cheung, & Tehrani, 1998). In the Emmons et al. (1998) study, these relations were stronger for women than for men, in accord with the literature on gender differences in religion and SWB. Spiritual strivings were also rated as more important, requiring more effort, and engaged in for more intrinsic reasons than were nonspiritual strivings. Investing goals with a sense of sacredness confers on them a power to organize experience and to promote well-being that is absent in nonsacred strivings (Mahoney et al., 1999).

Taken together, then, the findings on goal content and well-being indicate that when it comes to the positive life, not all goals are created equally (Ryan, Sheldon, Kasser, & Deci, 1996). Rather, certain clusters of goals consistently tend to foster higher levels of well-being than other types of goals. Intimacy, generativity, and spirituality are intrinsically rewarding domains of goal activity that render lives meaningful and purposeful, particularly compared to power strivings or strivings for self-sufficiency. Tillich (1951) spoke of "existential disappointment," which he saw as the result of giving ultimate concern to that which is merely transitory and temporal. Each of these three goal types reflects an active engagement with the world, a sense of connectedness to others, to the future, to the transcendent, and thus contain a glimpse of eternity. Spirituality has been virtually ignored in contemporary models of motivation and well-being (e.g., Ryan & Deci, 2000), yet there are compelling empirical and theoretical reasons for its inclusion in any comprehensive account of human well-being (Emmons, 1999; Piedmont, 1999).

INTRINSIC AND EXTRINSIC GOAL ORIENTATIONS

Another fruitful research program has demonstrated that the relative importance of different types of goals within a person's overall goal hierarchy profoundly affects well-being. Kasser and Ryan (1993, 1996) have distinguished between goals that serve intrinsic needs and goals that are extrinsic in that they serve other, less inherently satisfying needs. These researchers have demonstrated that the rated importance of the extrinsic goals of financial success, social recognition, and physical attractiveness were negatively related to several measures of well-being, including vitality and self-actualization. In addition, in Kasser and Ryan (1996), the rated importance of these extrinsic goals was positively associated with measures of anxiety, depression, narcissism, and physical illness symptomatology. Alternatively, research participants who possessed the intrinsic goals of personal growth and community contribution reported higher levels of SWB. The authors concluded that there is a "dark side to the American dream"—that a relative emphasis on fame, fortune, and success to the neglect of intrinsically meaningful goals is likely to lead to psychological and interpersonal problems. An overvaluation of materialistic pursuits detracts from the "good life" in at least two domains: positive subjective experience and fulfilling interpersonal relationships. Other studies have demonstrated that income is moderately correlated with well-being, from which it has been argued that increases in income beyond a base level fail to improve well-being (Myers, 2000).

The link between extrinsic goals and lower SWB appears to hold even when the current perceived attainment of these goals is high (Sheldon & Kasser, 1998). Sheldon and Kasser showed in a 12-week study that goal attainment toward intrinsic goals enhanced well-being, whereas progress toward extrinsic goals was unrelated to well-being. A related finding, reported by Brunstein, Schultheiss, and Graessman (1998), is that progress toward motive-congruent goals predicts SWB, but commitment toward motive-incongruent goals detracts from SWB. When it comes to psychological well-being, what people are striving for—the content of their aims and ambitions—does matter. Not all goals *are* created equal, and not all goal attainment is equally healthy. At first glance, this observation might seem blatantly obvious, yet goal theories of affect have been known to indiscriminately equate goal attainment with positive affective outcomes, regardless of goal content (Locke & Kristof, 1996).

In a recent, important cross-cultural replication and extension of the research by Kasser and Ryan (1993, 1996), Ryan and colleagues (1999) found that lower self-esteem, lower self-actualization, and lower life satisfaction were each associated with a greater investment in extrinsic goals in Russian college students. Furthermore, the perceived likelihood of attaining extrinsic and intrinsic aspirations was also associated with well-being in the predicted direction: Attainment of intrinsic goals facilitated well-being, whereas attaining extrinsic goals had no effect on well-being. This study is notable in that it points to potential culturally invariant relationships between patterns of goal striving and well-being. A commitment to extrinsic, materialistic goals, even when these goals are attainable, detracts from overall well-being. On the other hand, a commitment to intrinsic goals appears to favor well-being even in countries newly exposed to market economies. These results remind us that culture plays a formative role in the development of striving systems and that people's life goals reflect, to a certain degree, the economic and cultural systems within which they are embedded.

The influence of materialistic goals on well-being was also examined by Diener and Fujita (1995), who proposed that personal strivings mediate the relationship between resources and well-being. They hypothesized that resources such as money, good looks, health, and intelligence should be related to well-being *only* to the extent to which these resources enable the individual's personal strivings. Research participants rated the relevance of each of 21 resources for the attainment of each of their strivings. Significant correlations were found between the goal relevance of resources and negative affect and life satisfaction; higher correlations were also observed between goal-relevant resources and SWB than between less relevant resources and well-being. In other words, they found evidence for an interaction between material resources and well-being. The possession of resources per se, independent of goal strivings, was unrelated to well-being. Thus, the greater the congruence between a person's goals and his or her resources, the higher the well-being. Strivings mediated the relationship between resources and well-being. It is interesting to note that consistent with the research of Kasser and Ryan cited earlier, the "intrinsic" resources of self-confidence, social skills, and self-discipline received the highest relevance ratings, whereas the "extrinsic" resources of material possessions, physical attractiveness, and money were rated as mostly irrelevant to the attainment of one's goals. Both studies seriously question that the proverbial "American Dream" of fame, fortune, and image is a desirable state of affairs toward which to strive. Yet the latter class of goals remains a powerful draw in the lives of many despite their inability to provide lasting satisfaction. This suggests that either people's implicit theories of the types of outcomes that will lead to happiness is wrong, or that anticipated happiness and satisfaction are not the primary motivations for establishing and pursuing goals. Whether or not these relationships would hold for less educated samples or for people in dire financial situations remains to be seen. A recent study found that experimentally activating feelings of anxiety led research participants to increase their estimate of their future earnings and the amount of money they would spend on possessions, suggesting that certain aspects of low emotional well-being might drive materialistic goal pursuits (Kasser & Sheldon, 2000).

GOAL ORIENTATION: THE "HOW" OF GOAL-STRIVING

The second way in which personal goals are related to SWB is through goal orientation. Goal orientation refers to individual differences in the manner in which goals are represented consciously by the individual and described linguistically when communicating these goals to others. Thus, orientation refers to individual differences in the mental representations of goals. Although it might be argued that this distinction is purely a semantic one, with no practical significance, it does appear that there are psychological benefits (and conversely, psychological costs) associated with different forms of goal framing.

One goal orientation that appears to have important consequences for SWB is the degree to which individuals are striving for positive, desirable goals as opposed to striving to avoid negative, aversive goals (Cochran & Tesser, 1996; Elliott & Sheldon, 1998; Elliott, Sheldon, & Church, 1997; Emmons & Kaiser, 1996). The distinction between approach and avoidance is fundamental and basic to the study of human behavior and motivation. The difference between these two orientations is whether positive or negative outcomes are used as a benchmark for self-regulatory activity. Approach goals are positive incentives to be sought after and moved toward whereas avoidant goals are negative consequences to be avoided or prevented. For instance, a person may be trying to "spend time with others" versus "avoid being lonely," or "trying to avoid letting anything upset me" versus "trying to stay calm even under trying circumstances," "trying to contribute to the field of positive psychology" versus "trying to avoid focusing on remedial psychology." On average, between 10 and 20% of a person's goals tend to be avoidance goals (Emmons, 1999). A number of studies have now documented that avoidant striving is associated with less positive psychological outcomes as compared to approach striving (see Emmons, 1999, chap. 3, for a review).

Emmons and Kaiser (1996) found that individuals whose striving lists contain a large number of avoidant strivings experienced more psychological distress, particularly anxiety, than individuals with predominantly appetitive striving systems. Negative or inhibitory strivings appears to be a risk factor for psychological and physical distress, although in some cases they may lead to more effective self-regulation (Cochran & Tesser, 1996). Elliot et al. (1997) found that the pursuit of avoidance goals over time was negatively associated with SWB, as measured by affect and life satisfaction ratings. Moreover, mediational analyses revealed that the link between avoidance striving and SWB was mediated through perceived progress, with avoidance striving relating to less perceived progress. Elliot, Chirkov, Kim, and Sheldon (2001) extended this line of research cross-culturally. They found that avoidance goals negatively predicted subjective well-being in individualistic countries but not in collectivist countries.

Additional evidence suggests that avoidant goals may play a role in interpersonal as well as intrapersonal satisfaction. In a sample of married couples (King & Emmons, 1991), marital satisfaction was significantly negatively related to the proportion of the spouse's avoidant strivings. A person is likely to be less satisfied with his or her marriage if his or her spouse is predominantly concerned with avoiding negative outcomes. Thus, avoidant striving appears to exact an interpersonal as well as an intrapersonal toll on well-being.

There is also evidence that avoidance striving is related to poorer perceptions of physical health. Elliott and Sheldon (1998) found that avoidance personal goals are associated with both retrospective reports of physical symptomatology and an increase in symptoms over time. Rather than rely on expert coding, participants in this study classified their own goals by selecting whether each goal represented attaining a positive outcome (e.g., "to excel in my workplace") versus a focus on avoiding a negative outcome (e.g., "to avoid excessive partying"). Pursuing negative, avoidant goals was associated with experiencing more physical health complaints over time. Mediational analyses revealed that perceived progress, controlledness, and autonomy mediated the relationship between avoidant striving and subsequent ill health. In other words, participants who pursued a greater number of avoidance goals were less likely to attain those goals and felt a greater sense of external pressure to achieve them. Although not all avoidance goals may be inherently harmful, in general avoidance goals must be considered a psychological vulnerability that places individuals at risk for emotional and physical ill-being. Elliot and Sheldon (1998) concluded that "personal goals represent, in essence, the vehicles through which individuals negotiate their daily lives . . . some vehicles (approach goals) are better suited to the terrain of everyday life than others (avoidance goals)" (p. 1294).

PERSONAL GOALS IN THE LIVES OF PERSONS WITH NEUROMUSCULAR DISEASE

Having documented that there are substantial and replicable relationships between individual variations in people's goals and indicators of SWB in healthy populations, an important practical question becomes, Can the study of goal-striving within particular health populations be informative for understanding how goals contribute to well-being? Goals and goal-system variables have been used in several lines of research to examine positive and negative functioning within clinical health populations. Goal variables have been identified as a key determinant of both health promotion and health endangerment (Ewart, 1991; Karoly, 1991) and have been linked to conditions as diverse as heart disease, cancer, diabetes, alcohol and tobacco abuse, chronic pain, and hypochondriasis. For example, Affleck et al. (1998) found that perceived progress toward personal goals attenuated the effect of pain on well-being in women with fibromyalgia. Women who reported more progress toward their goals on a given day experienced an increase in emotional well-being for that day that was independent of pain or fatigue levels. Thus, a personal-goals approach has potential to lead to new insights into understanding the effects of chronic illness on emotional and psychological well-being.

We have recently begun a project to examine how a personal-goals perspective can be applied to understanding issues related to the quality of life and SWB of people with post-polio syndrome (PPS). PPS is a neuromuscular disease (NMD), which as a broader category includes more than 200 diseases that affect the neuromuscular organ system. NMDs are estimated to affect approximately four million people in the United States (National Institute of Health, 1998). PPS is a condition that can strike polio survivors anywhere from 10 to 40 years after recovery from an initial attack of the poliomyelitis virus. It is characterized by an additional weakening of muscles that were previously injured by polio infection. Symptoms include fatigue, slowly progressive muscle weakness, muscle and joint pain, and muscular atrophy. Some patients experience only minor symptoms, and others develop spinal muscular atrophy or what appears to be, but is not, a form of amyotrophic lateral sclerosis. PPS is rarely life-threatening. PPS is a very slowly progressing condition marked by long periods of stability and an unpredictable course.

Few studies have systematically examined what determines the quality of life of individuals with neuromuscular disease. Objective indicators such as functional ability in daily living, occupational status, and social activities are typically the focus of rehabilitation specialists. These indexes, however, fail to account for much variance in SWB (Abresch, Seyden, & Wineinger, 1998). By assisting people in their identification of their current priorities and commitments, by examining the sense of meaning and purpose goals provide as well as their manageability, stressfulness, and support, a personal-goals approach serves to examine what is possible and desirable to obtain. Framing subjective quality of life outcomes such as personal well-being in terms of goals may lead to new possibilities for understanding adaptation to physical disabilities.

With this rationale in mind, we administered a lengthy survey consisting of the Personal Strivings Assessment Packet (Emmons, 1999), measures of SWB, health status, functional ability, and a variety of other variables relevant to quality of life to 54 individuals with PPS. Participants were located through the University of California, Davis, Medical Center Neuromuscular Disease Clinic. Because of the special needs of this population with respect to achieving integration into their communities, specific measures were created to assess the degree to which their personal goals enabled them to feel connected to and integrated into their communities. We wanted to see if this goal-based measure explained more variance in SWB than standard questionnaire measures of community integration (Willer, Ottenbacher, & Coad, 1994). We also examined other social–ecological goal variables, including the degree to which others are aware of the striving (visibility), the degree to which others are supportive of the striving (support), the degree to which others hinder the striving (hindrance), and the degree to which the striving causes strain or tension in everyday interactions (strain).

Regression analyses indicated that the goal-based measure of integration was the strongest predictor of overall levels of well-being (a composite of life satisfaction, positive affect, and vitality) of any of the goal variables. Community integration through goals, perceived meaningfulness, and low goal difficulty were the strongest predictors of life satisfaction. Goal meaningfulness and low goal difficulty were the strongest predictors of positive affect. In other words, as goals increase in meaningfulness and attainability, persons with PPS feel more satisfied with their lives. A goal-based measure of spirituality (self-ratings of the degree to which the goal brings the person closer to God) was positively associated with life satisfaction and positive affect. The degree to which pain interfered with the person's ability to work toward his or her goals was predictive of psychological distress (negative affect), as was the amount of interpersonal strain perceived by the person to be caused by the striving. In contrast, a global rating of pain was unrelated to well-being, suggesting that the goal-relevant pain measure is a more sensitive indicator of quality of life than is a global rating of overall degree of pain. Overall, the goal variables accounted for 39 to 44 percent of the variance in SWB ratings. This finding dovetails with the study by Affleck et al. (1998), who found that goal pursuit is a key motivational–cognitive construct for chronic pain in patients with fibromyalgia. It is interesting to note that in their study, effort toward health and fitness goals was not diminished on days with increasing pain, but effort and progress toward interpersonal goals was, indicating that pain does not affect all goals equally.

The personal strivings of two of the participants in our study are shown in Exhibit 5.3. These two individuals were also the highest (top half of the exhibit) and lowest (bottom half of the exhibit) in the sample in terms of overall life satisfaction. Given the relationship between investment in certain goal domains and SWB described earlier, it is apparent why these two people differ in life satisfaction. Themes of spirituality and intimacy are prevalent in the first person's list, whereas the second person is bereft of these self-transcendent strivings. By contrast, the second individual is characterized by a preponderance of negative, avoidant strivings, focused largely on emotional management and minimizing impact on others. It is interesting to note that the two were not different on a questionnaire measure of functional independence, suggesting that differences in SWB are not a result of differences in physical status.

These results, taken as a whole, suggest that a goal-based approach to community integration is viable and invites further exploration into the role of personal goals as workable clinical units of analysis for understanding the quality of life in the lives of persons with post-polio disease. Improving the quality of life of persons with neuromuscular disease has always been a goal of rehabilitation medicine (Abresch et al., 1998). Yet little information has been provided regarding what factors are critical to achieving a high quality of life. Facilitating the patient's identification of personally meaningful, attainable strivings and developing workable strategies for their accomplishment becomes a priority for rehabilitation providers, enabling the person to "live happily and productively on the same level as their neighbors" (Abresch et al., 1998, p. 233).

EXHIBIT 5.3
Personal Goals of Individuals High and Low in Life Satisfaction, Postpolio Study

High life satisfaction:
    Live my life at all times for God.
    Watch what I say, so I don't hurt someone.
    Help people that need help.
    Pray for people I don't know, when I'm asked.
    Thank God for everything on earth and sea.
    Try to make people forget their problems.
    Give a happy call to make someone happy.
    Even though I'm in a wheelchair, show people it does not get me down.
    Teach crafts to people.
    Have fun and enjoy life because God gave me this life.

Low life satisfaction:
    Communicate with my children.
    Not be a burden to my family.
    Help my children.
    Not be a complainer.
    Maintain my friendships.
    Not depend too much on others.
    Be as independent as possible.
    Be well-informed.
    Think positive thoughts.
    Not get down in the dumps.
    Keep a smile on my face.
    Not overeat.

VIRTUE AND GOAL STRIVING: INTERNAL MECHANISMS FOR GOAL SUCCESS

As vital as goals are for leading a positive life, they are not the entire story. Even meaningful and manageable goals, as important as those two components are, do not guarantee optimal life management. Psychologists have tended to focus on the psychological structures and processes that underlie goal striving. Self-regulatory strategies and plans have been among the favorite units of analysis for goals researchers (see, e.g., Cantor & Zirkel, 1990, for a comprehensive review). Undoubtedly cognitive strategies are important regulators of successful goal pursuit, yet they may not be enough for understanding the many ways in which goals contribute to positive life functioning. An approach that identifies the cognitive virtues that enable a person to effectively pursue conduct directed toward higher purposes and goals might be a productive approach to take.

To move toward a comprehensive formulation of the positive person and the good life in terms of goals, I would argue that we must look to the virtues underlying goal striving. Virtues are essential person characteristics that can differentiate successful from unsuccessful goal strivers. Virtues are acquired excellences in character traits, the possession of which contributes to a person's completeness or wholeness (Zagzebski, 1996). Several theorists have brought the ancient Greek notion of *arête* into the 21st century, defining virtues as any psychological process that consistently enables a person to think and act so as to yield benefits for him- or herself and society (McCullough & Snyder, 2000, p. 3). Although a good many worthy virtues have been identified over the centuries, let me close this chapter by suggesting the relevance of the following trio for goal striving: prudence, patience, and perseverance. Each of these reflects a disposition that can counsel goal-directed action. Each of these is involved in self-regulation, which involves setting appropriate goals and persisting in the face of setbacks and failure (Baumeister, Leith, Muraven, & Bratslavsky, 1998).

Prudence

Prudence is normally conceived of as an intellectual virtue. Jeffries (1998) defined it as "the use of reason to correctly discern that which helps and that which hinders realizing the good" (p. 154). When applied to goal striving, prudence is foresight, future-mindedness, and the reasoned pursuit of long-term goals (Haslam, 1991). Haslam (1991) identified five components of prudence: (a) It is concerned with the choice, planning, and pursuit of long-term, virtuous ends; (b) it invokes a concern with identity, self-continuity, and personal integration as one projects oneself into the future; (c) it involves the rational pursuit of appropriate ends; (d) it involves maximizing the satisfaction of multiple goals; and (e) it seeks the good of the individual's self-interest without being collectively destructive. Little empirical work on the concept of prudence exists, and no individual difference measure of prudence exists. Goal theorists would themselves be prudent to dip into the well of collective wisdom that has accrued from rich philosophical accounts of this concept and to apply the concept to understanding individual differences in goal selection and life management.

Patience

Patience is commonly said to be a virtue, but it is not a virtue commonly included in contemporary discussions of the good life. Patience is the "ability to dwell gladly in the present moment" (Roberts, 1984, p. 53) when one would rather be doing something else. Patience is not just aimlessness, an absence of striving. Patience enables people to be attentively responsive to others, to be responsive to opportunities for goal attainment. Roberts contends that patience "is a necessary condition for the accomplishment of anything worthwhile" (p. 54). Harned (1997) discussed four primary meanings of patience: (a) suffering with calmness or composure, (b) forebearance and tolerance of others, (c) willingness to wait without resentment, and (d) constancy and consistency in effort (what I refer to below as perseverance). One might view patience as a necessary counterforce for the frenzied activity that future orientation and goal striving can sometimes produce. Much like prudence, psychologists have paid scant attention to this virtue, although they have studied it under related guises (e.g., delay of gratification in children).

Perseverance

Although patience is about the present, perseverance focuses on the future. Perseverance is the ability to keep commitments, to be steadfast, to endure despite obstacles, to make sacrifices, and to resist temptations to give up (Brickman, 1987). For the good life, perseverance must be combined with the right kind of goals. Without the right goals perseverance is useless, or worse: "A person who is merely persistent may be a carping, pestering, irksome annoyance, having no salutary effect whatsoever" (Bennett, 1993, p. 528). In the right combination with other virtues, perseverance is "an essential ingredient in human progress" (Bennett, 1993, p. 528). In contrast to prudence and patience, psychologists have shown more interest in the concept of perseverance and related constructs such as commitment (e.g., Brickman, 1987).

Future research on goals and SWB (and more broadly, the study of human motivation and emotion) might profit by incorporating the language and constructs of virtue ethics. Far from being the quaint vestigial remains of a bygone era, these constructs are powerful tools for research in positive psychology. The study of virtue as an aspect of personality is enjoying something of a renaissance in contemporary research (Cawley, Martin, & Johnson, 2000; Peterson & Seligman, 2000; Snyder & McCullough, 2000). In addition to facilitating self-regulatory activity, individual differences in these virtues might have a direct, main effect on SWB (Dube, Kairouz, & Jodoin, 1997).

CONCLUSION

In a systematic review of the goals construct in clinical psychology, Karoly (1999) concluded that a motivational perspective centered around personal goals could articulate "a vision of a troubled human life." It has been my thesis in this chapter that a goals orientation to human functioning might also articulate a vision of "the good life" and the "positive person." Happiness and life satisfaction, two spheres of subjective experience of concern to psychologists articulating a vision of the good life, are influenced in deep ways by the goals that people are committed to. Thanks to the efforts of a young cadre of researchers, considerable progress has been made in the development of integrative theoretical models for understanding motivational influences on well-being.

Space limitations prevent me from reviewing all of the literature on goal constructs and well-being. Furthermore, many of the conclusions that I have reached in this chapter need to be appropriately qualified. Certain life goals may fail to meet basic human needs (Ryan & Deci, 2000). Inflexible striving for unattainable or foolhardy goals can bring misery and suffering rather than joy and fulfillment. Goals, when they fulfill individualistic but not collective or societal needs, may ultimately lead to lower quality of life and a worsening of interpersonal relationships. Even usually positive characteristics can have harmful consequences. For example, spirituality, when it results in excessive self-preoccupation, can discourage generative actions such as responsible parenting (Dollahite, 1998). Furthermore, excessive choices, when it comes to available goals and pathways to achieve them, may be disabling instead of empowering (Schwartz, 2000).

I therefore end this chapter with a call for wisdom. Along with the virtues discussed in this chapter, to know which goals are out of reach, which are not in our best interest, and which really matter is essential for the good life. The late philosopher Robert Nozick (1989) defined wisdom as "being able to see and appreciate the deepest significance of whatever occurs and understanding not merely the proximate goods but the ultimate ones, and seeing the world in this light" (p. 276). A wise person knows which goals are ultimately fulfilling and which offer only the illusion of fulfillment and thus will order his or her life accordingly. According to the research reviewed in this chapter, wisdom would be manifested in the choice to pursue positively framed, self-transcendent strivings in a prudent, patient, and persevering manner. And lest we get too caught up in the process of setting and strivings for goals, I would be remiss if I failed to mention the importance of savoring, appreciating, and celebrating the pursuit of one's goals.

We now know a lot about how goals make life meaningful, valuable, and worth living. Using this information for prevention, for the diagnosis of human strengths, as well as for intervention, should be among the meaningful and manageable goals of a positive psychology.

REFERENCES

Abresch, R. T., Seyden, N. K., & Wineinger, M. A. (1998). Quality of life: Issues for persons with neuromuscular disease. *Physical Medicine and Rehabilitation Clinics of North America, 9,* 233–248.

Ackerman, S., Zuroff, D. C., & Moskowitz, D. S. (2000). Generativity in midlife and young adults: Links to agency, communion, and subjective well-being. *International Journal of Aging & Human Development, 50,* 17–41.

Affleck, G., Tennen, H., Urrows, S., Higgins, P., Abeles, M., et al.(1998). Fibromyalgia and women's pursuit of daily goals: A daily process analysis. *Health Psychology, 17,* 40–47.

Austin, J. T., & Vancouver, J. B. (1996). Goal constructs in psychology: Structure, process, and content. *Psychological Bulletin, 120,* 338–375.

Baumeister, R. F. (1991). *Meanings of life.* New York: Guilford Press.

Baumeister, R. F., Leith, K. P., Muraven, M., & Bratslavsky, E. (1998). Self-regulation as a key to success in life. In D. Pushkar (Ed.), *Improving competence across the lifespan* (pp. 117–128). New York: Plenum Press.

Bennett, W. J. (1993). *The book of virtues.* New York: Simon and Schuster.

Brickman, P. (Ed.). (1987). *Commitment, conflict, and caring.* Englewood Cliffs, NJ: Prentice Hall.

Brunstein, J. C., Schultheiss, O. C., & Graessman, R. (1998). Personal goals and emotional well-being: The moderating role of motive dispositions. *Journal of Personality and Social Psychology, 75,* 494–508.

Cantor, N., & Zirkel, S. (1990). Personality, cognition, and purposive behavior. In L. A. Pervin (Ed.), *Handbook of personality: Theory and research* (pp. 135–164). New York: Guilford Press.

Carver, C. S., & Scheier, M. F. (1990). On the origins of positive and negative affect: A control-process view. *Psychological Review, 97,* 19–35.

Cawley, M. J., Martin, J. E., & Johnson, J. A. (2000). A virtues approach to personality. *Personality and Individual Differences, 28,* 997–1013.

Cochran, W., & Tesser, A. (1996). The "what the hell effect": Some effects of goal proximity and goal framing on performance. In A. Tesser & L. Martin (Eds.), *Striving and feeling: Interactions among goals, affect, and self-regulation* (pp. 99–120). New York: Plenum Press.

Compton, W. C., Smith, M. L., Cornish, K. A., & Qualls, D. L. (1996). Factor structure of mental health measures. *Journal of Personality and Social Psychology, 71,* 406–413.

Csikszentmihalyi, M. (1990). *Flow: The psychology of optimal experience.* New York: HarperCollins.

Debats, D. L. (1996). Meaning in life: Clinical relevance and predictive power. *British Journal of Clinical Psychology, 35,* 503–516.

DeNeve, K. M., & Cooper, H. (1998). The happy personality: A meta-analysis of 137 personality traits and subjective well-being. *Psychological Bulletin, 124,* 197–229.

Diener, E., Emmons, R., Larsen, R., & Griffin, S. (1985). The Satisfaction with Life Scale. *Journal of Personality Assessment, 49,* 71–75.

Diener, E., & Fujita, F. (1995). Resources, personal strivings, and subjective well-being: A nomothetic and idiographic approach. *Journal of Personality and Social Psychology, 68,* 926–935.

Diener, E., Suh, E. M., Lucas, R. E., & Smith, H. L. (1999). Subjective well-being: Three decades of progress. *Psychological Bulletin, 125,* 276–302.

Dollahite, D. C. (1998). Fathering, faith and spirituality. *Journal of Men's Studies,* 7, 3–15.

Dube, L., Kairouz, S., & Jodoin, M. (1997). Commitment: A gauge of happiness? *Revue Quebecoise de Psychologie,* 18, 211–237.

Ebersole, P. (1998). Types and depth of written life meanings. In P. T. P. Wong & P. S. Fry (Eds.), *The human quest for meaning: A handbook of psychological research and clinical applications* (pp. 179–191). Mahway, NJ: Erlbaum.

Elliot, A. J., Chirkov, V. I., Kim, Y., & Sheldon, K. M. (2001). A cross-cultural analysis of avoidance (relative to approach) personal goals. *Psychological Science,* 12, 505–510.

Elliot, A. J., & Sheldon, K. M. (1998). Avoidance personal goals and the personality-illness relationship. *Journal of Personality and Social Psychology,* 75, 1282–1299.

Elliot, A., Sheldon, K., & Church, M. (1997). Avoidance personal goals and subjective well-being. *Personality and Social Psychology Bulletin,* 23, 915–927.

Emmons, R. A. (1991). Personal strivings, daily life events, and psychological and physical well-being. *Journal of Personality,* 59, 453–472.

Emmons, R. A. (1999). *The psychology of ultimate concerns: Motivation and spirituality in personality.* New York: Guilford Press.

Emmons, R. A., Cheung, C., & Tehrani, K. (1998). Assessing spirituality through personal goals: Implications for research on religion and subjective well-being. *Social Indicators Research,* 45, 391–422.

Emmons, R. A., & Kaiser, H. (1996). Goal orientation and emotional well-being: Linking goals and affect through the self. In A. Tesser & L. Martin (Eds.), *Striving and feeling: Interactions among goals, affect, and self-regulation* (pp. 79–98). New York: Plenum Press.

Ewart, C. K. (1991). Social action theory for a public health psychology. *American Psychologist,* 46, 931–946.

Fava, G. A. (1999). Well-being therapy: Conceptual and technical issues. *Psychotherapy and Psychosomatics,* 68, 171–179.

French, S., & Joseph, S. (1999). Religiosity and its association with happiness, purpose in life, and self-actualisation. *Mental Health, Religion & Culture,* 2, 117–120

Frisch, M. B. (1998). Quality of life therapy and assessment in health care. *Clinical Psychology: Science and Practice,* 5, 19–40.

Harned, D. B. (1997). *Patience: How we wait upon the world.* Cambridge, MA: Cowley.

Haslam, N. (1991). Prudence: Aristotelian perspectives on practical reason. *Journal for the Theory of Social Behaviour,* 21, 151–169.

Igreja, I., Zuroff, D. C., Koestner, R., & Saltaris, C. (2000). Social motives, social support, and distress in gay men differing in HIV status. *Journal of Research in Personality,* 34, 287–304.

Jeffries, V. (1998). Virtue and the altruistic personality. *Sociological Perspectives,* 41, 151–167.

John, O. P., & Srivastava, S. (1999). The Big Five Trait taxonomy: History, measurement, and theoretical perspectives. In L. A. Pervin & O. P. John (Eds.), *Handbook of personality: Theory and research* (2nd ed., pp. 102–138). New York: Guilford Press.

Karoly, P. (1991). Goal systems and health outcomes across the life span: A proposal. In H. E. Schroeder (Ed.), *New directions in health psychology assessment* (pp. 65–91). New York: Hemisphere.

Karoly, P. (1999). A goal systems–self-regulatory perspective on personality, psychopathology, and change. *Review of General Psychology, 3,* 264–291.

Kasser, T., & Ryan, R. M. (1993). A dark side of the American dream: Correlates of financial success as a central life aspiration. *Journal of Personality and Social Psychology, 65,* 410–422.

Kasser, T., & Ryan, R. M. (1996). Further examining the American dream: Differential correlates of intrinsic and extrinsic goals. *Personality and Social Psychology Bulletin, 22,* 280–287.

Kasser, T., & Sheldon, K. M. (2000). Of wealth and death: Materialism, mortality salience, and consumption behavior. *Psychological Science, 11,* 348–351.

Keyes, C. L. M. (1998). Social well-being. *Social Psychology Quarterly, 61,* 121–140.

Keyes, C. L. M., & Ryff, C. D. (1998). Generativity in adult lives: Social structural contours and quality of life consequences. In D. P. McAdams & E. de St. Aubin (Eds.), *Generativity and adult development: How and why we care for the next generation* (pp. 227–263). Washington, DC: American Psychological Association.

King, L. A., & Emmons, R. A. (1991). Psychological, physical, and interpersonal correlates of emotional expressiveness, conflict, and control. *European Journal of Personality, 5,* 131–150.

Klausner, E. J., Clarkin, J. F., Spielman, L., & Pupo, C. (1998). Late-life depression and functional disability. The role of goal-focused group psychotherapy. *International Journal of Geriatric Psychiatry, 13,* 707–716.

Klinger, E. (1998). The search for meaning in evolutionary perspective and its clinical implications. In P. T. P. Wong & P. S. Fry (Eds.), *Handbook of personal meaning: Theory, research, and application* (pp. 27–50). Mahwah, NJ: Erlbaum.

Lawton, M. P. (1996). Quality of life and affect in later life. In C. Magai & S. H. McFadden (Eds.), *Handbook of emotion, adult development, and aging* (pp. 327–348). San Diego, CA: Academic Press.

Locke, E. A., & Kristof, A. L. (1996). Volitional choices in the goal achievement process. In P. M. Gollwitzer & J. A. Bargh (Eds.), *The psychology of action: Linking cognition and motivation to behavior* (pp. 365–384). New York: Guilford Press.

Mahoney, A., Pargament, K. I., Jewell, T., Swank, A. B., Scott, E., et al. (1999). Marriage and the spiritual realm: The role of proximal and distal religious constructs in marital functioning. *Journal of Family Psychology, 13,* 321–338.

McAdams, D. P., & de St. Aubin, E. (1992). A theory of generativity and its assessment through self-report, behavioral acts, and narrative themes in autobiography. *Journal of Personality and Social Psychology, 62,* 1003–1015.

McAdams, D. P., & de St. Aubin, E. (Eds.). (1998). *Generativity and adult development: Psychosocial perspectives on caring for and contributing to the next generation.* Washington, DC: American Psychological Association.

McAdams, D. P., de St. Aubin, E., & Logan, R. L. (1993). Generativity among young, midlife, and older adults. *Psychology and Aging, 8,* 221–230.

McCullough, M. E., & Snyder, C. R. (2000). Classical sources of human strength: Revisiting an old home and building a new one. *Journal of Social and Clinical Psychology, 19,* 1–10.

Myers, D. G. (2000). The funds, friends, and faith of happy people. *American Psychologist, 55,* 56–67.

National Institute of Health. (1998). *Post-polio syndrome, fact sheet.* Bethesda, MD: National Institute of Neurological Disorders and Stroke.

Nozick, R. (1989). *The examined life.* New York: Simon and Schuster.

Oishi, S., Diener, E., Suh, E., & Lucas, R. E. (1999). Value as a moderator in subjective well-being. *Journal of Personality, 67,* 157–184.

Pascal, B. (1950). *The Pensees.* (Trans, H. F. Stewart). New York: Pantheon. (Original published 1660)

Pavot, W., & Diener, E. (1993). Review of the Satisfaction With Life Scale. *Psychological Assessment, 5,* 164–172.

Peterson, C., & Seligman, M. E. P. (2000). *The VIA taxonomy of human strengths and virtues.* Unpublished manuscript, University of Pennsylvania.

Piedmont, R. (1999). Does spirituality represent the sixth factor of personality? Spiritual transcendence and the Five-Factor Model. *Journal of Personality, 67,* 985–1013.

Reker, G. T., & Wong, P. T. P. (1988). Aging as an individual process: Toward a theory of personal meaning. In J. E. Birren & V. L. Bengston (Eds.), *Emergent theories of aging* (pp. 214–246). New York: Springer.

Robak, R. W., & Griffin, P. W. (2000). Purpose in life: What is its relationship to happiness, depression, and grieving? *North American Journal of Psychology, 2,* 113–119.

Roberts, R. C. (1984). *The strengths of a Christian.* Philadelphia: Westminster Press.

Ryan, R. M. Chirkov, V. I., Little, T. D., & Sheldon, K. M. (1999). The American dream in Russia: Extrinsic aspirations and well-being in two cultures. *Personality and Social Psychology Bulletin, 25,* 1509–1524.

Ryan, R. M., & Deci, E. L. (2000). Self-determination theory and the facilitation of intrinsic motivation, social development, and well-being. *American Psychologist, 55,* 68–78.

Ryan, R. M., Sheldon, K. M., Kasser, T., & Deci, E. L. (1996). All goals are not created equal: An organismic perspective on the nature of goals and their regulation. In J. A. Bargh & P. M. Gollwitzer (Eds.), *The psychology of action: Linking motivation and cognition to behavior* (pp. 7–26). New York: Guilford Press.

Ryff, C. D. (1989). Happiness is everything, or is it? Explorations on the meaning of psychological well-being. *Journal of Personality and Social Psychology, 57,* 1069–1081.

Ryff, C. D., & Keyes, C. L. M. (1995). The structure of psychological well-being revisited. *Journal of Personality and Social Psychology, 69,* 719–727.

Schwartz, B. (2000). Self-determination: The tyranny of freedom. *American Psychologist, 55,* 79–88.

Seeman, M. (1991). Alienation and anomie. In J. P. Robinson, & P. R. Shaver (Eds.), *Measures of personality and social psychological attitudes* (pp. 291–371). San Diego, CA: Academic Press.

Seligman, M. (1998, Oct.). Positive social science. *APA Monitor, 2,* 5.

Seligman, M. (1999, Aug.). *Positive psychology.* Presidential address delivered at the 107th Annual Convention of the American Psychological Association, Boston.

Seligman, M., & Csikszentmihalyi, M. (2000). Positive psychology: An introduction. *American Psychologist, 55,* 5–14.

Sheldon, K. M., & Elliot, A. J. (1999). Goal striving, need satisfaction, and longitudinal well-being: The self-concordance model. *Journal of Personality and Social Psychology, 76,* 482–497.

Sheldon, K. M., & Kasser, T. (1998). Pursuing personal goals: Skills enable progress, but not all progress is beneficial. *Personality & Social Psychology Bulletin, 24,* 1319–1331.

Snyder, C. R., & McCullough, M. E. (2000). Classical sources of human strength: Revisiting an old home and building a new one. *Journal of Social and Clinical Psychology, 19,* 1–10.

Tillich, P. (1951). *Christianity and the problem of existence. Three lectures.* Washington, DC: Henderson Services.

Willer, B., Ottenbacher, K. J., & Coad, M. L. (1994). The community integration questionnaire: A comparative examination. *American Journal of Physical Medicine and Rehabilitation, 73,* 103–111.

Wong, P. T. P. (1998). Spirituality, meaning, and successful aging. In P. T. P. Wong & P. S. Fry (Eds.), *The human quest for meaning* (pp. 359–394). Mahwah, NJ: Erlbaum.

Wong, P. T. P., & Fry, P. S. (Eds.). (1998). *Handbook of personal meaning: Theory, research, and application.* Mahwah, NJ: Erlbaum.

Zagzebski, L. T. (1996). *Virtues of the mind.* New York: Cambridge.

6

TOWARD A POSITIVE PSYCHOLOGY OF RELATIONSHIPS

HARRY T. REIS AND SHELLY L. GABLE

There's an old joke that goes something like this: No one on their deathbed ever said that they should have spent more time at the office. This joke, like most jokes that find their way into the literature, illustrates a principle that has received extensive empirical support: Relationships are an important, and perhaps the most important, source of life satisfaction and emotional well-being (see Berscheid & Reis, 1998, for a review). For example, a survey of more than 2000 Americans conducted in 1971 concluded that marriage and family life were the best predictors of overall life satisfaction among the major domains of human activity (Campbell, Converse, & Rodgers, 1976). Diener (2001), in a review of cross-national studies of the sources of subjective well-being, found that only one factor consistently predicted subjective well-being in every country studied: social relationships. People routinely list successful close relationships among their most important life goals and aspirations (e.g., Emmons, 1999; Little, 1989), and not doing so is significantly correlated with undesirable outcomes (e.g., Kasser & Ryan, 1996). When describing the factors that give life meaning, most people mention close relationships more so than other activities (e.g., Klinger, 1977). Evidence supporting this conclusion notably includes the late-life reminiscences of Terman's Gifted Children sample, a group of men who had exceptional career success and who therefore might have been expected to emphasize work, personal accomplishment, and self-expression (Sears, 1977).

Likewise, and almost without exception, theories of psychological well-being include positive relationships with others as a core element of mental health and well-being. Most theories view satisfying relationships as a determinant of well-being, much as the realization of any important goal or aspiration would predict emotional health. Some theories go so far as to posit "positive relations with others" as an intrinsic component of psychological well-being and not just as a cause of it (e.g., Keyes, 1998; Ryff, 1995). These theories vary, or in some cases are silent, about precisely what constitutes a positive relationship. Some construe positive relationships in terms of primary close relationships like marriage and parenting; others highlight process variables such as intimacy or secure attachment; and still others point more broadly to the critical role played by friendships and social networks throughout the life cycle (Hartup & Stevens, 1997). The benefits of relationships are not limited to mental health. The demonstrated value of social connections and social support for health, recovery from illness, and physiological functioning is clear (see Cohen & Herbert, 1996, for a review). These effects are not slight. House, Landis, and Umberson's (1988) review of several large, long-term prospective epidemiological studies concluded that low social integration (e.g., marriage, involvement in community groups) is a risk factor for mortality whose age-adjusted relative risk ratio exceeds that of cigarette smoking.

On the distress side of the spectrum, relationships are well-established as one of the most potent causes of human misery. More than half of the respondents in a large national survey asked to describe "the last bad thing that happened to you" recounted an interpersonal event, primarily disruption or conflict in a significant relationship (Veroff, Douvan, & Kulka, 1981). Death of a spouse is among the most traumatic of life events (Holmes & Rahe, 1967) and often affects psychological and physical health profoundly (Stroebe & Stroebe, 1987). Troubled relationships are the most common presenting problem in psychotherapy (e.g., Pinsker, Nepps, Redfield, & Winston, 1985), and the loss of, or failure to attain, desired relationships are a major source of depression, loneliness, alienation, and self-destructive behavior at all stages of the life cycle. The high rate of divorce and abuse in American families, the everyday absence of working parents from their children's lives in both single-parent and dual-parent families, and the decline in social and community participation noted by some observers (e.g., Putnam, 2000) are all thought to contribute to a variety of individual and social ills in American society. Finally, that destructive relationships also may have harmful health consequences is shown, for example, by the link between conflict and hostility with down-regulation of the immune system (e.g., Kiecolt-Glaser, 1999).

The weight of evidence is, in short, so compelling that one commentator referred to the association between relationships and well-being as a "deep truth" (Myers, 1992, p. 154). Virtually all reviews of this vast and diverse literature have concluded similarly (e.g., Argyle, 1987; Berscheid & Reis, 1998; Diener, Suh, Lucas, & Smith, 1999). Even economists and political scientists have begun to recognize the value and impact of close relationships, incorporating into their forecasts the economic and societal consequences of such relationship variables as the divorce rate, changing family constellations, and work-group interactions (Berscheid, 1999). That social relations exert broad and pervasive influence on human behavior and development is further evident in the role that the relationship context plays in many psychological processes. Reis, Collins, and Berscheid's (2000) review of theories and evidence led them to argue that because humans evolved in a social context, many of the most important basic processes with which humans have been endowed concern the tasks inherent in sociality, interaction, and ongoing relationships (see also Bugental, 2000). Their review shows how central processes of cognition, emotion, and motivation involve responses to, and regulation by, interpersonal relations. For example, social relations figure prominently and indispensably in phenomena such as emotion regulation, coping with stress, self-perception and identity formation, uncertainty reduction, collective task performance, and the fulfillment of personal aspirations. Relationships, in other words, provide a functional context that influences the operation of many, if not most, basic psychological processes.

Reviewing the voluminous literature on social relations and human well-being led Berscheid and Reis to conclude that

> despite the wealth of evidence that relationships are people's most frequent source of both happiness and distress, there is inadequate evidence of the causal mechanisms responsible and of the types of relationships that are most beneficial or harmful, even though these issues form the core of much theorizing and research. (1998, p. 243)

One reason for this lacuna may reside in the distinction on which this chapter is based—namely that existing research treats happiness and distress in relationships as opposing outcomes on a bipolar scale, as if happiness was simply the absence of distress and distress was simply the absence of happiness (chapter 13, this volume). Moreover, researchers sometimes seem to assume that the processes by which relationships are satisfying and beneficial are simply the inverse of, or reflect nothing more than the absence of, the processes by which relationships are distressing and harmful.

In this chapter, we argue that positive and negative processes in relationships may be better understood as functionally independent, not as opposites of each other. We will draw on similar positions supported in other areas of research, including emotion (Cacioppo & Gardner, 1999), motivation (Elliot, 1997), self-regulation (Higgins, 1998), and personality (Eysenck, 1981). Although specific phenomena differ from one research area to another, common among them is a fundamental distinction between rewarding (i.e., positive and desired) and punishing (i.e., negative and unwelcome) features of the social environment. We refer to these two dimensions as *appetite* and *aversion*, respectively, to capture simultaneously the evaluative and motivational properties of each system. Thus, the appetitive system pertains to goal-directed pursuit of desired, favorable outcomes whereas the aversive system relates to goal-directed avoidance of undesired, unfavorable outcomes.

Despite growing popularity in other areas of research, these issues have had relatively little impact on relationship research. Reconceptualizing positive and negative relationship processes as independent has the potential to clarify existing theories and research and to suggest new directions for theorizing, phenomena to be investigated, and applications to be developed. We will begin by discussing two questions inherent in this position. First, is bad stronger than good? That is, does the well-documented association between interpersonal circumstances and well-being arise because bad relationships cause distress, because good relationships produce well-being, or both? The second question concerns function. When it comes to relationships, do aversive and appetitive functions operate through a common process—in other words, a mechanism whose activation impels behavior in one direction for appetitive situations and a different direction for aversive circumstances—or do they require independent processes? Our goal is to demonstrate that positive processes have been underinvestigated by relationship researchers and to suggest several strategies for rectifying this unevenness. We propose that this involves conceptualizing positive relationship processes not as the opposite of negatives but rather as the result of a conceptually and functionally independent system. Toward this end, the later sections of this chapter will discuss several relationship processes that we believe exemplify the appetitive dimension that is central to a positive psychology of relationships.

IS BAD STRONGER THAN GOOD?

Relationship scientists have long been concerned with the relative impact of positive and negative factors. Christensen and Walczynski's conclusion is representative: "Once a relationship has been well established, conflict is the most important proximal factor affecting satisfaction in the relationship and ultimately its course" (1997, p. 250). Evidence supporting their conclusion is plentiful and diverse. For example, observational studies, which are used to objectively distinguish interaction patterns of distressed and nondistressed couples, have repeatedly identified negative-affect reciprocity as an indicator of marital dysfunction (Gottman, 1998). This construct refers to one spouse's reciprocation of negative affect expressed by the other, thereby escalating the existing level of negative affect while simultaneously impairing the couple's ability to resolve legitimate disagreements without additional damage to the relationship. This pattern contrasts sharply with the conflict-reducing and repair-oriented communication that characterizes nondistressed couples (Rusbult, Verette, Whitney, Slovik, & Lipkus, 1991).

Many research programs treat conflict and other negative interactions, and more particularly how couples manage these circumstances, as the *sine qua non* of relationship success. For example, in a classic diary study, Wills, Weiss, and Patterson (1974) had spouses keep track of positive and negative behaviors three times a day for 14 days. Negative behaviors, spanning both affectional and instrumental activity, accounted for 65% of the measurable variance in marital satisfaction. That displays of negative behavior are more highly correlated with satisfaction than are displays of positive behavior has been shown repeatedly since then (e.g., Gottman & Krokoff, 1989). Similarly, the well-documented downward trajectory in marital satisfaction that occurs in the first few years of marriage has been linked to increasing negativity of interaction (e.g., Gottman & Levenson, 1992; Huston & Vangelisti, 1991; Karney & Bradbury, 1997; Matthews, Conger, & Wickrama, 1999).[1]

Other examples of the importance of negative interactions in marriage include the belief by family systems theorists that "expressed emotion" (two of the three components of which are criticism and hostility) is the hallmark of dysfunctional family interaction; studies of the dispositional vulnerabilities that contribute to relationship dissatisfaction and instability, which show the strongest and most consistent evidence for the effects of negative affectivity (i.e., the tendency to experience emotional distress readily, often as an extreme reaction to mild or perceived provocation; see Karney & Bradbury, 1995, for a review); and communication studies such as that of Gottman (1994), who has found that the probability of divorce is substantially higher in couples whose communication is characterized by criticism, defensiveness, contempt, and stonewalling.

These examples describe destructive behaviors that arise in negative interactions, especially those involving conflict. Interdependence theorists argue that destructive behaviors are both more diagnostic about, and exert more influence on, relationship well-being because they create tension between the tendency to respond vindictively and the more pro-relationship response, whereas positive behaviors create no such tension. Thus, forgiveness and accommodation—tendencies to respond constructively to a partner's destructive behavior—are associated with commitment, satisfaction, and stability over time (e.g., Rusbult et al., 1991).

---

[1] Or, to paraphrase a character in the 1999 film, *The Story of Us*, "It's hard to French kiss someone you've just been arguing with about putting in the toilet paper roll so the paper comes over the top."

By no means is the evidence for the greater impact of negative interactions limited to marriage. For example, in both children and adults, the emotional impact of social rejection is greater than the emotional impact of social acceptance, a finding that is compatible with observations of many mammalian species. Other studies have compared the relative impact of interpersonal conflict and social support in such samples as widowed women, college students, and unemployed persons (Lepore, 1992; Rook, 1984; Vinokur & van Ryn, 1993). In each instance conflict had significantly stronger effects on individual well-being than did support.

In short, research on relationships and interpersonal events supports the same conclusion that Taylor (1991) drew in her review of the extensive literature on adaptation to life events: "Negative events appear to elicit more physiological, affective, cognitive, and behavioral activity and prompt more cognitive analysis than neutral or positive events" (1991, p. 67). It is therefore not surprising that studies of conflict and other negative interactions predominate in the literature relative to studies of more positive interactions: Researchers put their money where they believe the action lies (i.e., where the greatest percentage of variance is to be accounted), and insofar as relationships are concerned, the action appears to emphasize the dark side.

This emphasis has not been overlooked by the practice community. Two *Annual Review of Psychology* articles (Christensen & Heavey, 1999; Gottman, 1998) noted that marital therapy programs, which tend to emphasize communication skills involved in conflict management, are weighted toward helping spouses cope with negative situations rather than enhancing positive interactions and processes. As one self-help book put it,

> "Marital happiness has little to do with whom you marry and everything to do with how you cope with conflict" and "Simple truth #2: One zinger will erase twenty acts of kindness . . . it takes one put-down to undo hours of kindness you give to your partner." (Notarius & Markman, 1993, p. 20; 28)

Rather than striving to relate well, in other words, couples should simply seek to not relate badly.

AVERSIVE PROCESSES: A THEORETICAL PERSPECTIVE

Before considering an alternative position, it is important to acknowledge that this emphasis on relationship negatives may not be misplaced. Considerable supporting evidence exists across diverse areas of behavioral science, so that a reasoned case for the role of appetitive processes in the interpersonal realm must take these findings and theories into account.

Although this chapter cannot provide a comprehensive summary, a brief review of three popular theoretical models will set the stage for our position.

Evolutionary Adaptation

The basic premise of evolutionary psychology is that certain mechanisms became part of human nature because they solved specific adaptive problems related to survival and reproduction (Buss & Kenrick, 1998). In other words, mechanisms that enhanced the probability of survival or the production of capable offspring came to be included among the basic psychological processes with which all humans are innately endowed. Although the particulars remain to be documented, processes designed to contend with potentially damaging environmental circumstances likely had greater value during human evolution than did processes aimed at potentially beneficial environmental circumstances. This is because the former tended to have direct, immediate, and irreversible consequences for survival and reproduction, whereas the impact of beneficial circumstances is often indirect, delayed, or reversible. An imminent predator attack or the presence of sexual rivals has more direct adaptive consequences than the events that create joy and intimacy.

Emotions illustrate this distinction clearly. Emotions are innate mechanisms that orient the individual to attend to important environmental circumstances and prepare him or her to cope with them. Notwithstanding ongoing debate as to which particular emotions are "basic" (i.e., innate and not derivative of other affects), nearly all theories list more basic negative emotions than basic positive emotions. For example, Levenson and colleagues (1992) focused on four negative emotions—anger, fear, distress, and sadness—and one positive emotion—happiness—in a series of psychophysiological and cross-cultural studies. Lazarus (1994) discussed 15 basic emotions, 9 negative and 6 positive (of which three involve reactions to negative situations—relief, hope, and compassion). Conceptualizations of negative emotion tend to be more differentiated than conceptualizations of positive emotions, perhaps because the variability of diverse environmental threats requires a more differentiated response than environmental benefits do (Fiske & Taylor, 1991).

In a similar vein, Cosmides and Tooby (1992) argued that the human capacity for conditional reasoning reflects the need to detect cheaters—individuals who violate the social contract by benefiting themselves without reciprocally contributing to the group. In a series of elegant experiments, they demonstrated that this mechanism is specific to identifying cheaters—that is, it does not apply in situations without cost to the individual nor to the detection of altruists (i.e., people who contribute to the group without benefiting themselves). Presumably, identifying a single instance of social-contract cheating has direct and immediate implications for group living, whereas each instance of compliance is relatively uninformative.

Resource Mobilization

If threatening circumstances have more immediate and potentially graver consequences for the individual than beneficial circumstances do, it follows that physiological, affective, cognitive, and social resources should likewise be mobilized more quickly and extensively by the former than by the latter. Extensive evidence supports this supposition, as noted previously (Taylor, 1991). For example, traumatic life events such as death, illness, and unemployment generally produce stronger and more immediate responses than do birth, winning the lottery, or getting a job. People also invest more resources in getting out of a bad mood than in trying to create a good mood (Baumeister, Bratslavsky, Finkenauer, & Vohs, in press).

Research on opponent processes (Solomon & Corbit, 1974), which describes homeostatic neurological processes that subdue or suppress departures from hedonic neutrality, help explain this finding. Although opponent process models predict roughly equal responses to positive and negative events of the same magnitude, affective life is not normally distributed around a neutral zero—mood, everyday experiences, and social interaction tend to be mildly positive on average (e.g., Diener & Diener, 1996; Peeters & Czapinski, 1990). If so, the baseline to be restored is on average modestly positive rather than neutral, and a negative event of a given magnitude will tend to be more discrepant from baseline than a positive event of the same absolute magnitude. A stronger response is therefore required to return the individual to baseline. The irony of this explanation, of course, is that the overwhelming predominance of mild positive circumstances in everyday life is precisely what makes negative events more salient and influential.

Social Cognition

Laboratory studies of social judgment and decision making have repeatedly demonstrated negativity bias—a tendency to rely on negative cues more than on positive cues (see reviews by Peeters & Czapinski, 1990; Skowronski & Carlston, 1989). Given the methodological advantages of laboratory experimentation—experimental control of stimuli and random assignment—these studies provide compelling evidence for negativity bias and its putative causes. Several explanations have been supported. First, as mentioned previously, the sort of negative information that people encounter in everyday life tends to be more evaluatively extreme from the hypothetical neutral point than is positive information, which enhances its impact. Second, automatic (i.e., not consciously or deliberately mediated) vigilance tends to be greater with regard to negative stimuli than to positive stimuli (Pratto & John, 1991). Moreover, once noticed, negative stimuli influence automatic evaluative categorizations more than positive stimuli do, a stage of cognitive processing that precedes conscious awareness (Ito, Larsen, Smith, & Cacioppo, 1998). Manusov, Floyd, and Kerssen-Griep's (1997) finding that spouses were more likely to notice each others' negative nonverbal acts than their positive nonverbal acts is consistent with these findings.

Third, negative acts are believed to be more diagnostic about a person's inner qualities than are positive acts, which are more likely to be attributed to situational demands and social desirability (Vonk, 1994). Positive acts are considered to be less informative about an actor's attitudes and dispositions because politeness rules, social norms, and the desire to create favorable impressions tend to impel positive behavior by most people (Skowronski & Carlston, 1989). Negative actions run contrary to these strong situational demands and thereby are presumed to be more revealing about the person's inner states and dispositions. Being late for a date or job interview is more diagnostic than being on time.

Fourth, negativity bias involves the venerable concept of expectancy violation. Outcomes that deviate from expectations—what Helson (1964) called adaptation level and Thibaut and Kelley (1959) termed comparison level—tend to generate more pronounced reactions than do outcomes consistent with expectations. Extensive research supports this proposition—for example, acts that violate expectancies are more likely to be noticed, are more likely to require explanation and elaboration, influence impressions more strongly, and tend to produce stronger emotions (Olson, Roese, & Zanna, 1996). Given generally positive expectations about social interaction and close relationships—after all, friendships are pursued and deepened because they are rewarding and courtship typically turns into marriage because of the joy and fulfillment that partners experience in their relationship (in the Western world, at least)—hostile interactions are more likely to violate expectations than hospitable interactions are.

In long-term relationships, the expectancy violation process is commonly cited to explain why, as mentioned earlier, "one zinger will erase 20 acts of kindness" (Notarius & Markman, 1993, p. 28), and why spouses in successful marriages tend to exhibit at least a 5:1 ratio of positive to negative behaviors (Gottman, 1993). More often than not, spouses expect their partners to treat them well; negative acts therefore tend to deviate more from expectations than comparably extreme positive acts. Terms such as "reinforcement erosion" (Jacobson & Margolin, 1979) and "habituation and satiation" (Christensen & Heavey, 1999) have been used to describe the process by which the value of positive acts that were rewarding in the early stages of a relationship—gifts of a certain magnitude, loving gestures or favors—gradually subsides over time—that is, these acts become expected and thereby lose their power to delight. Negative acts, on the other hand—a forgotten birthday, a critical comment—retain their power. Precisely because of our extensive background of pleasing, positive interactions, both in general and with specific partners, negative acts acquire greater expectancy-violation potential than positive acts do. Ironically, it would seem, the better one treats a partner, the higher their expectations may rise and the more distressing the same mildly negative act may be.

IS THERE A PLACE FOR POSITIVE PROCESSES IN THESE THEORIES?

Given the aforementioned evidence, one might reasonably question the value of examining appetitive processes in close relationships. In the next section, we discuss several reasons why the situation may not be as one-sided as it appears. We propose that the field's inclination to treat negativity bias as received wisdom may have led it to neglect positivity, which, as we will argue, may have important implications for relationship functioning and well-being.

It may be useful to begin with a thought experiment. Expectancy violation implies a solution for marital distress: Lower the spouses' expectations. This intervention often occurs naturally—repeated unpleasant interactions tend to diminish partners' expectations about each other, so that over time, it would seem that they should fare better. But of course they do not: If anything, negativity tends to escalate over time. One reason is that expectations do not always produce the contrast effects discussed previously; under certain circumstances assimilation takes place. Rather than viewing a partner's unexpectedly positive act as a sign of caring or commitment, for example, distressed spouses often ignore or dismiss such acts, attributing them instead to external or circumstantial causes (Bradbury & Fincham, 1990)—bringing home flowers might be construed as a sign of guilt or as an accident of transient mood. Satisfied spouses, whose comparison level is higher, are more likely to give their partners attributional credit for positive acts. Thus it is the spouses with high expectations who tend to acknowledge their partners' positive acts while downplaying their negative acts, not those with low expectations, as the logic of expectancy violation would seem to imply.

The principle of expectancy violation further implies that a partner's positive acts should be more attributionally significant to the extent that an individual's interpersonal expectations are chronically lower. However, existing evidence suggests exactly the opposite: Persons predisposed to poorer expectations—for example, as represented in traits such as insecure attachment, low self-esteem, depression, pessimism, and negative affectivity—tend to be *more* dissatisfied with their friends, close relationships, and social life (mirroring their harsher assessments in most life domains; Karney & Bradbury, 1995). Thus, expectancy violation may not be as compelling an explanation for negativity bias as is often assumed, a conclusion also reached by Skowronski and Carlston (1989), who noted that in laboratory studies of social cognition, clear, well-established expectancies were about as likely to produce assimilation as contrast.

Bivariate, Not Bipolar

Considerable evidence has accumulated across diverse areas of research demonstrating the independence of two distinct functional systems, one concerned with appetitive processes, the other concerned with aversive processes. This literature suggests that the processes and mechanisms involved in responding to positive stimuli may be largely independent of those involved in responding to negative stimuli. In other words, rather than representing opposite ends of a single continuous "bad–good" dimension, it may be more fruitful to consider the processes implicated in confrontational and congenial social interaction as functionally and conceptually independent (see Figure 6.1). That is, they entail different eliciting circumstances, separate neural pathways, and behavioral mechanisms and they produce distinguishable outcomes. Bipolar models imply that high standing on one dimension requires low standing on the other; bivariate, two-dimensional models, in contrast, imply that high standing on one dimension tends to be relatively uninformative about the other.[2]

Functional independence of appetitive and aversive processes has been supported diversely. See the following examples.

Emotion

Studies of the structure of affects indicate that positive and negative affect are best represented as functionally independent dimensions (e.g., Watson, Wiese, Vaidya, & Tellegen, 1999). Belsky, Hsieh, and Crnic's (1995) analysis of infants' behavioral responses to affect-arousing situations found similar evidence for separate dimensions of positive and negative temperament, as did Gross and John's (1997) analysis of self-report data on adult emotional expressivity. Reflecting this and much more evidence,

---

[2]This does not mean that these two dimensions are necessarily uncorrelated. Most studies, in fact, find low to moderate negative correlations between them. This may occur, for example, when activation of one system inhibits operation of the other. For example, high levels of negative affect tend to inhibit positive affects and vice versa (Cacioppo & Gardner, 1999). Nevertheless, although appetitive and aversive processes may interact, they remain conceptually and functionally independent by virtue of using different operating systems.

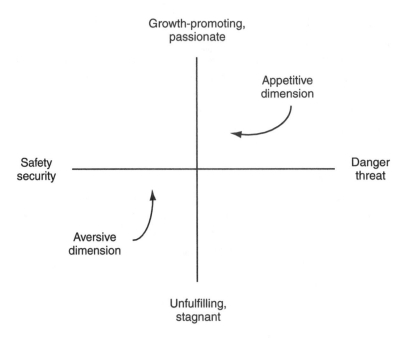

Growth-promoting,
passionate

Appetitive
dimension

Safety
security

Danger
threat

Aversive
dimension

Unfulfilling,
stagnant

Figure 6.1. Two-dimensional model of appetitive and aversive processes in relationships.

Cacioppo and Gardner (1999) concluded that independent biological and behavioral mechanisms appear to regulate experiences and expressions of positive and negative affect. Accumulating neurobiological evidence supports this position (e.g., Davidson, 1992; Sutton & Davidson, 1997).

Motivation

Several programs of research indicate that the fundamental hedonic principle of motivation—that people seek pleasure and avoid pain—involves independent systems, one regulating approach to desired outcomes, the other regulating avoidance of disliked outcomes (see Carver, 1996, for an overview). For example, Gray (1987, 1994) and Fowles (1994) described the same two orienting systems, one an approach system that activates responding to rewarding (i.e., appetitive) stimuli, the other an inhibition system that regulates responses to aversive stimuli. Similarly, in the achievement domain, Elliot (1997) distinguished approach goals, which concern obtaining success, and avoidance goals, which concern avoiding failure. The relative strength of approach and avoidance goals predicts various performance and affective outcomes (Elliot & Church, 1997). Social motivation may also be characterized in terms of distinct appetitive (hope for affiliation) and aversive (fear of rejection) drives (Boyatzis, 1973; Gable,

2000; Schmalt, 1999). Fincham and Linfield's (1997) suggestion that positive and negative feelings about marriage should be considered independent dimensions, rather than endpoints of a single dissatisfied-to-satisfied dimension, is consistent with this research.

Self-Regulation

Higgins and colleagues have described two forms of self-regulation, promotion and prevention (Higgins, 1998). Promotion refers to sensitivity to available positive outcomes, orients the individual to approaching these outcomes, and is concerned with growth and accomplishment. Prevention refers to sensitivity to the possibility of negative outcomes, orients the individual to avoiding these consequences, and is concerned with security and safety. Promotion and prevention are associated with distinctive feelings, perceptual sensitivities to positive and negative cues in the environment, adoption of behavioral strategies, decision-making processes, and task performance.

Social Judgment

The positive and negative attributes of an object are judged through different evaluative systems (Cacioppo, Gardner, & Bernston, 1997). These systems, both of which contribute to attitude formation, operate independently (although under some circumstances may influence each other).

Personality

The popular, extensively validated Big 5 model of personality identifies extraversion and neuroticism as distinct components (McCrae & Costa, 1987, 1997). Eysenck's proposal (e.g., Eysenck, 1981) that extraversion represents the person's relative sensitivity to reward cues (i.e., an appetition system) whereas neuroticism represents the person's relative sensitivity to punishment cues (i.e., an aversion system) has been supported in subsequent research (e.g., Lucas, Diener, Grob, Suh, & Shao, 2000; Watson & Clark, 1984).

Gable, Reis, and Elliot (2001) reasoned that these various examples may represent domain-specific manifestations of two general functional systems, one encompassing appetitive processes and the other encompassing aversive processes. They conducted a series of confirmatory factor analyses, each of which included variables from several of the domains listed previously. Their studies included self-reports and semiprojective measures, varied content and time frames, and different samples. In each analysis, regardless of which specific variables were included, the best-fitting model identified two latent variables, one composed of appetitive variables, the other composed of aversive variables. These results suggest that appetite and aversion may represent a fundamental distinction underlying various specific behavioral manifestations.

Considering the appetitive and aversive systems as independent suggests two basic conclusions. First, even if the same amount of negative stimulus produces larger changes than the same amount of positive stimulus, the operation of either system is generally uninformative about the other. Instead, these processes must be disentangled to be understood, both in terms of their distinct influences on social behavior and in terms of their interplay. As discussed later, in the area of relationships, current methods have not always allowed such fine-grained analysis. Second, the locus of action instigation may differ in an important way, as shown by Gable, Reis, and Elliot (2000). Rarely do people seek out negative events, but because they occur more or less inevitably, the aversive system regulates differential responses to what the environment offers. Positive events, on the other hand, often must be sought out, mandating that initiation plays a significant role in determining when opportunities are perceived, pursued, and capitalized on. The appetitive system, in other words, regulates differential exposure to positive events.

What does this model imply for the primary topic of this chapter, relationships? That the processes involved in obtaining desired positive, relationship outcomes may be distinct from those involved in avoiding negative, distressing outcomes. In practical terms, the absence of conflict and criticism in a relationship need not imply the presence of joy and fulfillment, just as the presence of joy and fulfillment need not denote the absence of conflict and criticism. We note that this is not a linguistic subtlety or theoretical hair-splitting. Our perspective suggests that the causes, operation, and consequences of negative processes in relationships should be considered separate and distinct from the causes, operation, and consequences of positive processes in relationships. As we argue later, the processes involved in relating well are not the same as those involved in not relating badly.

METHODOLOGICAL CONSIDERATIONS

In this light, how might one make sense of the consistent evidence favoring the greater impact of negativity? We suggest that several methodological issues may have inadvertently contributed to the primacy of negatives in the existing literature. In the section that follows, we briefly review a few of these issues, with particular attention to their implications for research on positivity in relationships. Rook (1998) provides a more extensive review of several of these factors.

What Is Investigated

Findings, of course, depend on where researchers choose to look, and today, researchers are more likely than not to investigate causal antecedents and consequences of negative processes in relationships, such as conflict, criticism, betrayal, stressful events, divorce, bereavement, rejection, social isolation, jealousy, violence, loneliness, and intrusiveness.[3] For example, the overwhelming majority of observational studies of marital interaction, considered by many researchers to be the methodological "gold standard," involve discussion of a significant conflict area. Protocols for observation and evaluation of affectionate behavior have yet to be developed (although see Roberts & Linney, 1999, for a promising development). Perhaps this focus reflects the clinical roots of relationship research (not to mention the impact of mental health funding): Many popular paradigms were designed to provide a scientific foundation for intervening with distressed couples and families. Nonetheless, if positive and negative processes are functionally independent, the failure to examine positive processes makes it unlikely that evidence for their impact will be found.

Several studies have sought to compare the relative impact of negative and positive interactions by including one examplar of each in the same study—typically conflict and social support, a well-established benefit of close relationships. But consider this ambiguity: Measures of enacted support assess the degree to which one partner effectively helps the other cope with an existing problem (from outside the relationship), which requires that both partners attend closely to and converse about distressing circumstances—an interaction likely to engender negative affect as well as the possibility of positive affect. Moreover, even if the supportive interaction succeeds, the germane affect is more likely to be relief (i.e., resolving a negative situation) than joy (i.e., experiencing a positive situation). Thus, social support may not be prototypical of the appetitive system in close relationships. Rook (1998) drew a related conclusion: The types of negative interaction typically studied tend to be broader than the types of positive interaction (which, more often than not, feature support given under distress). Rare are studies of interactions focused on purely positive interchange—affection, companionship, shared activity, and just plain fun.

---

[3] Such is the negativity bias in social science research that in a large and otherwise exemplary survey of mental health in America, Veroff, Douvan, and Kulka (1976) asked 2,267 respondents to describe "the last time something really bad happened to you." They did not ask respondents to describe the last time something really good had happened.

Extremity and Accumulation Biases

Establishing that negativity effects are stronger than positivity effects requires that the specific instances be equally extreme. Unfortunately, outside of true experiments, this is seldom the case. The negative events and interactions studied in relationship research tend to be more extreme than the positive events, and hence their greater potency may be unremarkable (Rook, 1998). Few positive events are equivalent in evaluative extremity to bereavement, spousal violence, sexual or emotional betrayal, or rejection by an admired other.[4] Thus, the predominant conclusion from existing work might be rephrased as "strong negatives are more potent than mild positives." Although this criticism may be less germane to experimental studies that use artificially constructed stimuli, even then, as Skowronski and Carlston (1989) noted, it is difficult to equate stimuli for their degree of positivity and negativity inasmuch as judges possess the same normative and extremity biases that research participants do.

Another issue concerns accumulation bias. Because positive interactions are more common in everyday life than negative interactions, examining the impact of events one at a time may understate the overall importance of positive events, given that the accumulation of more but weaker positive events may sum to a greater total effect than fewer but stronger negative events. Perhaps a year's worth of pleasantly affectionate conversation at the end of each day is more important than two major blow-outs simply because the former conversations occur more often. Laboratory observations typically overlook this issue of accumulation because of time constraints. Nonlaboratory methods are better suited to identifying strong, salient, and discrete events than to the accumulation of milder, less striking events—for example, studies that ask participants to recall events that took place in the past few weeks or months.

In contrast, researchers sometimes aggregate multiple events over short periods of time, such as a day or week. Little is known about how experience accumulates over time and situations into meaningful units, but one thing is clear: Simple averages and frequency counts, the predominant indexes in contemporary research, may be misleading. For example, two negative events of valence 1 and 5 have the same average impact rating of 3 as five positive events each rated as 3. Yet the former "5" is likely to be experienced as more influential than the latter "3s," as suggested by the "peak-end" rule (Feldman Barrett, 1997; Kahneman, Fredrickson, Schreiber, & Redelmeier, 1993).[5]

---

[4] Falling in love, discussed later, is one.

[5] That is, recollected general levels of affect tend to overemphasize moments of peak intensity as well as affect experienced at the end of a given episode or event.

Time Course of Impact

The predominance of cross-sectional research over longitudinal studies may have emphasized the impact of negative events. Generalizing from cross-sectional work requires assuming similarity in the time course of adaptation to positive and negative events. However, there is good reason to doubt this assumption. Although negative events may mobilize resources to a greater extent in the short run, subsequent minimizing processes may dampen their impact in the long run, presumably because effective everyday functioning is facilitated by an optimistic orientation (Taylor, 1991). Positive events require no mental dampening; in fact it may be adaptive to embellish them.

Two research programs document this asymmetry. First, in contrast to the ubiquitous information-processing advantage that negative stimuli possess in nearly all other aspects of social cognition, positive events tend to be remembered better than negative events (Matlin & Stang, 1978; Skowronski, Betz, Thompson, & Shannon, 1991). As noted earlier, it may be adaptive to attend to negative events when they occur but to dismiss them in the long run. Second, whereas short-term regrets tend to focus on acts of commission—something one did and wishes one had not done—long-term regrets tend to concern acts of omission—something one wishes one had done (Gilovich & Medvec, 1995). The former usually involve behaviors that have had negative consequences, whereas the latter typically refer to bypassed opportunities for desirable outcomes. Hence over time the emphasis of regrets shift from enacted negatives to foregone positives. This asymmetry may create negativity bias in surveys and interviews that ask participants to describe recent life events—that is, it may "accentuate the negative while eliminating the positive."

TOWARD A POSITIVE PSYCHOLOGY OF RELATIONSHIPS

We have suggested that positive, appetitive processes in social interaction and close relationships may be conceptually underappreciated and empirically underinvestigated. This assertion may seem odd to some readers, in view of recent critiques that attribute an unquestioning "relationships are intrinsically positive" attitude to the literature (e.g., Hoobler & Spitzberg, 1999). We find this critique somewhat ironic but not contradictory with our observations. Perhaps some researchers have seen less reason to investigate appetitive processes in relationships because they believe positivity is the norm, and deviations from the norm will engender more compelling research than the norm itself. In other words, the assumption of intrinsic positivity may have led some researchers to seek to understand the causes and consequences of destructive forces in relationships, treating positivity as a baseline or default condition not warranting investigation in its own right. We see little reason to concur with this assumption; most researchers readily acknowledge that relationships are often toxic and destructive (see Berscheid & Reis, 1998, for a review). Nonetheless, if positivity has been overlooked by relationship scientists because it is assumed, the need to attend more closely to these processes would be underscored. Of course, our contention that positive interpersonal processes and phenomena may be functionally independent from negative processes and phenomena suggests one possibility for rectifying the existing imbalance.

In the remainder of this chapter, we briefly discuss several directions that studies of the appetitive dimension in close relationships might take. As noted earlier, researchers interested in the positive side of close relationships have not always known where to look. The model of independent appetitive and aversive processes introduced earlier offers several suggestions. In interpersonal terms, these dimensions correspond to the pursuit of safety versus enrichment, respectively (Gable & Reis, 2001). The aversive dimension encompasses the desire to avoid danger and to feel safe and secure in relationships, implying a desire to avoid destructive interactions such as conflict and the possibility of rejection. On the other hand, the appetitive dimension involves the pursuit of growth, fulfillment, and pleasure in relationships. It is this latter dimension that is typically most salient when people initiate close relationships; few seek out others with the goal of avoiding negative outcomes.

Intimacy

Theories of human motivation and development typically posit some sort of innate process by which people seek to establish and maintain satisfying connections with others. For example, Baumeister and Leary (1995) described the "need to belong" and Deci and Ryan (1991) proposed a need for relatedness. That such needs may be more closely aligned with appetitive functions than with aversive functions is suggested by their stronger correlations with positive affect than with negative affect (Watson and Clark, 1984). Reis, Sheldon, Gable, Roscoe, and Ryan (2000) examined the degree to which satisfaction of three intrinsic needs—autonomy, competence, and relatedness—predicted daily fluctuations in affective well-being. Although satisfaction of all three needs predicted daily affect, relatedness was significantly associated only with positive affect, not with negative affect.[6] This asymmetry has been noted by others; as Watson concluded,

---

[6]This analysis was conducted within-persons—that is, it examined the daily ups and downs around each individual's baseline. Thus dispositional tendencies toward positive and negative affect are largely irrelevant to these findings.

"Positive affect—but not negative affect—is related to various indexes of social engagement and satisfaction" (1988, p. 129).

What sorts of interactions produce feelings of relatedness? Reis et al. (2000) also asked participants to describe the extent to which their three longest interactions of each day involved seven different types of social activity. Feeling understood and appreciated by partners was by far the strongest predictor of relatedness. Other activities also mattered (e.g., talking about something meaningful; sharing pleasant or fun activities), although conflict was uncorrelated with relatedness. This result follows directly from intimacy theory (Reis & Patrick, 1996; Reis & Shaver, 1988). Intimacy theory identifies several qualities that are central to feeling close and connected to others: revealing central aspects of the self (especially emotions) to partners through words, deeds, and nonverbal behavior; perceiving that partners are responsive to the self and the self's needs; and feeling understood, validated, and cared for. The theory includes both affective and cognitive components; thus believing that a partner understands the self is necessary because without it, a partner's response, no matter how positive, would not be experienced as relevant to the true self. Thus in practice intimacy is most likely to be experienced and reciprocated in long-term relationships, although the interaction process described by the theory may occur with any partner (i.e., with friends, acquaintances, romantic partners, coworkers, or therapists).

Among people's diverse social goals, intimacy tends to have high priority across the lifespan (although it assumes special importance in late-life; Carstensen, Isaacowitz, & Charles, 1999). From early adolescence on, when people discuss the kinds of relationships they want, intimacy is usually at or near the top of the list (e.g., "having a few special friends who care about you"), which helps explain why a large portion of goal-directed social activity is aimed at obtaining or enhancing intimacy (Reis, 1990). Describing intimacy as an actively sought social goal highlights its relevance to the appetitive dimension and suggests one way of characterizing this dimension—namely, in terms of qualities that promote growth, flourishing, positive affect, and movement toward personal ideals and goals in the context of an ongoing connection with others.

Other research conducted in our lab also illustrates the role of intimacy as an appetitive contribution to close relationships. In one study (Gable, 2000), married couples kept daily diaries reporting positive and negative behaviors they had enacted toward their partner, as well as whether their partner had enacted the same behaviors toward them (e.g., expressing affection or criticism). Participants also described their feelings about the relationship on that day. This research examined a wider range of positive and negative behaviors than earlier research has, to rectify the methodological biases discussed previously. The results revealed that positive and negative interactions made independent contributions roughly equivalent in magnitude to marital well-being. Furthermore, the positive behaviors that were most influential were those that contributed to a sense of intimacy—understanding, validation, and caring.

Another study directly compared the relative contribution of appetitive and aversive processes in a sample of dating couples (Gable, Asher, & Reis, 2000). Earlier research by Rusbult and her colleagues has shown that accommodation—the tendency to respond constructively to a partner's bad behavior—is related to important relationship outcomes (Rusbult et al., 1991). We reasoned that a parallel process pertaining to positive events may also be beneficial, which we call capitalization, or the experience of sharing personal positive experiences with partners (Langston, 1994). Perceiving a partner's genuine pleasure for one's personal good fortune connotes anticipated responsiveness and support for the self; in contrast, a partner's disinterested or jealous response, beyond dampening the experience itself, may signal distance and a lack of relatedness. Consistent with this reasoning, we found that capitalization was associated with positive relationship outcomes (i.e., satisfaction, intimacy, trust, and commitment) even when the degree of accommodation (which made significant contributions of its own) was controlled. In other words, reactions to both positive and negative events are relevant to relationship well-being.

Affection

Whereas the benefits of intimacy and relatedness may be available in various types of interaction and relationship, affection tends to occur primarily in close relationships, particularly romantic relationships. Affection has been studied in two ways—as an affect, usually called love, and in behavioral displays, typically assessed in reports of affectional acts. A sizable literature associates both forms pervasively and robustly with favorable relationship outcomes (see Berscheid & Reis, 1998, for a review), although the underlying causal processes are not well-understood. Perhaps as a result, when the relative contributions of affection and negativity are compared, affection usually fares poorly, typically accounting for relatively little variance over and above the effects of negativity. A common explanation involves inhibitory mechanisms—that conflict and criticism interfere with spouses' willingness to behave affectionately. Furthermore, an important component of affection—passion—tends to decrease in the early years of marriage, leading several theorists to suggest that the importance of passion is largely limited to initial attraction and relationship formation. Nonetheless, affection seems likely to play an important role in successful ongoing relationships. For example, in their longitudinal study of rural Pennsylvania newlyweds, Huston and Vangelisti (1991) showed that expressions of affection, especially by husbands, accounted for significant variance in marital satisfaction assessed two years later. Similarly, overt affection and expressions of love in the first two years of marriage predicted lower rates of divorce 13 years later (Huston, Caughlin, Houts, Smith, & George, 2001). Other investigators have reported similar findings.

Recent interest among neuroscientists in identifying causal pathways relevant to love and affiliation seem particularly promising. Heretofore, biologically oriented studies of dyadic interaction have emphasized conflict and social isolation, whose well-documented deleterious physiological effects include diminished immunological competence, heightened sympathetic activation, and increased neuroendocrine reactivity (see Kiecolt-Glaser, 1999, for a review). Recent—and still somewhat speculative—evidence suggests a comparable biological mechanism for more appetitive forms of interaction, involving the hypothalamic–pituitary–adrenal axis and particularly the neuropeptide oxytocin. Positive social interactions, notably those entailing affectionate contact, are associated with increases in oxytocin level (Carter, 1998), and in turn, oxytocin appears to stimulate affectionate contact as well as affiliation (Insel & Winslow, 1998) and nurturance (Taylor et al., 2000) in both humans and animals. Physical contact in the specific forms of touching, hugging, cuddling, breast-feeding, and sexual intercourse, as well as eye contact in an affectionate context, also tend to increase oxytocin levels in humans.

Oxytocin may be beneficial for several reasons: (a) By reducing stress responses in several bodily systems, oxytocin may confer substantial health benefits (and thereby may account for some of the health benefits of close relationships noted earlier; Seeman & McEwen, 1996); (b) release of oxytocin can be conditioned to psychological states or to imagery, thereby enhancing its effect in long-term relationships (Uvaes-Moberg, 1998); and (c) oxytocin may moderate the impact of endogenous opioids in the brain (Carter, 1998). For the purposes of this chapter, the major point is that oxytocin production appears to be stimulated by intense positive social interactions and not by the absence of negative interaction. If corroborated by additional research, these effects testify to the fundamental importance of positive interactions and relationships to human well-being.

Shared Fun

Evidence about the effects of shared marital recreation is inconsistent. Some studies report a positive correlation but others do not. Closer consideration of the kind of positive affects that are central to appetitive processes in social relations may help account for this discrepancy. The best evidence for the independence of positive and negative affect refers not to pleasant feelings but rather to activated positive affects, such as excitement, enthusiasm, and inspiration (e.g., Watson, Clark, & Tellegen, 1988). If so, shared recreation may benefit couple well-being only when activated positive affect is involved. Recent studies by Aron, Norman, Aron, McKenna, and Heyman (2000) showed that relationship quality (global ratings of satisfaction and passionate love) was improved by joint participation in a novel, arousing activity. In a series of experiments, spouses were asked to traverse an obstacle course as fast as possible while holding a cylindrical pillow between them without using their hands, arms, or teeth. When enacted separately, the same activities were not beneficial, nor were pleasant but not arousing shared activities (Aron, 2000). Presumably, activated positive affects are inherently reinforcing; sharing them with a partner ought to generalize, thereby bolstering and perhaps even augmenting a relationship.

Activated positive affect is also engendered by intrinsically motivated activities—pursuits enacted for the sheer pleasure of the activity itself (Deci & Ryan, 1985). Intrinsically motivated behavior is experienced as fun; it generates vitality, enthusiasm, and well-being, as well as the enjoyable sensation of "flow" (a state of absorption in an activity produced by an optimal balance of challenge and perceived personal efficacy; Csikszentmihalyi, 1990). The impact of shared intrinsically motivated activity on relationships, a topic well-suited to a positive psychology of relationships, has not been investigated. We speculate that such activity may be particularly relevant to appetitive processes in relationships for several reasons. First, intrinsically motivated activity involves central, self-determined goals, the sharing of which ought to enhance the perception of shared selves and responsiveness critical to intimacy. Also, because intrinsically motivated activity generates positive affect, partners may come to associate the relationship with the intrinsic enjoyment of the activity itself. This principle may be especially important when circumstances constrain opportunities—for example, during early parenthood or when economic resources are limited. New relationships deepen in part because of the excitement and personal fulfillment that derives from meshing one's life with that of another person; maintaining those gratifications once a relationship has become routine presents a key appetitive challenge to all close relationships.

CONCLUSION

It seems natural to attend to the many ways in which relationships can, and often do, go wrong. Representatives of popular media often remind us that bad news sells better than good news. There is certainly good reason to examine negativity effects in close relationships. Slightly more than half of this year's marriages are likely to end in divorce, and many more are likely to experience a substantial decline in satisfaction within the first few years. Isolation and alienation appear to be on the upswing among adolescents and the elderly. Americans' diminished sense of community is commonly cited to explain the myriad problems facing families, cities, neighborhoods, and government. Match-making is a growth industry in this era of suspicion and high-risk sexuality, and the toxic effects of relationship violence and abuse on children and adults are evident. In short, the profound distress that problematic relationships can cause is incontrovertible.

Yet to dwell on these and other negatives is at odds with several simple notions: that most interactions are at least mildly enjoyable and pleasant; that most people are fairly well-satisfied with their friendships, marriages, and family life; that when people reflect on the factors that make life meaningful and enjoyable, they emphasize friends and family; and that successful relationships are central to rewarding experiences at work, in school, in community life, and in recreation. The impact of aversive relating notwithstanding, there is much that is positive that we theoreticians and researchers need to investigate and understand. Such knowledge is critical not only for its own sake but for a critical social purpose as well: To help individuals, families, organizations, and society devise methods for facilitating the kind of positive relationships that can counter the destructive trends noted in the previous paragraph.

Tolstoy began *Anna Karenina* (1877/2000) by observing that, "Happy families are all alike, every unhappy family is unhappy in its own way" (p. 3). Ironically, bad news may be newsworthy because it is unusual, distinctive, unexpected, and attention-grabbing—precisely because, in other words, most of the time our interpersonal circumstances tend to be good. The downward comparison engendered by a focus on unhappy relationships may be tacitly reassuring, but it distracts us from better understanding of the normative case. As argued throughout this chapter, both sets of processes are fundamental to understanding relationships, and both need to be investigated vigorously.

Earlier we reviewed extensive evidence that negative interpersonal processes and events appear to be stronger than positive interpersonal processes and events. There is little reason to expect that this conclusion will be refuted; in the rush to explore positive processes, researchers should not lose sight of this canon. Nevertheless, the paucity of research into positive processes, especially, but not limited to, relationships, has not only forged an imbalanced literature, it has created conceptual lacunae that restrict the usefulness of existing research for describing the breadth and richness of human activity. The positive side of social life has much to tell us about human psychology, which becomes apparent when aversive and appetitive systems are considered as functionally independent systems. Even if bad is stronger than good, the importance of learning more about the factors that attract people to relationships and the processes that make interaction within those relationships fulfilling, enjoyable, and growth-producing is clear. Relating well is not the same as not relating badly.

REFERENCES

Argyle, M. (1987). *The psychology of happiness*. London: Methuen.

Aron, A. (2000, Oct.). *Self-expansion in relationships*. Paper presented at the Society for experimental social psychology meeting, St. Louis, MO.

Aron, A., Norman, C. C., Aron, E. N., McKenna, C., & Heyman, R. E. (2000). Couples' shared participation in novel and arousing activities and experienced relationship quality. *Journal of Personality and Social Psychology, 78, 273–284.*

Baumeister, R. F., Bratslavsky, E., Finkenauer, C., & Vohs, K. D. (2001). Bad is stronger than good. *Review of General Psychology, 5, 323–370.*

Baumeister, R., & Leary, M. R. (1995). The need to belong: Desire for interpersonal attachments as a fundamental human motivation. *Psychological Bulletin, 117, 497–529.*

Belsky, J., Hsieh, K. H., & Crnic, K. (1995). Infant positive and negative emotionality: One dimension or two? *Developmental Psychology, 32, 289–298.*

Berscheid, E. (1999). The greening of relationship science. *American Psychologist, 54, 260–266.*

Berscheid, E., & Reis, H. T. (1998). Attraction and close relationships. In D. T. Gilbert, S. T. Fiske, & G. Lindzey (Eds.), *The handbook of social psychology* (4th ed., Vol. 2, pp. 193–281). New York: McGraw-Hill.

Boyatzis, R. E. (1973). Affiliation motivation. In D. C. McClelland & R. S. Steele (Eds.), *Human motivation: A book of readings* (pp. 252–276). Morristown, NJ: General Learning Press.

Bradbury, T. N., & Fincham, F. D. (1990). Attributions in marriage: Review and critique. *Psychological Bulletin, 107, 3–33.*

Bugental, D. B. (2000). Acquisition of the algorithms of social life: A domain-based approach. *Psychological Bulletin, 126, 187–219.*

Buss, D. M., & Kenrick, D. T. (1998). Evolutionary social psychology. In D. T. Gilbert, S. T. Fiske, & G. Lindzey (Eds.), *The handbook of social psychology* (4th ed., pp. 982–1026). New York: McGraw-Hill.

Cacioppo, J. T., & Gardner, W. L. (1999). Emotion. *Annual Review of Psychology, 50, 191–214.*

Cacioppo, J. T., Gardner, W. L., & Berntson, G. G. (1997). Beyond bipolar conceptualizations and measures: The case of attitudes and evaluative space. *Personality and Social Psychology Review, 1, 3–25.*

Campbell, A., Converse, P. E., & Rodgers, W. L. (1976). *The quality of American life*. New York: Sage.

Carstensen, L. L., Isaacowitz, D. M., & Charles, S. T. (1999). Taking time seriously: A theory of socioemotional selectivity. *American Psychologist, 54,* 165–181.

Carter, C. S. (1998). Neuroendocrine perspectives on social attachment and love. *Psychoneuroendocrinology, 23,* 779–818.

Carver, C. S. (1996). Emergent integration in contemporary personality psychology. *Journal of Research in Personality, 30,* 319–334.

Christensen, A., & Heavey, C. L. (1999). Interventions for couples. *Annual Review of Psychology, 50,* 165–190.

Christensen, A., & Walczynski, P. T. (1997). Conflict and satisfaction in couples. In R. J. Sternberg & M. Hojjat (Eds.), *Satisfaction in close relationships* (pp. 249–274). New York: Guilford Press.

Cohen, S., & Herbert, T. B. (1996). Health psychology: Psychological factors and physical disease from the perspective of human psychoneuroimmunology. *Annual Review of Psychology, 47,* 113–142.

Cosmides, L., & Tooby, J. (1992). Cognitive adaptations for social exchange. In J. H. Barkow, L. Cosmides, & J. Tooby (Eds.), *The adapted mind: Evolutionary psychology and the generation of culture* (pp. 163–228). New York: Oxford University Press.

Csikszentmihalyi, M. (1990). *Flow.* New York: Harper.

Davidson, R. J. (1992). Emotion and affective style: Hemispheric substrates. *Psychological Science, 3,* 39–43.

Deci, E. L., & Ryan, R. M. (1985). *Intrinsic motivation and self-determination in human behavior.* New York: Plenum Press.

Deci, E. L., & Ryan, R. M. (1991). A motivational approach to self: Integration in personality. In R. Dienstbier (Ed.), *Nebraska symposium on motivation: Vol. 38. Perspectives on motivation* (pp. 237–288). Lincoln: University of Nebraska Press.

Diener, E. (2001, Feb.). *Subjective well-being.* Address presented at the annual meeting of the Society for Personality and Social Psychology, San Antonio, TX.

Diener, E., & Diener, C. (1996). Most people are happy. *Psychological Science, 7,* 181–185.

Diener, E., Suh, E. M., Lucas, R. E., & Smith, H. L. (1999). Subjective well-being: Three decades of progress. *Psychological Bulletin, 125,* 276–302.

Elliot, A. J. (1997). Integrating the classic and contemporary approaches to achievement motivation: A hierarchical model of approach and avoidance achievement motivation. In M. Maehr & P. Pintrich (Eds.), *Advances in motivation and achievement* (Vol. 10, pp. 143–179). Greenwich, CT: JAI Press.

Elliot, A. J., Church, M. A. (1997). A hierarchical model of approach and avoidance achievement motivation. *Journal of Personality and Social Psychology, 72,* 218–232.

Emmons, R. A. (1999). *The psychology of ultimate concerns: Motivation and spirituality in personality.* New York: Guilford Press.

Eysenck, H. J. (1981). *A model for personality*. Berlin: Springer-Verlag.

Feldman Barrett, L. F. (1997). The relationships among momentary emotion experiences, personality descriptions, and retrospective ratings of emotions. *Personality and Social Psychology Bulletin, 23,* 1100–1110.

Fincham, F. D., & Linfield, K. J. (1997). A new look at marital quality: Can spouses feel positive and negative about their marriage? *Journal of Family Psychology, 4,* 489–502.

Fiske, S. T., & Taylor, S. E. (1991). *Social cognition*. New York: McGraw-Hill.

Fowles, D. C. (1994). A motivational theory of psychopathology. In W. D. Spaulding (Ed.), *Nebraska Symposium on Motivation, Vol. 41: Integrative views of motivation, cognition, and emotion* (pp. 181–238). Lincoln: University of Nebraska Press.

Gable, S. L. (2000). *Appetitive and aversive social motivation*. Unpublished doctoral dissertation, University of Rochester.

Gable, S. L., Asher, E., & Reis, H. T. (2000). *Capitalization in romantic relationships*. Unpublished manuscript, University of Rochester.

Gable, S. L., & Reis, H. T. (2001). Appetitive and aversive social interaction. In J. H. Harvey & A. E. Wenzel (Eds.), *Close romantic relationship maintenance and enhancement* (pp. 169–194). Mahwah, NJ: Erlbaum.

Gable, S., Reis, H. T., & Elliot, A. (2000). Behavioral activation and inhibition in everyday life. *Journal of Personality and Social Psychology, 63,* 221–233.

Gable, S., Reis, H. T., & Elliot, A. (2001). *Evidence for bivariate systems: An empirical test of appetite and aversion across domains*. Unpublished manuscript, University of California, Los Angeles.

Gilovich, T., & Medvec, V. H. (1995). The experience of regret: What, when, and why. *Psychological Review, 102,* 379–395.

Gottman, J. M. (1993). The roles of conflict engagement, escalation, and avoidance in marital interaction: A longitudinal view of five types of couples. *Journal of Consulting and Clinical Psychology, 61,* 6–15.

Gottman, J. M. (1994). *What predicts divorce? The relationship between marital processes and marital outcomes*. Hillsdale, NJ: Erlbaum.

Gottman, J. M. (1998). Psychology and the study of marital processes. *Annual Review of Psychology, 49,* 169–197.

Gottman, J. M., & Krokoff, L. J. (1989). Marital interaction and satisfaction: A longitudinal view. *Journal of Consulting and Clinical Psychology, 57,* 47–52.

Gottman, J. M., & Levenson, R. W. (1992). Marital processes predictive of later dissolution: Behavior, physiology, and health. *Journal of Personality and Social Psychology, 78,* 1135–1149.

Gray, J. A. (1987). *The psychology of fear and stress* (2nd ed.). Cambridge: Cambridge University Press.

Gray, J. A. (1994). Three fundamental emotion systems. In P. Ekman & R. J. Davidson (Eds.), *The nature of emotion: Fundamental questions* (pp. 243–247). New York: Oxford University Press.

Gross, J. J., & John, O. P. (1997). Revealing feelings: Facets of emotional expressivity in self-reports, peer ratings, and behavior. *Journal of Personality and Social Psychology, 72,* 435–448.

Hartup, W. W., & Stevens, N. (1997). Friendships and adaptation in the life course. *Psychological Bulletin, 121,* 355–370.

Helson, H. (1964). *Adaptation-level theory.* New York: Harper & Row.

Higgins, E. T. (1998). Promotion and prevention: Regulatory focus as a motivational principle. In M. Zanna (Ed.), *Advances in experimental social psychology* (Vol. 30, pp. 1–46). San Diego, CA: Academic Press.

Holmes, T. H., & Rahe, R. H. (1967). The social readjustment rating scale. *Journal of Psychosomatic Research, 11,* 213–218.

Hoobler, G. D., & Spitzberg, B. H. (1999, June). *Communication and personal relationships research: Is the twilight settling or the dawn rising on a new millennium?* Paper presented at the International Network on Personal Relationship conference, Louisville, KY.

House, J. S., Landis, K. R., & Umberson, D. (1988). Social relationships and health. *Science, 241,* 540–545.

Huston, T. L., Caughlin, J. P., Houts, R. M., Smith, S. E., & George, L. E. (2001). The connubial crucible: Newlywed years as a predictor of marital delight, distress, and divorce. *Journal of Personality and Social Psychology, 80,* 237–252.

Huston, T. L., & Vangelisti, A. L. (1991). Socioemotional behavior and satisfaction in marital relationships. *Journal of Personality and Social Psychology, 61,* 721–733.

Insel, T. R., & Winslow, J. T. (1998). Serotonin and neuropeptides in affiliative behaviors. *Biological Psychiatry, 44,* 207–219.

Ito, T. A., Larsen, J. T., Smith, N. K., & Cacioppo, J. T. (1998). Negative information weighs more heavily on the brain: The negativity bias in evaluative categorizations. *Journal of Personality and Social Psychology, 75,* 887–900.

Jacobson, N. S., & Margolin, G. (1979). *Marital therapy: Strategies based on social learning and behavior exchange principles.* New York: Brunner/Mazel.

Kahneman, D., Fredrickson, B. L., Schreiber, C. A., & Redelmeier, D. A. (1993). When more pain is preferred to less: Adding a better end. *Psychological Science, 4,* 401–405.

Karney, B. R., & Bradbury, T. N. (1995). The longitudinal course of marital quality and stability: A review of theory, method, and research. *Psychological Bulletin, 118,* 3–34.

Karney, B. R., & Bradbury, T. N. (1997). Neuroticism, marital interaction, and the trajectory of marital satisfaction. *Journal of Personality and Social Psychology, 72,* 1075–1092.

Kasser, T., & Ryan, R. M. (1996). Further examining the American dream: Differential correlates of intrinsic and extrinsic goals. *Personality and Social Psychology Bulletin 22,* 80–87.

Keyes, C. L. M. (1998). Social well-being. *Social Psychology Quarterly, 61,* 121–140.

Kiecolt-Glaser, J. K. (1999). Stress, personal relationships, and immune function: Health implications. *Brain, Behavior, and Immunity, 12,* 61–72.

Klingler, E. (1977). *Meaning and void: Inner experience and the incentives in people's lives.* Minneapolis: University of Minnesota Press.

Langston, C. A. (1994). Capitalizing on and coping with daily-life events: Expressive responses to positive events. *Journal of Personality and Social Psychology, 67,* 1112–1125.

Lazarus, R. (1994). Appraisal: The long and the short of it. In P. Ekman & R. J. Davidson (Eds.), *The nature of emotion: Fundamental questions* (pp. 208–215). New York: Oxford University Press.

Lepore, S. J. (1992). Social conflict, social support, and psychological distress: Evidence of cross-domain buffering effects. *Journal of Personality and Social Psychology, 63,* 857–867.

Levenson, R. W., Ekman, P., Heider, K., & Friesen, W. V. (1992) Emotion and autonomic nervous system activity in the Minangkabau of West Sumatra. *Journal of Personality and Social Psychology, 62,* 972–988.

Little, B. R. (1989). Personal projects analysis: Trivial pursuits, magnificent obsessions and the search for coherence. In D. M. Buss & N. Cantor (Eds.), *Personality psychology: Recent trends and emerging directions* (pp. 15–31). New York: Springer-Verlag.

Lucas, R. E., Diener, E., Grob, A., Suh, E. M., & Shao, L. (2000). Cross-cultural evidence for the fundamental features of extraversion. *Journal of Personality and Social Psychology, 79,* 452–468.

Manusov, V., Floyd, K., & Kerssen-Griep, J. (1997). Yours, mine, and ours: Mutual attributions for nonverbal behaviors in couples' interactions. *Communication Research, 24,* 234–260.

Matlin, M. W., & Stang, D. J. (1978). *The Pollyanna principle: Selectivity in language, memory, and thought.* Cambridge, MA: Schenkman.

Matthews, L. S., Conger, R. D., & Wickrama, K. A. S. (1999). *Marital stability and marital interaction: Trajectories of growth and decline.* Unpublished manuscript, Iowa State University, Ames.

McCrae, R. R., & Costa, P. T. (1987). Validation of the five-factor model of personality across instruments and observers. *Journal of Personality and Social Psychology, 52,* 81–90.

McCrae, R. R., & Costa, P. T., Jr. (1997). Personality trait structure as a human universal. *American Psychologist, 52,* 509–516.

Myers, D. G. (1992). *The pursuit of happiness: Who is happy—and why.* New York: William Morrow.

Notarius, C., & Markman, H. (1993). *We can work it out: Making sense of marital conflict.* New York: G. P. Putnam's Sons.

Olson, J. M., Roese, N. J., & Zanna, M. P. (1996). Expectancies. In E. T. Higgins & A. W. Kruglanski (Eds.), *Social psychology: Handbook of basic principles* (pp. 211–238). New York: Guilford Press.

Peeters, G., & Czapinski, J. (1990). Positive-negative asymmetry in evaluations: The distinction between affective and informational negativity effects. *European Review of Social Psychology, 1*, 33–60.

Pinsker, H., Nepps, P., Redfield, J., & Winston, A. (1985). Applicants for short-term dynamic psychotherapy. In A. Winston (Ed.), *Clinical and research issues in short-term dynamic psychotherapy* (pp. 104–116). Washington, DC: American Psychiatric Association.

Pratto, F., & John, O. P. (1991). Automatic vigilance: The attention-grabbing power of negative social information. *Journal of Personality and Social Psychology, 61*, 380–391.

Putnam, R. D. (2000). *Bowling alone: The collapse and revival of American community.* New York: Simon & Schuster.

Reis, H. T. (1990). The role of intimacy in interpersonal relations. *Journal of Social and Clinical Psychology, 9*, 15–30.

Reis, H. T., Collins, W. A., & Berscheid, E. (2000). The relationship context of human behavior and development. *Psychological Bulletin, 126*, 844–872.

Reis, H. T., & Patrick, B. C. (1996). Attachment and intimacy: Component processes. In A. Kruglanski & E. T. Higgins (Eds.), *Social psychology: Handbook of basic principles* (pp. 523–563). New York: Guilford Press.

Reis, H. T., & Shaver, P. (1988). Intimacy as an interpersonal process. In S. Duck (Ed.), *Handbook of personal relationships* (pp. 367–389). Chichester, UK: John Wiley and Sons.

Reis, H. T., Sheldon, K. M., Gable, S. L., Roscoe, J., & Ryan, R. M. (2000). Daily well-being: The role of autonomy, competence, and relatedness. *Personality and Social Psychology Bulletin, 26*, 419–435.

Roberts, L. J., & Linney, K. D. (1999). *Development of a coding system for observing intimacy in the lab.* Unpublished manuscript, University of Wisconsin, Madison.

Rook, K. S. (1984). The negative side of social interaction: Impact on psychological well-being. *Journal of Personality and Social Psychology, 46*, 1097–1108

Rook, K. S. (1998). Investigating the positive and negative sides of personal relationships: Through a lens darkly? In B. H. Spitzberg & W. R. Cupach (Eds.), *The dark side of close relationships* (pp. 369–393). Mahwah, NJ: Erlbaum.

Rusbult, C. E., Verette, J., Whitney, G. A., Slovik, L. F., & Lipkus, I. (1991). Accommodation processes in close relationships: Theory and preliminary empirical evidence. *Journal of Personality and Social Psychology, 60*, 53–78.

Ryff, C. D. (1995). Psychological well-being in adult life. *Current Directions in Psychological Science, 4*, 99–103.

Schmalt, H. D. (1999). Assessing the achievement motive using the grid technique. *Journal of Research in Personality, 33*, 109–130.

Sears, R. R. (1977). Sources of life satisfactions of the Terman gifted men. *American Psychologist, 32*, 119–128.

Seeman, T. E., & McEwen, B. S. (1996). Impact of social environment characteristics on neuroendocrine regulation. *Psychosomatic Medicine, 58*, 459–471.

Skowronski, J. J., Betz, A. L., Thompson, C. P., & Shannon, L. (1991). Social memory in everyday life: Recall of self-events and other-events. *Journal of Personality and Social Psychology, 60*, 831–843.

Skowronski, J. J., & Carlston, D. E. (1989). Negativity and extremity biases in impression formation: A review of explanations. *Psychological Bulletin, 105*, 131–142.

Solomon, R. L., & Corbit, J. D. (1974). An opponent-process theory of motivation: I. Temporal dynamics of affect. *Psychological Review, 81*, 119–145.

Stroebe, W., & Stroebe, M. S. (1987). *Bereavement and health: The psychological and physical consequences of partner loss.* New York: Cambridge University Press.

Sutton, S. K., & Davidson, R. J. (1997). Prefrontal brain asymmetry: A biological substrate of the behavioral approach and inhibition systems. *Psychological Science, 8*, 204–210.

Taylor, S. E. (1991). Asymmetrical effects of positive and negative events: The mobilization-minimization hypothesis. *Psychological Bulletin, 110*, 67–85.

Taylor, S. E., Klein, L. C., Lewis, B. P., Gruenewald, T. L., Gurung, R. A. R., et al. (2000). Female responses to stress: Tend-and-befriend, not fight-or-flight. *Psychological Review, 107*, 411–429.

Thibaut, J.W., & Kelley, H. H. (1959). *The social psychology of groups.* New York: Wiley.

Tolstoy, L. *Anna Karenina.* New York: Modern Library. (Original published 1877)

Uchino, B. N., Cacioppo, J. T., & Kiecolt-Glaser, J. K. (1996). The relationship between social support and physiological processes: A review with emphasis on underlying mechanisms and implications for health. *Psychological Bulletin, 119*, 488–531.

Uvnaes-Moberg, K. (1998). Oxytocin may mediate the benefits of positive social interaction and emotion. *Psychoneuroimmunology, 23*, 819–835.

Veroff, J., Douvan, E., & Kulka, R. A. (1981). *Mental health in America: Patterns of help-seeking from 1957 to 1976.* New York: Basic Books.

Vinokur, A. D., & van Ryn, M. (1993). Social support and undermining in close relationships: Their independent effects on the mental health of unemployed persons. *Journal of Personality and Social Psychology, 65*, 350–359.

Vonk, R. (1994). Trait inferences, impression formation, and person memory: Strategies in processing inconsistent information about people. *European Review of Social Psychology, 5*, 111–149.

Watson, D. (1988). The vicissitudes of mood measurement: Effects of varying descriptors, time frames, and response formats on measures of positive and negative affect. *Journal of Personality and Social Psychology, 55*, 128–141.

Watson, D., & Clark, L. A. (1984). Negative affectivity: The disposition to experience aversive emotional states. *Psychological Bulletin, 96*, 465–490.

Watson, D., Clark, L., & Tellegen, A. (1988). Development and validation of brief measures of positive and negative affect: The PANAS scales. *Journal of Personality and Social Psychology, 54*, 1063–1070.

Watson, D., Wiese, D., Vaidya, J., & Tellegen, A. (1999). The two general activation systems of affect: Structural findings, evolutionary considerations, and psychobiological evidence. *Journal of Personality and Social Psychology, 76,* 820–838.

Wills, T. A., Weiss, R. L., & Patterson, G. R. (1974). A behavioral analysis of the determinants of marital satisfaction. *Journal of Consulting and Clinical Psychology, 42,* 802–811.

III

FIND FULFILLMENT IN CREATIVITY AND PRODUCTIVITY

7

CREATIVITY AND GENIUS

VINCENT J. CASSANDRO AND DEAN KEITH SIMONTON

Amid the pageantry of the recent turn-of-the-millennium celebrations were numerous newspaper articles and television reports ranking the most influential people of the century, if not the past 2000 years. Each of these lists, whether specific to science, leadership, or athletics, comprised individuals known for their remarkable impact on society, human behavior, and thought. The creative geniuses that top such lists exemplify the heights of human achievement, possibility, adaptability, and even destructive capacity—individuals as diverse as Thomas Edison, Albert Einstein, Martin Luther King, Jr., Napoleon Bonaparte, Pablo Picasso, and Eleanor Roosevelt. It is apparent from our fascination with such lists that our society holds the creative individual and the creative genius as a measure of its own value and well-being. In this chapter we describe the nature of both creativity and the creative genius, their relationship to the positive psychology movement, as well as the strategies that have been developed to measure these phenomena at the individual and sociocultural levels.

THE POSITIVE NATURE OF CREATIVITY AND GENIUS

The psychological study of creativity and genius fits nicely within the confines of the positive psychology movement. The subject matter entails behaviors that are indicative of psychological health, achievement, and optimal subjective experience. Indeed, at the level of the individual, creativity, originality, and talent are often listed among the general concerns of positive psychology (e.g., Seligman, 1998; Seligman & Csikszentmihalyi, 2000; Snyder & Lopez, 2002). Such concerns entail creativity as a characteristic of the positively flourishing individual as well as the impact of these individuals and the products that they produce on future generations. At the group level, the importance of creativity to the growth, health, and well-being of society cannot be understated. Just a brief scan of our current

163

environments reveals that we are constantly surrounded by a remarkable record of innovation. We are supported, cradled, and inspired by the thousands of creative treasures produced by the innovative minds of past generations, from the clothes that we wear to the antibiotics in our medicine cabinets, the pages of paper in the books that we are reading to the artwork on the walls around us, the furniture that we sit on to the car that transported us to our present locations, and countless others. This history of creative products and ideas can be thought of as an extension from past to future generations—a cross-generational interconnectedness fostered by the generative possibilities of the human mind.

Creativity and genius has been linked to optimal functioning and health by numerous researchers and theoreticians (Csikszentmihalyi, 1990; Maslow, 1968; May, 1975; Rogers, 1954). The best example of this tradition can be found in the humanistic psychology movement, led by Abraham Maslow and Carl Rogers. This movement describes creative behavior as a manifestation of positive mental health and also emphasizes that such behavior is a direct result of a positive home environment. At the apex of positive mental health is the self-actualized individual. Maslow (1970) examined the self-actualized personality by exploring the lives of such remarkable individuals as Goethe, Einstein, Eleanor Roosevelt, and Frederick Douglass. Self-actualization was hypothesized to give rise to a broad pattern of creative behavior, which Maslow (1968) termed "self-actualizing creativity." Moving away from common descriptions of domain-specific creativity (i.e., the idea that creative works are only produced by the talented artist, poet, scientist, or composer), Maslow described the self-actualized creator as displaying a predisposition to be creative across a broad number of nonspecific areas (e.g., humor, house-keeping, teaching). This broad-band creativity springs from the self-actualized individual's characteristic interest in the unfamiliar, the mysterious, and the complex. In addition, Maslow emphasized that these fully functioning, self-actualized creators have the ability to express ideas and impulses without fear of criticism, and thus are better able to produce and express creative ideas. Rogers (1954) theorized that creativity emerges from individuals nurtured in environments that emphasize "psychological safety" (i.e., an environment free of conditions of worth) and "psychological freedom" (i.e., an environment that permits complete freedom of symbolic expression). Research has thus far supported Rogers's beliefs that positive, free, and safe environments tend to produce later creative behavior (Harrington, Block, & Block, 1987). From this perspective, not only is creative behavior a possibility for everyone, but it is intimately entwined with optimal functioning and health. The humanistic movement describes the creative individual in almost idyllic terms—as generally healthy and well-adjusted, both interpersonally and intrapersonally.

From the sociocultural perspective, creativity is often recognized as a symbol of cultural vitality. The landscape of human history is marked by various peaks and troughs, described as either golden or dark ages, respectively. At their peaks, certain civilizations (e.g., Ancient Greece, Renaissance Italy, Enlightenment Europe) are known for their tremendous flow of creative products and tremendous diversity and wealth of ideas. At the pinnacle of each of these "golden" periods stands the creative genius. Genius is often conceived of as the absolute peak of human performance within a given domain (Simonton, 1994). Indeed, geniuses exist in all domains of human endeavor, including musical composition (e.g., Mozart), the arts (e.g., Shakespeare), sciences (e.g., Einstein), athletic performance (e.g., Michael Jordan), artistic performance (e.g., Martha Graham), and numerous others. The existence and number of geniuses in a given historical period allows for the identification and degree of prominence given to each golden period. We need only to mention the names of Michelangelo, Leonardo da Vinci, or Raphael to obtain an understanding of the tremendous accomplishments of Renaissance Italy; Picasso, Ernest Hemingway, or Gertrude Stein to understand the importance of Paris between the world wars. Detailed studies at the sociocultural level suggest that patterns in the fluctuations of such peaks and troughs in the historical record can be reliably predicted (Simonton, 1975a). For example, the amount of creativity in one generation is positively predicted by the number of geniuses found in the two previous generations—a finding that reveals the importance of role model availability to the creative development of children and adolescents (Simonton, 1975b). Ultimately, our conceptions of genius and cultural or societal vitality are deeply connected.

DEFINING CREATIVITY

Because of the ambiguities and complexities involved in identifying creativity as well as genius, it is common to encounter the folk belief that such concepts can only be identified intuitively (i.e., "I know it when I see it"). The rigors of empirical research, however, demand that we define such concepts with greater precision. Indeed, how we define such concepts directly affects our measurement strategies and the generalizability of our research conclusions. The construct of creativity has been defined in ways too numerous to describe, but most attempts to articulate this elusive concept usually entail three essential and product-focused criteria (see, for example, MacKinnon, 1962; Rogers, 1954; Stein, 1969).

First, and of greatest importance, is the criterion of *novelty*. A product or idea needs to be new, original, or even shocking to be considered as possibly "creative." An artistic forger may be able to replicate Vincent Van Gogh's "Starry Night" almost to the brushstroke, but as a copy it would not be considered novel and thus not particularly creative. Moreover, a product can be considered novel at a variety of social levels. A product or idea can be considered original to the individual creator, the individual's family or community, the individual's subculture or culture, or even the worldwide community. This novelty continuum has often been differentiated by the terms "little c creativity," which concerns the lower level of the construct, and "capital C creativity," which concerns a genius-level contribution. It is important to keep in mind that how we define creative behavior—in terms of its novelty—is dependent on the eye of the beholder.

Second is the criterion of *adaptiveness* or *appropriateness* to the problem at hand. Many remarkably novel ideas or behaviors are simply too absurd or ridiculous to ever merit the label "creative." For example, if an editor at a poetry magazine received a submission that included a series of 1,000 word poems that contain only the word "chicken," the probability that such works would find their way into the magazine's pages are quite low. A creative product should not only be novel but also appropriate to the demand of the task, situation, or problem. The boundaries of appropriateness are obviously set by the current standards of each domain.

Third is the criterion of *completeness*. For a work to be considered creative, the work must cross the unique threshold that each domain reserves for completed creative works. For example, an author may devote her career to writing the "Great American Novel," and she may compose one of the most unique chapters in the history of American literature. However, this very "American" chapter will neither receive the title "Great" nor "Novel" if the author fails to complete the entire work. Once the threshold for completeness is crossed, as nebulous as this boundary may be for a given domain, a product can be judged as creative (e.g., many of da Vinci's masterworks are incomplete, yet cross the artistic threshold for completed paintings).

DEFINING GENIUS

For individuals to receive the "creative genius" label, they must not only produce works that meet the previously stated creativity criteria but they must also possess a few key characteristics that differentiate them from the everyday creator. First, the genius is someone who possesses unique or distinctly characteristic creative ideas or behaviors—a concept that we will label *uniqueness*. The notion of uniqueness echoes the original Roman notion of "genius." (It was believed that each Roman possessed a guardian spirit or genius, which represented that which was unique about each person or family.) When extended to the realm of achievement, uniqueness refers to the characteristic stamp or impression that an individual makes on a particular field. Whether we are referring to Ludwig von Beethoven in musical composition, Babe Ruth in baseball, Isaac Newton in physics, Goethe in literature, or Napoleon on the battlefield, all geniuses have a unique, immediately recognizable way in which they compose their creative works, manipulate their bodies, or recombine their thoughts and ideas. The unique stamp of a genius is often apparent in the eponyms that follow a particularly important career—such as Darwinian thought, Shakespearean sonnet, or Pavlovian learning.

The second essential component of genius is an individual's social *impact*. The genius's thoughts, ideas, or products have a tremendous impact on the social environment, ranging from other members of the individual's field to the society as a whole. For instance, the genius of Shakespeare can be heard in all current verbal exchanges that use words that he first penned, including "watchdog," "assassination," and "fashionable." The genius is also part salesperson and must be able to convince others of the importance of the creative ideas, products, and behaviors that may change their lives. It is in this way that genius is synonymous with leadership, because an individual is deemed a leader by the very fact that he or she is able to affect an audience of followers. For example, genius inventors are individuals who have the ability to convince others that their lives will be better because of the genius's novel inventions.

These two components of genius are still lacking a third, crucial ingredient: the *quality of intellectual power*. There likely exist numerous cases of individuals who have displayed some unique ability that has distinguished them from others and has had some degree of impact on others; yet if these abilities lack a demonstrated intellectual power or importance, each creator may be doomed to obscurity. For example, the individual in the *Guinness Book of Records* (Russell, 1986) who can smoke hundreds of cigarettes simultaneously has displayed quite a unique ability and has probably acquired a few imitators. Yet this somewhat "impactful" smoker will never be known as a creative genius at smoking, for the power and importance of the act—and, arguably, the thought behind the act—is lacking.

Overall, the creative genius is an individual who brings into being products of undeniable novelty, adaptability to the particular problems of a domain, and completeness. In addition, these creative products bear the indelible stamp that is associated with each genius's unique style of thinking and being, a style that often pervades all aspects of his or her life. The products of genius also affect others—changing the way people think, behave, and experience their lives—and stand as a testament to the genius's tremendous intellectual power. The creative genius, by definition, is poised to have a tremendous and indelible impact on innumerable lives.

THE STUDY OF CREATIVE GENIUS AT THE LEVEL
OF THE INDIVIDUAL

Attempts to measure and identify creative genius usually fall into six somewhat related categories: those that emphasize productivity, eminence, intelligence, cognitive style, personality, or biography. Although psychologists most frequently emphasize the behavior and thoughts of individuals, researchers interested in genius and creativity often use creative products as their primary unit of analysis. Research using creative products has included a wide array of items including, but hardly limited to, poems (Simonton, 1989a; Skinner, 1939), scientific discoveries (Kulkarni & Simon, 1988), musical compositions (Jackson & Padgett, 1982; Simonton, 1995), and dramatic works (Derks, 1994; Simonton, 1983a). In the area of leadership, the creative product can be quantified using discrete legislative bills, elections, or military battles (Simonton, 1980; Suedfeld, Corteen, & McCormick, 1986). Indeed, it is the creative product that is often relied on to gauge productivity and eminence and may be used to infer creative processes in general.

Creative Products

The first quantitative analysis of creativity using productivity as a measure was published by the eminent social statistician Adolphe Quételet (1835/1968). Quételet was interested in the ebb and flow of dramatic productivity across the life spans of famous French and English playwrights. In particular, he examined issues regarding the relationship between the playwright's age and level of achievement, with achievement operationalized in terms of the playwright's productivity (i.e., the number of dramatic works produced). This quantitative approach allowed him to answer questions such as the following: At what age do individuals make their major creative contributions? At what age do they reach their peaks? At what age do their careers come to a close? In a similar tradition as Quételet, Harvey Lehman (1953, 1962) was interested in leadership products as well as creative products. He examined the ages at which leaders occupied various positions of power (e.g., prime ministers, cabinet members, presidents, ambassadors) and the ages at which military commanders led their troops into battle. Dennis (e.g., 1954, 1966) also examined the relationship between age and achievement across various disciplines, but with an emphasis on individual differences. For example, in a study of eminent psychologists, Dennis (1954) studied individual differences in output (in terms of publications) and how the level of output affects the field as a whole (e.g., if one is elected as American Psychological Association president as a result, at least in part, of this output). He found that the top handful of psychological thinkers were responsible for a disproportionate number of the overall publications produced by the discipline. The use of productivity in the identification of creative genius continues to be fruitfully applied to a variety of topics (see Simonton, 1990).

The primary advantage of using productivity as a measure concerns the convenience of ratio-scale measurement properties (Nunally, 1978). Even though ratio scales make up the bedrock of the physical sciences, interval and nominal scales dominate the measurement landscape of the social sciences. Measures of productivity, however, can assume meaningful values ranging from zero to hundreds of thousands, allowing for clear estimations of relative magnitude and meaningful interpretation. A number of concerns need to be addressed when choosing and measuring creative products. In fact, the primary disadvantage of this approach regards our operationalizations of creative products themselves. For example, should the researcher emphasize quantity at the expense of quality? When measuring the productivity of creative writers, for instance, should we restrict ourselves to only their successful fictional works or should we include all fictional works? Should we also include their works of nonfiction? And if we include their nonfiction works, should we also count the book reviews that they have written or their letters to the editor? Imagine how such questions become even more complex when applied to the realm of leadership. The productivity-centered approach is also limited to content that can be easily quantified. For example, is it possible to quantify everyday events of wit or humor? Unfortunately, some expressions of creativity may remain elusive.

Eminence

Identification strategies focused on creative genius have also used the concept of eminence (i.e., prominence or high position) as a primary criterion. Strategies that emphasize eminence select individuals who have established distinct and enduring reputations in a particular field. Such high reputation echoes our description of the creative genius as having widespread impact and influence on others. Sir Francis Galton was the first researcher to conduct a systematic investigation of genius using samples of eminent individuals. In his landmark book *Hereditary Genius*, Galton (1869) equated genius with reputation, in his words, "The reputation of contemporaries, revised by posterity" (p. 77). Moreover, he believed that reputation was generally heritable. Accordingly, Galton explored family pedigrees of the eminent, which allowed for easy access to a wealth of recorded information. Galton did not limit himself to prominent individuals in the arts and sciences but extended his examination of eminent family pedigrees to areas as diverse as statespersons, judges, divines, commanders, and even famous oarsmen and wrestlers of the North Country! As is apparent from Galton's work, a researcher who uses eminence as a selection criterion will be able to pick and choose from an abundance of information regarding creative genius.

The eminence strategy also allows for the quantification of creative genius. An early example of such quantification can be found in the work of James McKeen Cattell (1903). Cattell made the plausible assumption that as each creator's impact on a field and society increases, the amount of attention each receives in a reference work (e.g., biographical dictionary, encyclopedia) should also increase. Accordingly, Cattell (1903) measured the lines of text allotted to each creator across various international encyclopedias. In this manner, Cattell was able to produce an impressive ranking of the 1000 most influential individuals in human history—with Napoleon capturing the top position. Much work has followed the pioneering efforts of Galton and Cattell, successfully implementing eminence as an objective gauge of genius-level achievement (see Simonton, 1999).

There are numerous advantages to the use of eminence as our criterion of genius. The most salient advantage is that eminence measures result in quantitative and highly reliable estimates of an individual's impact on society. Studies of eminent scientists (Simonton, 1991a), visual artists (Simonton, 1984), philosophers (Simonton, 1976), and monarchs (Simonton, 1983b) have produced reliability coefficients indicative of tremendous consensus (i.e., alpha coefficients that hover around .90; see also Simonton, 1991b). This consensus is not limited to majority cultures or simply Western civilization. For example, the measured eminence of creative African Americans displays remarkable consistency across both majority-culture sources and reference works specific to African American culture (Simonton, 1998). Such consensus also cuts across cultural bounds, as can be seen in studies conducted on samples of eminent Japanese and Chinese creators (Simonton, 1988, 1992). Such quantification is certainly more satisfying than the turn of the century armchair rankings of influential individuals.

Equating eminence with creative genius has certain disadvantages as well. Consider that to appear within a reference work, an individual needs to reach a considerable level of recognition. Thus, using eminence as a criterion of genius may result in the exclusion of individuals with limited reputations but who may be potential genius-level creators. For example, women, minorities, and people from disadvantaged backgrounds are underrepresented in the ranks of those judged to be eminent. Researchers attempt to limit the impact of such sample biases by reaching beyond the confines of common reference works. Reference works devoted to the underrepresented and disadvantaged can be used to acquire a very broad sample of eminent individuals. For example, Simonton (1984) compiled a rather exhaustive and diverse sample of 772 artistic creators in his study of the social relationships of eminent visual artists. He achieved such a broad sample by selecting creators from 18 different sources, including general encyclopedias and field-specific biographical dictionaries and encyclopedias. Ultimately, however, the eminence criteria will only mature as a representative indicator of creative genius as the gaps in the historical record are explored and filled by historians, encyclopedists, and curious scholars.

Intelligence

For the past century, the concept of intelligence has been linked closely to genius. In fact, some dictionaries define genius as being synonymous with high scores on intelligence tests, or a high Intelligence Quotient (IQ; see, e.g., Mish, 1989). The linkage between genius and high intelligence can be traced back to Galton's original interest in the measurement of natural ability. In addition to his studies of eminent individuals, Galton (1883) was the first person to devise a reasonable set of tests to directly measure individual variation in intelligence. Galton developed numerous anthropometric instruments based on reaction time, the acuity of different sense modalities, and general perceptual abilities. However, these instruments failed as valid measures of intellectual functioning. It was not long after Galton's pioneering work that the first successful measure of intelligence was developed by Alfred Binet and Theodore Simon in 1905. At the foundation of their conception of intelligence was the relationship between a child's mental and chronological age. Mental age could be estimated by giving the child various age-specific tasks (i.e., tasks requiring complex mental functions and cultural knowledge) and simply comparing the child's score to that expected of his or her age group. Later, the ratio of mental to chronological age would be multiplied by 100 to produce what is now known as the IQ. Following this pioneering work, Lewis Terman brought the Binet-Simon test to America and used it to initiate the first longitudinal study of genius. As described in his *Genetic Studies of Genius*, Terman (1925) used his IQ test to identify and predict later occurrences of genius in his sample of gifted children. Terman set the IQ cutoff for inclusion at 140, and acquired a sample of 1528 children (857 males, 671 females) with an average IQ of 151. An IQ score of 140 represents the top 1% of scorers and is now generally considered to represent genius-level intellect. Needless to say, Terman's expectations were quite high for identifying and predicting genius in its youth.

As with measures of productivity and eminence, intelligence tests are also known for their good psychometric properties. In fact, intelligence tests are some of the most reliable tests produced by psychologists (Janda, 1998). However, these tests of intellectual functioning are best at predicting scholastic achievement, not real-world success (Tomlinson-Keasey & Little, 1990). The validity of IQ tests as an indicator of creative genius is also in doubt. The primary criticism of IQ tests in relation to high-level creative behavior is that they concern only a very narrow range of behaviors. In fact, there may be quite a few intelligences that are not captured by typical IQ tests but that are crucial to genius-level creative performance (Gardner, 1993; Sternberg & Lubart, 1991). For example, should we expect IQ tests, and the verbally oriented items that dominate their content, to predict genius in the visual arts, dramatic performance, athletics, or dance? An additional difficulty is that although IQ is a decent predictor of creativity at lower intelligence levels, IQ becomes a poor predictor of creative achievement after an IQ threshold of approximately 120 (Barron & Harrington, 1981). After the threshold of 120, any additional increase in IQ is less important than other factors, such as motivation and creative ability. Ironically, although great achievements were expected from the gifted individuals in Terman's sample, the only individual tested by Terman who received a Nobel prize—physicist William Shockley—was excluded from the sample because his IQ failed to meet the 140 point cut-off. Incidentally, the individual noted as having the highest IQ on record, an IQ of 228 achieved by columnist Marilyn Vos Savant, is notable not for her work on a cure for cancer or a better mouse trap but for answering reader questions in a Sunday magazine column. Ultimately, those qualities measured by IQ tests, without requisite levels of creativity and motivation, are unsatisfactory in their ability to capture creative genius.

Cognitive Style

It is clear that we must not rely entirely on intellect when attempting to conceive of genius. Genius demands the ingredient of imagination and creative thought. J. P. Guilford (1967) introduced a concept that addressed the distinction between intelligence and creative thought: divergent thinking. In particular, Guilford described intelligence as a cognitive orientation toward convergent thought, or the ability to focus on a single solution to a given problem. Such convergent thought processes are emphasized on most academic and IQ tests. In contrast, Guilford introduced the concept of divergent thought, which can be conceptualized as an individual's cognitive orientation toward the production of multiple solutions to a given problem. Although novel problem solutions are not guaranteed by such an orientation, the more directions that an individual's thought may range certainly increases the likelihood that a creative solution will be found. Guilford and a variety of others (see Runco, 1991) have developed tests to estimate an individual's divergent thinking abilities. Guilford's Alternate Uses Test (Christenson, Guilford, Merrifield, & Wilson, 1960) for example, requires research participants to generate a variety of uses for a common object (e.g., a toothpick, paper clip, or brick). Most commonly, the answers are then scored for originality (i.e., novelty as measured by statistical infrequency or observer ratings), fluency (i.e., the number of ideas given), and flexibility (i.e., the individual's ability to change set or categories). A similar theoretical orientation can be found in the work of Mednick (1962). Mednick's approach to divergent thought is grounded in his belief that creative thinkers are able to access a wider range of associated ideas than the narrow ranges found for less creative individuals. Mednick constructed a Remote Associates Test (RAT; Mednick & Mednick, 1969) to tap an individual's ability to connect remotely connected ideas. Each of the RAT items consist of three terms (e.g., blue, rat, cottage) that have one or two common associates (e.g., cheese). It was Mednick's belief that the analogical thinking ability required to achieve a high score on this creativity test may be the key to understanding an individual's creative problem-solving processes and ability.

Measures of divergent thinking generally demonstrate high reliability (Hovecar & Bachelor, 1989) and good discriminant validity in relation to intelligence tests (Wallach & Kogan, 1965). Yet the relationship between scores on divergent thinking tests and creative genius may be tenuous at best. Divergent thinking tests are, in general, not strong predictors of real-world creative behavior (Hovecar & Bachelor, 1989). Beyond psychometric concerns, however, is the more insidious assumption that divergent thinking tests are tapping a general creative ability—analogous to Spearman's G (Spearman, 1927) in intelligence research—that should predict creativity, regardless of the domain of creative activity. It is more likely that we should find little to no relationship between scores on divergent thinking tests (especially of the verbal type) and creative performance in domains as various as athletics, physics, or the visual and culinary arts. A demonstrated ability to generate or link remote ideas may be a necessary but not sufficient condition to generate creative performance of the highest degree in domains that range beyond the verbally centered professions. Creative thinking, including its components of information acquisition, expertise, and problem-solving strategies, may be much more domain-specific than previously assumed.

Personality and Biography

Beyond high intelligence and a creative cognitive style, other critical ingredients in the recipe of creative genius remain. The first study to emphasize the relative importance of personality characteristics (e.g., traits, motivations, interests, values) over intelligence was conducted by Catharine Cox (1926) as a part of Terman's larger exploration of intelligence. In contrast to Terman's longitudinal study of intelligence, Cox approached this issue retrospectively. Cox selected 301 of the most eminent individuals on Cattell's (1903) list of the top 1000. This select group contains individuals from a wide array of disciplines, nations, and centuries. The primary goal of her study was to explore the relationship between childhood intelligence and later creative success. Yet, for a subset of these geniuses, Cox collected a sizable amount of personality data and had each genius rated across 67 different personality characteristics. Although this portion of the study was immensely complex, Cox was able to condense her findings into the observation that creative genius requires high—but not the highest—intelligence, combined with tremendous persistence and motivation. Beyond the personality ratings used by Cox, the traits of creative individuals have been examined using a variety of measures. For instance, Anne Roe (1952) explored the personality characteristics of 64 eminent scientists using measures including the TAT (Murray, 1943) and Rorschach Ink Blot test (Rorschach, 1921). The Eysenck Personality Questionnaire has been used extensively by Hans Eysenck (1995) to tie genius to the personality construct of psychoticism (i.e., a predisposition for both mental illness and creative thinking ability). In addition, Raymond Cattell has used his 16PF personality questionnaire to explore creative individuals in a wide range of areas, from research scientists (Cattell, 1963) to Olympic medallists (Cattell, 1965). Much work on the personalities of creative individuals has revealed a number of defining characteristics, including the ability to persevere in the face of obstacles, an open orientation, the possession of broad interests, curiosity, task absorption, and a high level of intrinsic motivation (Tardiff & Sternberg, 1988). Cattell (1963) also extended his personality research to the realm of biographical data. Cattell began reading biographies of scientific geniuses (e.g., Charles Darwin, Johannes Kepler, Newton, Blaise Pascal) as a simple hobby, but soon realized the value of such detailed personality information and assigned 16PF ratings to each scientist as if each scientist had taken the test himself. Cattell found that the broad personality profile that marked contemporary research scientists was mirrored by the profile that characterized his scientific geniuses (e.g., above average intelligence, prudence, detachment, introversion).

Biographical material is not limited to the study of personality but presents the creativity researcher with a copious amount of other information that may be integral to achievement. For example, it is common for data to be collected regarding developmental experiences, family background, and educational history that may play a crucial role in the development of later creative behavior (see, e.g., Albert, 1980; Goertzel & Goertzel, 1962). Galton was the first researcher to examine these qualities in relation to later success. In particular, Galton (1874) created and successfully implemented the questionnaire as a means to acquire information regarding a variety of personal characteristics (e.g., birth order and its relation to achievement in the sciences). Galton (1874) found that great scientific minds are more likely to be a first born rather than a later born sibling. The pioneer sexologist Havelock Ellis was also interested in the study of biographical characteristics. Specifically, Ellis (1926) explored the lives of 1030 British geniuses and found similar results to that of Galton's regarding the importance of primogeniture. Even the past decade saw these particular research themes clarified in the work of Sulloway (1996). In addition, J. M. Cattell (1910) studied the biographical characteristics that predict eminence in psychology. Cattell found that father's occupation (e.g., professor or minister) was particularly important to the later success of psychologists.

As with previously discussed measures of creative genius, the primary advantage of personality measures can be found in their consistent demonstration of high reliability. Personality measures including the TAT, 16PF, EPQ, Q-sort, and many others have been extensively examined, normed, and are psychometrically sound (see, e.g., McCrae & Costa, 1997). Biographical information can be easily and objectively acquired on famous individuals, and the reliability of this data can be readily checked across sources. In fact, biographical checklists have been created that make data collection easy, efficient, and quite objective. Yet good biographical data is contingent on its availability and, in some cases, can lead to rather odd samples. For instance, Cox (1926) was forced to narrow her sample of geniuses to 301 because of gaping holes in the extant biographical information on many eminent historical figures. She excluded creators born before 1450 and had to put aside such mountainous intellects as Shakespeare, Machiavelli, and Rabelais because of insufficient childhood data. The most severe criticism of personality and biographical measures, however, is that they lack validity as indicators of creative genius.

It is clear from the variety of different definitions and conceptualizations of creative genius that this construct is complex and multidimensional in nature. Any single measure of creative genius—whether we emphasize productivity, eminence, intelligence, cognitive style, personality, or biography—is doomed to capture only a small portion of such a multifaceted construct. The best approach to conceptualizing and measuring creative genius may be to adopt a multiple measurement strategy. A suitable starting point for such a measure of creative genius may be found in a combination of the previously mentioned factors, such as a composite of personality, intelligence, and productivity measures.

THE STUDY OF CREATIVE GENIUS AT THE SOCIOCULTURAL LEVEL

Creativity and genius are not only considered characteristics of the individual but can be conceptualized and measured as unique features of a cultural and historical period. Primarily, cross-cultural and transhistorical analytical strategies have been used in the sociocultural exploration of creative genius. Cross-cultural strategies rely on the concept of *Ortgeist,* or the "spirit of the place," and emphasize the cultural factors that covary with indicators of creativity and genius. The transhistorical study of creative genius relies on the concept of *Zeitgeist*, or the "spirit of the times," and used historical period as its unit of analysis. This strategy emphasizes historical trends and cross-generational changes in the prevalence of creative genius.

Cross-cultural studies focus on the creative genius as a quantity specific to a particular culture or geographic region. An early example of this type of research can be found in Alphonse de Candolle's (1873) response to Galton's (1869) work on the heritability of creative genius. Contrary to Galton's work, Candolle was interested in the possible cultural and environmental factors that contribute to the prevalence of creative genius. Candolle's measures avoided common cultural and ethnocentric biases and allowed him to document a variety of important sociocultural predictors of genius (e.g., economic conditions, climate, political conditions). In addition, research has also revealed some interesting facts regarding the creativity of various cultures. For example, Carniero (1970) compared the complexity of various preindustrial societies and the creativity-related traits each possessed. Interestingly, Carniero found that creativity is a core trait in preindustrial societies—suggesting that these seemingly primitive cultures may have more creativity per capita (i.e., everyone contributes to the creative products of the culture) than industrialized societies that emphasize the solitary creative genius.

Transhistorical analyses of creative behavior are grounded in the observation that creative genius is not evenly distributed across the historical record. The history of humankind can be separated into "golden" and "silver" ages when creative genius is widespread and "dark" ages when the prevalence of creative genius reaches its nadir. Indeed, this ebb and flow of genius clusters has been studied in time-series periods ranging from years and generations to century-long spans (Simonton, 1990; Sorokin & Merton, 1935). Alfred Kroeber (1944) documented the historical peaks and troughs of genius, which he termed "cultural configurations," in every civilization known to have existed. Kroeber used his rich transhistorical data to decrease the prominence of genetic explanations of creative genius, for such fluctuations in genius would presuppose improbably rapid, periodic changes in the gene pool. Kroeber (1917) also studied the phenomenon of multiples in the historical record (i.e., an event entailing a simultaneous and independent discovery or invention by two or more individuals). It was Kroeber's contention that the sociocultural milieu, or *Zeitgeist*, not the individual genius, was responsible for the inevitability of various scientific innovations. Price (1963) extended Kroeber's work by fitting stochastic models to the occurrence of the phenomenon in the sciences and technologies. David McClelland (1961) also adopted a transhistorical approach in his influential work regarding human motivation. For example, McClelland examined the achievement motive in cultures as historically remote as Ancient Greece, Spain, and England, and compared them to contemporary cultures. He revealed that the positive relationship between demonstrations of the achievement motive (e.g., motives in children's stories, frequency of entrepreneurs) and economic prosperity is consistent across time and culture. Empirical research continues regarding both the transhistorical and cross-cultural predictors of creative genius within the tradition of historiometry (see Simonton, 1990).

The primary advantage of cross-cultural and transhistorical creativity research concerns its generalizability. The rather lofty goal of most scientific psychological research is to discern universal patterns of behavior (e.g., predictors of creative behavior across time and space). Accordingly, the importance of testing nomothetic hypotheses for their cross-cultural and transhistorical consistency cannot be understated. For instance, if we should find environmental predictors of creative behavior in the United States that fail to generalize to societies that feature different political systems, climates, or artistic traditions, our conclusions should not be acclaimed as behavioral universals. Alternatively, when a recurring pattern of creativity predictors is found across cultural, geographical, and temporal distance, its status as a universal phenomenon of human behavior should be commensurately applauded. The primary disadvantage to cross-cultural investigations of creativity and genius concern ethnocentric definitional biases. Unfortunately, Western conceptions and definitions of creativity and genius may lack appropriate analogs in other cultures. For example, if artistic creativity is defined in terms of per capita oil-painting production, a culture lacking a solid tradition of oil painting (e.g., Eskimo culture) may be evaluated as being less artistically creative than most. Narrow definitions that reflect Western values are bound to overlook cultures in which other artistic traditions, such as oral storytelling or ceremonial dance, may be clear demonstrations of cultural creativity. In addition, transhistorical analyses suffer the disadvantage of being reliant on the veracity and availability of historical data. Thus, the universal laws discerned by creativity and genius research must be qualified in relation to data adequacy concerns.

CONCLUSION

The psychological study of creative genius has produced a wealth of information concerning the lives of the most remarkable and influential individuals ever to have walked the Earth. These creators are not only examples of the heights of human potential, but they can be described also as the architects of the flourishing society. They are responsible for the majority of the products that surround us every day, the myriad ways in which we communicate, our understanding of the universe, and the ways in which we understand ourselves. A variety of research strategies at the individual and sociocultural levels have produced a clear and compelling portrait of these creative geniuses. Specifically, research has revealed the many cognitive (e.g., associationistic and divergent thought), personality (e.g., an open orientation, perseverance, risk-taking), developmental (e.g., education, early trauma), economic (e.g., high-status parental background), political (e.g., political turbulence, war), and social factors (e.g., mentor availability, collaborators) that characterize the creative genius across culture, time, and geography. Our broad understanding of the creative genius is beneficial not only to psychologists interested in the extremes of human potential but is also integral to our understanding of the everyday creator and optimally functioning human being.

Research regarding creative genius has directly affected the manner in which we conceptualize the everyday creator. For example, anecdotes and empirical studies of genius have helped to guide our understanding of the general features of the creative process (i.e., the preparation, incubation, illumination, and verification stages; see Wallas, 1926), important aspects of the creative person (e.g., flow, domain-relevant skills; see Csikszentmihalyi, 1996), and the environmental factors that give rise to creativity (e.g., factors predictive of intrinsic motivation; see Amabile, 1983). In addition, research regarding the narrow band of factors measured by ordinary IQ tests reveal that IQ alone is an inadequate predictor of genius. For societies to maximize human potential, emphasis must be placed on the combination of factors that result in genius (e.g., high motivation, adequately high intelligence, creative thinking skills, stimulating home environments). Cultures that place intelligence above creative thinking skills and other characteristics important to creative behavior are destined to fail in their quest to produce a future Marie Curie, W. E. B. Dubois, Mozart, or Shakespeare. At the present time, only a handful of academic institutions offer courses that concern creativity and creative thinking skills, and even fewer programs actually offer degrees in creative studies (e.g., The Center for Studies in Creativity at Buffalo State College). Whether or not such creativity-training programs will produce the geniuses of the future remains to be seen, but these programs are certainly contributing the essential ingredients that increase the creative potential and life satisfaction of their students. Regardless, the candle of genius burns bright enough to illuminate a path toward maximizing the potential of all human beings.

There is certain to be a place for creativity research within the positive psychology movement for some time to come. However, research concerning creativity and genius has yet to be recognized as a fully mainstream domain of psychological inquiry. We are certain that the celebrations marking the end of the twenty-first century will feature lists of the creative geniuses that have shaped society. We hope that such lists will be combined and complemented by the knowledge amassed by mainstream creativity and genius research. We might even wish that among those creative geniuses celebrated in 2099 will be at least one positive psychologist who fathomed the deeper secrets of this personally and socially valued human capacity.

REFERENCES

Albert, R. S. (1980). Family positions and the attainment of eminence: A study of special family positions and special family experiences. *Gifted Child Quarterly, 24*, 87–95.

Amabile, T. M. (1983). *The social psychology of creativity*. New York: Springer-Verlag.

Barron, F. X., & Harrington, D. M. (1981). Creativity, intelligence, and personality. *Annual Review of Psychology, 32*, 439–476.

Candolle, A. de. (1873). *Histoire des sciences et des savants depuis deux siècles*. Geneva: Georg.

Carniero, R. L. (1970). Scale analysis, evolutionary sequences, and the rating of cultures. In R. Naroll & R. Cohen (Eds.), *A handbook of method in cultural anthropology* (pp. 834–871). New York: Natural History Press.

Cattell, J. M. (1903). A statistical study of eminent men. *Popular Science Monthly, 62*, 359–377.

Cattell, J. M. (1910). A further statistical study of American men of science. *Science, 32*, 633–648.

Cattell, R. B. (1963). The personality and motivation of the researcher from measurements of contemporaries and from biography. In C. W. Taylor & F. Barron (Eds.), *Scientific creativity* (pp. 119–131). New York: Wiley.

Cattell, R. B. (1965). *The scientific analysis of personality*. Baltimore: Penguin.

Christenson, P. R., Guilford, J. P., Merrifield, P. R., & Wilson, R. C. (1960). *Alternate uses*. Beverly Hills, CA: Sheridan Psychological Services.

Cox, C. (1926). *The early mental traits of three hundred geniuses*. Stanford, CA: Stanford University Press.

Csikszentmihalyi, M. (1990). *Flow: The psychology of optimal experience*. New York: Harper Collins.

Csikszentmihalyi, M. (1996). *Creativity: Flow and the psychology of discovery and invention*. New York: Harper Collins.

Dennis, W. (1954). Predicting scientific productivity in later maturity form records of earlier decades. *Journal of Gerontology, 9*, 465–467.

Dennis, W. (1966). Creative productivity between the ages of 20 and 80 years. *Journal of Gerontology, 21*, 1–8.

Derks, P. L. (1994). Clockwork Shakespeare: The Bard meets the Regressive Imagery Dictionary. *Empirical Studies of the Arts, 12*, 131–139.

Ellis, H. (1926). *A study of British genius* (Rev. ed.). Boston: Houghton Mifflin.

Eysenck, H. J. (1995). *Genius: The natural history of creativity.* Cambridge: Cambridge University Press.

Galton, F. (1869). *Hereditary genius: An inquiry into its laws and consequences.* London: Macmillan.

Galton, F. (1874). *English men of science: Their nature and nurture.* London: Macmillan.

Galton, F. (1883). *Inquiries into human faculty and its development.* London: Macmillan.

Gardner, H. (1993). *Frames of mind: The theory of multiple intelligences* (2nd ed.). New York: Basic Books.

Goertzel, V., & Goertzel, M. G. (1962). *Cradles of eminence.* Boston: Little, Brown.

Guilford, J. P. (1967). *The nature of human intelligence.* New York: McGraw-Hill.

Harrington, D. M., Block, J. H., & Block, J. (1987). Testing aspects of Carl Roger's theory of creative environments: Child-rearing antecedents of creative potential in young adolescents. *Journal of Personality and Social Psychology, 52,* 851–856.

Hovecar, D., & Bachelor, P. (1989). A taxonomy and critique of measurements used in the study of creativity. In J. A. Glover, R. R. Ronning, & C. R. Reynolds (Eds.), *Handbook of creativity* (pp. 53–75). New York: Plenum Press.

Jackson, J. M., & Padgett, V. R. (1982). With a little help from my friend: Social loafing and the Lennon–McCartney songs. *Personality and Social Psychology, 8,* 672–677.

Janda, L. H. (1998). *Psychological testing: Theory and applications.* Boston: Allyn & Bacon.

Kroeber, A. L. (1917). The superorganic. *American Anthropologist, 19,* 163–214.

Kroeber, A. L. (1944). *Configurations of culture growth.* Berkeley: University of California Press.

Kulkarni, D., & Simon, H. A. (1988). The process of scientific discovery: The strategy of experimentation. *Cognitive Science, 12,* 139–175.

Lehman, H. C. (1953). *Age and achievement.* Princeton, NJ: Princeton University Press.

Lehman, H. C. (1962). More about age and achievement. *Gerontologist, 2,* 141–148.

MacKinnon, D. W. (1962). The nature and nurture of creative talent. *American Psychologist, 17,* 484–495.

Maslow, A. H. (1968). *Toward a psychology of being* (2nd ed.). New York: Van Nostrand Reinhold.

Maslow, A. H. (1970). *Motivation and personality* (2nd ed.). New York: Harper & Row.

May, R. (1975). *The courage to create.* New York: Harper.

McClelland, D. C. (1961). *The achieving society.* New York: Van Nostrand.

McCrae, R. R., & Costa, P. T. (1997). Personality trait structure as a human universal. *American Psychologist, 52,* 509–516.

Mednick, S. A. (1962). The associative basis of the creative process. *Psychological Review, 69,* 220–232.

Mednick, S. A., & Mednick, M. T. (1967). *Remote Associate Test: College adult form 1.* Boston: Houghton-Mifflin.

Mish, F. C. (Ed.). (1989). *Webster's ninth new collegiate dictionary.* Springfield, MA: Merriam Webster.

Murray, H. A. (1943). *Thematic apperception test.* Cambridge, MA: Harvard University Press.

Nunally, J. (1978). *Psychometric theory* (2nd ed.). New York: McGraw-Hill.

Quételet, A. (1968). *A treatise on man and the development of his faculties.* New York: Franklin. (Original work published 1835)

Price, D. (1963). *Little science, big science.* New York: Columbia University Press.

Roe, A. (1952). *The making of a scientist.* New York: Dodd, Mead.

Rogers, C. R. (1954). Toward a theory of creativity. *ETC: A Review of General Semantics, 11,* 249–260.

Rorschach, H. (1921). *Psychodiagnostik.* Berne: Bircher.

Runco, M. A. (1991). *Divergent thinking.* Norwood, NJ: Ablex.

Russell, A. (Ed.). (1986). *1987 Guinness book of world records.* New York: Sterling.

Seligman, M. E. P. (1998, Oct.). What is the "good life"? President's column. *APA Monitor,* 2.

Seligman, M. E. P., & Csikszentmihalyi, M. (2000). Positive psychology: An introduction. *American Psychologist, 55,* 5–14.

Simonton, D. K. (1975a). Interdisciplinary creativity over historical time: A correlational analysis of generational fluctuations. *Social Behavior and Personality, 3,* 181–188.

Simonton, D. K. (1975b). Sociocultural context of individual creativity: A transhistorical time-series analysis. *Journal of Personality and Social Psychology, 32,* 1119–1133.

Simonton, D. K. (1976). Philosophical eminence, beliefs, and zeitgeist: An individual-generational analysis. *Journal of Personality and Social Psychology, 34,* 630–640.

Simonton, D. K. (1980). Land battles, generals, and armies: Individual and situational determinants of victory and casualties. *Journal of Personality and Social Psychology, 38,* 110–119.

Simonton, D. K. (1983a). Dramatic greatness and content: A quantitative study of eighty-one Athenian and Shakespearean plays. *Empirical Studies of the Arts, 1,* 109–123.

Simonton, D. K. (1983b). Intergenerational transfer of individual differences in hereditary monarchs: Genes, role-modeling, cohort, or sociocultural effects? *Journal of Personality and Social Psychology, 44,* 354–364.

Simonton, D. K. (1984). Artistic creativity and interpersonal relationships across and within generations. *Journal of Personality and Social Psychology, 46,* 1273–1286.

Simonton, D. K. (1988). Galtonian genius, Kroeberian configurations, and emulation: A generational time-series analysis of Chinese civilization. *Journal of Personality and Social Psychology, 55,* 230–238.

Simonton, D. K. (1989). Shakespeare's sonnets: A case of and for single-case historiometry. *Journal of Personality, 57,* 695–721.

Simonton, D. K. (1990). *Psychology, science, and history: An introduction to historiometry.* New Haven, CT: Yale University Press.

Simonton, D. K. (1991a). Career landmarks in science: Individual differences and interdisciplinary contrasts. *Developmental Psychology, 27,* 119–130.

Simonton, D. K. (1991b). Latent-variable models of posthumous reputation: A quest for Galton's G. *Journal of Personality and Social Psychology, 60,* 607–619.

Simonton, D. K. (1992). Gender and genius in Japan: Feminine eminence in masculine culture. *Sex Roles, 27,* 101–119.

Simonton, D. K. (1994). *Greatness: Who makes history and why.* New York: Guilford Press.

Simonton, D. K. (1995). Drawing inferences from symphonic programs: Musical attributes versus listener attributions. *Music Perception, 12,* 307–322.

Simonton, D. K. (1998). Achieved eminence in minority and majority cultures: Convergence versus divergence in the assessments of 294 African Americans. *Journal of Personality and Social Psychology, 74,* 804–817.

Simonton, D. K. (1999). Significant samples: The psychological study of eminent individuals. *Psychological Methods, 4,* 425–451.

Skinner, B. F. (1939). The alliteration in Shakespeare's sonnets: A study in literary behavior. *Psychological Record, 3,* 186–192.

Snyder, C. R., & Lopez, S. J. (Eds.). (2002). *The handbook of positive psychology.* New York: Oxford University Press.

Sorokin, P. A., & Merton, R. K. (1935). The course of Arabian intellectual development, 700–1300 A.D. *Isis, 22,* 516–524.

Spearman, C. (1927). *The abilities of man.* London: Macmillan.

Stein, M. I. (1969). Creativity. In E. F. Borgatta & W. W. Lambert (Eds.), *Handbook of personality theory and research* (pp. 900–942). Chicago: Rand-McNally.

Sternberg, R. J., & Lubart, T. I. (1991). An investment theory of creativity and its development. *Human Development, 34,* 1–31.

Suedfeld, P., Corteen, R. S., & McCormick, C. (1986). The role of integrative complexity in military leadership: Robert E. Lee and his opponents. *Journal of Applied Social Psychology, 16,* 498–507.

Sulloway, F. J. (1996). *Born to rebel: Birth order, family dynamics, and creative lives.* New York: Pantheon Books.

Tardiff, T. Z., & Sternberg, R. J. (1988). What do we know about creativity? In R. J. Sternberg (Ed.), *The nature of creativity* (pp. 429–440). New York: Cambridge University Press.

Terman, L. M. (1925). *Genetic studies of genius: Vol. 1. Mental and physical traits of a thousand gifted children.* Stanford, CA: Stanford University Press.

Tomlinson-Keasey, C., & Little, T. D. (1990). Predicting educational attainment, occupational achievement, intellectual skill, and personal adjustment among gifted men and women. *Journal of Educational Psychology, 82,* 442–455.

Wallach, M. A., & Kogan, N. (1965). *Modes of thinking in young children.* New York: Holt Rinehart & Winston.

Wallas, G. (1926). *The art of thought.* New York: Harcourt Brace.

8

WORKING, PLAYING, AND EATING: MAKING THE MOST OF MOST MOMENTS

AMY WRZESNIEWSKI, PAUL ROZIN, AND GWEN BENNETT

Pleasure and fulfillment surely make for quality in life. The more of each, the more quality. Hence, the more pleasure and fulfillment are part of our most common daily activities, the better. It is probably true that work, leisure, and eating constitute the three major waking activities of most humans. From the economic point of view, work accounts for almost all of income, and food and leisure account for most expenditures—food in the developing nations and leisure in the developed nations (Samuelson, 1990). There is a great deal of variance, within and between cultures, in the enjoyment and personal fulfillment associated with work, leisure, and eating. It is reasonable to assume that the more positive these experiences, the better the quality of life (for evidence from the domain of work, see Campbell, Converse, & Rodgers, 1976; Wrzesniewski, McCauley, Rozin, & Schwartz, 1997).

We propose that intrinsic value and fulfillment are two critical characteristics of activities that enhance their positivity and contribution to the quality of life. Intrinsic value is found in the accomplishment of an activity for its own sake, as opposed to accomplishment for some other purpose, such as for its instrumental value (Deci & Ryan, 1985; Lepper, 1983). Fulfillment refers to a sense that one is a better person, in terms of personal or societal goals, as a result of participation in an activity. Fulfillment and intrinsic value are clearly related; indeed, a sense of fulfillment may encourage intrinsic value. On the other hand, they are opposed in the sense that

Thanks to the Edmund J. and Louise W. Kahn Chair research fund and to the NIH for support of some of the research described in this chapter.

185

fulfillment, especially when expressed as improving the world or the lives of others, has an instrumental quality.

In this chapter, we explore the role of fulfillment and intrinsic value in three major domains of life: work, leisure, and the domain of food and eating. We discuss the domain of work first, and analyze callings in terms of both the intrinsic value of work (enjoyed for its own sake) and often, the sense of improving the world and the self (fulfillment). In English, the word *callings* describes a positive framing of fulfilling work. We propose the word *passions* for our second domain, leisure activities, to correspond to callings in the work domain. We hold that passions combine intrinsic value and fulfillment. In the third section, we explore the domain of food and eating, where the focus is more about intrinsic value rather than fulfillment. We consider the question of whether food and eating are enjoyed for their own sake or are embedded in the worrisome instrumentalities of improved nutrition and avoidance of illness and obesity. Finally, we attempt to draw some conclusions from our analysis of the three major domains of life that we have analyzed.

THE DOMAIN OF WORK: CALLINGS

Work represents nearly half of waking life for most adults. Most people must work to make a living, which makes work an obligation rather than a choice. Even so, the experience of work is often quite varied, ranging from work as a drudging necessity to work as a source of joy. Traditionally, researchers have focused on either individual determinants of the experience of work (Dubin, 1956; Lodahl & Kejner, 1965; Roberson, 1990), such as expectations or values, or external characteristics of the job itself (Griffin, 1987; Hackman & Oldham, 1976, 1980), such as work tasks or social interaction at work. Both perspectives minimize the role that employees play in actively shaping the meaning of a job. Even in the most restricted and routine jobs, employees can exert some influence on framing the essence of the work.

The most common constructs studied in the meaning of work literature include work centrality (Dubin, 1956; MOW, 1987), work commitment (Loscocco, 1989), job involvement (Lodahl & Kejner, 1965), work involvement (Kanungo, 1982), intrinsic–extrinsic motivation (Kanungo, 1981; Kanungo & Hartwick, 1987; Roberson, 1990), and work values (Nord, Brief, Atieh, & Doherty, 1990). Some researchers define work centrality in terms of how work compares with other life spheres in its importance (Dubin, 1956), whereas work commitment is defined as "the relative importance work has to people's sense of self" (Loscocco, 1989, p. 370). Kanungo (1982) defined job involvement as attachment to work, whereas work involvement has to do with a normative belief about the importance of work in life (Kanungo, 1982, p. 342). Herzberg (Herzberg, Mausner, & Snyderman, 1959) was the first to identify the intrinsic and extrinsic motivations for working. In the original conceptualization, intrinsic motivations for working included opportunities for advancement, achievement, and recognition, whereas more recent definitions have focused on interesting work, creativity, and fulfillment (Kanungo & Hartwick, 1987). Extrinsic motivations for working include pay, working conditions, and job security. Finally, work values have been defined as the "end states people desire and feel they ought to be able to realize through working" (Nord et al., 1990, p. 21).

Clearly, there is a great deal of overlap between the constructs listed and how all of them relate to either the importance or salience of work in the context of the rest of life or to the specific aims, goals, or reasons people have for working. For half a century, much attention has been paid to the relative importance of work in people's lives, and researchers have charted trends showing that most people are likely to continue with their work without pay if they had all the money they would need (Morse & Weiss, 1955), although this trend has decreased in recent decades (Vecchio, 1980). In fact, the current thinking among many meaning-of-work researchers is that work is no longer at the center of the values and fabric of our society (Castillo, 1997; Vecchio, 1980).

Such findings raise the question of how the meaning of work is shaped and what effects it has in peoples' lives. An ongoing debate in the meaning of work literature centers on whether the meaning of work is determined internally (i.e., within the individual) or externally (i.e., by the job and wider environment). Are the changing meanings of work a function of changing work environments, or have people's needs in these work environments changed? Loscocco (1989) has investigated the influence of both the job and the person in shaping commitment to work. According to the first perspective, the jobs people have exert strong influences on their work commitment (Kohn, Schooler, Miller, Miller, & Schoenberg, 1983). In effect, it is the features of the job that are the primary determinants of the nature of our attachment to the job. Such a view is aligned with a job characteristics perspective of the experience of work. Oldham and Hackman (1981) claimed that it is the characteristics of a job that should have the greatest influence on work commitment. Another perspective takes the opposite argument—that it is the individual's personality that determines work commitment (Alderfer, 1972; Staw, Bell, & Clausen, 1986). According to this view, individual needs, demographic, and social class background affect commitment to work. Loscocco (1989) found that both external and internal influences affected work commitment. Thus, people make meaning of their work, and forge their attachments to their work, under the influence of multiple forces.

The external characteristics of the job that are likely to affect attachment and attitudes toward work have long been a focus of organizational research. Two dominant perspectives—the job characteristics model and social information processing theory—have laid out different sources of job attitudes. The job characteristics model represents the experience of work as a function of objective features of the job, such as skill variety, task identity and significance, autonomy and feedback (Hackman & Lawler, 1971; Hackman & Oldham 1976, 1980). In contrast, social information processing theory (Salancik & Pfeffer, 1978) acknowledges that tasks are not purely objective but rather are socially constructed with others on the job. In effect, the cues that others give in the social environment about how the tasks and environment of the job should be interpreted by the employee are thought to be powerful influences on the experience of the job. Our focus in this chapter is on the individual determinants of how people make meaning of their experiences of work, regardless of the task characteristics and reactions of others that the work involves.

The kinds of meaning people make of their work make up a primary focus of this chapter. Recent research suggests that people tend to frame their relationship to work in different ways. More specifically, sociologists (Bellah, Madsen, Sullivan, Swidler, & Tipton, 1985) and psychologists (Baumeister, 1991; Schwartz, 1986, 1994; Wrzesniewski et al., 1997) have argued for a tripartite model of people's orientations to their work. These general orientations toward work partially determine the experience of work and its accompanying thoughts, feelings, and behaviors. The orientations represent more of an individual differences view of work attitudes, but one's orientation toward work may also be shaped by the job. As such, work orientation represents the interplay between the person and the job.

Bellah and colleagues (1985; see also Schwartz, 1986, 1994) described three dominant orientations that reflect the experience of work in the United States. In the first work orientation, people view work as a job, focusing on the material benefits of work to the relative exclusion of other kinds of meaning and fulfillment. The work is simply a means to a financial end that allows people to enjoy their time away from work. Usually, the interests and ambitions of those with jobs are expressed outside of the domain of work (Wrzesniewski et al., 1997) and involve hobbies and other interests. In contrast, those with career orientations work for the rewards that come from advancement through an organizational or occupational structure. For those with careers, the increased pay, prestige, and status that come with promotion and advancement are a dominant focus in their work. Advancement brings higher self-esteem, increased power, and higher social standing (Bellah et al., 1985, p. 66). Finally, those with calling orientations work not for financial rewards or for advancement but for the fulfillment that doing the work brings. In callings, the work is an end in itself and is associated with the belief that the work makes the world a better place.

Although callings have traditionally meant being "called" by God to do morally and socially significant work (Weber, 1958, 1963), in modern times the term has lost its religious connotation and acquired a focus on doing work that contributes to the world (Davidson & Caddell, 1994). Whether the work actually does contribute to making the world a better place is defined by the individual worker: A physician who views the work as a job and is simply interested in making a good income does not have a calling, whereas a garbage collector who sees the work as making the world a cleaner, healthier place could have a calling. Our focus in this chapter is on those who work in callings, because they are maximally engaged in and passionate about their work.

In an initial investigation of work orientation, Wrzesniewski and colleagues (Wrzesniewski et al., 1997) operationalized the job, career, and calling orientations, created measures of each, and surveyed 196 people from a variety of occupations. The measures took two forms: (a) a set of three paragraphs that described a prototypical job, career, and calling person; (b) a set of 18 items that were designed to reflect the thoughts, feelings, and behaviors that were likely to accompany each work orientation. For example, it was expected that those with job orientations would report that work was largely a way to get income and that they were not deeply involved with or passionate about their work. For those with career orientations, it was expected that work would be approached with a focus on advancement, moving between jobs, and seeing one's current job as a stepping stone to other things. Finally, it was expected that those with callings would report that work was a deeply involving domain in life that they enjoyed very much and would continue in without pay if financially possible. In addition, those with callings were expected to feel that their work contributed to the world in a meaningful way.

Respondents were surprisingly unambiguous in reporting that they experienced their work as job, career, or calling. The sample was nearly evenly divided into thirds, with each third feeling that their work fit into one of the three categories. Within the sample, there was a group of 24 administrative assistants who worked in the same organization with similar levels of pay, education, and tenure. In this subsample, as in the full sample, each work orientation was represented by a third of the administrative assistants such that they were nearly evenly divided into the three work orientations. This finding suggests that even in the same job done in the same organization, there are quite meaningful differences in how people experience their work.

Overall, it appears that those with calling orientations have a stronger and more rewarding relationship to their work, which is associated with spending more time in this domain and gaining more enjoyment and satisfaction from it (Wrzesniewski et al., 1997; Wrzesniewski & Landman, 2000). These studies have not been longitudinal, thus it is impossible to posit causal relationships (i.e., does the experience of the work produce the orientation, or does the orientation shape the experience of the work?). Because we have found all three work orientations among administrative assistants (Wrzesniewski et al., 1997) and evidence of both calling and job orientations among hospital cleaners (Wrzesniewski & Dutton, 2001), it is clear that there is some effect of the individual on shaping the work experience.

The three work orientations reflect different types of connections to the domain of work—connections that vary in their intrinsic and instrumental focus and in their implications for other domains of life. Those with jobs are not likely to have a passionate connection with their work, because the work primarily represents a means to an end. Those with careers may be more deeply engaged with their work, because the work is a source of achievement in the rewards, positions, and power it yields. Only for those with callings is work a wholly enriching and meaningful activity that is a passion in its own right.

Indeed, correlates of calling orientations support this point. Many people with callings put more time in at work (Wrzesniewski et al., 1997), whether or not this time is compensated. As well, those with callings report higher job and life satisfaction than those with jobs or careers (Wrzesniewski et al., 1997). They also derive more satisfaction from the domain of work than the domain of leisure. It is interesting to note that those with jobs and careers rank the satisfaction they get from their leisure time (i.e., hobbies and friends) as higher than the satisfaction they get from work. The differences between those with callings and the other two groups are significant on each dimension. Clearly, for those with callings, work is one's passion, whereas for those with jobs and careers, the deeper satisfactions are found in leisure or in relationships outside of the workplace.

It seems likely that people with callings may demonstrate good psychological health along any number of dimensions. Traits such as optimism (Gillham, Shatte, Reivich, & Seligman, 2001), mastery (Rawsthorne & Elliott, 1999), and conscientiousness (McCrae & Costa, 1999) may be associated with having a calling. This raises the question of whether people with these traits tend to enter a line of work they view as a calling or if any line of work is likely to be viewed as such. Staw and his colleagues (1986) have found that job attitudes are highly stable over time and different kinds of jobs; thus, it may be that a calling orientation is a portable benefit of those who tend to have a more positive outlook on life in general.

THE DOMAIN OF LEISURE: PASSIONS

Unlike work, which for most people is a necessity, leisure activities have an optional quality. One would and should be surprised that people did not get pleasure out of their leisure activities. This pleasure usually means that leisure activities have intrinsic value; it is usually the case that we engage in them for the enjoyment they inspire.[1] Nonetheless, there are important differences in leisure activities with respect to how fulfilling they are and hence the extent to which they enrich life. There would seem to be two aspects to fulfillment in leisure activities. One has to do with mastery, self-improvement, and the richer pleasures that come from accomplishment and expertise. There is a sense in which a highly educated musical listener or football fan may get more out of these leisure activities than one without expertise might. A second aspect is the sense of purpose or moral accomplishment that comes from feeling that one contributes to a better life for those close to one or those far away. Both mastery and contribution add to the meaning of life. Mastery seems more important than moral fulfillment in most of the passions we have identified, with the exception of volunteer work.

There is a surprising absence of systematic investigation of passions, leisure activities, or hobbies in psychology (see Csikszentmihalyi, 2000, for a discussion of enjoyable activity). We have begun to collect descriptive data on what we call passions: a certain type of intense, focused leisure activity. For our respondents, we defined passions as follows:

> A *passion* is an overwhelming interest in some object or situation. This interest becomes one of the major foci of life, is one of the principal sources of engagement, and often costs a good percentage of one's income. On retirement, people often devote their lives to their passions. The passion can concern anything other than another human being. Examples of passions included hobbies, activities–sports (participant or spectator–fan), collecting, (e.g., stamps, bottles), artistic–creative activities, puzzles–games (including video games), books, exercise, participation in an organization, house, clothing, food–cuisine, travel. A passion is sufficiently intense that it is the principal way one spends one's leisure time. Passions must last at least one month to qualify.

Note that we excluded specific relationships with other people, leaving out romantic relationships, good friends, and family as passions. We recognize that these activities may serve some of the same functions and may possess some of the same attributes as passions, but we think that they may be

---

[1] It is possible that some leisure activities are engaged in toward some external goal, such as meeting other people or building one's resume. In this chapter, we consider those leisure activities that are ends in themselves.

distinctively different (e.g., they involve basic human bonds and are less likely to involve a substantial outlay of income). In retirement, family dedication, along with passions, probably constitute the major meaningful activities in life in the Western-developed world.

A survey that asked respondents to indicate their passions and provide some information about them was given to 235 University of Pennsylvania undergraduates (152 female, 81 male, 2 of unreported gender) and to 47 adult family members and friends (25 female, 22 male, mean age of 46 years, primarily parents) of a subset of these students. The results, by category of activity, are displayed in Table 8.1. The table lists the most common passions described by respondents, who were permitted to list up to six passions. We retained those categories that accounted for at least 4% of the responses given in one of the two groups (students and adults).

In both the student and adult samples, women and men reported similar numbers and patterns of passions. The 152 women in the student sample reported 823 passions (5.4 per person), and the 24 women in the adult sample reported 91 passions (3.8 per person). Comparable data from 81 male students included 409 passions (5.0 per person), and the 22 male adults reported 76 passions (3.5 per person).

In the student sample, women had a significantly greater number of passions related to the arts (χ^2 = 37.78; p < .001), whereas men reported

TABLE 8.1
Most Common Passions

Passion	College Students (n = 235)[a]	Adults (n = 47)[b]
Number of listed passions	1242[c]	167[d]
Sports	23% (287)**	25% (41)
Academics (reading, writing, poetry)	15% (183)	16% (26)
Art	11% (140)**	10% (16)
Music	9% (114)*	3% (5)
Entertainment (fun, games, entertainment, computer activities)	8% (102)**	7% (12)
People, social, volunteering	7% (91)	7% (11)
Collecting	6% (72)	7% (11)
Food	4% (50)	5% (9)*
Travel	4% (50)	7% (11)
Hobbies/cars	2% (21)	5% (9)
Percentage of all passions listed, constituted by above categories	87%	89%

Note. An asterisk indicates a significant sex difference: * p < .05; ** p < .001.
[a] For gender analysis, n = 233.
[b] For gender analysis, n = 46.
[c] For gender analysis, n = 1232.
[d] For gender analysis, n = 167.

a significantly greater number of passions related to entertainment (χ^2 = 11.05; $p < .001$), sports (χ^2 = 12.24; $p < .001$), and music (χ^2 = 5.18; $p < .05$). The adult sample size was small and only allows for limited conclusions on passions in relation to gender. However, the data show that female adults report a significantly greater number of passions for food than male adults. Overall, the frequency and distribution of passions is surprisingly similar across gender.

Respondents in the student and adult samples were asked to describe the effects of their strongest or most recent passion, and the results for both groups were similar. Both groups described their passions as being positive, enriching activities in their lives that offered an outlet for amusement and fun. Specifically, respondents felt that their passions sustained their mental health by offering them an outlet for stress and emotions, boosting their self-esteem, providing an escape, and offering a way to achieve focus, control, and creative expression.

From these data, we conclude that people in our sample (principally upper-middle-class Americans) generally had a positive attitude toward their passions—that is, they were glad they had them and thought that the passions enriched their lives. We recognize that this is a preliminary study on a nonrepresentative sample of Americans. However, we believe it opens the door to the study of an important part of human life, a part that has much to do with the quality of life.

Passions may have a particularly important function in retirement, when leisure activities come to dominate waking life and when the social and other rewards of work disappear. In this context, passions enrich life by personal and societal fulfillment (the latter as in volunteer work) and usually connect people into social networks of like-minded folk.

There is, of course, a relationship between callings and passions. For people with callings, work takes on most of the characteristics of passions; some describe work as their passion and intentionally allow their work to consume their leisure time. Self-realization, intrinsic value, and social fulfillment all play major roles in passions and callings. Indeed, it is possible that people with callings are less inclined to have other passions, because of the overwhelming time commitments demanded by their callings. On the other hand, the personality characteristics that incline a person to a calling, including perhaps desire for challenge and variety and motivation to improve the world, also might incline the same people to have passions and callings. We might expect, if this is true, that people with callings develop strong passions if or when they retire.

Our results suggest some intriguing hypotheses about the relationship between callings and passions. If those with callings report that work satisfactions crowd out other sources of satisfaction, then perhaps a compensatory or zero-sum relationship exists between callings and passions. In effect, those with callings may not have other passions, because their passion is their work. Such a compensatory model is supported by findings that suggest that a high degree of involvement in one's work is associated with feeling that one's leisure is unsatisfactory (Gee & Baillie, 1999). Support for the compensatory model of work and leisure has been established by others as well (Melamed & Meir, 1981; Miller & Weiss, 1982). Other research suggests that spillover between work and leisure occurs as well, such that the experience of work is reflected in the experience of leisure and vice versa (Rothbard, 1999; Rousseau, 1978). However, no research in this area addresses extremes in experiences of work and leisure. Thus, research is needed to determine if those with callings tend to have passions outside of work as well (i.e., spillover) or instead if those with passions are compensating for a work experience that reflects a job or career orientation (Wrzesniewski et al., 1997).

Support for the hypothesis that callings *are* passions to those who have them comes from recent research on the effect of work orientations on employment transitions (Wrzesniewski, 1999). When talking about their experience of the jobs they had recently found, people with calling orientations talked about their work in ways that were strikingly different from how those with job orientations talked about work. Although both groups generally found their work likable, the ways they talked about the work in their jobs were rather different. For example, one respondent from the calling orientation group of our study explicitly rejected calling her job "work," instead saying,

> It's not (work). Work, as work goes, I could do without it.
> I have enough to do here at home to keep me happy for the rest of my life. I get my satisfaction from the people I'm with, my patients and their families. Work itself, forget it.
> (Do you consider that work, when you're with the patients and families?)
> No, not when I'm there, no.

Another respondent from the calling group talked about her sense of calling and its close relationship with helping others:

> (What do you like most about your job?)
> I'm fulfilling a personal call. It is ultimately, enduringly fulfilling. It's like I just said, I like people and I like to see people get helped. And we've seen a lot of people helped.

THE DOMAIN OF FOOD: FOOD AS FUN OR FRIGHTENING

Callings and passions are human inventions. They are afforded by lives in which work options are highly varied, leisure time is plentiful, and the options for engagement during leisure are legion. In contrast, pleasure at eating is something we inherit from our mammalian and primate progenitors. It is one aspect of the general adaptive tendency, in evolution, to link pleasure with the satisfaction of basic biological needs. We did not invent the pleasure–eating link, and, on the contrary, are at risk for spoiling it. Thus, in terms of quality of life, our aim is to preserve something old rather than to create something new.

For most of human history, for almost all people in developing nations today, and for many people in developed nations, food remains something anticipated and enjoyed. For our ancestors and less fortunate contemporaries, the negative side of food and eating comes from the risk of not having enough food to eat. But just as we have created a world in which our work can be infinitely interesting and broad-ranging and our leisure can bring us into new and exciting worlds and challenges, we have also created a developed world in which food is plentiful, accessible (indeed, hard to avoid), varied, highly palatable, and relatively cheap. Built to find, consume, and conserve food, we (in the developed world) are now immersed in a world full of food. We are ill-suited to be in a world with such temptations, which satisfy our deep biological needs for nutrition and for storing away food for leaner times.

The abundance of food has been accompanied by a number of other social "advances" that help to create a worrisome side to eating. The epidemiological revolution, caused by the conquest of many infectious diseases by antibiotics, sanitation, and other environmental innovations and early detection of these diseases has produced much longer life expectancy. In the developing world people now usually die of degenerative rather than infectious diseases. Many modern diseases are typically insidious in onset and slow in course, unlike the formerly rapid effects of food poisoning. Although we might have felt "safe" hours or days after eating a primeval meal, we now wonder about the lingering effects of our diets, slowly building up arterial plaques, the likelihood of cancer, and other ills. We are fostered in these concerns by the availability, in the last decades of the 20th century, of substantial epidemiological and experimental evidence, of a sort never generally available before. We hear constantly about risky activities, particularly risky foods, and in the United States have come to the point where risk factors (e.g., high blood pressure and cholesterol) are treated as if they are diseases.

The abundance of cheap and tasty food has collaborated with other societal advances, which have made it possible for us to go through life, working and playing, while hardly moving. Cars, electric garage door openers, phones, television, and the Internet all allow us to do what we have to do without much physical activity. The combination of plentiful food and relative inactivity has led to an increased prevalence of obesity in the developed world, especially in the United States. Obesity has two negative consequences: It increases some health risks, about which we worry, and it makes us less attractive in our own eyes and in the eyes of others. As a result, we have widespread dieting, especially in women. Dieting itself is not necessarily problematic with respect to the quality of life, except that dieting is usually unsuccessful, resulting in both a deprivation of pleasure and a sense of failure (Seligman, 1994). In the United States, a fair percentage of college students (25 to 30) confess that they would choose a nutritive, inexpensive pill as an alternative to eating (Rozin, Bauer, & Catanese, 2002; Rozin, Fischler, Imada, Sarubin, & Wrzesniewski, 1999). It would not be pleasurable, but it might put temptation to rest and would likely produce desirable weight loss.

Thus, in the United States, and to a lesser extent other Western countries, we are faced with major food ambivalence, especially in women. Food is necessary for life and fun, but it also causes obesity and, in the eyes of many, is a source of major disease risk factors: fats, sugars, and a myriad of potential toxins, including pesticides, synthetic chemicals, and (perish the thought) naturally harmful compounds. It is our view that for many Americans, worries about eating have come to dominate the pleasures of eating; there is little doubt that these worries have eroded the quality of life and reduced the intrinsic and largely innate pleasures of eating. However, such worries are often unfounded or at least exaggerated: For health, eating is still better than not eating. Americans seem to have come to believe that food itself is a risk factor. They have, in our view, come to exaggerate the admittedly significant effect of diet on disease. Worry about diet may have positive health consequences insofar as it leads to an improved diet, but the worry per se is surely not good for the pleasure of life, and may itself be harmful to health. Thus, worry about diet and dieting has both costs and benefits.

The French seem to have found a different way to balance the costs and benefits of eating (Rozin, 1999; Rozin et al., 1999). The French are legendary for their love of food and wine, their care in preparing it, and the richness and variety of their cuisine. Meals are occasions of note in France. But, at least in the view of American doctors and the average American, this apparent food indulgence should come at a price. However, French life expectancy is slightly higher than American life expectancy. In what has been termed the "French paradox" (Renaud & Logeril, 1992), the French have a much lower mortality from cardiovascular disease than Americans. How do the French manage this miracle, and can we learn from them?

Americans seem to think diet is responsible for most of their ills, and have therefore gravitated to the idea that it is wine, a food, that protects the French from the ravages that their diet would otherwise take out upon them. Wine is the most popular account for the French paradox. Although wine may contribute to the relatively healthier lifestyle of the French, there are many things we can learn from the French, in addition to moderate wine drinking.

First, and perhaps most critically, although the French diet is modestly higher in fat than the American diet (Drewnowski et al., 1996), it is lower in calories. The French simply eat less food, and by most accounts, it is calories that are the single biggest threat to health (and surely to our national waistline). But how is it that the French eat less than we do, with all that delicious food and all that time spent at the table? The French face their plates, and their meal companions, for much more time than Americans do. It is well-known that the more time one faces palatable food, the more one will eat. We do not want to claim that French food is unpalatable, as that seems highly unlikely. Thus, the paradox deepens.

How, then, is it that the French eat less food than Americans? Much of the answer has to do with tradition and ecology. The French tradition is to eat slowly and for a long time in a positive social environment. The tradition is to pay attention to the food one is eating, as opposed to shoveling it in the mouth while talking about other matters. The tradition is to not eat between meals. These traditions are represented in the ecology; in the fact that restaurants expect meals to take hours, in the lower chance that a television set dominates the dining room, and in the much lower availability of street food. Eating slowly allows satiation to increase during the meal. The upshot is that the French seem to get more experience of tasting food while eating less of it. They enjoy more while eating less. Perhaps the major determinant of how much we eat is how much we put in front of people. The French put less food in front of people; their portion sizes, whether in restaurants or individual containers of yogurt, are noticeably smaller than those in the United States (Rozin, Kabnick, Pete, Fischler, & Shields, 2002).

In a similar way, the French traditions and ecology discourage driving and encourage walking and bicycling. The necessities of life are closer at hand, gas is expensive, and parking is often difficult. Getting the car out of a crowded garage is time consuming, often involving getting in and out of the car two or three times to open and close doors.

As Peter Stearns (1997) has pointed out in his excellent comparison of the evolution of French and American culture over the past 100 years, there is a strong tradition of moderation in France, contrasted with a strong tradition of excess in the United States. The American Thanksgiving dinner, which is a failure if people can get up from the table, is totally foreign to the French view of a celebratory meal. This difference clearly maps into issues such as portion size.

Another reason for the relative success of the French in the domain of food is that the French are less concerned with the instrumental aspects of eating: nutrition, and more critically, risks associated with particular foods. Although the American view (especially in the upper and upper-middle-classes) often frames food in terms of risks and benefits, or conflicts between pleasure and health, the French view is more unimodal and positive. The French recognize that, in general, food and eating are good for health, whereas Americans behave as if they are not so sure. These attitude differences are illustrated in a recent study that compared French and American attitudes to food and eating (Rozin et al., 1999). The French appeared to eat less of foods modified to be healthier (e.g., fat removed) and to be more food-focused, less worried about health and diet, and more inclined to think of foods in terms of the experience of eating them rather than their physiological effects.

American ambivalence about food is demonstrated in free associations to the word "chocolate" in France and the United States. Although about 20% of U.S. college students mention a fat word (fat, fatty, fattening) as one of the first three words that comes to mind when they think of chocolate, only about 5% of French college students offer such a word (Rozin, Kurzer, Lee, & Cohen, 2000). In free associations to the word "food," fat is the third most common word among American college females, and falls much lower in France (Rozin, Kurzer, & Cohen, in press). Among American college females, some 12 to 15% admit to being embarrassed about *buying* a bar of chocolate (*we* were embarrassed to ask this question in France!; Rozin et al., 2000). When college student respondents are asked whether they associate chocolate cake with guilt or celebration, 22% of Americans, versus 14% of French, choose guilt. These and other effects we describe reliably show higher ambivalence in females than males, in both the United States and France.

Another major difference between French and Americans has to do with the importance of food in life, within a positive context. Given a choice for a vacation between a week at a luxury hotel with average food or a hotel with a normal comfort level with gourmet food, for the same price, 76% of Americans choose the luxury hotel, in comparison to 10% of the French. For the example mentioned previously, of a choice of an inexpensive, nutritive pill or eating, 28% of the American students choose the pill, but only 10% of comparable French respondents do. These and other results (Rozin et al., 1999) suggest that eating and enjoying food is a moderately ambivalent experience for Americans, whereas it is much more of a unidimensionally positive experience in France. A consequence is more pleasure and less worry about food in France than in the United States. It remains to be seen whether this more pleasure-oriented and relaxed attitude extends to other domains in which entertainment and health may be in opposition.

Of course, if the Americans are right about the risks of eating even moderate amounts of "bad" foods, then the French are trading short-term pleasure for a shorter life. But, as the record shows, the French do not pay this price. Some combination of their modest food intake, low stress and worry in the food domain (and perhaps others), particular food choices (e.g., red wine), and perhaps genetics, medical system, and other institutional factors seem to promote both health and the good life. It is also possible that Americans and the American medical profession exaggerate the admittedly substantial effects of diet on health.

Food is clearly a source of pleasure, and is also clearly related to health. So are driving, mountain climbing, walking, living in urban environments, marriage, and a myriad of other human activities. The French–American comparison raises the suggestion that any society may balance these risks and benefits in a nonoptimal way, and that it is possible for societies to learn from one another.

CONCLUSION

The total amount of time spent working, in leisure activities, and in eating surely varies greatly across age, social class, and culture. Retired people spend less time working than younger adults, French spend more time eating than Americans (while eating less!), people in developing nations may spend less time at leisure activities than people in developed nations. Our claim is that in all of these domains, the time spent can be more or less pleasant and fulfilling. Eating is more about pleasure (and filling, but not fulfilling), whereas there is more of a combination of pleasure and fulfillment in work and leisure. Work and eating are necessities of life; the question is how much positive experience we can make out of a necessity. Leisure is a luxury, in which pleasure is presumed, and the question is the degree of pleasure and the amount of fulfillment that can be attained. Ideally, one enjoys a leisure experience as it is occurring and at the same time feels a sense of personal and moral fulfillment.

Tibor Scitovsky (1976) made the important distinction between plea-sures and comforts. According to Scitovsky, comforts are background im-provements in life, such as air conditioning, which make life generally easier but which are things we adapt to. Pleasures are unique events, like good meals, evenings with friends, vacations, and concerts, which have the type of variety and distinctiveness to which we do not adapt. As a result, it is proposed that pleasures contribute more to the quality of life than do com-forts. This difference is no doubt enhanced when we consider not only experienced pleasure but also anticipated pleasure and remembered pleasure

(Kahneman, Wakker, & Sarin, 1997). We do not remember or anticipate our car air conditioning or its quietness in the same way that we do concerts or meals. As Scitovsky pointed out, cultures differ in the degree to which they apportion time and expenditures to these two broad domains, and it seems clear (to Scitovsky and us, at least) that Americans favor comforts much more than do Europeans.

The French food example suggests an important and largely ignored dimension that operates to enhance pleasure and perhaps fulfillment as well. This has to do with the ecology of the environment of artifacts created by each culture. The traditions of long, social meals, no snacking, and attention to food are manifested environmentally, in the design of restaurants and the absence of street food. Walking and bicycle riding, as alternatives to driving, are promoted by high gas prices, inconvenient parking, locally accessible food and other stores, and the difficulties of getting the car from the garage to the street.

Similarly, passions, and most critically, passions that are both self- and other-fulfilling, are promoted by cultural valuation of such activities, the availability of such activities in one's environment, and their presence in family and friendship networks. Most people develop passions by exposure to them, often through admired others (Bandura, 1977). The ecology of the work environment is, perhaps, less determinative of the development of callings than ecology is for play and eating. But it must be true that the social environment, including the example of callings in one's fellow workers, has some influence on the individual.

The forms that passions can take are likely more varied than the picture offered by our data. We surveyed students and adults from an upper-middle-class population, and although there was a wide range of passions reported, others may be represented in greater numbers among those from other class groups. For example, passions for academics and travel may be unavailable or unimportant to a large percentage of the population. It remains an interesting empirical question to determine the form and function of passions across a wide spectrum of society.

As it happens, distinctive pleasures and actions (e.g., special meals, special acts of kindness, special accomplishments in passions or at work) often produce the ideal result with respect to improving the quality of life. They provide some or all of experienced pleasure, pleasant memories, pleasant anticipations, a sense of personal fulfillment or accomplishment, and a sense of moral fulfillment by making the world, or somebody else's world, a better place. In at least some of these cases, these special pleasures are compatible with, or even promoting of, good health. This is a substantial package of rewards that is bound to improve the quality of life. It is definitely, in Robert Wright's (2000) sense, a non–zero-sum game.

Overall, the more we know about the acquisition of intrinsic value, the development of values that extend beyond the self, and the way that the cultural ecology promotes these, the more we will be able to make the most of most moments in our waking lives.

REFERENCES

Alderfer, C. (1972). *Human needs in organizational settings*. New York: Free Press.

Bandura, A. (1977). *Social learning theory*. New York: Prentice-Hall.

Baumeister, R. F. (1991). *Meanings of life*. New York: Guilford Press.

Bellah, R. N., Madsen, R., Sullivan, W. M., Swidler, A., & Tipton, S. M. (1985). *Habits of the heart: Individualism and commitment in American life*. New York: Harper & Row.

Campbell, A., Converse, P., & Rodgers, W. (1976). *The quality of American life: Perceptions, evaluations, and satisfactions*. New York: Russell Sage Foundation.

Castillo, J. J. (1997). Looking for the meaning of work. *Work and Occupations, 24*, 413–425.

Csikszentmihalyi, M. (2000). *Beyond boredom and anxiety*. San Francisco: Jossey-Bass.

Davidson, J. C., & Caddell, D. P. (1994). Religion and the meaning of work. *Journal for the Scientific Study of Religion, 33*, 135–147.

Deci, E. L., & Ryan, R.M. (1985). *Intrinsic motivation and self-determination in human behavior*. New York: Plenum Press.

Drewnowski, A., Henderson, S. A., Shore, A. B., Fischler, C., Preziosi, P., et al. (1996). Diet quality and dietary diversity in France: Implications for the French paradox. *Journal of the American Dietetic Association, 96*, 663–669.

Dubin, R. (1956). Industrial workers' worlds: A study of the "central life interests" of industrial workers. *Social Problems, 3*, 131–142.

Gee, S., & Baillie, J. (1999). Happily ever after? An exploration of retirement expectations. *Educational Gerontology, 25*, 109–128.

Gillham, J. E., Shatte, A. J., Reivich, K. J., & Seligman, M. E. P. (2001). Optimism, pessimism, and explanatory style. In E. C. Chang (Ed.), *Optimism and pessimism: Implications for theory, research, and practice* (pp. 53–75). Washington, DC: American Psychological Association.

Griffin, R. W. (1987). Toward an integrated theory of task design. *Research in Organizational Behavior, 9*, 79–120.

Hackman, J. R., & Lawler, E. E. (1971). Employee reactions to job characteristics. *Journal of Applied Psychology, 55*, 259–286.

Hackman J. R., & Oldham, G. R. (1976). Motivation through the design of work: Test of a theory. *Organization Behavior and Human Decision Processes, 16*, 250–279.

Hackman, J. R., & Oldham, G. R. (1980). *Work redesign*. Reading, MA: Addison-Wesley.

Herzberg, F., Mausner, B., & Snyderman, B. B. (1959). *The motivation to work*. New York: Wiley.

Kahneman, D., Wakker, P. P., & Sarin, R. (1997). Back to Bentham? Explorations of experienced utility. *The Quarterly Journal of Economics, 112,* 375–405.

Kanungo, R. N. (1981). Work alienation and involvement: Problems and prospects. *International Review of Applied Psychology, 30,* 1–15.

Kanungo, R. N. (1982). Measurement of job and work involvement. *Journal of Applied Psychology, 67,* 341–349.

Kanungo, R. N., & Hartwick, J. (1987). An alternative to the intrinsic–extrinsic dichotomy of work rewards. *Journal of Management, 13,* 751–766.

Kohn, M. L., Schooler, C., Miller, J., Miller, K. A., & Schoenberg, R. (1983). *Work and personality: An inquiry into the impact of social stratification*. Norwood, NJ: Ablex.

Lepper, M. R. (1983). Social-control processes and the internalization of social values: An attributional perspective. In E. T. Higgins, D. N. Ruble, & W. W. Hartup (Eds.), *Social cognition and social development* (pp. 294–330). New York: Cambridge University Press.

Lodahl, T. M., & Kejner, M. (1965). The definition and measurement of job involvement. *Journal of Applied Psychology, 49,* 24–33.

Loscocco, K. A. (1989). The interplay of personal and job characteristics in determining work commitment. *Social Science Research, 18,* 370–394.

McCrae, R. R., & Costa, P. T. (1999). A five-factor theory of personality. In L. A. Pervin (Ed.), *Handbook of personality: Theory and research* (2nd ed., pp. 139–153). New York: Guilford Press.

Meaning of Work International Research Team (MOW). (1987). *The meaning of working*. New York: Academic Press.

Melamed, S., & Meir, E. I. (1981). The relationship between interests-job incongruity and selection of a vocational activity. *Journal of Vocational Behavior, 18,* 310–325.

Miller, L. E., & Weiss, R. M. (1982). The work-leisure relationship: Evidence for the compensatory hypothesis. *Human Relations, 35,* 763–771.

Morse, N. C., & Weiss, R. S. (1955). The function and meaning of work and the job. *American Sociological Review, 20,* 191–198.

Nord, W. R., Brief, A. P., Atieh, J. M., & Doherty, E. M. (1990). Studying meanings of work: The case of work values. In A. Brief & W. Nord (Eds.), *Meanings of occupational work: A collection of essays* (pp. 21–64). Lexington, MA: Lexington Books.

Oldham, G. R., & Hackman, J. R. (1981). Relationships between organizational structure and employee reactions: Comparing alternative frameworks. *Administrative Science Quarterly, 26,* 66–83.

Rawsthorne, L. J., & Elliott, A. J. (1999). Achievement goals and intrinsic motivation: A meta-analytic review. *Personality & Social Psychology Review, 3*, 326–344.

Renaud, S., & Logeril, M. de. (1992). Wine, alcohol, platelets, and the French paradox for coronary heart disease. *Lancet, 339*, 1523–1526.

Roberson, L. (1990). Functions of work meanings in organizations: Work meanings and work motivation. In A. Brief & W. Nord (Eds.), *Meanings of occupational work: A collection of essays* (pp. 107–134). Lexington, MA: Lexington Books.

Rothbard, N. P. (1999). *Enriching or depleting? The dynamics of engagement in work and family.* Unpublished doctoral dissertation, University of Michigan, Ann Arbor.

Rousseau, D. M. (1978). Relationship of work to nonwork. *Journal of Applied Psychology, 63*, 513–517.

Rozin, P. (1999). Food is fundamental, fun, frightening, and far-reaching. *Social Research, 66*, 9–30.

Rozin, P., Bauer, R., & Catanese, D. (2002). *Attitudes to food and the role of food in life in American college students: Comparison of six regions and campuses.* Submitted manuscript.

Rozin, P., Fischler, C., Imada, S., Sarubin, A., & Wrzesniewski, A. (1999). Attitudes to food and the role of food in the U.S.A., Japan, Flemish Belgium and France: Possible implications for the diet-health debate. *Appetite, 33*, 163–180.

Rozin, P., Kabnick, K., Pete, E., Fischler, C., & Shields, C. (2002). *Naturalistic measurements of French versus American interactions with food.* Unpublished manuscript.

Rozin, P., Kurzer, N., & Cohen, A. (in press). Free associations to "food": The effects of gender, generation, and culture. *Journal of Research in Personality.*

Rozin, P., Kurzer, N., Lee, D., & Cohen, A. (2000). *Free associations to "chocolate": The effects of gender, generation, and culture.* Unpublished manuscript.

Salancik, G. R., & Pfeffer, J. (1978). A social information processing approach to job attitudes and task design. *Administrative Science Quarterly, 23*, 224–253.

Samuelson, R. J. (Ed.). (1990). *The Economist book of vital world statistics.* New York: Random House.

Scitovsky, T. (1976). *The joyless economy: An inquiry into human satisfaction and consumer dissatisfaction.* New York: Oxford University Press.

Schwartz, B. (1986). *The battle for human nature: Science, morality, and modern life.* New York: W. W. Norton.

Schwartz, B. (1994). *The costs of living: How market freedom erodes the best things in life.* New York: W. W. Norton.

Seligman, M. E. P. (1994). *What you can change and what you can't.* New York: Knopf.

Staw, B. M., Bell, N. E., & Clausen, J. A. (1986). The dispositional approach to job attitudes. *Administrative Science Quarterly, 31*, 56–77.

Stearns, P. (1997). *Fat history: Bodies and beauty in the modern West.* New York: New York University Press.

Vecchio, R. P. (1980). The function and meaning of work and the job: Morse and Weiss (1955) revisited. *Academy of Management Journal, 23*, 361–367.

Weber, M. (1958). *The Protestant ethic and the spirit of capitalism*. New York: Scribner.

Weber, M. (1963). *The sociology of religion*. Boston: Beacon.

Wright, R. (2000). *Non-zero: The logic of human destiny*. New York: Random House.

Wrzesniewski, A. (1999). *Jobs, careers, and callings: Work orientation and job transitions*. Doctoral dissertation, University of Michigan, Ann Arbor.

Wrzesniewski, A., & Dutton, J. E. (2001). Crafting a job: Revisioning employees as active crafters of their work. *Academy of Management Review, 26*, 179–201.

Wrzesniewski, A., & Landman, J. (2000). *Occupational choice and regret: Decision antecedents and their outcomes*. Unpublished manuscript.

Wrzesniewski, A., McCauley, C. R., Rozin, P., & Schwartz, B. (1997). Jobs, careers, and callings: People's relations to their work. *Journal of Research in Personality, 31*, 21–33.

9

WELL-BEING IN THE WORKPLACE AND ITS RELATIONSHIP TO BUSINESS OUTCOMES: A REVIEW OF THE GALLUP STUDIES

JAMES K. HARTER, FRANK L. SCHMIDT, AND COREY L. M. KEYES

Two lines of research characterize the study of the effects of organizational environment on workers' quality of life and performance. The first line originates with the study of stress and health and is best represented by the theory of person–environment fit (see French, Caplan, & Van Harrison, 1982). Proponents of the stress perspective argue that worker performance and quality of life are hindered by strain (too much challenge) or boredom (too little challenge). When demands exceed or fall below the resources, individuals experience undesirable states (e.g., strain or boredom) that hinder the quality and quantity of performance as well as their well-being. From the stress perspective, a healthy work force means the absence of strain or boredom (see also Edwards, Caplan, & Van Harrison, 1998).

A second line of research on worker quality of life and performance originates with the behavioral, cognitive, and health benefits of positive feelings and positive perceptions (Isen, 1987; Warr, 1999). Proponents of the well-being perspective argue that the presence of positive emotional states and positive appraisals of the worker and his or her relationships within the workplace accentuate worker performance and quality of life. When environments provide and people seek out interesting, meaningful, and challenging tasks, individuals in these situations are likely to have what Brim (1992) has called manageable difficulties and Csikszentmihalyi (1997)

The authors gratefully acknowledge the support of The Gallup Organization. We dedicate this chapter to Dr. Donald O. Clifton, who has pioneered the theory and application of positive psychology in business. We also thank Jon Haidt and Amy Wrzesniewski for their helpful comments on an earlier draft of this chapter.

has described as optimal states. That is, when demands match or slightly exceed resources, individuals experience positive emotional states (e.g., pleasure, joy, energy) and they perceive themselves as growing, engaged, and productive (Waterman, 1993). From the well-being perspective, a healthy work force means the presence of positive feelings in the worker that should result in happier and more productive workers.

In this chapter we focus on the well-being approach to understand the benefits of promoting the well-being of workers. We present the results of a meta-analysis of the relationships between employee workplace perceptions and business-unit outcomes. We investigate and demonstrate that the presence of positive workplace perceptions and feelings are associated with higher business-unit customer loyalty, higher profitability, higher productivity, and lower rates of turnover. Our chapter relates to the reemergence of interest in the happy–productive worker hypothesis. This hypothesis positions organizations to capitalize on changing trends in a work force that is increasingly seeking greater purpose and growth through their work, and, as well, has increasing choice in where to work.

We see *well-being* as a broad category that encompasses a number of workplace factors. Within the overall category of well-being we discuss a hypothesized model that employee engagement (a combination of cognitive and emotional antecedent variables in the workplace) generates higher frequency of positive affect (job satisfaction, commitment, joy, fulfillment, interest, caring). Positive affect then relates to the efficient application of work, employee retention, creativity, and ultimately business outcomes.

WELL-BEING AND EMPLOYEES IN THE WORKPLACE

The well-being of employees is in the best interest of communities and organizations. The workplace is a significant part of an individual's life that affects his or her life and the well-being of the community. The average adult spends much of his or her life working, as much as a quarter or perhaps a third of his waking life in work. As much as a fifth to a quarter of the variation in adult life satisfaction can be accounted for by satisfaction with work (Campbell, Converse, & Rodgers, 1976). Measures of job satisfaction tend to correlate in the range of .50 to .60 with measures of life satisfaction (Judge & Watanabe, 1993; Spector, 1997). The nature of work, such as its routinization, supervision, and complexity, has been linked causally to an individual's sense of control and depression (Kohn & Schooler, 1982). It is now recognized that depression is second only to ischemic heart disease in contributing to reductions in productive and healthy years of life (Murray & Lopez, 1996). The ability of the workplace to prevent mental illness and to promote well-being is compatible with the mission of the public's health, as outlined by the surgeon general (U.S. Department of Health and Human Services, 1999).

However, the well-being of employees is also in the best interests of employers who spend substantial resources hiring employees and trying to generate products, profits, and maintain loyal customers. To succeed in hiring, employers must provide tangible benefits. However, employees want more than a stable job with pension and benefits. Surveys of recent and upcoming generations of employees clearly show a majority of employees desire greater meaning and personal development from their work and suggest many workers see their work as a calling—enjoyable, fulfilling, and socially useful (Avolio & Sosik, 1999; Wrzesniewski, McCauley, Rozin, & Schwartz, 1997; see also chapter 8, this volume).

Studies now clearly suggest that the well-being of employees may be in the best interest of the employer. In particular, researchers have studied the relationship of individual-level job satisfaction to individual-level performance (Iaffaldano & Muchinsky, 1985; Judge, Thoresen, Bono, & Patton, 2001). Meta-analyses reveal positive relationships between job satisfaction and individual performance, particularly facets such as satisfaction with one's supervisor and satisfaction with one's work. Still, questions of the direction and causality of these relationships have not been resolved completely. Spector's (1997) review suggested that more satisfied employees are more cooperative, more helpful to their colleagues, more punctual and time-efficient, show up for more days of work, and stay with the company longer than dissatisfied employees. Investigation of the happy–productive worker clearly links emotional well-being with work performance. Employees who report experiencing a greater balance of positive emotional symptoms over negative emotional symptoms received higher performance ratings from supervisors than employees who report feeling more negative than positive symptoms of emotion (Wright & Bonnett, 1997; Wright & Cropanzano, 2000; Wright & Staw, 1999).

In sum, work is a pervasive and influential part of the individual and the community's well-being. It affects the quality of an individual's life and his or her mental health, and thereby can affect the productivity of entire communities. The ability to promote well-being rather than engender strains and mental illness is of considerable benefit not only to employees in the community but also to the employer's bottom line. The emotional well-being of employees and their satisfaction with their work and workplace affect citizenship at work, turnover rates, and performance ratings. However, researchers have conceived employee well-being broadly and often not in a way that is intuitively actionable for managers and employees. Moreover, few studies have linked a measure of employee well-being to business-unit outcomes, such as employee turnover, customer loyalty, productivity, and profitability.

ELEMENTS OF WELL-BEING THAT CAN BE INFLUENCED BY MANAGERS AND EMPLOYEES

Over the course of the past 30 years, Gallup researchers have qualitatively and quantitatively assessed the most salient employee perceptions of management practices. Researchers with The Gallup Organization have conducted hundreds of qualitative focus groups across a wide variety of industries. The methodology underlying this research has been centered on the study of success—the study of productive work groups and individuals rather than the study of failure in organizations. In developing measures of employee perceptions, researchers have focused on the consistently important human resource issues that managers can influence. From this, a simple and focused employee survey consisting of 12 statements has evolved from a number of qualitative and quantitative studies. The meta-analysis reviewed in this chapter is part of an ongoing study of the performance relatedness and utility of these core aspects of employee satisfaction and engagement across organizations. The technical details of this meta-analysis can be found in Harter and Schmidt (2000) and Harter, Schmidt, and Hayes (2002). The 12 survey statements included in the Gallup Workplace Audit (GWA) are as follows:[1]

1. I know what is expected of me at work.
2. I have the materials and equipment I need to do my work right.
3. At work, I have the opportunity to do what I do best every day.
4. In the last seven days, I have received recognition or praise for doing good work.
5. My supervisor or someone at work seems to care about me as a person.
6. There is someone at work who encourages my development.
7. At work, my opinions seem to count.
8. The mission/purpose of my company makes me feel my job is important.
9. My associates (fellow employees) are committed to doing quality work.
10. I have a best friend at work.
11. In the last six months, someone at work has talked to me about my progress.
12. This last year, I have had opportunities at work to learn and grow.

---

[1] These 12 statements are proprietary and copyrighted by The Gallup Organization. They cannot be reprinted or reproduced in any manner without the written consent of The Gallup Organization. Copyright © 1992–1999, The Gallup Organization, Princeton, NJ. All rights reserved.

As a current quality standard, these 12 statements are asked of each employee (census survey) with six-response options (5 = strongly agree, 1 = strongly disagree, 6 = don't know/does not apply option score). Although these items measure issues that can be influenced by the manager or supervisor, only one item contains the word "supervisor." This is because it is realistic to assume that numerous people in the workplace can influence whether someone's expectations are clear, they feel cared about, and so forth. However, the manager or supervisor is in a position in which he or she can take the lead in establishing a culture that values behaviors that support these perceptions.

Although many variables can be studied and many methodologies used, it is important that survey tools can be used to create meaningful change in the workplace. Not surprisingly, a recent study demonstrates that giving feedback on surveys relates to improvement in upward (direct report to manager) feedback scores (Walker & Smither, 1999). As well, in Gallup's organizational work, we have found the importance of the supervisor in the feedback process is critical. The variability in workplace perceptions across work groups within the typical company is nearly as wide as the variation across work groups in all companies. Therefore, what managers actually do to influence engagement likely varies widely within companies.

The GWA items are measures of antecedents to positive affective constructs such as "job satisfaction" and, theoretically, positive emotions. We refer to the GWA as a measure of employee "engagement," which assumes both cognitive and emotional antecedents to broader affective and performance outcomes. Others (e.g., Diener, 2000) have studied and written about the broader construct of subjective well-being (life satisfaction), of which the workplace is one part. The broader psychological and social well-being definition has, interestingly, some parallel to our definition of workplace well-being (personal growth, purpose in life, positive relations with others, environmental mastery, social integration, and social contribution; Keyes, 1998).

Before looking more closely at the strengths of the connections of GWA items to business outcomes, it is important to explore why they may exist in productive environments and their potential roots and causes.

THEORETICAL FOUNDATIONS OF EMPLOYEE ENGAGEMENT IN THE WORKPLACE

Referring back to the initial perspective of stress versus well-being, cognitive–emotional research sheds some light on why positive and negative emotions interact differently with cognition. Ellis and Ashbrook (1989) reviewed how depressed mood states interact with memory. Depressed research participants, when compared to neutral participants, demonstrate poorer recall of difficult (high-effort) material and no loss in recall from low-effort materials. Depression can filter cognition, particularly when complex cognition is needed, like that in most work environments. Although negative emotions, such as depression, may limit cognition, positive affect may "loosen" information-processing strategies (Fiedler, 1988; Schwarz & Bless, 1991) and broaden cognitive potential. As well, positive affect influences creative thinking (Fredrickson, 1998; Isen, 1987; Ziv, 1976).

We can understand how this contrast between positive and negative emotion plays out in the workplace if we consider how ongoing organizational changes are dealt with in differing ways by management and the resulting consequences. In focus group transcripts from one work group within an organization experiencing some restructuring changes, employees said,

> We have undergone many changes, but our manager has kept us informed of the changes, why they are occurring, and asked us for our advice. . .about how we can keep meeting our clients' needs. Being involved in the business frees us up to get to know one another and makes our solutions more creative.

Another workgroup within the same organization experienced something very different:

> The change in restructuring that our organization has undergone scares us. Many good people left the company and the new people that have taken over don't know the business . . . our history was having very loyal people, that bleed [the company colors]. In our new culture it isn't there . . .we have moved from two-way communication to becoming order takers. Decisions would be more effective, and there would be more ownership if decisions were made listening to those close to the customer. Basically, we're being told "don't think . . . just do," and we lose our innovation . . . many people feel they will get fired if they make a good change.

We can see how this difference between the positive management in the first scenario leads to higher frequency of positive emotions and the second scenario leads to higher frequency of negative emotions.

Frederickson (1998) proposed a "broaden and build" model that describes how positive emotions "broaden people's momentary thought action repertoires" and "build their enduring personal resources" (p. 300). Positive emotions broaden scope of attention, cognition, and action, and build physical, intellectual, and social resources. Frederickson theorizes that positive emotion has evolutionary roots. Although many negative emotions may lead to fight or flight actions and a narrowing of cognitive activity, it is possible that the broadening of scope of attention that is realized through positive emotions leads to more enduring thoughts and actions that then relate to successful business outcomes within organizations. This suggests that positive emotions have connections to our most basic emotional needs in the workplace. In the workplace, positive emotions occur through daily experiences and predisposed traits; for instance, conscientiousness has a positive relationship to workplace engagement, and it is likely the interaction of traits and daily experiences that ultimately influences the frequency of positive emotions.

In considering workplace attitudes that relate most highly to business outcomes, among the four positive emotions highlighted by Frederickson (1998)—joy (happiness, amusement, elation), interest (curiosity, intrigue, excitement, or wonder), contentment (tranquility or serenity), and love (emotions felt toward specific individuals)—it seems joy, interest, and love (or caring) come closest to describing employees' emotions in high-performing business units. On the surface, it may seem easy to equate the broad construct of job satisfaction with contentment (high certainty and low effort). More specifically, in observing a variety of high-performing workplaces across industries and job types, it became clear that the definition of employee engagement that cut across companies, boundaries, even cultures represented high cognitive and emotional activity. As such, we can see that daily occurrences that bring about joy, interest, and love (or caring) lead to a bonding of individuals to each other, their work, and their organization. To managers, when they pay attention and respond to each unique individual they manage, the daily experiences lead to higher frequency of joy, interest, and love (or caring) among their employees. This appears to be a very important, active, ongoing endeavor on the part of management and employees. Over time, this serves to build a bond between the individual employee and other employees in the organization, some at a local level and others that represent other higher level authorities or agents to the company. Per Kahn's (1990) conceptualization, employees become more cognitively and emotionally engaged when their basic needs are met. Parallels can be found in the study of student engagement (Skinner, Wellborn, & Connell, 1990), which suggests engagement as a basic human need mediating the relationship between the environment and performance. The positive emotions that result when basic needs are met in the workplace serve to broaden the employees' attention, cognition, and action in areas related to the welfare of the business. Our experience is that most employees have an inherent need to contribute to an organization or larger entity. In most situations, their needs and that of the organization can be fulfilled simultaneously.

Basic needs in the workplace start with clarity of expectations and basic materials and equipment being provided. To some extent, these needs, when met, reflect the credibility of the organization to the employee. "Is the company helping me understand the ultimate outcomes and supplying me with what I need to get it done?" In transcripts of employee interviews, one employee said, "My manager lets me handle some situations my way, but the ultimate outcomes that I am to achieve are clear between me and her." Another said, "I always know what I need to do when I show up. The managers take good care of me." Contrast this to an employee who said, "I was never taught how to handle my responsibilities in this job and never told what I am expected to do," or "I feel there is no opportunity for me to succeed in my job. The company's changing policies get in the way." If expectations are not clear and basic materials and equipment not provided, negative emotions such as boredom or resentment may result, and the employee may then become focused on surviving more than thinking about how he can help the organization succeed. In contrast, when expectations are clear and basic material needs provided, positive emotions such as interest may result.

Second, it is important that employees feel that they are contributing to the organization. Perhaps the most important basic element of this contribution is person–environment fit. Do the individual employees have an opportunity to do what they do best in their current roles? Numerous studies have documented the utility of selection of the right people for particular jobs (Fredrickson, 1998; Hunter & Schmidt, 1983; Huselid, 1995; Schmidt, Hunter, McKenzi, & Muldrow, 1979; Schmidt & Rader, 1999). It is important that what the employee is asked to do is something he or she inherently enjoys. As one employee said, "I like working in a company where my talents, knowledge, and skill are understood and put to good use and respected." Contrast this to an employee who said, "The lack of interaction with people that comes with my current job gets boring without having long human contact." Many employees do not get bored without long human contact. As well, frequent and immediate recognition for good work is important to create positive emotions that reinforce success. When individuals hear from others how they have succeeded, it appears to open their mind and broaden their thinking about how they can do more. An important element of recognition appears to be the understanding of how each person prefers to be recognized, to make it objective and real by basing it on performance, and to do it frequently. Feelings of contribution are also heavily influenced by relationships and developmental opportunities. For each person, feeling cared about may mean something different, depending on their unique traits, values, and whether or not their manager listens to them and responds to their needs. Great managers appear to be very keen at finding the connection between the needs of the individual and the needs of the organization, which can lead to greater frequency of positive emotions such as joy, interest, and love (caring).

Third, a sense of belonging to something beyond oneself is an important element of employee engagement and a basic human need (Baumeister &

Leary, 1995). When decisions are made in the workplace that affect employees, having their opinions heard and involving them in the decisions can influence interest, which broadens the scope of thinking and acting. As well, employees who can connect their work to a larger, meaningful mission or purpose of the overall organization are likely to have higher levels of interest (Wrzesniewski et al., 1997) and ownership for organizational outcomes. As the individual is doing his or her work, he or she is constantly reminded (through the common mission or purpose) of the big-picture impact of what the work relates to, whether it is the customer, safety in the workplace, or the general public. Friendships at work also appear to be vital and a key differentiator between successful work groups and less successful work groups. When negative situations occur at work, strong friendships help to build social resources that can be relied on to perhaps undo the effects of negative emotions. As one employee said, "The people I work with are now some of my best friends, and that makes working fun, and that gets passed on to our customers." The positive emotions that occur through friendships (love–caring) at work likely build resources that reinforce creativity and communication. Great managers appear to be very good at creating opportunities for people at work to get to know one another.

Fourth, creating an environment in which employees have opportunities to discuss their progress and grow leads to positive emotions that can build intellectual resources at work. How these intellectual resources are built when learning opportunities and progress discussions occur may be dependent on the positive emotions that result from basic needs being met, feelings of contribution, and belonging. When these positive emotions are present in the workplace, the filter through which employees learn and discuss their progress becomes more focused on the organization's functioning and is applied in a way that helps the organization learn and improve important outcomes.

Positive emotions are facilitated by actions within organizations that support clear outcome expectancies, give basic material support, and encourage individual contribution and fulfillment, a sense of belonging, and a chance to progress and learn continuously. All of these elements together can be called employee engagement. These elements are measured by the 12 GWA statements listed earlier. Each statement taps into one of these elements.

THE META-ANALYSIS

This section summarizes the findings of a meta-analysis of the relationship between employee engagement and business outcomes. A meta-analysis is a statistical integration of data accumulated across many different studies.

It provides uniquely powerful information because it controls for measurement and sampling errors and other idiosyncracies that distort the results of individual studies. Individual studies can often appear to have conflicting conclusions when, in fact, differences are a result only of sampling error, measurement error, and other artifactual sources of variation in the effects. A meta-analysis eliminates bias and provides an estimate of the true relationship between the variables studied. As indicated, this chapter will not provide a full review of meta-analysis. For more information on meta-analysis, see Bangert-Drowns (1986); Hunter and Schmidt (1990); Lipsey and Wilson (1993); Schmidt (1992); and Schmidt, Hunter, Pearlman, and Rothstein-Hirsh (1985).

Because The Gallup Organization surveys hundreds of work forces around the world, many organizations are able to provide business-unit-level measures of performance that are comparable from one business unit to another. Such business-unit-level measures have included employee turnover, customer satisfaction–loyalty, productivity, and profitability. As of the 2000 meta-analysis, 36 independent companies are included in Gallup's inferential database of such studies, estimating the relationship of the GWA measures of employee engagement to business-unit outcomes. This database includes both studies in which employee engagement and outcomes were collected in the same year and studies in which employee engagement was collected in Year 1 and subsequent performance collected in Year 2 (predictive). The current database includes studies from 21 different industries, including financial, manufacturing, retail, services, and transportation–public utilities organizations. Business units and work units included bank branches, call centers, departments, city center offices, dealerships, health care units, hotels, plants, restaurants, regional territories, sales teams, schools, stores, and other team designations that are relevant to the company being studied. The overall database includes 7,939 business units within which are 198,514 respondents. This study is ongoing and updated periodically.

As part of the meta-analysis study, we estimated the correlation of employee engagement at the item and composite level, with business outcomes correcting for measurement error in the dependent variables. As well, validity generalization estimates were calculated to understand whether the relationships across companies were consistent or different. One very clear finding throughout was that the relationships, for all items, were generalizable to multiple outcomes across companies. This adds substantial evidence to the argument that there are basic human needs in the workplace that transcend company and industry boundaries.

Table 9.1 provides a summary review of items that have positive and generalizable relationships across organizations. Relationships that show bolded Xs indicate the strongest relationships to each of the various outcomes, and the less bold Xs indicate positive, generalizable relationships.

One interesting finding is that basic needs, such as expectations and materials and equipment, have relationships to basic outcomes, such as customer satisfaction–loyalty and employee turnover–retention, which are outcomes that ultimately influence larger business outcomes like profitability. In addition, there were six items that had substantial relationships to three or more of the performance criteria:

- I know what is expected of me at work.
- At work, I have the opportunity to do what I do best every day.
- My supervisor, or someone at work, seems to care about me as a person.
- At work, my opinions seem to count.
- My associates (fellow employees) are committed to doing quality work.
- This last year, I have had opportunities at work to learn and grow.

Within business units, when employees have clear expectations and the basic materials and equipment they need to do their work, the stage is set. In addition, there appear to be higher level needs that ultimately relate to profitability, such as the fit of the person to his or her job, having other individuals at work who care about and listen to the employees, having respect for fellow coworkers with an end toward quality, and having ongoing opportunities to learn and grow as individuals.

Our goal was to understand what the practical utility was of the generalizable relationships across organizations. If one thinks of a work unit or manager as working toward many outcomes simultaneously, we consider

TABLE 9.1

Items With Meta-Analytic *R*s That Are Generalizable Across Organizations

Item	Turnover	Customer	Productivity	Profit
Know what is expected	x	x	x	
Materials and equipment	x	x		
Opportunities to do what I do best	x	x	x	x
Recognition/praise	o	o	o	x
Cares about me	x	x	x	o
Encourages development	o	x	o	x
Opinions count	o	x	x	x
Mission/purpose	o	o	x	x
Committed—quality	x	o	x	x
Best friend		x	o	x
Talked about progress		o	o	
Opportunities to learn and grow	x	x	x	x

Notes. o = Positive, generalizable relationship.
x = Strongest generalizable relationships.

an aggregate of the four outcomes in Table 9.1 as a composite measure of business-unit performance. That is, work units may never be fully sustainable unless all four of these outcomes are achieved simultaneously. For instance, in the short-term, a work unit may be profitable, but if customers are not satisfied and employees are leaving the work unit, profitability is likely to suffer in the long-term. Profitability may be achievable in the short-term through quick fixes by management and factors outside the scope of employee engagement. But in the long-term, turnover and disloyal customers will have direct financial consequences to the business unit. For this reason, we calculated a composite performance measure to understand how overall composite employee engagement (the mean of responses from the 12 statements) related to composite performance in a correlational and probability framework.

The meta-analytic correlation of business-unit employee engagement to composite performance is .26 within companies and .33 for business units across companies (correcting for measurement error in the dependent variables). Within a given company, business units above the median on employee engagement realize .5 standard deviation units higher performance than those below the median. For business units across companies, this difference is .6 standard deviation units in performance.

Employee engagement defines one part of overall business-unit performance, and it is important to understand what a business unit's probability of success is when employee engagement is high versus low.

Table 9.2 provides the probability of a business unit being successful (above-average composite performance) if it has employee engagement at various levels for its own company and for various levels across companies. For instance, business units with employee engagement at the 95th percentile for a given company have a 67% probability of success. Random success would be 50%, given we define performance at the median. This represents 34% improvement over the median. Comparing work units above the median with those below the median, those in the top half of employee engagement for a given company have a 70% higher probability of success than those in the bottom half. Work units at the 95th percentile have more than double the success rate of those at the 5th percentile. For business units across companies, this difference is even greater. Business units at the 95th percentile have improved their odds of success by 42% over the median business unit and by 145% over the 5th percentile business unit. This indicates that work units with high levels of employee engagement have a much greater chance of business unit success, as measured by our composite criterion.

Other forms of expressing the practical meaning behind the effects from the study include utility analysis methods (Schmidt & Rauschenberger,

TABLE 9.2
Probability of Business Unit Success as a Function of
Employee Engagement

Employee engagement percentile	Success rate (within companies)[a]	Success Rate (across companies)[b]
99	73%	78%
95	67%	71%
75	57%	59%
50	50%	50%
25	43%	41%
5	33%	29%
1	27%	22%

[a]Success rate (within) = percentage of business units with composite performance above the median of business units *within* a company.
[b]Success rate (across) = percentage of business units with composite performance above the median of business units *across* companies.

1986). To understand the practical utility of employee engagement in relationship to employee turnover, customer satisfaction–loyalty, productivity, and profitability, three basic elements are needed. First is to understand the relationship between employee engagement and the outcome (defined earlier). Second is to understand variability in the dependent variable. Third, one must estimate potential change in the independent variable. For purposes of illustration, we compared differences (Table 9.3) between top and bottom quartile business units within five companies (with similar outcome metrics) for each of the outcomes studied (a more detailed table of this analysis is provided in Harter et al., 2002). For the turnover outcome, we studied high-turnover organizations (with more than 60% average turnover) and low-turnover organizations (from 10 to 20% average turnover).

Perhaps the most concrete and direct day-to-day outcome to study is turnover. Referring to Table 9.3, for high-turnover companies (with annualized turnover about 60%), the difference between the average unit in the top quartile on employee engagement to the average unit in the bottom quartile ranged from 14 to 51 percentage points (average of 29 percentage points). For lower turnover companies, the difference was from 4 to 19 points (average of 10 percentage points). If we assume 4 percentage points difference, the smallest difference in a lowest turnover company, assuming a business unit of 100 employees and a cost of turnover of $30,000 per person, this difference equates to $120,000 per business unit. A more typical difference is a 10-percentage point difference between top and bottom quartile units, which equates to $300,000 per business unit per year. Cost of turnover calculations vary by type of position and company. For high-turnover companies, the typical difference between highly engaged and less

TABLE 9.3
Utility Analysis Examples: Five Companies Per Outcome

Difference per business unit on outcome measure (e.g., customer loyalty) between top and bottom quartile on employee engagement (as measured by GrandMean—or sum—of GWA items).

Turnover (high)	Difference
mean	29%
range	14–51%

Turnover (low)	Difference
mean	10%
range	4–19%

Customer satisfaction/ loyalty measures[a]	Difference
mean	2.9%
range	1.9–4.4%

Productivity measures	Difference
mean	$162k
range	$80k–$393k

Profitability measures (% of sales)	Difference
mean	2.0%
range	.87%–4.24%

[a]Scale is percentage of satisfied/loyal customers.
Source: Summarized from Table 6 in Harter, Schmidt, & Hayes (2002). Copyright 2002 by the American Psychological Association. Adapted by permission.

engaged work units represents approximately 20 percentage points annualized turnover and in lower turnover companies, the difference is more typically 5 to 10 percentage points.

For customer satisfaction–loyalty, the difference between top and bottom quartiles on employee engagement ranges from two to four points per business unit (average of 2.9 percentage points). To calculate the dollar impact for a given organization, one would need to know the average number of customers per business unit and the average number of dollars spent per customer, assuming loyalty perceptions result in loyalty behavior. Within most organizations with a large number of business units, this equates to millions of dollars when one compares business units in the top quartile to those in the bottom quartile on employee engagement.

Similar results are provided for productivity (revenue or sales), which are average sales volume per month figures. Business units in the top quartile on employee engagement averaged $80,000 to $120,000 higher revenue or sales; for one organization, the difference was more than $300,000 per month.

Assuming the $80,000 difference per month per business unit translates into $960,000 per year per business unit. This is substantial revenue to most organizations.

For the profitability measures (which were all calculated as a percentage profitability of sales), the difference between employee engagement top and bottom quartiles ranged from approximately 1 to 4 percentage points in profitability. On average, business units in the top quartile on the employee engagement measure produced 1 to 4 percentage points higher profitability. For many organizations in a highly competitive market, 1 to 4 points per business unit is quite substantial and represents the difference between success and failure.

When calculating the business utility and the probability of business units being successful as a function of employee engagement, the relationships are clearly nontrivial. Business units that use principles of positive psychology may be able to influence employee engagement, and this then may enhance the bottom line.

CONCLUSION

Well-being in the workplace is, in part, a function of helping employees do what is naturally right for them by freeing them up to do so—through behaviors that influence employee engagement and therefore that increase the frequency of positive emotions. Short-term fixes through negative reinforcement that may result in behavior that helps the organization financially in the short-term may narrow the ownership and creativity of employees that limits long-term benefits to the organization. Alternatively, behaviors that increase the frequency of positive emotions lead to increasing clarity of expectations, the understanding and use of resources that is congruent with company goals, individual fulfillment in work, a bonding of individuals through a sense of caring, ownership for the altruistic and tangible impact of the company, and learning that is in line with this shared mission. In the long run, this is what is good for the employee and the company.

One real and important element in the workplace we have not yet addressed is monetary pay and benefits. Managers vary in how they can affect their employees' pay and benefits. Yet it is a factor important to nearly everyone; people often choose to join and leave organizations based in part on tangible rewards. Our evidence suggests that employee engagement is related to how people perceive their tangible rewards. Employee engagement is a leading indicator of intent to stay within a given organization. However, when employees are not engaged, pay may enter in as a more critical factor. Employees heavily underpaid relative to others they perceive as in like jobs may place a different weight on pay. However, when engagement is low, monetary satisfiers seem to become more important, which may relate to staying or leaving but less to productivity. The problem in many organizations is that the monetary satisfiers can easily be matched or topped by competing organizations. Relying exclusively on these short-term satisfiers results in a quick-fix mentality that does not fully address the basic human need of fulfillment and feeling of impact and contribution.

In the evolutionary time frame, our ancestors may have been successful at survival because they were good at cooperating with each other (broadening each other's thought–action repertoires) and gathering resources together. When employees are in a position in which their only satisfaction comes from gathering their survival resources alone, it does not feel as good and is not sustainable to the benefit of the larger organization. Even the most independent of entrepreneurs and sales people rely on others for sustainable growth and celebration. Providing employees the opportunity to expand their monetary rewards—by clarifying outcomes, providing material support to achieve these rewards, and putting them into positions in which they can do what they do best and contribute to the organization—expands the chance for positive emotions to occur more frequently and opens employees' minds to how they can most efficiently build their own resources and expand relationships to build more in-depth consideration for how resources can be applied.

Methodologically, we have not yet addressed issues of statistical causality. Getting to the heart of causal inferences is never absolute in any one study and involves research from many different angles. The body of evidence included in the meta-analysis reviewed includes many case studies in which statistical causal issues have been addressed—studies of change over time, predictive relationships, and path analyses (Harter, 2000). Our evidence is that employee engagement is likely a leading indicator of multiple outcomes, as opposed to a trailing result, but that the relationship is somewhat reciprocal. In addition, as Gallup representatives have worked with organizations in applying employee engagement measures into practice, combining the measurement with education for managers within business units, and partnering with companies on change initiatives and dialogue surrounding the 12 items referenced, companies have experienced (from the first to second year) on average one-half standard deviation growth on employee engagement and often times a full standard deviation growth and more after three or more years. At the business-unit level of analysis, there is evidence that growth in engagement relates to growth in business outcomes (Harter, 2000). There is certainly more research that can be conducted in understanding issues of causality, including complimentary quantitative and qualitative designs. An important element in the utility of any applied instrument and process is the extent to which the variable under study can be changed. Our current evidence is that employee engagement, as measured with the

GWA, is changeable and varies widely by business unit within nearly any company. Therefore, the need to create change in many business units is substantial.

Another important consideration of employee engagement is that its partial causes may be individual-level psychological traits. Although it is possible that traits may account for individual differences in job satisfaction or engagement (i.e., emotional stability or neuroticism—reverse scored—and conscientiousness), business-unit aggregate scores of employee engagement average out most individual-level personality differences (average of 25 individuals per business unit). Therefore, business-unit measures of employee engagement provide a more construct-valid definition of the attitudinal component of engagement, which may explain why we have observed changes in engagement over time across many business units.

We conclude from this study that the well-being perspective is quite applicable to business and that, as managers and employees focus on satisfying basic human needs in the workplace—clarifying desired outcomes and increasing opportunity for individual fulfillment and growth—they may increase the opportunity for the success of their organization. We have provided a theoretical framework to describe why this may occur. The data indicate that workplaces with engaged employees, on average, do a better job of keeping employees, satisfying customers, and being financially productive and profitable. Workplace well-being and performance are not independent. Rather, they are complimentary and dependent components of a financially and psychologically healthy workplace.

REFERENCES

Avolio, B. J., & Sosik, J. J. (1999). A life-span framework for assessing the impact of work on white-collar workers. In S. L. Willis & J. D. Reid (Eds.), *Life in the middle: Psychological and social development in middle age* (pp. 251–274). San Diego, CA: Academic Press.

Bangert-Drowns, R. L. (1986). Review of developments in meta-analytic method. *Psychological Bulletin, 99*(3), 388–399.

Baumeister, R. F., & Leary, M. F. (1995). The need to belong: Desire for interpersonal attachments as a fundamental human motivation. *Psychological Bulletin, 117*(3), 497.

Brim, O. G. (1992). *Ambition: How we manage success and failure throughout our lives.* New York: Basic Books.

Campbell, A., Converse, P. E., & Rodgers, W. L. (1976). *The quality of American life: Perceptions, evaluations, and satisfactions.* New York: Russell Sage.

Csikszentmihalyi, M. (1997). *Finding flow: The psychology of engagement with everyday life.* New York: Basic Books.

Diener, E. (2000). The science of happiness and a proposal for a national index. *American Psychologist, 55*(1), 34–43.

Edwards, J. R., Caplan, R. D., & Van Harrison, R. (1998). Person-environment fit theory: Conceptual foundations, empirical evidence, and directions for future research. In C. L. Cooper (Ed.), *Theories of organizational stress* (pp. 29–67). New York: Oxford University Press.

Ellis, H. C., & Ashbrook, P. W. (1989). The state of mood and memory research. In D. Kuiken (Ed.), *Mood and memory: Theory, research, and applications.* (Special Issue) *Journal of Social Behavior and Personality, 4*(2), 1–21.

Fiedler, K. (1988). Emotional mood, cognitive style, and behavior regulation. In K. Fiedler & J. P. Forgas (Eds.), *Affect, cognition and social behavior* (pp. 100–119). Toronto, Canada: Hogrefe.

Fredrickson, B. L. (1998). What good are positive emotions? *Review of General Psychology, 3*, 300–319.

French, J. R. P., Caplan, R. D., & Van Harrison, R. (1982). *The mechanisms of job stress and strain.* New York: Wiley.

Harter, J. K. (2000). The linkage of employee perception to outcomes in a retail environment: Cause and effect? *The Gallup Research Journal-Special Issue on Linkage Analysis, 3*(1), 25–38.

Harter, J. K., & Schmidt, F. L. (2000). *Validation of a performance-related and actionable management tool: A meta-analysis and utility analysis.* Lincoln, NE: Gallup Technical Report.

Harter, J. K., Schmidt, F. L., & Hayes, T. L. (2002). Business unit-level relationship between employee satisfaction, employee engagement, and business outcomes: A meta-analysis, *Journal of Applied Psychology, 87*(2), 268–279.

Hunter, J. E., & Schmidt, F. L. (1983). Quantifying the effects of psychological interventions on employee job performance and work-force productivity. *American Psychologist, 38*, 473–478.

Hunter, J. E., & Schmidt, F. L. (1990). *Methods of meta-analysis: Correcting error and bias in research findings.* Newbury Park, CA: Sage.

Huselid, M. A. (1995). The impact of human resource management practices on turnover, productivity and corporate financial performance. *Academy of Management Journal, 38*(3), 635–672.

Iaffaldano, M. T., & Muchinsky, P. M. (1985). Job satisfaction and job performance: A meta-analysis. *Psychological Bulletin, 97*, 251–273.

Isen, A. M. (1987). Positive affect, cognitive processes, and social behavior. In L. Berkowitz (Ed.), *Advances in experimental social psychology* (Vol. 20, pp. 203–253). San Diego, CA: Academic Press.

Judge, T. A., Thoresen, C. J., Bono, J. E., & Patton, G. K. (2001). The job satisfaction-job performance relationship: A qualitative and quantitative review. *Psychological Bulletin, 127*, 376–407.

Judge, T. A., & Watanabe, S. (1993). Another look at the job satisfaction-life satisfaction relationship. *Journal of Applied Psychology, 78*(6), 939–948.

Kahn, W. A. (1990). Psychological conditions of personal engagement and disengagement at work. *Academy of Management Journal, 33,* 692–724.

Keyes, C. L. M. (1998). Social well-being. *Social Psychological Quarterly, 61,* 121–140.

Kohn, M. L., & Schooler, C. (1982). Job conditions and personality: A longitudinal assessment of their reciprocal effects. *American Journal of Sociology, 87,* 1257–1286.

Lipsey, M. W., & Wilson, D. B. (1993). The efficacy of psychological, educational, and behavioral treatment. *American Psychologist, 48,* 1181–1209.

Murray, C. J. L., & Lopez, A. D. (Eds.). (1996). *The global burden of disease: A comprehensive assessment of mortality and disability from diseases, injuries, and risk factors in 1990 and projected to 2020.* Cambridge, MA: Harvard School of Public Health.

Schmidt, F. L. (1992). What do data really mean? Research findings, meta-analysis, and cumulative knowledge in psychology. *American Psychologist, 47,* 1173–1181.

Schmidt, F. L., Hunter, J. E., McKenzie, R. C., & Muldrow, T. W. (1979). Impact of valid selection procedures on work-force productivity. *Journal of Applied Psychology, 64,* 609–626.

Schmidt, F. L., Hunter, J. E., Pearlman, K., & Rothstein-Hirsh, H. (1985). Forty questions about validity generalization and meta-analysis. *Personnel Psychology, 38,* 697–798.

Schmidt, F. L., & Rader, R. (1999). Exploring the boundary conditions for interview validity: Meta-analytic validity findings for a new interview type. *Personnel Psychology, 52,* 445–464.

Schmidt, F. L., & Rauschenberger, J. (1986, April). *Utility analysis for practitioners.* Paper presented at the First Annual Conference of The Society for Industrial and Organizational Psychology, Chicago.

Schwarz, N., & Bless, H. (1991). Happy and mindless, but sad and smart? The impact of affective states on analytic reasoning. In J. P. Forgas (Ed.), *Emotion and social judgement* (pp. 55–71). Oxford: Pergamon Press.

Skinner, E. A., Wellborn, J. G., & Connell, J. P. (1990). What it takes to do well in school and whether I've got it: A process model of perceived control and children's engagement and achievement in school. *Journal of Educational Psychology, 82,* 22.

Spector, P. E. (1997). *Job satisfaction: Application, assessment, cause, and consequences.* Thousand Oaks, CA: Sage.

U.S. Department of Health and Human Services. (1999). *Mental health: A report of the Surgeon General.* Rockville, MD: Author.

Walker, A. G., & Smither, J. W. (1999). A five-year study of upward feedback: What managers do with their results matters. *Personnel Psychology, 52,* 393–419.

Warr, P. (1999). Well-being and the workplace. In D. Kahneman, E. Deiner, & N. Schwarz (Eds.), *Well-being: The foundations of hedonic psychology* (pp. 392–412). New York: Russell Sage.

Waterman, A. S. (1993). Two conceptions of happiness: Contrasts of personal expressiveness (eudaimonia) and hedonic enjoyment. *Journal of Personality and Social Psychology, 64,* 678–691.

Wright, T. A., & Bonnett, D. G. (1997). The role of pleasantness and activation-based well-being in performance prediction. *Journal of Occupational Health Psychology, 2,* 212–219.

Wright T. A., & Cropanzano R. (2000). Psychological well-being and job satisfaction as predictors of job performance. *Journal of Occupational Health Psychology, 5,* 84–94.

Wright, T. A., & Staw, B. M. (1999). Affect and favorable work outcomes: Two longitudinal tests of the happy-productive worker thesis. *Journal of Organizational Behavior, 20,* 1–23.

Wrzesniewski, A., McCauley, C., Rozin, P., & Schwartz, B. (1997). Jobs, careers, and callings: People's relations to their work. *Journal of Research in Personality, 31,* 21–33.

Ziv, A. (1976). Facilitating effects of humor on creativity. *Journal of Educational Psychology, 68,* 318–322.

IV

LOOKING BEYOND ONESELF

10

DOING WELL BY DOING GOOD: BENEFITS FOR THE BENEFACTOR

JANE ALLYN PILIAVIN

"For it is in giving that we receive."

Saint Francis of Assisi

On my office door I have an old Red Cross poster that reads, "Give blood. All you'll feel is good." Is this truth in advertising? And can we generalize this assertion—beyond its rather transparent attempt to downplay the physical pain of blood donation—to other forms of community service and to other benefits to the benefactor than simply "feeling good"? Are there payoffs for doing good in the coinage of higher self-esteem, decreased depression, or even longer life? To foreshadow my conclusions, the answer to this first basic question is essentially yes: One does well by doing good.

For the purpose of this chapter, I will restrict my definition of community service to mean taking actions, carried out within an institutional framework, that potentially provide some service to one or more other people or to the community at large. Cleaning up a park, giving blood, coaching little league, tutoring children, being a Big Brother or Sister, fundraising for the American Cancer Society, volunteering in a food pantry, or working on a Rape Crisis Center hotline all qualify for this definition. Simply being a member of an organization that carries out such actions does not "count" as community service under this definition. Visiting a sick neighbor or caring for an ailing parent on one's own also does not fall under this definition, because it is not done in an institutional framework.

THEORETICAL APPROACHES

Space allows for only a cursory presentation of the theories that can be applied to understand the positive relationship between community service and mental and physical health. Sociologists have proposed for many years that there are benefits of social participation. In the 19th century, Durkheim (1951/1898) argued convincingly for the importance of group ties, norms, and social expectations in protecting individuals from suicide. The role-accumulation approach within role theory (Marks, 1977; Sieber, 1974; Thoits, 1986) assumes that social roles provide status, role-related privileges, and ego gratification, as well as identities that provide meaning and purpose and thus enhance psychological well-being. Within this tradition, Thoits (1992, 1995) suggested that voluntary roles, such as friend or group member, may be more responsible for the positive effects of multiple roles than are obligatory roles such as parent or spouse.

Within psychology, research by Langer and Rodin (1976; Rodin & Langer, 1977) has indicated that simply doing things, being the cause of action, and being in control provides protection against morbidity and mortality. Snyder, Clary, and Stukas (2000) have been carrying out a systematic program of research focused on understanding volunteer motivation. They have identified six functions that volunteering serves: value-expressive, social, knowledge, defensive, enhancement, and career. They have consistently found greater satisfaction on the part of volunteers based on meeting their motivational needs. Cialdini has argued that individuals are socialized to take pleasure from helping others (e.g., see Cialdini & Fultz, 1990; Cialdini, Kenrick, & Baumann, 1982). Individuals should thus feel better when they help, which could lift the spirits of those who are depressed and could—if the psychoneuroimmunologists are correct—strengthen the immune system and lead to reduced morbidity and mortality.

Thus, both sociological and psychological theories predict that performing community service will have benefits for the helper. Mechanisms are suggested from the very macro, based on integration into society, to the very micro—psychoneuroimmunologic. From both sets of theories we are led to believe that the impact will vary depending on a "fit" between the helper's needs and the nature of the actions performed. And both sets of theories suggest that having a feeling of volition and control will enhance the positive effects.

DOES HELPING OTHERS LEAD TO POSITIVE EMOTIONS?

Although there is little direct evidence that helping others makes you feel good, there is indirect evidence. Harris (1977) presented survey data indicating that college students believe that altruistic actions have a mood-enhancing component. Newman, Vasudev, and Onawola (1985) interviewed 180 older adults (55 to 85) volunteering in three school programs in New York, Los Angeles, and Pittsburgh. Sixty-five percent reported improved life satisfaction, 76% better feelings about themselves, and 32% improved mental health. In response to the question, "How has the volunteer experience affected you?" the authors received many answers such as, "It is an experience that I will keep with me as long as I live . . . it has enriched my life. I think that associating with children is rejuvenating; it is energizing. . . . " (p. 125).

The most direct evidence that helping leads to positive feelings comes from a series of laboratory experiments by Weiss et al. (Weiss, Boyer, Lombardo, & Stich, 1973; Weiss, Buchanan, Altstatt, & Lombardo, 1971). They demonstrated that being able to terminate shock to another student (clearly helping that person) served as a reinforcer, in a classic operant conditioning setting involving what was essentially a bar-pressing response. They concluded that "altruism is rewarding" (1971, p. 1262). The other side of the coin is demonstrated in a study by Batson and Weeks (1996), in which undergraduate women who tried to help but were unsuccessful showed negative mood changes. The changes were particularly significant among research participants high in empathy.

The only type of real world helping for which there is direct evidence of enhanced positive mood is blood donation. Piliavin and Callero (1991) reported on several longitudinal studies of blood donors from high school, college, and the general public. In interviews with our college sample 18 months after their first donation we asked how they expected to feel at the time of their next donation. Moods measured before and after the first donation[1] predicted those expected feelings. Donors who had given four or more times showed much lower levels of expected nervousness and higher expectations of good feelings than did those who had given fewer times. Most critically, both expecting to feel good and saying those good feelings were a reason for donation were related to a commitment to continued donation.[2] The conclusion I draw is that at least this form of helping can lead to feeling better emotionally and feeling better about oneself and that those feelings are rewarding and can lead individuals to engage in additional helping. I turn now to the potential for more long-lasting effects of community service.

ARE THERE LONG-TERM POSITIVE EFFECTS OF COMMUNITY SERVICE?

This review will be organized by life cycle stage, because the dependent variables that have been investigated are different for people of different

---

[1]Mood was measured using modifications of scales developed by Nowlis (1970).
[2]Controlling for the number of previous donations and several other factors that predict continued donation.

stages, and the forms of helping are also often different. Adolescents and the elderly have been the focus of most of this research, and it is easy to see why this might be. Adolescents have not yet developed all of their cognitive and social skills or been socialized completely to their social roles, and their sense of self is particularly unstable. Thus engaging in helping has the potential to help them develop desirable personality traits, skills, and habits and to internalize helping roles as part of their self-concept. They may even be young enough to still be learning that helping can make you feel good. In addition, they are not yet fully integrated into social structures, and there is often serious concern that they may be alienated and looking for trouble. The elderly are generally thought of as fully socialized but potentially alienated by virtue of retirement, loss of family roles, and decreasing physical abilities. Thus the focus of research on the elderly has been not on development issues but on issues of integration in society, the avoidance of depression, and even physical health and mortality.

Another reason for organizing this review by life cycle stage is that this is how the literature itself appears to be organized. Perhaps because of the age segregation of American life, researchers have often picked a life-cycle stage to study and stuck with it. There is an unstated assumption behind this organization—namely, that community service serves different functions for different age groups.

Effects of Helping and Volunteering on Youth and College Students

There are good reasons to believe that participation in many forms of extracurricular activities will be healthy for children. First, any productive use of time can simply interfere with the opportunity to engage in antisocial or otherwise undesirable activities (Eccles & Barber, 1999). This is the main rationale for "midnight basketball" and supervised nighttime clubs for teenagers. Larson (1994), for example, has found a suppression of delinquency among students who engage in the arts and hobbies and who participate in youth organizations. It is also argued that such programs can have effects on the growth of intellect, mastery, social responsibility, social skills, and leadership abilities.

Focusing specifically on the potential impact of community service activities, Moore and Allen (1996) stated, "By enhancing these competencies in adolescents, volunteering may also increase adolescents' resistance to other problems, such as teenage pregnancy, school drop-out, and delinquency" (p. 233) These authors stressed that formal volunteer service programs usually have a variety of components other than volunteering, and that it is thus impossible to separate out the specific causal impact of volunteering. However, the best designed of these programs do appear to have a number of positive effects.

Effects on Behavior

Moore and Allen reviewed two major programs designed to decrease social problems among teenagers. The San Antonio, Texas, Valued Youth Program focused on children in middle school, all of whom scored below grade level on reading tests. They were randomly assigned to a control group or to do tutoring of younger children and were compared at the beginning and end of a two-year evaluation period on a number of dimensions. Positive effects were found on dropout rates (1% of tutors versus 12% of control students), reading grades, self-concept, and attitudes toward school. The results of this study could in part be a result of increased valuing of academics based on the greater engagement with the material.

In the Teen Outreach Program, students took part in volunteer work that was meaningful to them for an average of 31 hours over an academic year (slightly less than an hour a week). Participants were an ethnically diverse group aged 11 to 21 who were expected to be at risk for problem behaviors. An eight-year longitudinal evaluation included 237 sites, 3986 participants, and 4356 comparison students (Allen, Philliber, & Hoggsen, 1990; Allen, Philliber, Herrling, & Kuperminc, 1997). Results showed that Teen Outreach students had "a 5% lower rate of course failure in school, an 8% lower rate of school suspension, a 33% lower rate of pregnancy, and a 50% lower rate of school dropout" (Moore & Allen, 1996, p. 235).[3] Most critically for our purposes, the study found that programs in which students did more intensive volunteer work showed better outcomes on a scale of problem behaviors. This seems like a classic "dose-response" curve—greater effects with more exposure to the treatment. The program also involved classroom-based discussions of a variety of issues such as family stress, human growth, and values. However, there was no comparable effect of the amount of classroom instruction.

Uggen and Janikula (1999) noted that several studies in the literature on volunteer work and antisocial behavior show correlations and apparent causal effects of volunteer service on recidivism. They present a longitudinal analysis, using the Youth Development Study, begun in 1988 with a panel of 1139 St. Paul, Minnesota, adolescents then in ninth grade, who were followed for eight years. Measures of volunteer activity were based on the third- and fourth-wave data obtained in their junior and senior years. The dependent variable is self-reported first arrest data for ages 17 to 21, measured when they were 21. Many control measures were also used, including pro-social attitudes, helping personality, substance abuse, school misconduct,

---

[3] These effects were statistically significant, controlling for a number of demographics and for preprogram problem behavior.

socioeconomic status, and employment obtained in the first wave. Their bottom line conclusion is, "Only 3% of the volunteers were arrested in the four years following high school compared to 11% of the nonvolunteers" (p. 344). Although there was no random assignment, the authors controlled for many factors that might predispose students either to do volunteer work or to be arrested.

Finally, Calabrese and Schumer (1986) divided students who wanted to do community service randomly into three groups: a control and two volunteer groups, one short-term (10 weeks) and one long-term (20 weeks). They found both lower levels of discipline problems and lower levels of alienation while the students were doing volunteer work. Alienation increased again in the group that stopped volunteering after 10 weeks.

Effects on Attitudes, Self-Concept, and Well-Being

If children have learned, by adolescence, that helping others makes one feel good about oneself, the experience of helping others should lead to positive changes in self-concept. Johnson, Beebe, Mortimer, and Snyder (1998), using the same data set used by Uggen and Janikula (1999), found that volunteering in grades 10 to 12 increased intrinsic work values, the perceived importance of a career, and the importance of community involvement.[4] Volunteering was *not* associated with later depressive affect, academic or other self-esteem, and many other well-being factors, controlling for 9th-grade levels of these variables.

Conrad and Hedin (1981, 1982) investigated the social and psychological development of junior and senior high students as a function of "experiential education," which involved either volunteering, political and social action, internships, or research activities, compared to self-selected control groups. Similarly, Newmann and Rutter (1983) studied 11th and 12th grade students in eight public schools in which some students spent at least four hours per week volunteering and a minimum of two hours per week in a school class connected to the program. A control group in each school consisted of students who were planning to take the program in a future semester. These two studies measured many of the same dimensions—including moral development, self-acceptance, positive attitudes toward adults, being active in the community, competence in helping, reports of actual performance relevant to volunteering, and belief in responsibility to help people in need—and each found positive impacts, but on different

---

[4] It would be interesting to know whether these variables mediate the effects on delinquency reported by Uggen and Janikula (1999).

variables. Future research needs to focus more on what aspects of programs are responsible for what kinds of effects.

In a longitudinal study of the impact of the first year of college, Lee (1997) found no impact of volunteering on self-esteem or academic self-efficacy. Students' self-esteem generally went down over the year, and the most powerful variable contributing to this was grade point average. Participating in volunteer work did have a significant impact on volunteer role identity. That is, such participation strengthened students' self-concept as volunteers. Perhaps at this critical life turning point, academics assume a highly focal position, such that other activities can have little impact on overall evaluation of the self. Astin and Sax (1998) also carried out a longitudinal study of students from an array of colleges. They found that there were positive effects of service participation on civic responsibility, educational attainment, life skills, and commitment to community service in the future. The students who participated also *perceived* greater changes in social self-confidence and a variety of other abilities. The more service students did, the larger the effects were—again, an apparent dose-response curve.

Effects of Cross-Age and Peer Tutoring

The practice of peer and cross-age tutoring has been so common from elementary grade levels through college since at least the 1970s that I thought it worth a separate examination. The technique involves having either a same-age or an older child assist another in a school task, as in the Valued Youth study discussed earlier. The intention is to help both the tutor and the learner, both academically and socially. A meta-analysis specifically focused on reading outcomes provides good evidence that such tutoring reaches its educational goal for both partners (Elbaum, Vaughn, Hughes, & Moody, 1999).

Support for claims of positive emotional, self-esteem, and attitude outcomes for tutors is, however, mixed. Yogev and Ronen (1982) and Gardner (1978) both found increases in self-esteem among participants in cross-age tutoring; one study was done in Israel and the other in a Detroit inner-city school. However, a review of research done between 1970 and 1985 using handicapped students as tutors (Osguthorpe & Scruggs, 1986) found more convincing effects on academic achievement than on self-esteem. A similar review of work done with behaviorally or emotionally disturbed children as tutors (Scruggs, Mastropieri, & Richter, 1985) also found some positive academic effects but no consistent impact on self-esteem. One more recent individual study (Winter, 1996) did find increases in self-esteem and general self-worth among girls and gains in intrinsic motivation to learn among all students.

Effects of "Service Learning"

In the 1990s, the concept of service learning became very popular both in secondary school and at the college level. Service learning is usually defined as academic experiences in which students engage both in social action and in reflection on their experiences in performing that action. Stukas, Clary, and Snyder wrote,

> It is the reflection component and the surrounding educational context that serves to highlight the reciprocal nature of the community service activities at the center of service-learning programs. . . . In other forms of service and helping, it may not be nearly as clear that both the recipient of help . . . and the helper receive benefits from their partnership. (1999, p. 2–3)

Stukas et al. frame their review of the literature in terms of their functional approach to volunteering, which assumes that volunteers receive a variety of benefits related to six possible goals for volunteering: self-enhancement, understanding of self and the world, value expression, career development, social experiences, and ego protection. They concluded that service learning *can* have effects related to all six of the functions. In terms of self-enhancement—feeling better about oneself—they noted that service learning can affect personal efficacy, self-esteem, and confidence (Giles & Eyler, 1994, 1998; Williams, 1991, Yates & Youniss, 1996b). In terms of understanding, there is evidence that service learning can influence students' appreciation for and attitudes toward diverse groups in society (Blyth, Saito, & Berkas, 1997; Yates & Youniss, 1996a), including elderly individuals (Bringle & Kremer, 1993) and people of other cultures and races (Myers-Lipton, 1996a, 1996b). Specific learning of course content may be enhanced (Hamilton & Zeldin, 1987), and more general effects on the ability to connect academic concepts to real situations have been claimed (Kendrick, 1996; Miller, 1994).

In terms of value expression, some studies have shown an increase in altruistic motivation (Yogev & Ronen, 1982) and social and personal responsibility (Sax & Astin, 1997). With regard to career development, there is some evidence that "volunteer work predicted intrinsic work values, the importance of a career, and the importance of community involvement, even when factors related to self-selection . . . were taken into account" (Johnson et al., 1998, as cited in Stukas et al., p. 8). Finally, in terms of protection—by which Stukas et al. mean reduction of stress, feelings of alienation, or guilt—service learning can distract students from personal problems and perhaps give them an opportunity to work through those problems. Follman and Muldoon (1997) claimed that some benefits of service learning are stronger for "at-risk" students. Such students may be able to compare themselves to others with even worse problems, for example, which allows them to put their personal failings in perspective. The authors stress that the studies reviewed in many if not most cases do not have random assignment to programs and control conditions, and that selection factors undoubtedly contaminate many of the claimed effects.

Stukas et al. emphasized four features of the programs that appear to be related to positive effects if learning is to be enhanced. These are as follows: (a) being autonomy-supportive—that is, allowing participants a voice in determining the details of service activities; (b) matching goals and activities—that is, allowing students' needs and interests to help shape the activities to contribute to the attainment of goals; (c) attention to the relationship among all participants, involving mutual respect among instructors, students, and community members; and (d) inclusion of opportunities for reflection, which "cement the link between experience and theory" (1999, p. 14).

Overall, then, there is considerable evidence that community service has positive impacts on youth. Various forms of service decrease delinquency and other social problem behaviors and increase commitment to positive social values. Cross-age tutoring seems to teach the skills the tutors teach. The evidence for positive effects on self-esteem or other mental health measures is weaker in both these literatures. Service learning has a variety of positive intellectual, social, and psychological outcomes. There are many moderators of the effects, including some evidence that effects are stronger for students most at risk. What is almost completely lacking is information on the mechanisms by which these effects take place.

Effects of Volunteering and Helping on Adults

As with studies of adolescents and college students, most of the research on volunteering and well-being is correlational, but in some of the studies other relevant variables are statistically controlled. In much of the research, "voluntary association membership" is the independent variable measured, not actual participation. Gecas and Burke (1995) found membership to be related to self-esteem; Brown, Gary, Green, & Milburn (1992) to decreased depression; Ellison (1991) to personal happiness and life satisfaction; and Burman (1988) to improved well-being. Reitschlin (1998) found that as the number of voluntary association memberships (including work-related, church-related, recreational, fraternal, and civic) increased, the level of depression decreased. He also found a significant effect of memberships in buffering the impact of stress on depression.[5]

---

[5] He used controls for mastery, self-esteem, social support, church attendance, and a number of demographic factors.

These studies tell us little, however, about volunteering per se. Keyes (1998) found that respondents who had volunteered in the past year reported higher levels of social well-being (i.e., a sense of social contribution) than did those who had volunteered over a year previously or had never volunteered. Van Willigen (1998) found effects both of attending voluntary association meetings and of hours of volunteer work on life satisfaction (positive) and depression (negative).

The most comprehensive investigation to date of the impact of volunteering on well-being is presented by Thoits and Hewitt (2001), who simultaneously investigate the question of the impact of well-being on volunteering and the reverse. Using the two-wave national sample of adults collected by House and reported in *Americans' Changing Lives* (House, 1995), the authors carry out multiple regressions of the number of volunteer hours at time 1 (1986) and the change in volunteer hours from time 1 to time 2 (1989) on six measures of well-being: happiness, life satisfaction, self-esteem, mastery, depression, and physical health at time 2. Although there are positive effects on all six measures, the most highly significant are on life satisfaction and feelings of mastery.[6] The authors noted that some important remaining question are, "What are the structural conditions which move willing workers into service activities?" and "How are the beneficial effects of volunteer work on well-being generated?" They concluded,

> Better understanding of the structural conditions which encourage volunteerism and how the positive consequences of community service occur might suggest ways to facilitate recruitment as well as to enhance volunteers' service experiences, to the benefit of all. (House, 1995, p. 22)

Effects of Volunteering on Elderly Individuals

Older volunteers, like adolescents and adults in general, believe that volunteering is beneficial to them. But what is the evidence that this is actually the case?

Helping and Mental Health

In a recent meta-analysis, Wheeler, Gorey, and Greenblatt (1998) found 37 studies of the impact of volunteer activities, defined as "voluntary association membership, indirect and direct helping roles" for which they

---

[6]Controls for demographic factors as well as for other forms of community participation (and change in participation), such as church attendance and participation in other organizations do not eliminate the impact of volunteer participation on the well-being measures at time 2. The authors also study the impact of the six measures of well-being and change in those measures to time 2, three years later, on volunteer hours at time 2, controlling for hours at time 1. There are significant effects here as well. That is, well-being and volunteering have a reciprocal relationship.

could calculate effect sizes.[7] Of these, 20 were cross-sectional, 9 were pre-experimental, seven were quasi-experimental, and only one was a true experiment. The average correlation between helping (or membership) and some measure of well-being, most commonly life satisfaction, was .252 ($p < .001$), with a range from 0 to .582.

In studies that adjusted for health or socioeconomic status, the average correlation was smaller (.186 vs. .322, $p < .05$), but still, "it remained significant in both a practical and statistical sense" (p. 74). Those who engaged in direct helping (12 studies) "seemed to derive greater rewards from volunteering . . . than other elders engaged in more indirect or less formally 'helping' roles" (p. 75). The average correlations for those two kinds of studies were .358 and .173, respectively, ($p < .01$), indicating some greater effect of doing something as compared to simply being a member. This analysis is informative but hardly conclusive of an actual causal relationship.

Midlarsky and Kahana (1994) carried out a survey of 200 community-dwelling and 200 residential elderly individuals on family, neighborly, and volunteer helping, followed four years later by a much smaller experimental intervention designed to increase helping behavior. Helping was significantly related to higher subjective affect–balance (essentially good feelings), social integration, morale, and self-esteem. An interesting but unexpected finding is that the relationship of empathy with both morale and affect–balance is *negative* once helping is entered into the equation. The authors suggested that highly empathic elderly individuals may be at some risk of negative emotional outcomes if exposed to serious suffering, such as long-term illness.

An experimental test would be highly desirable—one in which some elderly individuals are randomly assigned to engage in helping and others are not. Midlarsky and Kahana did the nearest thing to this by randomly assigning 60 elderly respondents to receive an extremely strong, individualized persuasive appeal to volunteer[8] and another 60 were assigned to a control group. This intervention led to increases in perceptions of volunteer opportunities and in all forms of helping that were measured: familial, neighborly, and formal volunteering. Finally, there was a significant effect of all types of helping on affect–balance and self-esteem, and a significant effect of volunteering on morale and subjective social integration.

Effects on Morbidity and Mortality

Researchers have also looked at the impact of volunteering on health and mortality among elderly individuals. Young and Glasgow (1998) analyzed

---

[7]The inclusion of voluntary association membership is unfortunate, but it is only a small minority of the studies (eight).

[8]Each experimental participant "heard a standardized message in which his or her help was solicited . . . [I]ndividualized brochures were prepared with the help of personal information obtained . . . during the initial telephone contact . . . Information in the brochures was very specific, containing

a sample of 629 nonmetropolitan elderly individuals engaged in either "instrumental" or "expressive" social participation. Instrumental participation included political activities, volunteering, and club memberships.[9] Expressive activities included recreation, cultural events, and education— activities with a more self-oriented focus. Self-reported health status increased as instrumental social participation increased for both men and women; expressive social participation was related to health only for women. Clearly, however, the causal relationship could lead from health to participation rather than the reverse.

Moen, Dempster-McClain, and Williams (1989), studying a sample of women who had been between the ages of 25 and 50 when interviewed in 1956, found that those who had participated in clubs and volunteer activities were less likely to have died by 1986. The analysis controlled for many other relevant factors, including the number of other roles and health in 1956, and the article makes clear that the activities were indeed largely community-oriented (PTA, scouting, book drives, etc.). In a second more complex analysis based on interviews done in 1986 with the 313 surviving women in the sample, Moen, Dempster-McClain, and Williams (1992) found effects on three health measures: self-appraised health, time to serious illness, and functional ability. There is a significant, or nearly significant, effect of organizational participation in 1956 on all three measures, providing strong evidence for the causal impact of community service on health.

Oman, Thoresen, and McMahon (1999) also examined volunteering and mortality in a 1990 to 1991 prospective study of 2025 community-dwelling elderly individuals aged 55 and older in Marin County, California. Mortality was assessed through November 1995. Controlling for health habits, physical functioning, religious attendance, social support, and many other factors, high volunteers (two or more organizations) had 44% lower mortality than nonvolunteers.[10] The impact of volunteering on mortality increased with increasing age—that is, those most at risk were helped the most.

Moderating and Mediating Factors

Musick, Herzog, and House (1999) have taken the first serious step in attempting to track down the mechanisms by which volunteering by

---

names and telephone numbers of contact persons, types of persons and skills specifically being requested, the nature of the tasks and duties, why the help is needed, and what people are expected to benefit ..." (Midlarsky & Kahana, 1994, p. 197).

[9] I have tried to focus on actions rather than memberships in defining community service, but here the clubs are at least described as having "community-oriented purposes" (Young & Glasgow, 1998, p. 349).
[10] Their measure of volunteering was developed from two questions, whether respondents did "any volunteer work at the present time" and then "how many voluntary organizations are you involved with?"

elderly individuals might decrease mortality. These authors tracked respondents aged 65 and older at the first wave of the *Americans' Changing Lives* (House, 1995) data set, using the National Death Index, from the year of the survey (1986) through March 1994. They then explored the effect of the amount of volunteering done in the year preceding the survey on mortality. Controlling for health, race, age, income, physical activity, and initial health and impairment, moderate volunteering (fewer than 40 hours per year or for only one organization) had a protective function. Volunteering more than that was no more beneficial than not volunteering at all. Of this effect, the authors stated,

> This curvilinear effect for volunteering supports both the role enhancement and the role strain perspectives. In terms of the former, the findings indicated that simply adding the volunteering role was protective of mortality. To gain the protective effect one did not have to volunteer to a great extent. Indeed, volunteering at higher levels provided no protective effect. This finding is consonant with the role strain hypothesis, which would argue that for older adults, taking on too much volunteering activity incurs just enough detriments to offset the potential beneficial effects of the activity. (House, 1995, p. S178)

The authors admitted that with their data they could not actually test this role-strain hypothesis. They suggested, "Future analyses should attempt to resolve the issue with more specific data on the nature and experience of volunteer work and other forms of productive activity" (p. S19).

Of perhaps greater interest, the protective effect was found only among those low in informal social interaction,[11] conceptualized as a measure of social integration. The role perspective suggests that one mechanism by which volunteering could lead to better physical and mental health is by preventing alienation and anomie, consistent with Durkheim's suicide findings.

In an even more recent study using all three currently available waves of *Americans' Changing Lives*,[12] Musick and Wilson (in press) investigated the role of volunteering in depression. Although there is a strong effect of volunteering, they find only a small mediating effect of social and psychological resources measured at time 2 on depression at time 3. They also discover a dose-response curve: Volunteering in all three waves has a highly significant effect, whereas volunteering in only one wave is unrelated to depression at time 3. It also appears that volunteering for religious organizations has a stronger protective effect than volunteering for only secular causes. In their analysis, the volunteering effect is significant only among those over 65.

---

[11] This is measured by how often they talk on the telephone with friends, neighbors, or relatives in the typical week and how often they get together with them.
[12] 1986, 1989, and 1994.

Comparing Effects of Helping on Elderly Individuals and Adults in General

Van Willigen (2000) used the first two waves of the same data, comparing the relative benefits of volunteering in 1986 for the life satisfaction and perceived health of older and younger adults in 1989. This study again allows us to begin to look at interaction effects and thus to get a hint of mechanisms. Using ordinary least squares (OLS), she estimated four regressions: on each of the two dependent variables and separately for volunteers under and over age 60. Within each regression, she presented separate models using volunteer–nonvolunteer, time volunteering, or number of organizations volunteered for as the independent variable. Results are clear. For both older and younger adults, volunteering predicts greater life satisfaction and better perceived health. This is true regardless of what measure of volunteering is used. However, the relationships are significantly stronger in the elderly sample using two of the three independent variable measures. That is, volunteering makes more of a difference in life satisfaction and perceived health for those over the age of 60.

There appear to be different stories to tell regarding the two different dependent variables. (a) Life satisfaction increases linearly for the older respondents with more hours of volunteering and with a wider range of volunteer activities—more is better, in other words. For the younger sample, life satisfaction (which is significantly lower overall than for the elderly) increased only up to 100 hours of volunteer work per year, and the curve turns negative after 140 hours. Similarly, although working for one organization provides benefits, working for two does not increase them. (b) Perceived health—which is significantly better for the younger group—shows quite a different pattern. Simply being a volunteer improves perceived health 2.5 times more for elderly individuals than for young adults, and the number of organizations also shows positive effects only in this group. However, the number of hours is curvilinearly related to perceived health for seniors but is linearly related for young adults—exactly the reverse of the relationship for life satisfaction. Why?

Van Willigen suggested, "Young adults who are heavily committed may be particularly likely to have high levels of responsibility, including supervising other volunteers, which may lead to stress, whereas particularly high levels of volunteer commitment may be physically taxing for some senior adults" (2000, p. S 316). In other words, there may be role strain for the younger group when they take on too many volunteer tasks, leading to expressions of low life satisfaction. Seniors, who have fewer roles, may find increasing life satisfaction with increasing involvement, but it may wear them down physically. Remember that this is almost the same group of respondents for whom Musick et al. found a mortality benefit for light volunteering but no benefit for heavier involvement.

The inescapable conclusion regarding volunteering by elderly individuals is that it is highly beneficial. There appears to be a strong and consistent effect, such that the more an elderly person volunteers, the higher is his or her life satisfaction. The impact is greater on those who need it most. Similarly, some volunteering enhances physical health and even can stave off death. The only caveat appears to be that for physical health, more is not always better. Volunteering in moderation that does not physically tax the elderly individual appears to be best—as with exercise, food, and wine, moderation in all things.

CONCLUSION

In doing this review I have been interested to see the different foci that research on volunteering has taken depending on the age of the people being studied. In studies of youth, the emphasis has been mainly on two kinds of potential outcomes: negative behaviors and intellectual, psychological, and social growth. That is, one focus has been on how volunteering can prevent youth from doing things that are damaging to them, both in the present and in the future—premarital sex, drugs, drinking, crime. The other focus has been on how volunteering can teach something—citizenship, problem-solving, moral reasoning, empathy, or how it can make kids feel better about themselves. The explosion of programs integrating volunteering and academic work—service learning and peer tutoring—are particularly illustrative of this trend. School is a child's work, and it is where children spend most of their daylight hours. Service learning is a way to extend those hours in both time and space and to bring the community into the school and vice versa.

The emphasis in work on adults, including elderly individuals, is mainly in terms of the role that voluntary organization membership and volunteering plays in social integration and the buffering of stress. The typical dependent variables are life satisfaction, depression, physical health, and even mortality. Issues of psychological growth, or learning, are essentially ignored. And certainly nobody talks about how volunteer work can keep these populations from harming themselves! The positive effects with youth do, however, suggest a possible approach to rehabilitation of adult offenders, substance abusers, and other problem populations.

Looking beyond the basic finding that there are positive effects of prosocial actions, we need to ask why and how these benefits accrue. What are the mediators, social, psychological, and physiological, by which community service is translated into health benefits? That is, for example, does increased life satisfaction come from feeling more efficacious or from basking in positive social feedback? Does it come from enhanced meaning or from just getting out and about? Furthermore, we need to explore whether different benefits result for volunteers at different stages of the life cycle, because of their developmental tasks and different social locations, for different kinds of community service, or for different personality types. That is, we need to discover moderators of the effect.

Midlarsky (1991) has proposed five "analytically distinguishable reasons that helping others may benefit the helper" (p. 240): (a) by providing a distraction from one's own troubles, (b) by enhancing the sense of meaningfulness and value in one's life, (c) by having a positive impact on self-evaluations, (d) by increasing positive moods, and (e) through enhanced social integration based on social skills and interpersonal connections. Clary et al. (1998) suggested that what makes one satisfied—and thus presumably happier and possibly even healthier—will depend on one's goals and one's actual volunteer experience. There is a wide-open field for investigation, but it will require pretesting volunteers on Clary et al.'s scales (some of which strongly resemble Midlarsky's possible mechanisms).

What about the effects on physical health and mortality? How might these come about? Oman et al. (1999) suggested that several of Midlarsky's proposed mechanisms (e.g., improved morale, self-esteem, and positive affect) could influence the body through psychoneuroimmunologic pathways, thus reducing mortality in aging populations. They also caution us that they and others have found interactions of the protective "volunteer effect" with other factors. They found greater effects for the very old and for those who were more religious, for example. At least some of these interactions could be related to compromised immune function in the subpopulations that appear to benefit the most. Here again is a fruitful field for additional investigation.

Finally, different kinds of volunteering and helping may well have different effects on health, and not all forms of helping may be beneficial. In the work on adolescents, the suggestion was made that the most positive effects come when the volunteer feels some autonomy and choice. The literature on multiple roles points out that not all roles are the same. Specifically, Thoits (1992, 1995) has suggested that obligatory roles may have fewer positive effects than voluntary roles, and Baruch and Barnett (1986) cautioned us that we must think about role quality. For example, half of the AIDS volunteers in Snyder and Omoto's (1991) research drop out within a year, because such work is emotionally debilitating.

As the population ages, more and more caregivers and volunteers will be exposed to obligatory, unrewarding, and in fact depressing forms of helping behavior.[13] We already hear of the "sandwich generation," caught between the needs of their children and those of their parents. Society will need to develop institutions such as respite care to provide some relief for those who will be taking on these highly burdensome roles. However, the fact that helping does not always feel good is far outweighed by the preponderance of evidence in the foregoing review that helping and volunteering can improve mood, increase self-esteem, and contribute to mental and physical health. The message of the Red Cross poster—"all you'll feel is good"—may be an overstatement, but on many levels—psychologically, socially, and even physically—one indeed does "do well by doing good."

REFERENCES

Allen, J. P., Philliber, S., Herrling, S., & Kuperminc, G. P. (1997). Preventing teen pregnancy and academic failure: Experimental evaluation of a developmentally based approach. *Child Development, 64,* 729–742.

Allen, J. P., Philliber, S., Hoggson, N. (1990). School-based prevention of teenage pregnancy and school dropout: Process evaluation of the national replication of the Teen Outreach Program. *American Journal of Community Psychology, 18,* 505–524.

Astin, A. W., & Sax, L. J. (1998). How undergraduates are affected by service participation. *Journal of College Student Development, 39,* 251–262.

Baruch, G. K., & Barnett, R.C. (1986). Role quality, multiple role involvement, and psychological well-being in midlife women. *Journal of Personality and Social Psychology, 51,* 578–585.

Batson, C. D., & Weeks, J. L. (1996). Mood effects of unsuccessful helping: Another test of the *empathy-altruism* hypothesis. *Personality and Social Psychology Bulletin, 22,* 148–157.

Blyth, D. A., Saito, R., & Berkas, T. (1997). A quantitative study of the impact of service-learning programs. In A. S. Waterman (Ed.), *Service-learning: Applications from the research* (pp. 39–56). Mahwah, NJ:. Erlbaum.

Bringle, R. G., & Kremer, J. F. (1993). Evaluation of an intergenerational service-learning project for undergraduates. *Educational Gerontology, 19,* 407–416.

Brown, D. R., Gary, L., Green, A., & Milburn, N. (1992). Patterns of social affiliation as predictors of depressive symptoms among urban blacks. *Journal of Health and Social Behavior, 33,* 242–253.

Burman, P. (1988). *Killing time, losing ground: Experiences of unemployment.* Toronto: Thompson Educational.

---

[13] The cited review on psychoneuroimmunology specifically noted negative immune system effects among Alzheimer caregivers.

Calabrese, R. L., & Schumer, H. (1986). The effects of service activities on adolescent alienation. *Adolescence, 21,* 675–687.

Cialdini, R. B., & Fultz, J. (1990). Interpreting the negative mood/helping literature via Mega-analysis. *Psychological Bulletin, 107,* 210–214.

Cialdini, R. B., Kenrick, D. T., & Baumann, D. J. (1982). Effects of mood on prosocial behavior in children and adults. In N. Eisenberg (Ed.), *The development of prosocial behavior* (pp. 339–359). New York: Academic Press.

Clary, E. G., Snyder, M., Ridge, R. D., Copel, J., Stukas, A. A., et al. (1998). Understanding and assessing the motivations of volunteers: A functional approach. *Journal of Personality and Social Psychology, 74,* 1516–1530.

Conrad, D., & Hedin, D. (1981). *National assessment of experiential education: A final report.* Minneapolis, MN: Center for Youth Development and Research.

Conrad, D., & Hedin, D. (1982). The impact of experiential education on adolescent development. *Child and Youth Services, 4,* 57–76.

Durkheim, E. (1951). *Suicide* (Trans. J. Spalding & G. Simpson). New York: Free Press. (Original work published 1898)

Eccles, J. S., & Barber, B. L. (1999). Student council, volunteering, basketball, or marching band: What kind of extracurricular involvement matters? *Journal of Adolescent Research, 14,* 10–43.

Elbaum, B., Vaughn, S., Hughes, M., & Moody, S. W. (1999). Grouping practices and reading outcomes for students with disabilities. *Exceptional Children, 65,* 399–415.

Ellison, C. G. (1991). Religious involvement and subjective well-being. *Journal of Health and Social Behavior, 32,* 80–99.

Follman, J., & Muldoon, K. (1997). Florida learn and serve 1995–96. *NAASP Bulletin, 81,* 29–36.

Gardner, W. E. (1978). Compeer assistance through tutoring and group guidance activities. *Urban Review, 10,* 45–54.

Gecas, V., & Burke, P.J. (1995). Self and identity. In K. S. Cook, G. A. Fine, & J. S. House (Eds.), *Sociological perspectives on social psychology* (pp. 41–67). Boston: Allyn and Bacon.

Giles, D. E., Jr., & Eyler, J. (1994). The impact of a college community service laboratory on students' personal, social, and cognitive outcomes. *Journal of Adolescence, 17,* 327–339.

Giles, D. E., Jr., & Eyler, J. (1998). A service learning research agenda for the next five years. *New Directions for Teaching and Learning, 73,* 65–72.

Hamilton, S. F., & Zeldin, R. S. (1987). Learning civics in the community. *Curriculum Inquiry, 17,* 407–420.

Harris, M. B. (1977). Effects of altruism on mood. *Journal of Social Psychology, 91,* 37–41.

House, J. S. (1995). *Americans' changing lives: Waves I and II, 1986 and 1989.* Ann Arbor, MI: Inter-University Consortium for Political and Social Research.

Johnson, M. K., Beebe, T. , Mortimer, J. T., & Snyder, M. (1998). Volunteerism in adolescence: A process perspective. *Journal of Research on Adolescence, 8,* 309–332.

Kendrick, J. R., Jr. (1996). Outcomes of service-learning in an introduction to sociology course. *Michigan Journal of Community Service Learning, 3,* 72–81.

Keyes, C. L. M. (1998). Social well-being . *Social Psychology Quarterly, 61,* 121–140.

Langer, E. J., & Rodin, J. (1976) The effects of choice and enhanced personal responsibility for the aged: A field experiment in an institutional setting. *Journal of Personality and Social Psychology, 34,* 191–198.

Larson, R. (1994). Youth organizations, hobbies, and sports as developmental contexts. In R. K. Silbereisen & E. Todt (Eds.), *Adolescence in context: The interplay of family, school, peers, and work in adjustment* (pp. 46–65). Boulder, CO: Westview Press.

Lee, L. (1997). *Change of self-concept in the first year of college life: The effect of gender and community involvement.* Unpublished doctoral dissertation, University of Wisconsin, Madison.

Marks, S. R. (1977). Multiple roles and role strain: Some notes on human energy, time and commitment. *American Sociological Review, 42,* 921–936.

Midlarsky, E. (1991). Helping as coping. In M. C. Clark (Ed.), *Prosocial behavior: Review of personality and social psychology* (Vol. 12, pp. 238–264). Newbury Park, CA: Sage.

Midlarsky, E., & Kahana, E. (1994). *Altruism in later life.* Thousand Oaks, CA: Sage.

Miller, J. (1994). Linking traditional and service-learning courses: Outcome evaluations utilizing two pedagogically distinct models. *Michigan Journal of Community Service Learning, 1,* 29–36.

Moen, P., Dempster-McClain, D., & Williams, R. M., Jr. (1989). Social integration and longevity. *American Sociological Review, 54,* 635–647.

Moen, P., Dempster-McClain, D., & Williams, R. M., Jr. (1992). Successful aging: A life-course perspective on women's multiple roles and health. *American Journal of Sociology, 97,* 1612–1638.

Moore, C. W., & Allen, J. P. (1996). The effects of volunteering on the young volunteer. *The Journal of Primary Prevention, 17,* 231–258.

Musick, M. A., Herzog, A. R., & House, J. S. (1999). Volunteering and mortality among older adults: Findings from a national sample. *The Journals of Gerontology: Psychological sciences and social sciences, 54B,* S173–S180.

Musick, M. A., & Wilson, J. (in press). Volunteering and depression: The role of psychological and social resources in different age groups. *Social Science and Medicine.*

Myers-Lipton, S. J. (1996a). Effect of service-learning on college students' attitudes toward international understanding. *Journal of College Student Development, 37,* 659–668.

Myers-Lipton, S. J. (1996b). Effect of a comprehensive service-learning program on college students' level of modern racism. *Michigan Journal of Community Service Learning, 3*, 44–54.

Newman, S., Vasudev, J., & Onawola, R. (1985). Older volunteers' perceptions of impacts of volunteering on their psychological well-being. *Journal of Applied Gerontology, 4*, 123–127.

Newmann, F. A., & Rutter, R. A. (1983). *The effects of high school community service programs on students' social development: Final report.* Madison: Wisconsin Center for Educational Research.

Nowlis, V. 1970. Mood: Behavior experience. In M. Arnold (Ed.), *Feelings and emotions* (pp. 61–77). New York: Academic Press.

Oman, D., Thoresen, E., & McMahon, K. (1999). Volunteerism and mortality among the community-dwelling elderly. *Journal of Health Psychology, 4*, 301–316.

Osguthorpe, R. T., & Scruggs, T. E. (1986). Special education students as tutors: A review and analysis. *Remedial and Special Education, 7*, 15–25.

Piliavin, J. A., & Callero, P. L. (1991). *Giving blood: The development of an altruistic identity.* Baltimore: Johns Hopkins University Press.

Reitschlin, J. (1998). Voluntary association membership and psychological distress. *Journal of Health and Social Behavior, 39*, 348–355.

Rodin, J., & Langer, E. (1977). Long-term effects of a control-relevant intervention with the institutionalized aged. *Journal of Personality and Social Psychology, 35*, 897–902.

Sax, L. J., & Astin, A. W. (1997). The benefits of service: Evidence from undergraduates. *Educational Record, 78*, 25–32.

Scruggs, T. E., Mastropieri, M. A., & Richter, L. (1985). Peer tutoring with behaviorally disordered students: Social and academic benefits. *Behavioral Disorders, 10*, 283–294.

Sieber, S. D. (1974). Toward a theory of role accumulation. *American Sociological Review, 39*, 567–578.

Snyder, M., Clary, E. G., & Stukas, A. A. (2000). The functional approach to volunteerism. In G. R. Maio & J. M. Olson (Eds.), *Why we evaluate: Functions of attitudes* (pp. 365–393). Hillsdale, NJ: Erlbaum.

Snyder, M., & Omoto, A. M. (1991). Who helps and why? The psychology of AIDS volunteerism. In S. Spacapan & S. Oskamp (Eds.), *Helping and being helped: Naturalistic studies* (pp. 213–239). Newbury Park, CA: Sage.

Stukas, A. A., Clary, E. G., & Snyder, M. (1999). Service learning: Who benefits and why? *Social Policy Report: Society for Research in Child Development, 8*, 1–19.

Thoits, P. A. (1986). Social support and psychological well-being: Theoretical possibilities. In I. G. Sarason & B. R. Sarason (Eds.), *Social support: theory, research, and application* (pp. 51–72). Dordrecht, The Netherlands: Martinus Nijhoff.

Thoits, P. A. (1992). Multiple identities: Examining gender and marital status differences in distress. *Social Psychology Quarterly, 55,* 236–256.

Thoits, P. A. (1995). Identity-relevant events and psychological symptoms: A cautionary tale. *Journal of Health and Social Behavior, 36,* 72–82.

Thoits, P. A., & Hewitt, L. N. (2001). Volunteer work and well-being. *Journal of Health and Social Behavior, 42,* 115–131.

Uggen, C., & Janikula, J. (1999). Volunteerism and arrest in the transition to adulthood. *Social Forces, 78,* 331–362.

Van Willigen, M. (1998, Aug. 20–22). *Doing good, feeling better: The effect of voluntary association membership on individual well-being.* Paper presented at the annual meeting of the Society for the Study of Social Problems, San Francisco.

Van Willigen, M. (2000). Differential benefits of volunteering across the life course. *Journals of Gerontology: Social Sciences, 55B,* S308–S318.

Weiss, R. F., Boyer, J. L., Lombardo, J. P., & Stich, M. H. (1973). Altruistic drive and altruistic reinforcement. *Journal of Personality and Social Psychology, 25,* 390–400.

Weiss, R. F., Buchanan, W., Altstatt, L., & Lombardo, J. P. (1971). Altruism is rewarding. *Science, 11,* 1262–1263.

Wheeler, J. A., Gorey, K. M., & Greenblatt, B. (1998). The beneficial effects of volunteering for older volunteers and the people they serve: A meta-analysis. *International Journal of Aging and Human Development, 47,* 69–79.

Williams, R. (1991). The impact of field education on student development: Research findings. *Journal of Cooperative Education, 27,* 29–45.

Winter, S. (1996). Paired reading: Three questions. *Educational Psychology in Practice, 12,* 182–189.

Yates, M., & Youniss, J. (1996a). Community service and political-moral identity in adolescents. *Journal of Research on Adolescence, 6,* 271–284.

Yates, M., & Youniss, J. (1996b). A developmental perspective on community service in adolescence. *Social Development, 5,* 85–11.

Yogev, A., & Ronen, R. (1982). Cross-age tutoring: Effects on tutors' attributes. *Journal of Educational Research, 75,* 261–268.

Young, F. W., & Glasgow, N. (1998). Voluntary social participation and health. *Research on Aging, 20,* 339–362.

11

THE INTERMARRIAGE OF WISDOM AND SELECTIVE OPTIMIZATION WITH COMPENSATION: TWO META-HEURISTICS GUIDING THE CONDUCT OF LIFE

PAUL B. BALTES AND ALEXANDRA M. FREUND

The notion of flourishing has a long history in the social sciences and the humanities (P. Baltes & Baltes, 1999; P. Baltes & Staudinger, 2000). Philosophers and humanists in particular have attempted to specify its meaning. Concepts such as *eudaimonia* (happiness) and a good life, for instance, were central to early Greek and other early humanist writings. To illustrate, consider a citation from the work of Amelie O. Rorty, a scholar on Greek philosophy: "Happiness is defined . . . as an activity of the soul in accordance with rationality and virtue" (1980, p. 3; see also Kekes, 1995; Nussbaum, 1994; Rice, 1958; Robinson, 1990).

Another important distinction of Greek philosophical thought is the differentiation between the theoretical and the practical sciences, a distinction often associated with Aristotle (Dittmann-Kohli & Baltes, 1990; Nussbaum, 1994; Robinson, 1990). Especially relevant for this chapter is the application of the theoretical–practical distinction to the concept of wisdom. Theoretical wisdom *(sophia)*, in this tradition, is knowledge as knowledge about the phenomena and causes of truth and the human condition. Practical wisdom *(phronesis)*, on the other hand, deals with knowledge translated into action and producing real outcomes. In the spirit of this historical evolution, a central tenet of this chapter is that psychological work on ideas such as flourishing and a good life benefit from consideration of philosophical and humanist work. We argue that several disciplines are required to elaborate the concept, in the same way that the coordination of several senses and representational modes are needed to grasp the meaning of an elephant, as the old chestnut illustrates.

Keeping in mind the fertility of interdisciplinary work on the meaning and conduct of life, this chapter is our first effort at marrying two research programs (research on wisdom and research on the theory of selection, optimization, and compensation) conducted at the Berlin Max Planck Institute for Human Development. Specifically, we propose that wisdom—knowledge about the fundamental aspects of the human condition—offers the most general meta-frame of the nature of optimal human development. Furthermore, we propose that the implementation of such wisdom-related knowledge is achievable on the behavioral level by selection, optimization, and compensation (SOC). Finally, we suggest that during ontogenesis, wisdom and SOC can engage each other in mutually facilitative ways.

As illustrated in Figure 11.1, wisdom defines the most general space of developmentally, ethically, and morally appropriate goals and means associated with the conduct and meaning of life. This most general space provided by wisdom is the foundation on which goals and means are seen as desirable in principle. SOC, on the other hand, is basically value-neutral as far as goals and means are concerned. The model of SOC outlines an ensemble of behavioral strategies by which goals and means can be pursued and attained. In this sense, the SOC model specifies ways of implementing wisdom. A successful life, then, is enhanced by a joint consideration of wisdom and SOC.

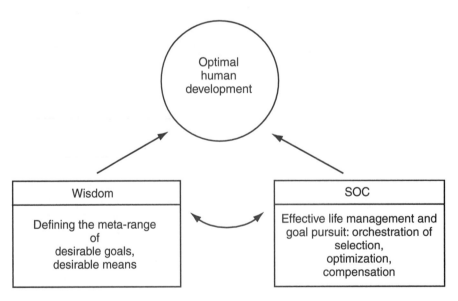

Figure 11.1. The concept of human strength as the integration of wisdom, the knowledge about fundamental pragmatics of life, and the life-management strategies of selection, optimization, and compensation.

THEORETICAL BACKGROUND OF WISDOM

The most general definition of wisdom implies that wisdom entails a convergence of means and ends toward excellence involving the personal and the common good. In this sense, wisdom is a concept that aims at the peak of human functioning (P. Baltes, Dittmann-Kohli, & Dixon, 1984; P. Baltes & Smith, 1990; P. Baltes & Staudinger, 2000; Dittmann-Kohli & Baltes, 1990; Kekes, 1995; Sternberg, 1990; see also Exhibit 11.1). Theoretical wisdom, which is knowledge about what is good and right for humans, and the application and realization of this knowledge in the conduct of one's life (practical wisdom) is purported to produce happiness and life satisfaction. The origins of this notion lie in the distant past of civilization (P. Baltes & Staudinger, 1993, 2000). For instance, in the philosophical tradition of the ancient Greeks, wisdom and its realization are often regarded as virtue, a key concept in which the question of happiness is concerned (Kekes, 1995; Lehrer, Lum, Slichta, & Smith, 1996; Oelmüller, 1989; Rice, 1958; Welsch, 1995).

According to Aristotle, for instance, the highest and purest form of happiness is theoretical wisdom. In Ancient Greece, philosophers often argued that this highest form of happiness lies exclusively in the realm of the gods or the divine ideals. Humans can only achieve the "second best" form of happiness (practical wisdom), which is a function of both *knowing* what is good and right and the conceptual and specific *realization*—the pragmatic aspect—of this knowledge. Similarly, the philosophical school *Stoa* taught that virtue is the knowledge of what is good and bad and, accordingly, of what ought and ought not to be done. Virtue is the practical and therefore realizable knowledge about the conditions of life. In one form or another, theoretical and practical wisdom need to converge. The result is a good life and happiness in the Greek sense of *eudaemonia*.

Note in this context that the wisdom-related use of the concept of happiness or similar concepts is not at all identical with psychologists' versions of happiness, well-being, life satisfaction, and the like (see, e.g., Kahnemann, Diener, & Schwarz, 1999; Ryff, 1989; Staudinger 1999b). Psychologists tend to focus on the study of well-being and life satisfaction *without* an explicit consideration of an underlying dimension of truth or societally based evaluation concerning which forms of manifested happiness, well-being, or life satisfaction are morally or ethically appropriate (but see Keyes, 1998).

There are arguably good reasons for this abstinence of psychologists from normative prescription—such as their preference for pluralism and tolerance. Full abstention, however, is not possible. When psychologists approach the question of evaluation, they use more indirect evidence of moral–ethical evaluation. One example is the concept of social desirability. Thus, for instance, psychologists might argue that there is a high correlation between social-desirability ratings and the indicators used to measure well-being and that, therefore, there is a high likelihood that the behaviors expressed are also positive in terms of ethics and morality.

Another and more direct example is research driven by developmental conceptions associated with higher stages of functioning à la Erikson or Piaget (Kramer, 1990; Labouvie-Vief, 1990, 1995). In this vein, the work of Ryff (1989) is relevant. In the Eriksonian tradition, Ryff postulated several facets along which well-being can be evaluated beyond an individual's self-report of being more or less happy or more or less satisfied. One of the facets, for instance, is the conception of personal growth. Despite these worthwhile indirect efforts, we need to acknowledge that the classical philosophical conception of happiness or similar concepts (such as a good life) is fundamentally distinct from this moral-neutral or desirability-based approach practiced by mainstream psychology.

THE BERLIN WISDOM PARADIGM

In our work, we define wisdom as an expert knowledge system concerning the fundamental pragmatics of life, including knowledge and judgment about the conduct and meaning of life (P. Baltes & Smith, 1990; P. Baltes & Staudinger, 2000). By fundamental pragmatics, we mean knowledge and judgment about the most important (fundamental) aspects of the human condition and the ways and means of planning, managing, and understanding a good life. As the gestalt of descriptions and Exhibit 11.1 signal (see also Pasupathi & Baltes, 2000; Staudinger & Baltes, 1994), wisdom is a construct that has a very rich and multifaceted meaning; its facets are bound together to identify a coordinated ensemble.

In our work, the quality of wisdom and the capacity for judgment in the fundamental pragmatics of life are defined through a set of five criteria. The two general criteria (*factual* and *procedural knowledge*) are characteristic of all types of expertise and stem from the tradition of expertise research (Ericsson & Smith, 1991). Applied to this subject area, these criteria are rich factual (declarative) knowledge and rich procedural knowledge about the fundamental pragmatics of life.

In addition to these two basic criteria that are generally relevant for expertise, we have, based on lifespan theory, formulated three meta-criteria that we consider specific to wisdom. The first, *lifespan contextualism*, is meant to identify knowledge that considers the many themes and contexts of life (e.g., education, family, work, friends, leisure, the public good of society, etc.), their interrelations and cultural variations, and in addition, incorpo-

EXHIBIT 11.1
Wisdom Criteria: General Criteria Derived From Cultural–Historical Analysis and Specific Criteria (Berlin Wisdom Paradigm) Used to Analyze Wisdom-Related Products

General Criteria Outlining the Nature of Wisdom

- Wisdom addresses important and difficult questions and strategies about the conduct and meaning of life.
- Wisdom includes knowledge about the limits of knowledge and the uncertainties of the world.
- Wisdom represents a truly superior level of knowledge, judgment, and advice.
- Wisdom constitutes knowledge with extraordinary scope, depth, and balance.
- Wisdom involves a perfect synergy of mind and character—that is, an orchestration of knowledge and virtues.
- Wisdom represents knowledge used for the good or well-being of oneself and of others.
- Wisdom, though difficult to achieve and to specify, is easily recognized when manifested.

Criteria Used in Berlin Wisdom Paradigm to Operationalize Wisdom as Expertise in the Fundamental Pragmatics of Life

- Rich factual knowledge about life.
- Rich procedural knowledge about life.
- Lifespan contextualism.
- Relativism of values and life priorities.
- Recognition and management of uncertainty.

Source: From P. Baltes and Staudinger (2000).

rates a lifetime temporal perspective (i.e., past, present, and future). The second wisdom-specific meta-criterion, *relativism of values and life priorities*, is the acknowledgment of and tolerance for value differences and the relativity of life priorities. Wisdom, of course, is not meant to imply full-blown relativity of values and value-related life priorities. On the contrary, it includes an explicit concern with the topic of virtue and the common good in contrast to exclusively considering one's own personal good.

The third meta-criterion, the *recognition of and management of uncertainty*, is based on the ideas that (a) the validity of human information processing itself is essentially limited (constrained); (b) individuals have access only to select parts of reality; and (c) the future cannot be fully known in advance. Wisdom-related knowledge and judgment offer ways and means to deal with such uncertainty about human insight and the conditions of the world, individually and collectively.

Empirical Research

So far, the Berlin wisdom paradigm has focused primarily on life-management tasks and their assessment by think-aloud protocols. These were evaluated by application of the five criteria listed in the bottom part of Exhibit 11.1. Note in this context that for a response to approach wisdom, it needs to qualify for high scores on each of the five criteria. Based on our past research on wisdom (P. Baltes & Staudinger, 2000), Exhibit 11.2 gives an illustration of two responses that would be scored as high or low on wisdom. The responses are think-aloud protocols from two individuals for the life problem "A 15-year-old girl wants to get married right away."

The available research on the ontogeny and expression of wisdom also addressed questions such as age, gender, professional training, personality, and experiential characteristics associated with individual differences in levels of wisdom-related knowledge. Thus, we know that the body of knowledge and cognitive skills associated with wisdom has its largest rate of change gradient in late adolescence and young adulthood (Pasupathi & Baltes, 2000; Staudinger, 1999a). Subsequent age changes are a result of specific circumstances of life and nonintellectual attributes. For instance, the development of wisdom-related knowledge during adulthood is more conditioned by personality, cognitive style, and life experience than by psychometric intelligence (Staudinger, Maciel, Smith, & Baltes, 1998). In principle, wisdom-related knowledge can continue to flourish into early old age (P. Baltes, Staudinger, Maercker, & Smith, 1995). Aside from a general state of brain health, whether wisdom-related knowledge continues to evolve is dependent on wisdom-salient life experiences, including professional skills and opportunities for practice and being mentored (Smith, Staudinger, &

EXHIBIT 11.2
Berlin Wisdom Paradigm: Illustration of Wisdom-Related Tasks With Examples of Extreme Responses (Abbreviated)[a]

A 15-year-old girl wants to get married right away. What should one/she consider and do?

Low Wisdom-Related Score

A 15-year-old girl wants to get married? No, no way, marrying at age 15 would be utterly wrong. One has to tell the girl that marriage is not possible. (After further probing) It would be irresponsible to support such an idea. No, this is just a crazy idea.

High Wisdom-Related Score

Well, on the surface, this seems like an easy problem. On average, marriage for 15-year-old girls is not a good thing. But there are situations where the average case does not fit. Perhaps in this instance, special life circumstances are involved, such that the girl has a terminal illness. Or the girl has just lost her parents. And also, this girl may live in another culture or historical period. Perhaps she was raised with a value system different from ours. In addition, one has to think about adequate ways of talking with the girl and to consider her emotional state.

[a]See also P. Baltes and Staudinger (2000).

Baltes, 1994). Finally, the expression of wisdom-related knowledge involves a strong "interactive minds" or social–collaborative component (Staudinger, 1996; Staudinger & Baltes, 1996).

WISDOM AS META-HEURISTIC

Recently, P. Baltes and Staudinger (2000) have enlarged this definitional frame to also include wisdom as a cognitive and motivational meta-heuristic. As a meta-heuristic or meta-pragmatic concept, wisdom is aimed at organizing and guiding the overall conduct of life toward excellence. A key challenge is how to understand the link between wisdom as knowledge (theoretical wisdom) and wisdom as behavioral expression (practical wisdom). To this end, P. Baltes and Staudinger (2000; see also Kunzmann & Baltes, 2002) have started to elaborate on the question of how wisdom-related knowledge is translated into behavioral manifestations.

Specifically, we highlighted the importance of wisdom as a heuristic. In the tradition of the psychology of heuristics (e.g., Gigerenzer, Todd, & the ABC Group, 1999), we claim that wisdom is a *meta-heuristic with fast, efficient, and broad applicability*. Following Gigerenzer et al. (1999), for instance, a heuristic can be defined as a "useful shortcut, an approximation, or a rule of thumb for guiding search" (p. 28). In the area of cognitive judgments and decisions, Gigerenzer et al. (1999) have demonstrated the adaptiveness of a number of simple, cognitive heuristics in everyday life. They label these as "fast and frugal" heuristics.

If wisdom as a meta-heuristic operates effectively, the expectation is that its use creates the cognitive and motivational foundation from which well-being can be achieved. In this sense, wisdom can be seen as the embodiment of the best subjective beliefs about laws of life that a culture has to offer and that individuals under favorable conditions are able to acquire. Note in this context again that aging by itself does not produce wisdom. An everyday saying (personal communication, John R. Nesselroade, Aug. 2001) tells this story: "It's easier to get old than to get wise."

In our view, then, wisdom as a meta-heuristic coordinates the bodies of knowledge that individuals possess about the fundamental pragmatics of life and about the general ways and means toward human excellence. In other words, wisdom provides at the highest level of cognitive and behavioral representation a frame within which strategies and goals involving the conduct and meaning of life can be elaborated. The meaning context of wisdom, then, forms the most general space of goals and means within which specific elaborations of the ways and means of living a good life can proceed.

The SOC model specifies strategies of life management that make the delineation and pursuit of goals possible in any domain of functioning. In this sense, SOC is also relevant for the translation of wisdom into practical behavior.

We argued earlier that wisdom at the highest level of analysis is a heuristic for the "what" and "how" of leading a good life. Now we argue that SOC is also such a simple and fast and frugal heuristic—this time at the level of behavioral implementation. So far, we are not aware that such simple heuristics have been identified for the area of life planning (Smith, 1996). There is relevant work, of course, on effective behavior implementation strategies (e.g., Bargh & Gollwitzer, 1994; H. Heckhausen, 1991; H. Heckhausen & Gollwitzer, 1987; Oettingen, 1996). Most definitely this research has furthered our understanding of important factors for the occurrence and maintenance of behavior. However, it does not address the question of an overall and broadly applicable guiding rule for life management in the sense of achieving a wisdom-like good life that prescribes what ends and means are acceptable in principle or more or less desirable from a moral–ethical point of view.

In theory, SOC is an effort to achieve behavioral implementation using a set of three concepts that are derived from lifespan psychology (M. Baltes & Carstensen, 1996; P. Baltes, 1997; P. Baltes & Baltes, 1990; Freund & Baltes, 2000, 2002; Marsiske, Long, Baltes, & Baltes, 1995). On the basis of the SOC model, we argue that there are three "simple" heuristics that, in their coordinated orchestration, promote successful life-management. On a very general level, these guiding rules are as follows:

- *Select*: Delineate the range of possible alternative options or ends (articulate, develop, and commit to a set of goals).
- *Optimize*: Acquire and invest–apply means to achieve the ends or goals selected.
- *Compensate*: When confronted with loss or other forms of blockage of previously available goal-relevant means, acquire and invest alternative means to maintain functioning or goal attainment.

These definitions are general, and additional specification requires a concrete behavioral context and a specific theory that is appropriate for the goal domain under consideration. For instance, the processes of selection, optimization, and compensation differ whether applied to functions such as perception, cognitive problem solving, achievement motivation, personal control (see, e.g., J. Heckhausen, 1999; J. Heckhausen & Schulz, 1995), or the regulation of sensori-motor behavior (Li, Lindenberger, Freund, & Baltes,

2001). Note also that the processes associated with each of the three components can be conscious or unconscious, active or passive, internally or externally driven. In the next section, we will sketch how these guiding rules might function in promoting successful development.

To highlight the specific function of SOC in the present line of inquiry, we offer an intermediate summary: Although SOC-related rules give guidelines for *how* to proceed in a given situation involving means–ends relations, SOC does not specify what goals one "should" select from a moral–ethical point of view or what means might be ethically and morally appropriate for goal pursuit or maintenance in the face of loss. Mafia bosses as well as someone such as Mother Teresa can make use of SOC. The concept of wisdom is required to know which goals to pursue and which path of goal pursuit promotes one's own well-being as well as the well-being of others—that is, to live a good life.

EXCURSUS: AN ACTION-THEORETICAL ACCOUNT OF SOC

The aim of this section is to provide a more detailed account of SOC if, as one paradigm sample case, one takes an *action-theoretical* approach (e.g., Boesch, 1991; Brandtstädter, 1999; Eckensberger & Meacham, 1984; Gollwitzer & Bargh, 1996) to the specification and elaboration of SOC (Freund & Baltes, 2000, 2002; Freund et al., 1999). Action-theoretical paradigms emphasize conceptions of behavior that include intentionality, goal intention, goal pursuit, and goal attainment. This approach allows integrating motivational processes of goal selection and goal pursuit into a lifespan perspective. Summaries of other areas or theories of application of SOC are available in B. Baltes and Dickson (2001), M. Baltes and Carstensen (1998), P. Baltes (1997), Freund and P. Baltes (1998, 2000), Freund, Li, and Baltes (1999), Lerner, Freund, de Stefanis, and Habermas (2001), and Marsiske et al. (1995).

In the following, we present evidence on the operation of the three fundamental processes (selection, optimization, and compensation) that we postulate is necessary to organize and optimize the developmental process. Note again that this approach based in action theory is but one way to specify and operationalize SOC.

Selection

Throughout the lifespan, biological, social, and individual opportunities and constraints specify a range of alternative domains of functioning (see also J. Heckhausen, 1999). Within this great variety of options that is usually larger than the amount of resources available to the individual, people actively and passively, consciously and unconsciously select domains in which to focus their resources and efforts. In action theory, the domains selected are conceptualized as goals. Selection of goals operates as a precondition for (a) specialized "canalization" and (b) the additional acquisition of resources in the sense of development as optimization. Developing, elaborating, and committing to a goal—in other words, selection—directs development. These personal goals guide and organize behavior across situations and time (e.g., Emmons, 1996).

There are various ways to taxonomize goals. One important distinction is between approach and avoidance goals. In this vein, it has been repeatedly shown in cognitive research on judgment and decision making (e.g., Tversky & Kahnemann, 1981) as well the motivational literature (e.g., Emmons, 1996; Higgins, Grant, & Shah, 1999) that it is important to distinguish between a "gain" and a "loss" focus when investigating goal-related processes. Impending or actual losses seem to affect people more strongly than gains (Hobfoll, 1989). On the other hand, the goal literature has also shown that the pursuit of avoidance rather than approach goals is detrimental for both well-being and actual attainment of goals (e.g., Coats, Janoff-Bulman, & Alpert, 1996; Elliot & Sheldon, 1997; Elliot, Sheldon, & Church, 1997).

This fundamental distinction between a gain focus and a loss focus is captured in the SOC-model by distinguishing between two modes of selection, *elective selection* and *loss-based selection*. Throughout the lifespan, individuals encounter losses in goal-relevant resources affecting their positive functioning. Note that losses in means may not be a result of permanent losses in basic potential but may also be a response to temporary blockage or negative transfer because of the pursuit of other means. Consider as an illustration the example of a loss in athletic skills when a high school student invests more time and effort into the pursuit of academic goals. Presumably, with a redirection of efforts, the athletic skills could be reacquired.

Elective selection is the delineation of goals to advance the match of a person's needs and motives with the given or attainable resources and opportunity structures. With elective selection, individuals aim at achieving higher levels of functioning (i.e., a gain focus). In contrast, loss-based selection occurs as a response to losses in previously available goal-relevant means, threatening the maintenance of goal attainment. Loss-based selection involves changes in goals or the goal-system such as reconstructing one's goal hierarchy, focusing on the most important goal(s), adapting standards, or searching for new goals (cf., assimilative coping, Brandtstädter & Wentura, 1995; compensatory secondary control, J. Heckhausen, 1999).

The hypothesis that selection of goals promotes positive development and a sense of flourishing is supported by empirical research. On the one hand, to hold and feel committed to goals contributes to believing that one's life has a purpose and thereby gives meaning to life (e.g., Klinger, 1977; B. Little, 1989; Staudinger, 1999b). On the other hand, goals organize behavior into action sequences. Goals reduce the complexity of any given situation as they guide attention and behavior. In other words, goals can also be seen as permanently available decision rules ("implemental mind-set," Gollwitzer, 1994) for directing attention (which of the numerous stimuli or information are goal-relevant?) and for behavior selection (which of the many behavioral options in this situation are goal-relevant?). As such, goals, like wisdom, are heuristics although at a more microlevel of behavior than would be true for wisdom: Instead of deliberating about all of the possible alternatives one has in any given situation, people—consciously or unconsciously—scan their environment for possibilities to pursue their goals.

Optimization

Whereas selection of goals is the first step toward positive functioning, the SOC model posits that, for achieving desired outcomes in the domains selected, it is crucial to acquire, apply, and refine goal-relevant means (i.e., optimization). What means are best suited for achieving one's goals varies according to the specific goal domain (e.g., academic versus social domain), personal characteristics (e.g., gender, temperament), and the sociocultural context (e.g., availability of institutional support systems or cultural modes of adaptive fitness).

It is possible, however, to identify a number of general processes involved in the acquisition, application, and refinement of goal-relevant means (see M. Baltes & Carstensen, 1996; P. Baltes, 1997; Freund & Baltes, 2000, 2002; Freund et al., 1999). On the most general level, some sort of monitoring between the actual state and the desired state (goal) needs to take place (Carver & Scheier, 1995; Miller, Galanter, & Pribram, 1960). This continuous monitoring that might occur outside of conscious awareness (Wegner, 1992) allows a constant adaptation of goal-related action. Progress toward the goal indicates the continuation of the invested goal-relevant means; whereas no progress or even a greater distance from the goal indicates that other means might be better suited for achieving the respective goal (Boesch, 1976, 1991).

How does a person "know" what means are best suited for achieving ones' goal? Cultural knowledge about means–ends beliefs, for instance, is important for goal pursuit because it provides information about which internal and external causal factors lead to a given goal. Means–ends beliefs (Little, 1998; Skinner, Chapman, & Baltes, 1988) vary by domains or contexts, such as school, friendship, or work. Moreover, goal-relevant means can be acquired in a number of different ways (Bandura, 1995), such as observing and modeling successful others, instruction by more experienced others (e.g., parents, teachers, coaches, peers, experts), reading manuals about the effectiveness of means, or direct experience.

To act on one's beliefs, however, people also need to believe that they are, in general, able to achieve a given outcome or goal (control beliefs) and have access to and can apply the required goal-relevant means. This is the topic of perceived control, agency, and efficacy (Bandura, 1995; Little, Oettingen, Stetsenko, & Baltes, 1995; Skinner, 1995). One of the most important theories in this field is Bandura's notion of self-efficacy. His program of research demonstrates the importance of agency and control beliefs for acquiring goal-relevant means, for engaging in goal-related actions, and for positive functioning (see also Flammer, 1990; Seligman, 1991).

An additional example for general processes that are closely related to optimization is the ability to delay immediate gratification for the sake of more long-term payoff (e.g., Mischel, Cantor, & Feldman, 1996). Long-term goals often require investing resources with no immediate gain (e.g., studying for good SAT scores instead on partying tonight). Resisting temptations that offer short-term gratifications is thus a precondition for persistently pursuing a goal over an extended period of time. The importance of the ability to delay gratification for positive functioning is also underscored by a finding reported by Mischel et al. (1996) that impulse control (delay of gratification) in children predicts academic performance about a decade later.

Another very general conception of an optimization mechanism is that of physical theories of practice and associated advances in expertise toward peak performance (Ericsson & Smith, 1991). As already expressed in folk knowledge: "Practice makes perfect." There is strong empirical evidence for this view, although for practice to be effective certain conditions of learning and motivational commitment need to be fulfilled. For instance, Ericsson (1996) highlighted the significance of "deliberate" practice. Practice leads not only to the refinement of skill components but also to their integration. Repeated practice also leads to the automation of skills that become less resource-demanding and free resources that can be devoted to other goal-related means.

Although the role of practice might be most obvious in domains with a clear achievement aspect, such as academic achievement, sports, or music (Ericsson, 1996), practice is also important for domains with less clearly defined skills and criteria. For instance, the literature on marital therapy shows that many marital problems occur because partners lack the skills to communicate effectively with each other. After practicing the application of such skills over extended periods of time, these skills positively affect the marriage (e.g., Markman, Floyd, Stanley, & Storaasli, 1988). Thus, practice of skills can be considered central for achieving desired outcomes in most, if not all, life domains.

Compensation

Compensation has many sources but always occurs in response to a loss in means that are relevant for goal attainment. Its behavioral function is to maintain a given level of goal attainment. Some losses in means are a result, for instance, to a redirection of attention, others to more or less permanent losses in biological capacity. One relevant strategy to regulate loss was already mentioned earlier in the context of changes in goal structures—that is, loss-based selection.

In the SOC model, compensation designates another loss-based component that focuses on ways to overcome losses in means without changes in goals. In SOC theory, when goals are maintained despite losses or blockages of previously effective means—for instance, by using alternative means—we speak of compensation. Typical instances are the substitution of previously available goal-relevant means by acquiring new means (e.g., glasses to compensate for loss in visual acuity), activating unused internal or external resources, such as notebooks as external aids for the case of memory or the use of social partners as providers of means (cf., M. Baltes, 1996; Bäckman & Dixon, 1992; Carstensen, Hanson, & Freund, 1995; Marsiske et al., 1995; Schönpflug, 1998).

From a lifespan developmental perspective, the maintenance of positive functioning by compensatory means is as important for successful developmental regulation as a growth focus (optimization). This is the case because development at any point in the lifespan can be characterized as always comprising both gains and losses (P. Baltes, 1987, 1997; P. Baltes, Baltes, Freund, & Lang, 1999; Brandtstädter & Wentura, 1995; Labouvie-Vief, 1981). However, it is also true that with age, there might be an increasing need to invest more resources into maintenance and resilience of functioning rather than into processes of increased adaptive fitness or growth (M. Baltes & Carstensen, 1996, 1998; P. Baltes, 1997; Dixon & Bäckman, 1995; Staudinger, Marsiske, & Baltes, 1995).

In other words, compensation is not only conspicuous in old age, as SOC originally maintained (P. Baltes & M. Baltes, 1980), but also infants, children, and adults. Examples are compensatory behaviors in child motor development, or the negative transfer that results from massive attention to goals selected for primary expertise, or the shift in efficacy of means that results from redirecting one's attention to new developmental tasks.

As was discussed in the context of optimization, what means are best suited for maintaining a given level of functioning in the face of loss or an otherwise neglected or blocked means depends on the domain of functioning and the adaptive affordances of the context. In each instance, SOC theory assumes the origin of compensation to be a deficit or a loss. There are cases, however, in which the dynamics of compensation are such that their functional consequences may in the long run result in positive outcomes beyond maintaining the level of functioning that gave rise to compensation. In other words, what once originated as a compensatory behavior may subsequently become part of a system of optimization involving other targets or goals of development (see P. Baltes, 1997; Freund et al., 1999; Marsiske et al., 1995, for additional exposition of SOC as a dynamic and changing system of adaptive self-organization).

From a motivational perspective, the origin of compensation (i.e., the pursuit of avoidance goals) might have less positive consequences than optimization (i.e., the pursuit of approach goals). A number of studies (Coats, Janoff-Bulman, & Alpert, 1996; Elliot, & Sheldon, 1997; Elliot et al., 1997; Emmons, 1996) have shown that trying to achieve gains and growth is associated with a higher degree of self-efficacy and leads to positive emotions and well-being whereas trying to avoid losses and decline is related to negative emotions and distress.

This pattern of less positivity of avoidance goals, however, might change over developmental time for at least two reasons. First are the subsequent positive consequences of compensation that might come about as the compensatory means becomes part of the ensemble of resources that individuals use to move forward in development. Second are the losses, with aging, that increase and the resulting experiential and adaptive focus more on maintenance rather than additional growth (cf., P. Baltes, Staudinger, & Lindenberger, 1999; Freund & Baltes, 2000; J. Heckhausen, 1991; J. Heckhausen, Dixon, & Baltes, 1989). In this instance, effective use of compensatory behavior may become part of an overall positive goal system. In fact, Freund, Wiese, and Baltes (1999) have shown that older adults, in contrast to younger adults, seem to consider their involvement in compensatory behaviors as pleasing, whereas younger adults do not show evidence of positive emotions when asked to engage in compensatory behavior.

EMPIRICAL EVIDENCE ON EFFECTIVENESS OF SOC

Is there any empirical evidence that SOC serves as a heuristic for successful life management? And is there evidence that the application and realization of that knowledge—in other words, the engagement in SOC—actually promotes positive functioning (see also Freund & Baltes, 1998, 2000; Marsiske et al., 1995; Wiese, Freund, & Baltes, 2000)?

Knowledge of SOC

In research on naive theory or folk psychology, proverbs are viewed as a body of crystallized (folk) knowledge about human life (Haselager,

1997; Mieder, 1993, 1997; Peng & Nisbett, 1998; Rogers, 1990). Proverbs are short statements summarizing advice on how to deal effectively or in morally correct ways with situations of everyday life (e.g., Mieder, 1997). In this sense, then, the effective use of proverbs can be linked to theories of practical wisdom (P. Baltes, Smith, & Staudinger, 1992; Baltes & Staudinger, 2000).

If cultural knowledge about the fundamental processes of successful life management as conceptualized by the model of selection, optimization, and compensation exists, it should also be possible to identify proverbs that contain knowledge or prescriptions (in the sense of specific heuristics) related to SOC. Consistent with this expectation, Ostrop (1996), in a thesis conducted in our laboratory, found that there is a substantial number of proverbs containing statements about behaviors that one can designate as selection, optimization, and compensation. Examples of such proverbs are for selection "Jack of all trades, master of none," for optimization "Practice makes perfect," for compensation "When there's no wind, grab the oars."

In a subsequent study, we (Freund & Baltes, in press) examined whether people, when asked to respond to life problems displayed on a computer screen, have access to proverbs that contain SOC-related knowledge. Specifically, we asked young and old adults to decide on the degree of match between problems of life and a pool of proverbs. Participants had to chose between a proverb reflecting strategies of selection, optimization, or compensation and proverbs reflecting other strategies of life management (e.g., "Everything comes to those who wait"). Alternative and SOC-targeted proverbs were matched on other criteria relevant for preference judgments such as familiarity, desirability, and perceived usefulness.

Results of this study confirmed our expectation. Participants chose SOC-related proverbs more frequently than alternative proverbs. Moreover, young and old adults chose proverbs reflecting SOC faster than proverbs reflecting alternative strategies of life management. In our view, this finding suggests that young and older adults hold subjective theories about life-management strategies that converge with SOC.

Adaptive Consequences of SOC

There is beginning evidence for a link between SOC-related knowledge and behavioral outcomes. On the one hand, as reviewed by Marsiske et al. (1995), there exists a large literature that is consistent with SOC and indirectly supports the SOC model (see also B. Baltes & Dickson, 2001; Freund & Baltes, 2000). Direct empirical investigation of SOC conducted in our laboratory has focused on a self-report measure, the SOC questionnaire (P. Baltes et al., 1999). This questionnaire assesses the component processes of SOC using a forced-choice format opposing two statements, one describing a behavior reflecting either selection, optimization, or compensation; the other one describing an alternative, non-SOC behavior.

In this way, the SOC-questionnaire assesses a person's reported preference for SOC-behaviors over alternative strategies of life management. Sample items are, for elective selection: "I concentrate all my energy on few things." (This is contrasted with, "I divide my energy among many things.") For loss-based selection: "When things don't go as well as before, I choose one or two important goals." (This is contrasted with, "When things don't go as well as before, I still try to keep all my goals.") For optimization: "I make every effort to achieve a given goal." (This is contrasted with, "I prefer to wait for a while and see if things will work out by themselves.") For compensation: "When things don't go as well as they used to, I keep trying other ways until I can achieve the same result I used to." (This is contrasted with, "When things don't go as well as they used to, I can accept it.")

Using this instrument, several studies have shown that self-reported SOC is associated with positive functioning. In old and very old age, a time in life when resources such as health, life-time, and the number of social partners become more restricted, for instance, selection, optimization, and compensation were positively related to subjective indicators of successful aging such as positive emotions, satisfaction with aging, and absence of loneliness (Freund & Baltes, 1998, 2002). In addition, M. Baltes and Lang (1997) have demonstrated that older adults who have more resources exhibit a tendency to display SOC-like behaviors.

Evidence for the functional usefulness of SOC is also available for young adults, arguably at their prime with regard to resources in many areas of life. They also seem to profit from engaging in the life-management strategies of selection, optimization, and compensation. In a study by Wiese et al. (2000), young adults reporting SOC behaviors scored higher on multiple subjective indicators of well-being, positive emotions, and success. In this study, the focus was on life management in two central life domains in young adulthood, namely work and family–partnership. Abraham and Hansson (1995) provided further evidence that SOC promotes positive functioning in the work domain. They observed a positive association between the use of SOC strategies and subjective ratings of competence-maintenance and goal attainment in the occupational domain (see also B. Baltes & Dickson, 2001).

Cognitive experimental work on dual-task allocations associated with sensorimotor and memory functioning in old age is a final example. In old age, one of the major adaptive tasks of life is how to allocate cognitive–attentional resources—for instance when both walking and thinking are required. In this case, data show that older adults in situations of high challenge express a preference of allocating resources into sensorimotor over memory behavior

(Lindenberger, Marsiske, & Baltes, 2000). This preference may be a result of the greater risk component of motor behavior in old age (negative consequence of falling, for instance). In a follow-up study (Li et al., 2001), compensatory components were added to the dual-task situation of motor versus memory functioning. It could be shown how individuals make increasingly more use of compensatory aids as the system of performance is challenged because of conditions of testing the limits.

Taken together, the empirical evidence on SOC suggests that selection, optimization, and compensation are available as bodies of knowledge. They can be considered as adaptive strategies of life management promoting both general as well as domain-specific positive functioning across adulthood.

CONCLUSION

We began this chapter by referring to the concept of virtue in the wisdom-related philosophical tradition of the ancient Greeks. Aristotle claimed that humans could achieve happiness by *knowing* what is good and right on the most general level of judgment (theoretical wisdom) and the approximate *realization* of this knowledge in terms of behavioral expression (practical wisdom).

We accepted this distinction as a general frame. We proffered that wisdom is the most general heuristic for defining the good of the what (ends) and the how (means) in lifespan development. In addition, to move to a more concrete level of analysis and behavioral implementation, we suggested that SOC is a general heuristic that organizes how means–ends connections are formed and nurtured over time to achieve a well-functioning system of life-long and broadly based goal attainments. We also presented evidence to show (a) how SOC operates when goals are pursued; (b) that individuals use this knowledge (in the form of proverbs) when they are confronted with situations requiring a decision; and (c) that individuals who report the use of SOC do better in several aspects of their lives.

This program of research is unfolding, and additional work needs to be done to identify the causes, temporal linkages, and dynamic systems of self-organization associated with wisdom and SOC. In closing, we offer examples from everyday life as additional support for the approach suggested.

A first example involves the maintenance of a goal such as piano playing in old age despite losses in mechanical speed (see also Krampe & Ericsson, 1996). Consider what the 80-year-old pianist, Arthur Rubinstein, hinted at when asked about the ways and means of staying on top as a concert pianist. He suggested, among other things, that he played fewer pieces (selection), practiced these more often (optimization), and used tempo contrasts to hide his loss in mechanical speed (compensation).

The second case study is based on reports by Brim (1992) about the way his father managed old age. Brim's report (1988) under the heading of "My Father's Window Box" is a moving and persuasive example of this principle. After his retirement, a college professor decided to live on a farm in a valley surrounded by lovely hills. Taking care of this farm and its surroundings became a central component of his daily life. With increasing age, and as physical limitations appeared, his psychological horizon of expectations was reduced step by step. First, care of the hills had to cease; the meadows in the valley and the garden followed. The man became very old. When he reached 100, his expectation and daily activity concentrated on the window box in his living room. This window box became the primary locus of his attention and productivity.

The reader will have noted that these examples are anecdotal and not scientific evidence. Moreover, in the examples the specification of and linkage between theoretical wisdom (in the form of SOC) and practical wisdom is not as rigorous and explicit as we would like. The examples are better illustrations of SOC as practical wisdom than of theoretical wisdom as the guiding frame defining the pursuit of ends and means (but see Exhibit 11.2 for an example of high versus low scoring answers on wisdom task; see also Colby & Damon, 1992; Damon, 1996). Yet, as we attempt to advance our work in this area, these examples serve as guideposts of encouragement for the lifelong pursuit of flourishing and lend intuitive support to our belief that the wisdom–SOC connection is more than a promissory note.

REFERENCES

Abraham, J. D., & Hansson, R. O. (1995). Successful aging at work: An applied study of selection, optimization, and compensation through impression management. *Journal of Gerontology: Psychological Sciences, 50B*, P94–P103.

Bäckman, L., & Dixon, R. A. (1992). Psychological compensation: A theoretical framework. *Psychological Bulletin, 112*, 1–25.

Baltes, B. B., & Dickson, M. W. (2001). Using life-span models in industrial/ organizational psychology: The theory of selective optimization with compensation. *Applied Developmental Science, 5*, 51–61.

Baltes, M. M. (1996). *The many faces of dependency in old age*. New York: Cambridge University Press.

Baltes, M. M., & Carstensen, L. L. (1996). The process of successful ageing. *Aging and Society, 16*, 397–422.

Baltes, M. M., & Carstensen, L. L. (1998). Social psychological theories and their applications to aging: From individual to collective. In V. L. Bengtson & K. W. Schaie (Eds.), *Handbook of theories of aging* (pp. 209–226). New York: Springer.

Baltes, M. M., & Lang, F. R. (1997). Everyday functioning and successful aging: The impact of resources. *Psychology and Aging, 12,* 433–443.

Baltes, P. B. (1987). Theoretical propositions of life-span developmental psychology: On the dynamics between growth and decline. *Developmental Psychology, 23,* 611–626.

Baltes, P. B. (1997). On the incomplete architecture of human ontogeny: Selection, optimization, and compensation as foundation of developmental theory. *American Psychologist, 52,* 366–380.

Baltes, P. B., & Baltes, M. M. (1980). Plasticity and variability in psychological aging: Methodological and theoretical issues. In G. E. Gurski (Ed.), *Determining the effects of aging on the central nervous system* (pp. 41–66). Berlin: Schering.

Baltes, P. B., & Baltes, M. M. (1990). Psychological perspectives on successful aging: The model of selective optimization with compensation. In P. B. Baltes & M. M. Baltes (Eds.), *Successful aging: Perspectives from the behavioral sciences* (pp. 1–34). New York: Cambridge University Press.

Baltes, P. B., & Baltes, M. M. (1999). Harvesting the fruits of age: Growing older, growing wise. *Science & Spirit, 10,* 12–14.

Baltes, P. B., Baltes, M. M., Freund, A. M., & Lang, F. (1999). *The measurement of selection, optimization, and compensation (SOC) by self report: Technical report 1999.* Berlin: Max Planck Institute for Human Development.

Baltes, P. B., Dittmann-Kohli, F., & Dixon, R. A. (1984). New perspectives on the development of intelligence in adulthood: Toward a dual-process conception and a model of selective optimization with compensation. In P. B. Baltes & O. G. Brim, Jr. (Eds.), *Life-span development and behavior* (Vol. 6, pp. 33–76). New York: Academic Press.

Baltes, P. B., & Smith, J. (1990). The psychology of wisdom and its ontogenesis. In R. J. Sternberg (Ed.), *Wisdom: Its nature, origins, and development* (pp. 87–120). New York: Cambridge University Press.

Baltes, P. B., Smith, J., & Staudinger, U. M. (1992). Wisdom and successful aging. In T. Sonderegger (Ed.), *Nebraska symposium on motivation* (Vol. 39, pp. 123–167). Lincoln: University of Nebraska Press.

Baltes, P. B., & Staudinger, U. M. (1993). The search for a psychology of wisdom. *Current Directions in Psychological Science, 2,* 75–80.

Baltes, P. B., & Staudinger, U. M. (2000). Wisdom: A metaheuristic to orchestrate mind and virtue toward excellence. *American Psychologist, 55,* 122–136.

Baltes, P. B., Staudinger, U. M., & Lindenberger, U. (1999). Lifespan psychology: Theory and application to intellectual functioning. *Annual Review of Psychology, 50,* 471–507.

Baltes, P. B., Staudinger, U. M., Maercker, A., & Smith, J. (1995). People nominated as wise: A comparative study of wisdom-related knowledge. *Psychology and Aging, 10,* 155–166.

Bandura, A. (1995). *Self-efficacy in a changing society.* New York: Cambridge University Press.

Bargh, J. A., & Gollwitzer, P. M. (1994). Environmental control of goal-directed action: Automatic and strategic contingencies between situations and behavior. In W. D. Spaulding (Ed.), *Nebraska Symposium on Motivation: Vol. 41. Integrative views of motivation, cognition, and emotion* (pp. 71–124). Lincoln: University of Nebraska Press.

Boesch, E. E. (1976). *Psychopathologie des Alltags* (Psychopathology of everyday life). Bern: Huber.

Boesch, E. E. (1991). *Symbolic action theory and cultural psychology.* Heidelberg: Springer.

Brandtstädter, J. (1999). The self in action and development: Cultural, biosocial, and ontogenetic bases of intentional self-development. In J. Brandtstädter & R. M. Lerner (Eds.), *Action and self development: Theory and research through the life span* (pp. 37–65). Thousand Oaks, CA: Sage.

Brandtstädter, J., & Wentura, D. (1995). Adjustment to shifting possibility frontiers in later life: Complementary adaptive modes. In R. A. Dixon & L. Bäckman (Eds.), *Compensating for psychological deficits and declines: Managing losses and promoting gains* (pp. 83–106). Hillsdale, NJ: Erlbaum.

Brim, O. G., Jr. (1988). Losing and winning: The nature of ambition in everyday life. *Psychology Today, 9,* 48–52.

Brim, O. G., Jr. (1992). *Ambition: How we manage success and failure throughout our lives.* New York: Basic Books.

Carstensen, L. L., Hanson, K. A., & Freund, A. M. (1995). Selection and compensation in adulthood. In R. A. Dixon & L. Bäckman (Eds.), *Compensating for psychological deficits and declines: Managing losses and promoting gains* (pp. 107–126). Hillsdale, NJ: Erlbaum.

Carver, C. S., & Scheier, M. F. (1995). *On the self-regulation of behavior.* Cambridge: Cambridge University press.

Coats, E. J., Janoff-Bulmann, R., & Alpert, N. (1996). Approach versus avoidance goals: Differences in self-evaluation and well-being. *Personality and Social Psychology Bulletin, 22,* 1057–1067.

Colby, A., & Damon, W. (1992). *Some do care: Contemporary lives of moral commitment.* New York: Free Press.

Damon, W. (1996). The lifelong transformation of moral goals through social influence. In P. B. Baltes & U. M. Staudinger (Eds.), *Interactive minds: Lifespan perspectives on the social foundation of cognition* (pp. 198–220). New York: Cambridge University Press.

Dittmann-Kohli, F., & Baltes, P. B. (1990). Toward a neofunctionalist conception of adult intellectual development: Wisdom as a prototypical case of intellectual growth. In C. Alexander & E. Langer (Eds.), *Higher stages of human development: Perspectives on adult growth* (pp. 54–78). New York: Oxford University Press.

Dixon, R. A., & Bäckman, L. (Eds.). (1995). *Compensating for psychological deficits and declines: Managing losses and promoting gains.* Mahwah, NJ: Erlbaum.

Eckensberger, L., & Meacham, J. A. (1984). Action theory, control and motivation. *Human Development, 27,* 163–210.

Elliot, A. J., & Sheldon, K. M. (1997). Avoidance achievement motivation: A personal goal analysis. *Journal of Personality and Social Psychology, 73,* 171–185.

Elliot, A. J., Sheldon, K. M., & Church, M. A. (1997). Avoidance personal goals and subjective well-being. *Personality and Social Psychology Bulletin, 23,* 915–927.

Emmons, R. A. (1996). Striving and feeling: Personal goals and subjective well-being. In P. M. Gollwitzer & J. A. Bargh (Eds.), *The psychology of action: Linking cognition and motivation to behavior* (pp. 313–337). New York: Guilford Press.

Ericsson, K. A. (1996). *The road to excellence: The acquisition of expert performance in the arts and sciences, sports and games.* Mahwah, NJ: Erlbaum.

Ericsson, K. A., & Smith, J. (Eds.). (1991). *Towards a general theory of expertise: Prospects and limits.* New York: Cambridge University Press.

Flammer, A. (1990). *Erfahrung der eigenen Wirksamkeit: Einführung in die Psychologie der Kontrollmeinung* (Experiencing self-efficacy: Introduction to the psychology of control beliefs). Bern: Hans Huber.

Freund, A. M., & Baltes, P. B. (1998). Selection, optimization, and compensation as strategies of life-management: Correlations with subjective indicators of successful aging. *Psychology & Aging, 13,* 531–543.

Freund, A. M., & Baltes, P. B. (2000). The orchestration of selection, optimization, and compensation: An action-theoretical conceptualization of a theory of developmental regulation. In W. J. Perrig & A. Grob (Eds.), *Control of human behavior, mental processes, and consciousness* (pp. 35–58). Mahwah, NJ: Erlbaum.

Freund, A. M., & Baltes, P. B. (2002). Life-management strategies of selection, optimization, and compensation: Measurement by self-report and construct validity. *Journal of Personality and Social Psychology, 82,* 642–662.

Freund, A. M., & Baltes, P. B. (in press). The adaptiveness of selection, optimization, and compensation as strategies of life management: Evidence from a preference study on proverbs. *Journals of Gerontology: Psychological Sciences.*

Freund, A. M., Li, K. Z. H., & Baltes, P. B. (1999). Successful development and aging: The role of selection, optimization, and compensation. In J. Brandtstädter & R. M. Lerner (Eds.), *Action and self-development: Theory and research through the life span* (pp. 401–434). Thousand Oaks, CA: Sage.

Freund, A. M., Wiese, B. S., & Baltes, P. B. (1999, Sept.). *Die entwicklungsregulative Funktion von Zielauswahl und Zielverfolgung: Beispiele aus dem Erwachsenenalter* (The regulatory function of goal-setting and goal-pursuit for development: Examples from adulthood). Paper presented at the Conference for Developmental Psychology, Fribourg, Switzerland.

Gigerenzer, G., Todd, P. M., & the ABC Group. (1999). *Simple heuristics that make us smart.* New York: Oxford University Press.

Gollwitzer, P. M. (1994). Goal achievement: The role of intentions. In W. Stroebe & M. Hewstone (Eds.), *European review of social psychology* (Vol. 4, pp. 141–185). London: Wiley.

Gollwitzer, P. M., & Bargh, J. A. (Eds.). (1996). *The psychology of action: Linking cognition and motivation to action.* New York: Guilford Press.

Haselager, W. F. G. (1997). *Cognitive science and folk psychology: The right frame of mind.* London: Sage.

Heckhausen, H. (1991). *Motivation and action.* New York: Springer.

Heckhausen, H., & Gollwitzer, P. M. (1987). Thought contents and cognitive functioning in motivational versus volitional states of mind. *Motivation and Emotion, 11,* 101–120.

Heckhausen, J. (1991). Adults' expectancies about development and its controllability: Enhancing self-efficacy by social comparison. In R. Schwarzer (Ed.), *Self-efficacy: Thought control of action* (pp. 107–126). Washington, DC: Hemisphere.

Heckhausen, J. (1999). *Developmental regulation in adulthood: Age-normative and sociostructural constraints as adaptive challenges.* New York: Cambridge University Press.

Heckhausen, J., Dixon, R. A., & Baltes, P. B. (1989). Gains and losses in development throughout adulthood as perceived by different adult age groups. *Developmental Psychology, 25,* 109–121.

Heckhausen, J., & Schulz, R. (1995). A life-span theory of control. *Psychological Review, 102,* 284–304.

Higgins, E. T., Grant, H., & Shah, J. (1999). Self-regulation and quality of life: Emotional and non-emotional life experiences. In D. Kahnemann, E. Diener, & N. Schwarz (Eds.), *Well-being: The foundation of hedonic psychology* (pp. 244–266). New York: Russell Sage Foundation.

Hobfoll, S. E. (1989). Conservation of resources. *American Psychologist, 44,* 513–524.

Kahnemann, D., Diener, E., & Schwarz, N. (Eds.). (1999). *Well-being: The foundation of hedonic psychology.* New York: Russell Sage Foundation.

Kekes, J. (1995). *Moral wisdom and good lives.* Ithaca, NY: Cornell University Press.

Keyes, C. L. M. (1998). Social well-being. *Social Psychology Quarterly, 61,* 121–140.

Klinger, E. (1977). *Meaning and void: Inner experience and the incentives in people's lives.* Minneapolis: University of Minnesota Press.

Kramer, D. A. (1990). Conceptualizing wisdom: The primacy of affect-cognition relations. In R. J. Sternberg (Ed.), *Wisdom: Its nature, origins, and development* (pp. 121–141). New York: Cambridge.

Krampe, R. T., & Ericsson, K. A. (1996). Maintaining excellence: Deliberate practice and elite performance in young and older pianists. *Journal of Experimental Psychology: General, 125*(4), 331–359.

Kunzmann, U., & Baltes, P. B. (2002), *Wisdom-related knowledge: Emotional, motivational, and interpersonal correlates.* Unpublished manuscript.

Labouvie-Vief, G. (1981). Proactive and reactive aspects of constructivism: Growth and aging in life-span perspective. In R. M. Lerner & N. A. Busch-Rossnagel (Eds.), *Individuals as producers of their development* (pp. 197–230). New York: Academic Press.

Labouvie-Vief, G. (1990). Wisdom as integrated thought: Historical and developmental perspectives. In R. J. Sternberg (Ed.), *Wisdom: Its nature, origins, and development* (pp. 52–83). New York: Cambridge University Press.

Labouvie-Vief, G. (1995). *Psyche and eros: Mind and gender in the life course.* New York: Cambridge University Press.

Lehrer, K., Lum, B. J., Slichta, B. A., & Smith, N. D. (Eds.). (1996). *Knowledge, teaching and wisdom.* Dordrecht: Kluwer.

Lerner, R. M., Freund, A. M., de Stefanis, I., & Habermas, T. (2001). The selection, optimization, and compensation model as a frame for understanding developmental regulation in adolescence. *Human Development, 44,* 29–50.

Li, K. Z. H., Lindenberger, U., Freund, A. M., & Baltes, P. B. (2001). Walking while memorizing: A SOC study of age-related differences in compensatory behavior under dual-task conditions. *Psychological Science, 12,* 230–237.

Lindenberger, U., Marsiske, M., & Baltes, P. B. (2000). Memorizing while walking: Increase in dual-task costs from young adulthood to old age. *Psychology and Aging, 15,* 417–436.

Little, B. R. (1989). *Personal projects analysis: Trivial pursuits, magnificent obsessions, and the search for coherence.* New York: Springer-Verlag.

Little, T. D. (1998). Sociocultural influences on the development of children's action-control beliefs. In J. Heckhausen & C. S. Dweck (Eds.), *Motivation and self-regulation across the life span* (pp. 281–315). New York: Cambridge University Press.

Little, T. D., Oettingen, G., Stetsenko, A., & Baltes, P. B. (1995). Children's action-control beliefs about school performance: How do American children compare with German and Russian children? *Journal of Personality and Social Psychology, 69,* 686–700.

Markman, H. J., Floyd, F. J., Stanley, S. M., & Storaasli, R. D. (1988). Prevention of marital distress: A longitudinal investigation. *Journal of Consulting and Clinical Psychology, 56,* 210–21.

Marsiske, M., Lang, F. R., Baltes, M. M., & Baltes, P. B. (1995). Selective optimization with compensation: Life-span perspectives on successful human development. In R. A. Dixon & L. Bäckman (Eds.), *Compensation for psychological defects and declines: Managing losses and promoting gains* (pp. 35–79). Hillsdale, NJ: Erlbaum.

Mieder, W. (1993). *Proverbs are never out of season: Popular wisdom in the modern age.* New York: Oxford University Press.

Mieder, W. (1997). *The politics of proverbs.* Madison: University of Wisconsin Press.

Miller, G. A., Galanter, E., & Pribram, K.-H. (1960). *Plans of structure of behavior.* New York: Holt, Rinehart, & Winston.

Mischel, W., Cantor, N., & Feldman, S. (1996). Principles of self-regulation: The nature of willpower and self-control. In E. T. Higgins & A. W. Kruglanski (Eds.), *Social psychology: Handbook of basic principles* (pp. 329–360). New York: Guilford Press.

Nussbaum, M. C. (1994). *The therapy of desire: Theory and practice in hellenistic ethics*. Princeton, NJ: Princeton University Press.

Oelmüller, W. (1989). *Philosophie und Weisheit* (Philosophy and wisdom). Paderborn, Germany: Schöningh.

Oettingen, G. (1996). Positive fantasy and motivation. In P. M. Gollwitzer & J. A. Bargh (Eds.), *The psychology of action: Linking cognition and motivation to action* (pp. 236–259). New York: Guilford Press.

Ostrop, G. (1996). *Die Wahl und Nutzung von Sprichwortern in der Erforschung des Wissens über Selektion, Optimierung und Kompensations* (On the choice and usage of proverbs in research on selection, optimization, level compensation). Master's thesis at the Free University of Berlin, Germany.

Pasupathi, M., & Baltes, P. B. (2000). Wisdom. In A. E. Kazdin (Ed.), *Encyclopedia of psychology* (Vol. 8, pp. 249–253). New York: Oxford University Press.

Peng, K., & Nisbett, R. E. (1998). *Naive dialectism and reasoning about contradiction*. Unpublished manuscript.

Rice, E. F., Jr. (1958). *The renaissance idea of wisdom*. Cambridge, MA: Harvard University Press.

Robinson, D. N. (1990). Wisdom through the ages. In R. J. Sternberg (Ed.), *Wisdom. Its nature, origins, and development* (pp. 13–24). New York: Cambridge University Press.

Rogers, T. B. (1990). Proverbs as psychological theories . . . Or is it the other way around? *Canadian Psychology, 31*, 195–207.

Rorty, A. O. (1980). Introduction. In A. O. Rorty (Ed.), *Essays on Aristotle's "Ethics"* (pp. 1–6). Berkeley: University of California Press.

Ryff, C. D. (1989). Happiness is everything, or is it? Explorations on the meaning of psychological well-being. *Journal of Personality and Social Psychology, 57,* 1069–1081.

Schönpflug, W. (1998). Improving efficiency of action control through technical and social resources. In M. Kofta, G. Weary, & G. Sedek (Eds.), *Personal control in action. Cognitive and motivational mechanism* (pp. 299–314). New York: Plenum Press.

Seligman, M. E. P. (1991). *Learned optimism*. New York: Knopf.

Skinner, E. A. (1995). *Perceived control* (Vol. 8). Thousand Oaks, CA: Sage.

Skinner, E. A., Chapman, M., & Baltes, P. B. (1988). Control, means-ends, and agency beliefs: A new conceptualization and its measurement during childhood. *Journal of Personality and Social Psychology, 54*, 117–133.

Smith, J. (1996). Planning about life: Toward a social interactive perspective. In P. B. Baltes & U. M. Staudinger (Eds.), *Interactive minds: Life-span perspectives on the social foundation of cognition* (pp. 242–275). New York: Cambridge University Press.

Smith, J., Staudinger, U. M., & Baltes, P. B. (1994). Occupational settings facilitating wisdom-related knowledge: The sample case of clinical psychologists. *Journal of Consulting and Clinical Psychology, 62*, 989–999.

Staudinger, U. M. (1996). Wisdom and the social-interactive foundation of the mind. In P. B. Baltes & U. M. Staudinger (Eds.), *Interactive Minds: Life-span perspectives on the social foundation of cognition* (pp. 276–318). New York: Cambridge University Press.

Staudinger, U. M. (1999a). Older and wiser? Integrating results from a psychological approach to the study of wisdom. *International Journal of Behavioral Development, 23,* 641–664.

Staudinger, U. M. (1999b). Social cognition and a psychological approach to an art of life. In F. Blanchard-Fields & B. T. Hess (Eds.), *Social cognition and aging* (pp. 343–375). New York: Academic Press.

Staudinger, U. M., & Baltes, P. B. (1994). Psychology of wisdom. In R. J. Sternberg (Ed.), *Encyclopedia of human intelligence* (Vol. 2, pp. 143–152). New York: Macmillan.

Staudinger, U. M., & Baltes, P. B. (1996). Interactive minds: A facilitative setting for wisdom-related performance? *Journal of Personality and Social Psychology, 71,* 746–762.

Staudinger, U. M., Maciel, A. G., Smith, J., & Baltes, P. B. (1998). What predicts wisdom-related performance? A first look at personality, intelligence, and facilitative experiential contexts. *European Journal of Personality, 12,* 1–17.

Staudinger, U. M., Marsiske, M., & Baltes, P. B. (1995). Resilience and reserve capacity in later adulthood: Potentials and limits of development across the life span. In D. Cicchetti & D. Cohen (Eds.), *Developmental psychopathology* (Vol. 2, pp. 801–847). New York: Wiley.

Sternberg, R. J. (Ed.). (1990). *Wisdom: Its nature, origins, and development.* New York: Cambridge University Press.

Tversky, A., & Kahneman, D. (1981). The framing of decisions and the psychology of choice. *Science, 211,* 453–458.

Wegner, D. M. (1992). You can't always think what you want: Problems in the suppression of unwanted thoughts. In M. Zanna (Ed.), *Advances in experimental social psychology* (Vol. 25, pp. 193–225). San Diego, CA: Academic Press.

Welsch, W. (1995). *Vernunft: Die zeitgenössische Vernunftkritik und das Konzept der transversalen Vernunft* (Rationality: The modern critique of rationality and the concept of transversal rationality). Frankfurt am Main: Suhrkamp.

Wiese, B. S., Freund, A. M., & Baltes, P. B. (2000). Selection, optimization, and compensation: An action-related approach to work and partnership. *Journal of Vocational Behavior, 57,* 273–300.

12

ELEVATION AND THE POSITIVE PSYCHOLOGY OF MORALITY

JONATHAN HAIDT

The power of positive moral emotions to uplift and transform people has long been known, but not by psychologists. In 1771, Thomas Jefferson's friend Robert Skipwith wrote to him asking for advice on what books to buy for his library, and for his own education. Jefferson sent back a long list of titles in history, philosophy, and natural science. But in addition to these obviously educational works, Jefferson advised the inclusion of some works of fiction. Jefferson justified this advice by pointing to the beneficial emotional effects of great fiction:

> Every thing is useful which contributes to fix us in the principles and practice of virtue. When any ... act of charity or of gratitude, for instance, is presented either to our sight or imagination, we are deeply impressed with its beauty and feel a strong desire in ourselves of doing charitable and grateful acts also. On the contrary when we see or read of any atrocious deed, we are disgusted with its deformity and conceive an abhorrence of vice. Now every emotion of this kind is an exercise of our virtuous dispositions; and dispositions of the mind, like limbs of the body, acquire strength by exercise. (Jefferson, 1771/1975, pp. 349–350)

Jefferson goes on to say that the physical feelings and motivational effects caused by a good novel are as powerful as those caused by real episodes:

> [I ask whether] the fidelity of Nelson, and generosity of Blandford in Marmontel do not dilate [the reader's] breast, and elevate his sentiments

I thank Sara Algoe, Gerald Clore, and Jayne Riew for helpful comments, and I thank my collaborators for their ideas and enthusiasm: Sara Algoe, Yuki Amano, E. Carter Chandler, Zita Meijer, and Anita Tam. Finally I thank David Whitford for his beautiful words and for permission to reprint them.

as much as any similar incident which real history can furnish? Does he not in fact feel himself a better man while reading them, and privately covenant to copy the fair example? (1771/1975, p. 350)

I have quoted this passage at length because it serves as an abstract for this chapter. Jefferson identified, more than 200 years ago, the major features of an emotion that I have begun to call "elevation" (Haidt, 2000). Elevation is elicited by acts of virtue or moral beauty; it causes warm, open feelings ("dilation"?) in the chest; and it motivates people to behave more virtuously themselves (to "covenant to copy the fair example"). Elevation therefore seems to fit easily into modern appraisal theories of emotion (e.g., Frijda, 1986; Lazarus, 1991). Yet elevation, and some related positive moral emotions[1] (e.g., awe, gratitude, admiration), have received almost no attention from emotion researchers. I suggest that attention to such emotions is crucial for a full understanding of human morality, and I think that a major contribution of positive psychology will be to explore and publicize these positive moral emotions.

To explain how elevation works, and why no modern researcher has studied it, I must first discuss the three dimensions of social cognition: solidarity, hierarchy, and elevation. But to explain these three dimensions I must first take a detour to Flatland.

THE THIRD DIMENSION OF SOCIAL COGNITION

Flatland is a mythical two-dimensional world created by Edwin Abbott, an English mathematician and novelist (Abbott, 1884/1952). The inhabitants of Flatland are two-dimensional geometric figures, including the protagonist of the novel, a square. One day the square is visited by a stranger from a three-dimensional country called Spaceland. The visitor is a sphere, but when a sphere comes to Flatland, all that is visible is the transection of the sphere as it passes through the plane of Flatland—in other words, a circle. The square is amazed by the way this circle is able to grow or shrink at will (by rising or sinking into the plane of Flatland) and even to disappear and reappear in a different place. The sphere tries to explain the concept of the third dimension to the two-dimensional square, but the square is

---

[1] The moral emotions can be defined as "those emotions that are linked to the interests or welfare either of society as a whole or at least of persons other than the judge or agent" (Haidt, in press). Positive moral emotions are emotions that are triggered by the good or admirable deeds of others and that motivate people to do good or admirable deeds themselves.

mystified. The sphere presents analogies and geometrical demonostrations, but in every case the square fails to grasp that his "side" is not his front, back, left, or right.

The square's difficulty in understanding the third dimension of physical space illustrates the difficulty that I believe many Westerners have in understanding a third dimension of social space. Many social theorists have talked about two dimensions of social space (Brown & Gilman, 1960; Hamilton & Sanders, 1981; Kemper, 1990; Sahlins, 1965). The first is a horizontal dimension of solidarity, referring to the fact that some people are closer to the self, others are farther, both in terms of affection and mutual obligation. The second dimension that is commonly discussed is a vertical dimension of hierarchy, power, or status. In classic social psychology, people were well-aware of both of these dimensions. Brown and Gilman (1960) showed how forms of address vary along exactly these two dimensions, even in languages such as English that do not have pronouns like *tu* versus *vous* to mark them explicitly. These two dimensions appear to be universals of human social cognition. All cultures behave and feel differently toward kin and friends than they do toward strangers. And even among groups that despise hierarchy, such as egalitarian hunter–gatherers (Boehm, 1999) or American liberals (Lakoff, 1996), people notice hierarchy, and their social interactions are strongly influenced (in culturally variable ways) by the relative standings of the interactants.

Yet there is a third dimension along which people can vary, which appears to be nearly as ubiquitous as solidarity and hierarchy. This third dimension might be called "purity versus pollution," or as will be explained shortly, "elevation versus degradation." Social practices, emotions, and the underlying logic of purity and pollution are somewhat similar across widely disparate cultures, religions, and eras. The basic logic seems to be that people vary in their level of spiritual purity as a trait (some are high, such as priests and saints; others are low, such as prostitutes or those who work in "dirty" jobs) and as a state (one is high after bathing and meditating; one is low after defecating or when in a state of anger). Purity and pollution practices seem designed to ensure that people interact with each other, and with sacred objects and spaces, in ways that keep the impure (low) from contaminating the pure (high). In this way God and those closest to God are protected from desecration and defilement.

For example, the Old Testament is full of prescriptions and proscriptions for handling spiritual pollution and for protecting sacred objects and spaces from pollution. According to the book of Leviticus (12:4), when a woman gives birth she is highly polluted and must undergo purification rites. "She shall continue in the blood of purification three and thirty days; she shall touch no hallowed thing, nor come into the sanctuary, until the days of her purification be fulfilled."[2] Similar concerns about purity and pollution are common in the Muslim world (see Abu-Lughod, 1986) and in ancient Greece (Parker, 1983).

PURITY AND POLLUTION IN INDIA

Arguably the world's experts on purity and pollution, the culture with the longest tradition of practice and scholarship on the subject is Hindu India. Written in the 2nd century BCE, The Laws of Manu (Doneger & Smith, 1991) is a guide for high-caste Hindus, telling them how to live and worship properly. The *Laws* include many rules about purity and pollution. For example, Brahmins are urged to "not even think about" reciting the Vedas in the following situations, all of which would be incompatible with the purity and sacredness of the holy scriptures:

> while expelling urine or excrement, when food is still left on his mouth and hands. . . . or when (the planet) Rahu causes a lunar or solar eclipse . . . [or] when one has eaten flesh or the food of a woman who has just given birth, when there is fog, when arrows are whizzing by, at either of the twilights. . . . He should not recite in a cremation ground, a village, or a cowpen; nor while wearing a garment that he has worn in sexual union, nor while accepting anything at a ceremony for the dead. . . . Nor in the midst of an army or a battle; nor when one has just eaten or has not digested (his food) or has vomited or belched; nor without the permission of one's guest; nor when the wind blows strongly; nor when blood flows from one's limbs or when one has been wounded by weapons. (pp. 121–122)

It must be noted that not all of these concerns involve purity and pollution. Some involve concerns about auspiciousness or astrology. But the basic point is that the words of the holy scriptures must be protected from contamination or degradation by a diverse set of threats, many of which involve the human body and its biological processes. One must not even have holy words in mind while engaged in polluting activities.

These rules about purity and pollution have been modified in some ways over the past 2200 years, but the basic logic is still very much in place in traditional Hindu culture. In 1993, I interviewed 20 priests and monks in the Eastern Indian state of Orissa about their concepts of purity and pollution and about why it is important morally and spiritually to regulate one's bodily processes. Their responses revealed that the concept of purity

---

[2] It is interesting to note that if a woman gives birth to a girl, the waiting period is doubled to 66 days, presumably because for the ancient Hebrews, as for many traditional societies, girls and women are seen as more polluting than boys and men.

(*shuddha*) reflects concerns both about biological processes and about socio-moral behavior. As one holy man (*sanyasi*) put it: "Before I was a [religious devotee], I had this instinct of violence, and I was involved in many evil activities. They are impure [*ashuddha*]. To do evil things with girls, or to eat fish and meat, or to kill an animal, these are impure things." In other words, one can become polluted by food, sex, or violence. Purity covers a broad domain of biological and social behaviors.

Why do Hindu Indians combine bodily and social actions and see both as potentially polluting? The answer seems to be that Hinduism very explicitly places all creatures onto a vertical dimension, running from the gods above to the demons below. People rise and fall on this vertical dimension based on the degree to which they behave like gods or demons in this life. The life one is reborn into depends on the karma one accumulated in the previous round of life on earth. As one of my most eloquent informants put it, while explicating the concept of purity:

> We ourselves can be gods or demons. It depends on karma, if a person behaves like a demon, for example he kills someone, then that person is truly a demon. . . . a person who behaves in a divine manner, because a person has divinity in him, he is like a god. . . . What is wrong with being like a demon? What is going on nowadays, it is demonic. Divine behavior means not cheating people, not killing people. Complete character. You have divinity, you are a god.

So one behaves in a pure and godlike way by treating people well, as well as by being careful about one's eating habits, sexual practices, and other bodily transactions. One behaves like a demon, or (more mildly) like an animal, when one fails to heed rules of conduct and ethics.

This vertical dimension of purity versus pollution is critical for understanding Hindu ethics. Swami Vivekananda, an Indian spiritual leader in the late nineteenth century, even made this dimension into a kind of Hindu categorical imperative, which can be used to guide all action:

> To give an objective definition of duty is entirely impossible. Yet there is duty from the subjective side. Any action that makes us go Godward is a good action and is our duty; any action that makes us go downward is evil and is not our duty. (quoted by Yatiswarananda, 1979, p. 74)

Note that evil actions are explicitly said to draw us "down," away from God on a vertical dimension.

THE THIRD DIMENSION IN THE UNITED STATES

I have taken the time to discuss Hindu ethics because it illustrates so clearly a vertical dimension of social cognition that is operating, I believe, in most or all human cultures. Once we know what to look for, we can find evidence of this dimension in modern Western cultures as well. Issues of elevation and purity appear unexpectedly in our otherwise two-dimensional social world, just as the three dimensional sphere appeared in the two dimensional world of Flatland. Knowing about this third dimension can help us explain phenomena that otherwise would be mysterious.

For example, why do Americans moralize drugs and sexuality? Given their strong endorsement of personal autonomy and liberty, one might expect a national consensus that individuals have the right to engage in whatever activities they choose, as long as those activities are harmless, consensual, and private. Yet there is no such consensus (Haidt & Hersh, 2001).

In earlier times, Americans felt quite comfortable condemning sexuality and drug use in a language of purity and pollution. For example, in 1904 Dr. Sylvanus Stall, in a best-selling book of advice for young men, wrote, "God has made no mistake in giving man a strong sexual nature, but any young man makes a fatal mistake if he allows the sexual to dominate, to degrade, and to destroy that which is highest and noblest in his nature" (p. 35). Even in the hard sciences, a vertical–moral dimension was assumed. A chemistry textbook from 1867 (Steele, p. 191), after describing the chemical structure of ethyl alcohol, adds that alcohol has the effect of "dulling the intellectual operations and moral instincts; seeming to pervert and destroy all that is pure and holy in man, while it robs him of his highest attribute—reason."

To modern ears such evocations of purity and all that is highest and holy in human beings sound old-fashioned. Secular Americans do not talk that way anymore. Yet my research into moral judgment shows that secular Americans still *feel* that way—they just cannot talk about it in a language of purity and pollution. They therefore resort to a makeshift language of fabricated health concerns and far-fetched potential harms. When I interviewed Americans and Brazilians about harmless violations of food, sex, and drug traditions (e.g., eating one's already dead pet; consensual sibling incest using birth control; or private use of nonaddictive drugs) I repeatedly found that many people condemned the actions immediately, and then struggled to find supporting reasons (Haidt, 2001; Haidt & Hersh, 2001; Haidt, Koller, & Dias, 1993). Many of these supporting reasons were patently absurd (e.g., that eating fully cooked dog meat will make a person sick). When cross-examined, participants often dropped these post-hoc reasons, yet did not change their minds. Instead they became "morally dumbfounded"—that is, they had strong moral intuitions that an action was wrong, and they were shocked to find that they could not find reasons to support their intuitions.

Moral dumbfounding in these cases is readily explained by the intrusion of intuitions about purity and pollution into a subculture that has lost the language of purity and pollution. Feelings of disgust toward certain behaviors inform people that someone else is moving "down" on the third dimension. In fact, research on the emotion of disgust shows it to be the paradigmatic emotion of spiritual pollution. Rozin, Haidt, and McCauley (2000) have found that there are nine classes of disgust elicitors: food, animals, body products, sexuality, body envelope violations (including gore and bleeding), death, hygiene, interpersonal contamination, and social disgust. It is quite striking that the list of prohibitions from the *Laws of Manu* (quoted earlier) includes six of the first seven elicitors (all but animals), and in interviews I conducted in Orissa I found that all of the other categories (animals, interpersonal contamination, and social disgust) are frequent causes of pollution as well. Rozin et al. (2000) argued that disgust is best understood as a complex emotion that protects the body and the soul from degradation. The word "soul" is not meant to imply anything supernatural; it is meant to capture the fact that people sometimes experience disgust as a kind of degradation, debasement, or bringing down of a nonphysical, moral component of their selves. Our minds, hearts, and stomachs are sensitive to the third dimension of social cognition, even though our mouths can no longer explain these feelings.

THE POSITIVE HALF OF THE THIRD DIMENSION

If disgust is the emotional reaction that we feel when we see people move down on the third dimension, then is there a corresponding emotion we feel when we see people move up? I believe that there is. One of the basic themes of positive psychology is that psychology has focused too much on what is negative in human nature and has often missed the brighter and more beautiful side. My own research on disgust illustrates this point. It was not until I had studied disgust for eight years that it even occurred to me to ask about the opposite of disgust, an emotion triggered by people behaving in a virtuous, pure, or superhuman way. I have called this emotion "elevation" (Haidt, 2000), because seeing other people rise on the third dimension seems to make people feel higher on it themselves. Once I began looking for elevation I found it easily. I found that most people recognize descriptions of it, that the popular press and Oprah Winfrey talk about it (as being touched, moved, or inspired), and that research psychologists had almost nothing to say about it. Here are some of the things I have learned in my first three years of research on elevation.

The Basic Features of Elevation

To begin, my students and I did a simple recall study: We asked college students to recall and write about times when they had been in one of four positive emotion-arousing situations (Haidt, Algoe, Meijer, & Tam, 2002). The prompt for elevation was to "think of a specific time when you saw a manifestation of humanity's 'higher' or 'better' nature." Control conditions included instructions to "think of a specific time when you were making good progress towards a goal," which is the appraisal condition described by Lazarus (1991) as the elicitor of happiness. In a second study we induced elevation in the lab by showing participants 10-minute video clips, one of which was about the life of Mother Teresa. (Control conditions included an emotionally neutral but interesting documentary and a comedy sequence from the television show "America's Funniest Home Videos"). In both studies we found that participants in the elevation conditions reported different patterns of physical feelings and motivations when compared to participants in the happiness and other control conditions. Elevated participants were more likely to report physical feelings in their chests, especially warm, pleasant, or "tingling" feelings, and they were more likely to report wanting to help others, to become better people themselves, and to affiliate with others. In both studies happiness energized people to engage in private or self-interested pursuits, whereas elevation seemed to open people up and turn their attention outward, toward other people. Elevation therefore fits well with Fredrickson's (1998) "broaden and build" model of the positive emotions, in which positive emotions are said to motivate people to cultivate skills and relationships that will help them in the long run.

Elevation Reports From India and Japan

Elevation does not appear to be a uniquely Western emotion. In 1997, I conducted eight interviews in a small village in Orissa, India. I asked informants to discuss six potentially emotional situations they had experienced, one of which was "a time when you saw someone do something wonderful, a very good deed, to someone else, but not to you." Six of the informants described clear cases of witnessing a good deed, and in all six cases at least some of the hallmarks of elevation were present (i.e., warm or tingly feelings, positive affect, and a motivation to help others). One such case came from the 36-year-old principal of a primary school. He described a time when a teacher was wrongly accused of having stolen some books, because they had disappeared under his care. But the people around him knew he was honest, and one of them stepped forward to buy replacement books and to talk to the district supervisor to plead the man's case. When asked to describe his own feelings on witnessing this event, the principal said, "It created a kind of emotion for the person who helped the teacher. Seeing his quality of kindness towards others, seeing such acts of doing good things to others, a feeling of joy [*ananda*] was generated." When asked if this event included any feelings in his body, he replied, "A kind of tingling sensation in the body. I mean, another person is doing something for someone, and I wish I could do that. He is doing a good thing, and I feel like this: If I had done this, how much more joy I would have felt!"

In 1998 Yuki Amano, a Japanese American student working with me, conducted similar interviews with 15 people from varied backgrounds in Japan. She found that informants were emotionally responsive to the good deeds of others in ways that resembled the responses of Americans and Indians. Many of the interviews revolved around Japanese words for heart (*kimochi, kokoro*) and for times when the heart is moved (*kandou*). Informants described a variety of situations that moved their hearts, such as seeing a gang member giving up his seat on the train to an elderly person, seeing news about Mother Teresa, and watching the band in the movie *Titanic* playing on courageously as the ship sank. For example, when interviewing a 46-year-old housewife, the following exchange took place:

> **Q:** Have you ever had positive feelings due to something others did?
> **A:** Yes I have. For example, when there is a natural disaster in another country, those who actually go there and help people as volunteers. Also those who do things within [their limits], such as collecting money and food and clothes for those who are suffering from disaster.
> **Q:** You feel positive feelings when you hear stories about those people?
> **A:** Yes.
> **Q:** Can you explain the feelings in detail?
> **A:** I wonder if there is anything that I can do with my own strength. For example, donating money, giving clothes, and I have done that before myself. . . . I think how I could join those people even though what I have done is not much compared to what they do.
> **Q:** When you have these feelings, do you have any physical feeling?
> **A:** When I see news of a disaster, I feel pain in my chest, and tears actually come out when I read the newspaper. Then after that, seeing volunteers and finding out that there are helping people out there, the pain goes away, the heart brightens up [*akarui*] and I feel glad [*yokatta*], relieved [*anshin*], admiration [*sugoi*], and respect [*sonkei*]. When I see volunteers, the heart heavy from sad news becomes lighter.

In these Japanese interviews, as in the Indian interviews, the same elements are conjoined: The perception of compassionate or courageous behavior by others causes a pleasurable physical feeling in the chest of movement, warmth, or opening, coupled with a desire to engage in virtuous action oneself.

JEFFERSON AND THE EMOTIONAL RESPONSE TO MORAL BEAUTY

It is a basic fact about human beings that we sometimes help others, even strangers, at some cost or risk to ourselves. Psychology has a lot to say about this basic fact, as altruism has been a major area of research for the past thirty years. It is also a basic fact about human beings that we are easily and strongly moved by the altruism of others. Psychology has almost nothing to say about this fact, and this is an oversight that positive psychology must correct. We cannot have a full understanding of human morality until we can explain why and how human beings are so powerfully affected by the sight of a stranger helping another stranger.

The usual impulse of experimental psychologists is to strive for parsimony, to explain away any apparently virtuous aspect of human nature as a covert manifestation of selfishness, libido, or "mood management" (e.g., Cialdini et al., 1987). But I would like to suggest that the overzealous application of Occam's razor—the principle that entities should not be multiplied needlessly—has grossly disfigured the field of psychology, blinding us to the times when new entities are truly needed. I would like to propose that Thomas Jefferson was right and that we must posit a built-in emotional responsiveness to moral beauty.

If we return to the quotation at the start of this chapter, we see that Jefferson's letter is not just poetic musings: It contains a surprisingly precise and modern description of an emotion. Most current emotion theories attempt to break each emotion down into a set of components, or slots in a script, such as an eliciting condition, a physiological response, a motivational tendency, and an affective phenomenology (e.g., Frijda, 1986; Lazarus, 1991; Shweder & Haidt, 2000). Based on my preliminary research on elevation, it appears that Jefferson got the major components exactly right. He described the eliciting condition for elevation as the presentation to our "sight or imagination" of any "act of charity or of gratitude." He described the motivational tendency as "a strong desire in ourselves of doing charitable and grateful acts also." He described the affective phenomenology (what it feels like) as feeling "elevated sentiments," and a feeling of moral improvement (feeling oneself to be a "better man"). Jefferson located the physiological response in the chest cavity, and he described it as a sort of "dilation." We still do not know exactly what happens in the chest when one experiences elevation, but it seems likely that the vagus nerve is at work, causing a variety of changes in the heart, lungs, and throat (Porges, 1995), which are qualitatively different from the more well-known effects of sympathetic arousal.

Jefferson even proposed, 230 years ago, that elevation is the opposite of social disgust (which he called the emotional reaction to seeing or reading about "any atrocious deed"). Table 12.1 shows the ways in which elevation and social disgust appear to be opposites of each other, including the fact that elevated people, such as saints, are sources of positive contamination (i.e., people want to touch or own things that have touched the saint), whereas socially disgusting people, such as Hitler, are sources of negative contamination (i.e., most people do not want to come into physical contact with anything that touched a murderer; see Rozin, Millman, & Nemeroff, 1986). I would even go so far as to suggest that saints are found in so many cultures because elevation is found in so many cultures. People whose actions cause widespread elevation are likely to be canonized.

CONCLUSION

One of the goals of positive psychology is to bring about a balanced reappraisal of human nature and human potential. We can grant that people are capable of perpetrating great cruelty on one another, but we must also grant, and study, the ways in which people are good, kind, and compassionate toward one another. How can positive psychology bring about this reappraisal? I offer four suggestions.

1. Begin with the positive emotions. Psychology already knows a lot about the negative moral emotions (anger, shame, guilt) and about reactions to suffering (sympathy–empathy). But the positive moral emotions are a new frontier, one with vast potential to improve the lives of individuals and the functioning of society. Only in the past few years has work begun to appear on gratitude (McCullough, Kilpatrick, Emmons, & Larson, 2001) and elevation (Haidt, 2000). In the next few years work will begin to appear on awe and admiration as well (Keltner & Haidt, in press). Guided by new theoretical perspectives on positive emotions (Fredrickson, 1998), positive psychologists

Table 12.1
Diametrically Opposed Features of Elevation and Social Disgust

Component	Elevation	Social disgust
Elicitor	People moving up, blurring human–god divide	People moving down, blurring human–animal divide
Motivation tendency	Merge, open up, help others	Separate, close off
Affective phenomenology	Feel lifted up, optimistic about humanity	Feel dragged down, cynical about humanity
Physical changes	Chest (warm glow)	Gut (nausea)
Contamination	Positive	Negative

can balance out what is known about the emotions that make us care about the actions of others (see Haidt, 2002, for a review of the moral emotions).

2. Look to other cultures and eras for guidance. It is a dictum of cultural psychology that different cultures are "experts" in different areas of human potential (Shweder, 1990). There is clearly not just one kind of flourishing, one kind of "good life," and one kind of coherent morality. Positive psychologists should look to other cultures and other historical eras for ideas and perspectives on virtue and the good life. For example, classical Hindu ideas of purity and pollution have helped me to understand the moral life of Americans. Classical Greek ideas of well-being *(eudamonia)* have informed modern research on happiness (Ryff, 1989; Waterman, 1990), including Seligman and Czikszentmihalyi's (1999) thinking about positive psychology. In particular, the world's religions offer highly developed and articulated visions of virtues, practices, and feelings, some of which may even be useful in a modern secular society (e.g., agape love, forgiveness, and meditation).

3. Apply what is learned for the common good. It is sometimes said that there is nothing as practical as a good theory, but I think there is nothing as practical as a good demonstration project. If positive psychologists can create moral or character education programs that work, or moral growth experiences for adults that can touch and enrich their lives, the world will beat a path to their doors. Given the widespread current interest in service learning and volunteerism, there is clearly a large market hungry for programs that will make a difference in the lives of adolescents. Moral education programs that focus on building strengths and triggering the positive moral emotions may be more effective than the more traditional reasoning-oriented interventions (e.g., Power, Higgins, & Kohlberg, 1989).

4. Examine peak experiences and moral transformations. Moral development is generally thought of as a slow and lifelong process. Yet many people have experienced moments of profound emotional power that left them changed forever. Maslow (1964) studied the changes that peak experiences can bring about in people's identities and in their spiritual lives, but since then there has been little empirical research on such issues. I believe that powerful experiences of elevation can be peak experiences. Powerful moments of elevation sometimes seem to push a mental "reset button," wiping out feelings of cynicism and replacing them with feelings of hope, love, and optimism and a sense of moral inspiration. This thought is for the moment an unproven hypothesis (one I refer to as the "inspire and rewire" hypothesis).

A clear description of such a case was recently sent to me. Several years ago, a Unitarian church in Massachusetts asked each of its members to write his or her own "spiritual autobiography"—that is, an account of how they came to be the spiritual people they are now. One member, David Whitford, sent me a section of his autobiography in which he puzzled over why he is so often moved to tears during the course of church services. He noticed that there were two kinds of tears. The first he calls "tears of compassion," such as those he shed during a sermon on Mothers' Day, on the subject of children who are growing up abandoned or neglected. These cases felt to him like "being pricked in the soul," after which "love pours out" for those who are suffering. But the second kind of tear is very different. He calls them "tears of celebration," but he could just as well have called them "tears of elevation." I will end this chapter with his words, which give a more eloquent description of elevation than anything I could write:

> There's another kind of tear. This one's less about giving love and more about the joy of receiving love, or maybe just detecting love (whether it's directed at me or at someone else). It's the kind of tear that flows in response to expressions of courage, or compassion, or kindness by others.
>
> A few weeks after Mother's Day, we met here in the sanctuary after the service and considered whether to become a Welcoming Congregation [a congregation that welcomes gay people]. When John stood in support of the resolution, and spoke of how, as far as he knew, he was the first gay man to come out at First Parish, in the early 1970s, I cried for his courage. Later, when all hands went up and the resolution passed unanimously, I cried for the love expressed by our congregation in that act. That was a tear of celebration, a tear of receptiveness to what is good in the world, a tear that says it's okay, relax, let down your guard, there are good people in the world, there is good in people, love is real, it's in our nature. That kind of tear is also like being pricked, only now the love pours in.

REFERENCES

Abbott, E. A. (1952). *Flatland.* New York: Dover.

Abu-Lughod, L. (1986). *Veiled sentiments.* Berkeley: University of California Press. (Original published 1884)

Boehm, C. (1999). *Hierarchy in the forest: The evolution of egalitarian behavior.* Cambridge, MA: Harvard University Press.

Brown, R., & Gilman, A. (1960). The pronouns of power and solidarity. In T. A. Sebeok (Ed.), *Style in language* (pp. 253–276). Cambridge: MIT Press.

Cialdini, R., Schaller, M., Houlihan, D., Arps, K., Fultz, J., et al. (1987). Empathy-based helping: Is it selflessly or selfishly motivated? *Journal of Personality and Social Psychology, 52,* 749–758.

Doneger, W., & Smith, B. K. (Eds.). (1991). *The laws of Manu* (Trans. W. Donegar & B. K. Smith). London: Penguin. (Original work written in the first few centuries BC)

Fredrickson, B. L. (1998). What good are positive emotions? *Review of General Psychology, 2,* 300–319.

Frijda, N. (1986). *The emotions*. Cambridge: Cambridge University Press.

Haidt, J. (2000). The positive emotion of elevation. *Prevention and Treatment, 3*, n.p.

Haidt, J. (2001). The emotional dog and its rational tail: A social intuitionist approach to moral judgment. *Psychological Review, 108,* 814–834.

Haidt, J. (in press). The moral emotions. In R. J. Davidson, K. Scherer, & H. H. Goldsmith (Eds.), *Handbook of affective sciences* (pp. 852–870). Oxford: Oxford University Press.

Haidt, J., Algoe, S., Meijer, Z., & Tam, A. (2002). *Elevation: An emotion that makes people want to do good deeds*. Unpublished manuscript, University of Virginia, Charlottesville.

Haidt, J., & Hersh, M. A. (2001). Sexual morality: The cultures and reasons of liberals and conservatives. *Journal of Applied Social Psychology, 31,* 191–221.

Haidt, J., Koller, S., & Dias, M. (1993). Affect, culture, and morality, or is it wrong to eat your dog? *Journal of Personality and Social Psychology, 65,* 613–628.

Hamilton, V. L., & Sanders, J. (1981). The effects of roles and deeds on responsibility judgements: The normative structure of wrongdoing. *Social Psychology Quarterly, 44,* 237–254.

Jefferson, T. (1975). Letter to Robert Skipwith. In M. D. Peterson (Ed.), *The portable Thomas Jefferson* (pp. 349–351). New York: Penguin. (Original published 1771)

Keltner, D., & Haidt, J. (in press). Approaching awe, a moral, spiritual, and aesthetic emotion. *Cognition and Emotion.*

Kemper, T. D. (1990). Social relations and emotions: A structural approach. In T. D. Kemper (Ed.), *Research agendas in the sociology of emotions* (pp. 41–51). Albany: SUNY Press.

Lakoff, G. (1996). *Moral politics: What conservatives know that liberals don't*. Chicago: University of Chicago Press.

Lazarus, R. S. (1991). *Emotion and adaptation*. New York: Oxford University Press.

Maslow, A. H. (1964). *Religions, values, and peak-experiences*. Columbus: Ohio State University Press.

McCullough, M. E., Kilpatrick, S. D., Emmons, R. A., & Larson, D. B. (2001). Is gratitude a moral affect? *Psychological Bulletin, 127,* 249–266.

Parker, R. (1983). *Miasma: Pollution and purification in early Greek religion*. Oxford: Oxford University Press.

Porges, S. W. (1995). Orienting in a defensive world: Mammalian modifications of our evolutionary heritage. A Polyvagal Theory. *Psychophysiology, 32,* 301–18.

Power, F. C., Higgins, A., & Kohlberg, L. (1989). *Lawrence Kohlberg's approach to moral education*. New York: Columbia University Press.

Rozin, P., Haidt, J., & McCauley, C. R. (2000). Disgust. In M. Lewis & J. M. Haviland-Jones (Ed.), *Handbook of emotions* (2nd ed., pp. 637–653). New York: Guilford Press.

Rozin, P., Millman, L., & Nemeroff, C. (1986). Operation of the laws of sympathetic magic in disgust and other domains. *Journal of Personality and Social Psychology, 50,* 703–712.

Ryff, C. D. (1989). Happiness is everything, or is it? Explorations on the meaning of psychological well-being. *Journal of Personality and Social Psychology, 57,* 1069–1081.

Sahlins, M. (1965). On the sociology of primitive exchange. In M. Banton (Ed.), *The relevance of models for social anthropology* (pp. 139–236). London: Tavistock.

Seligman, M., & Czikszentmihalyi, M. (1999). Positive psychology: An introduction. *American Psychologist, 55,* 5–14.

Shweder, R. A. (1990). Cultural psychology: What is it? In J. W. Stigler, R. A. Shweder, & G. Herdt (Ed.), *Cultural psychology: Essays on comparative human development* (pp. 1–43). New York: Cambridge University Press.

Shweder, R. A., & Haidt, J. (2000). The cultural psychology of the emotions: Ancient and new. In M. Lewis & J. M. Haviland-Jones (Ed.), *Handbook of emotions* (2nd ed., pp. 397–414). New York: Guilford Press.

Stall, S. (1904). *What a young man ought to know.* London: Vir.

Steele, J. D. (1867). *Fourteen weeks in chemistry.* New York: A. S. Barnes.

Waterman, A. S. (1990). The relevance of Aristotle's conception of eudaimonia for the psychological study of happiness. *Theoretical and Philosophical Psychology, 10,* 39–44.

Yatiswarananda, S. (1979). *Meditation and spiritual life.* Bangalore, India: Sri Ramakrishna Ashrama.

V

LOOKING AHEAD:
A CALL TO ACTION

13

COMPLETE MENTAL HEALTH: AN AGENDA FOR THE 21ST CENTURY

COREY L. M. KEYES

Congress passed the National Mental Health Act in 1946, which provided substantial funding for psychiatric research and education, and created the National Institute of Mental Health (NIMH; see Mechanic, 1989). From its inception, the NIMH's mission and modus operandi has been "To improve this nation's mental health ..." by supporting "... a wide range of research related to the etiology, diagnosis, treatment, and prevention of mental *disorders*" (U.S. Department of Health and Human Services, 1995, p. 1; emphasis added). Although the mission of improving the mental health should continue, this chapter will argue that the practice of doing so by focusing solely on mental illness must be amended to include an equal emphasis on mental health.

Despite more than 50 years of national commitment to mental health, very little has been learned about it. Instead, much has been learned about mental illness, which is a persistent and substantial deviation from normal functioning that impairs an individual's ability to execute their social roles (e.g., employee) and generates emotional suffering (Spitzer & Wilson, 1975). Depression, in particular, costs billions each year through lost productivity, health care costs, and premature mortality from suicide (Keyes & Lopez, 2002; Murray & Lopez, 1996; Mrazek & Haggerty, 1994; Rebellon, Brown, & Keyes, 2001; U.S. Department of Health and Human Services, 1998). Studies suggest that about 1 in 10 adults have an episode of major depression each year, and 5 in 10 adults experience at least one serious mental illness

Support for the research summarized in this chapter comes from the John D. and Catherine T. MacArthur Foundation's Program on Human and Community Development through membership in the Successful Midlife Development Research Network (MIDMAC), directed by Dr. Orville Gilbert Brim, Jr.

in their lifetime (Kessler et al., 1994; Robins & Regier, 1991, U.S. Department of Health and Human Services, 1999).

Though mental illness is prevalent, the statistics also suggest that many people do not "breakdown." About one half of the adult population will be free of serious mental illness throughout life, and about 90% will not experience major depression each year. Are these adults who remain free of mental illness necessarily mentally healthy? This is a paramount question for proponents of the mental health model who view mental health as a state that is not merely the absence of mental illness (Keyes, 2002; Ryff & Singer, 1998). According to the surgeon general, mentally healthy adults have *successful* mental function, *fulfilling* relationships, *productive* activities, and the *capacity for adaptation* (U.S. Department of Health and Human Services, 1999). This definition embraces the idea that mental health is the presence of positive levels of feelings and psychosocial functioning and not simply the absence of mental illness (see also Jahoda, 1958; Smith, 1959; World Health Organization, 1948).

The purpose of this chapter is to review the conception and diagnosis of mental health. Research is reviewed that clearly shows that there are grave reasons for concern about the mental health of adults in the United States. First, fewer than one quarter of adults between the ages of 25 and 74 fit the criteria for *flourishing* in life, which is defined as a state in which an individual feels positive emotion toward life and is functioning well psychologically and socially. Second, individuals diagnosed as flourishing have excellent emotional health, miss fewer days of work, cut back on work on fewer days, and have fewer physical limitations in their daily lives.

Third, the absence of mental health—a condition described as *languishing*—is more prevalent than major depression disorder. Languishing is defined as a state in which an individual is devoid of positive emotion toward life, is not functioning well psychologically or socially, and has not been depressed during the past year. In short, languishers are neither mentally ill nor mentally healthy. Languishing is a "disorder" that exists on the mental health continuum (see Keyes, 2002), constituting a life of quiet despair that parallels clinical accounts of patients who may describe their lives as "hollow" or "empty" (see, e.g., Cushman, 1990; Levy, 1984).

Fourth, languishing is associated with emotional distress and psychosocial impairment at levels that are comparable to the impairment associated with a major depressive episode.

In sum, there are compelling reasons that positive psychologists cannot overlook mental illness. However, languishing—a silent and debilitating epidemic in the United States—indicates that there are equally compelling reasons that behavioral and social scientists can no longer ignore the concept of mental health. This chapter begins with the current and historic conceptions of mental health, with special emphasis on the absence of mental health. Neither the surgeon general's definition of mental health nor historical accounts of positive mental health (e.g., Jahoda, 1958) have addressed the nature of the absence of mental health, and accounts of languishing stretch back through history.

THE ABSENCE OF MENTAL HEALTH

Languishing in Life

The Eighth Deadly Sin

To the ancients, and particularly Christian philosophers like Evagrius Ponticus, the state of languishing was the eighth deadly sin (Funk, 1998; Sutera, 1999). Acedia vanished from the list of deadly sins in the 6th century at the hands of Pope Gregory the Great. Derived from the Greek term *akdeia*, which denotes indifference, the concept of acedia denotes the absence of care and is similar to states of apathy and ennui. Acedia is spiritual sloth and physical idleness, which reasons the early Christians deemed it sinful. *The Oxford English Dictionary* (1991) defines acedia and languishing synonymously. Acedia is "sloth, torpor," and a "condition leading to listlessness and want of interest of life." Languishing is defined as "Suffering from, or exhibiting, weariness or ennui," and as "failing to excite interest" in life.[1]

Arrest of Life

Count Leo Tolstoy described what could only be considered a form of languishing in his autobiographical work titled, "A Confession." At the age of about 50, and at the height of his literary success, Tolstoy wrote the following account of his life:

> At first I experienced moments of perplexity and arrest of life, as though I did not know what to do or how to live; and I felt lost and became dejected. But this passed, and I went on living as before. Then these moments of perplexity began to recur oftener and oftener, and always in the same form. They were always expressed by the questions: What is it for? What does it lead to? At first it seemed to me that these were aimless and irrelevant questions. I thought that it was all well known, and that if I should ever wish to deal with the solution it would not cost me much effort; just at present I had no time for it, but when I wanted to, I should be able to find the answer. The questions however began to repeat themselves frequently, and to demand replies more and

---

[1] Thanks to Dr. Greg Fricchione, director of the Carter Center's mental health program, for the suggestion of *Acedia* as the historical equivalent of languishing.

more insistently, and like drops of ink always falling on one place they ran together into one black blot. (1882/1951, pp. 15–16)[2]

Tolstoy's moments of perplexity and dejection, inquiries about the purpose and meaning of life, and his comparison of the feelings as amounting to "one black blot" of ink suggests a person tormented by the absence of feeling for life rather than the presence of negative feelings toward life. Indeed, Tolstoy describes how the feelings of despair and emptiness occurred at a time of "complete good fortune." He characterized his life as consisting of a good wife, good children, and a large estate. He continued, "And far from being insane or mentally diseased, I enjoyed the contrary strength of mind and body ... mentally I could work for eight and ten hours at a stretch. ... " (pp. 18–19).[3]

Something More

There are contemporary accounts of languishing in life that parallel Tolstoy's confessions of emptiness. For example, the October 13, 1998, "Oprah Winfrey Show" was devoted to the topic of women's lives and wanting something more out of life. The backdrop for this discussion, however, was women's struggle with languishing in life.

The women who spoke clarified the meaning and challenge of languishing in life. These women had the trappings of success—good marriages, great children, good jobs, and nice homes in good neighborhoods. Yet these women clearly suffered from very low well-being. They felt empty, lost, lacking a purpose, and adrift without meaning in life ("The Oprah Winfrey Show," 1998, pp. 1–2).

These women described social conditions that should lead to the absence of mental disorders—in other words, married, employed, a good home, and healthy children. However, the feelings and functioning described by these women illustrate the conception of languishing in life. They described themselves as having unsettling feelings, a void in their souls. They attempted to fill the void with hedonistic pursuits that did not quench their desire for meaning, and pondered such ultimate questions as the purpose and meaning of life.

The Lost Children of Rockdale County

Between 1996, as the state of Georgia and city of Atlanta prepared to host the Olympics, and May 20, 1999, a series of events occurred in

---

[2] Reprinted by permission of Oxford University Press.
[3] Thanks to Dr. George Vaillant for the suggestion that Tolstoy was one of history's greatest languishers.

Rockdale County that reflected, in part, a social void and personal emptiness in youth. A 16-year-old boy was killed in a fight at a strip-mall parking lot. An adolescent boy, wielding a shotgun, went on a shooting rampage at Heritage High School (in Conyers, Georgia, May 20, 1999) wounding six fellow students. Moreover, 17 teenagers in Rockdale County between the ages of 14 and 17 tested positive for syphilis, and 200 teenagers were exposed to the sexually transmitted virus. The story of Rockdale County's "lost children" is one of economic prosperity and personal emptiness (cf. Myers, 2000).

Rockdale County is small and affluent, and comprises mostly Caucasian, suburban, and middle-class and upper-class families. The children of Rockdale lived physically comfortable, somewhat privileged lives. Heritage High School, where the shooting and several of the syphilis cases occurred, was ranked among the best schools in Georgia. However, the public health investigation of the syphilis outbreak unveiled a story of group sex, alcohol abuse, and drug use among the teenagers. Documented by Public Broadcasting's *Frontline* series and analyzed by the pundits, explanations for Rockdale County included the theme of languishing. *Frontline's* producer of the "Lost Children of Rockdale County," Rachel Dretzin Goodman, said that she and her colleagues "came to see the syphilis outbreak in Rockdale County as a kind of metaphor for a deeper malady afflicting so many adolescent today. Wherever we went, we met kids who were drifting, hungry for something to fill the void left by too much time on their own and too little structure in their lives."[4]

The absence of structure in the lives of Rockdale's youth was ironically a reflection of their parent's economic success. The parents were successful, busy, and hard-working individuals. These parents could therefore provide for their children's material needs but had little time or energy leftover to provide for their teenager's existential needs. Commenting on children's natural craving for attention, a former school guidance counselor in the Rockdale system, Peggy Cooper, noted how the absence of attention is particularly troubling for youth. She said that children naturally crave attention and "they'll get good attention as long as they can get it. If they can't get good attention, they'll get bad attention because the worst thing in the world to them is to have no attention. No attention is to lead a solitary life" (Frontline, 2002).[5] According to Michael Resnick, a professor of sociology and pediatrics at the University of Minnesota,

---

[4]Information and all quotations in this section are taken from the transcript of the Frontline documentary and the postscripts available on the Georgia Public Television's Lost Children of Rockdale County Webpage (www.pbs.org/wgbh/pages/frontline/shows/georgia). Retrieved July 15, 2002. Used by permission.

[5]Quoted by permission.

It certainly wasn't clear who was the more lost: the children or the parents of Rockdale County. . . . We heard a lot about emptiness. Houses that were empty and devoid of supervision, adult presence, oversight. There was in far too many of the adolescents a fundamental emptiness of purpose; a sense that they were not needed, not connected to adults, to tasks, to anything meaningful other than the raw and relentless pursuit of pleasure. (Frontline, 2002)[6]

What do the youth of Rockdale County, living life at the end of the 20th century in the affluence of the United States, share in common with the ancient notion of acedia or Tolstoy's confessions of his want for meaning in life? Whether sinning with a slothful soul or seized by questions of life's purpose, individuals have languished throughout history. People suffer a quiet despair that comes from the absence of meaning, the absence of purpose, and the absence of anything positive in life. Languishing is an overlooked malady that is the counterpart to mental health. Although languishers are stagnant and empty, flourishing individuals have an enthusiasm for life and are actively and productively engaged with others and in society.

MENTAL HEALTH OPERATIONALIZED

Symptoms and Syndrome

Mental health, like mental illness, should be viewed as a syndrome of symptoms. A state of health, like illness, is indicated when a set of symptoms at a specific level are exhibited for a period of time that coincides with distinctive mental and social functioning (Mechanic, 1999). The symptoms of mental health consist of an individual's subjective well-being. Subjective well-being reflects individuals' perceptions and evaluations of their own lives in terms of their affective states and their psychological and social functioning. Forty years of research on subjective well-being has yielded a taxonomy of mental health symptoms consisting of emotional well-being and functional well-being (Keyes, Shmotkin, & Ryff, 2002; Keyes & Waterman, 2003).

Emotional well-being is a cluster of symptoms reflecting the presence and absence of positive feelings about life (see Table 13.1). Symptoms of emotional well-being can be ascertained from individuals' responses to structured scales measuring the presence of positive affect (e.g., individual is in good spirits), the absence of negative affect (e.g., individual is not

---

[6]Quoted by permission.

TABLE 13.1.
Operational Definitions of Symptoms of Mental Health

Positive feelings: emotional well-being	Positive functioning: psychological well-being	Positive functioning: social well-being
Positive affect: Regularly cheerful, in good spirits, happy, calm and peaceful, satisfied, and full of life.	*Self-acceptance*: Positive attitude toward oneself and past life, and concedes and accepts varied aspects of self.	*Social acceptance*: Positive attitude toward others while acknowledging and accepting people's complexity.
Happiness: Feels happiness toward past or about present life overall or in domains of life.[a]	*Personal growth*: Insight into one's potential, sense of development, and open to challenging new experiences.	*Social actualization*: Cares and believes that, collectively, people have potential and society can evolve positively.
Life Satisfaction: Sense of contentment or satisfaction with past or present life overall or in life domains.[a]	*Purpose in life*: Has goals, beliefs that affirm sense of direction in life, and feels life has purpose and meaning.	*Social contribution*: Feels that one's life is useful to society and that one's contributions are valued by others.
	Environmental mastery: Has capability to manage complex environment and can choose or create suitable environs.	*Social coherence*: Has interest in society, feels it's intelligible, somewhat logical, predictable, and meaningful.
	Autonomy: Comfortable with self-direction, has internal standards, resists unsavory social pressures.	*Social integration*: Feels part of, and a sense of belonging to, a community, derives comfort and support from community.
	Positive relations with others: Has warm, satisfying, trusting relationships, and is capable of empathy and intimacy.	

[a]Examples of life domains are employment, marriage, and neighborhood.

hopeless), and perceived satisfaction or happiness with life. Measures of the expression of emotional well-being in terms of positive affect and negative affect are related but distinct dimensions (e.g., Bradburn, 1969; Watson & Tellegen, 1985). Last, measures of avowed (e.g., "I am satisfied with life") and expressed (i.e., positive and negative affect) emotional well-being are related but distinct dimensions (Andrews & Withey, 1976; Bryant & Veroff, 1982; Diener, 1984; Diener, Sandvik, & Pavot, 1991; Diener, Suh, Lucas, & Smith, 1999).

Ryff (1989) argued that well-being is more than happiness with life. In addition, subjective well-being includes measures of positive functioning in life. Since Ryff's (1989) operationalization of clinical and personality theory conceptions of positive functioning (Jahoda, 1958), the field has moved toward a broader set of measures of psychological well-being. Positive functioning consists of six dimensions: self-acceptance, positive relations with others, personal growth, purpose in life, environmental mastery, and autonomy (see Keyes & Ryff, 1999). Individuals are mentally healthy when they like all parts of themselves, have warm trusting relationships, see themselves developing into better people, have a direction in life, are able to shape their world to satisfy their needs, and have a degree of self-determination. The psychological well-being scales are reliable and validated (Ryff, 1989); the hypothesized six-factor structure has been confirmed in a large and representative sample of U.S. adults (Ryff & Keyes, 1995).

Keyes (1998) argued that positive functioning consists of more than psychological well-being. Functioning well in life includes social challenges and tasks that reflect an individual's social well-being (Keyes, 1998). Whereas psychological well-being represents more private and personal criteria for the evaluation of functioning, social well-being epitomizes the more public and social criteria whereby people evaluate their functioning in life. These social dimensions consist of social coherence, social actualization, social integration, social acceptance, and social contribution. Individuals are mentally healthy when they view social life as meaningful and understandable, when they see society as possessing potential for growth, when they feel they belong to their communities, are able to accept all parts of society, and when they see their lives as contributing to society. The social well-being scales have shown good construct validity and internal consistency, and the hypothesized five-factor structure has been confirmed in two studies of representative samples of adults in the United States (Keyes, 1998; Keyes & Shapiro, in press).

Diagnosis of Mental Health

Empirically, mental health and mental illness are not opposite ends of a single continuum. Measures of symptoms of mental illness (viz., depression) correlate modestly and negatively with various measures of subjective well-being. Specifically, measures of psychological well-being (in two separate studies reviewed in Ryff & Keyes, 1995) correlated on average −.51 with the Zung depression inventory and −.55 with the Center for Epidemiological Studies depression (CESD) scale. Indicators and scales of life satisfaction and happiness (i.e., emotional well-being) also tend to correlate around −.40 to −.50 with scales of depression symptoms (see Frisch, Cornell, Villanueva, & Retzlaff, 1992). In short, there is about 25% shared variance between common scales of depression and subjective well-being.

Confirmatory factor analyses of the subscales of the CESD and the scales of psychological well-being in a sample of U.S. adults supported the two-factor theory (Keyes, Ryff, & Lee, in press). That is, the best-fitting model was one in which the CESD subscales were indicators of the latent factor that represented the presence and absence of mental illness. The psychological well-being scales were indicators of a second latent factor that represented the presence and absence of mental health. These findings corroborate factor analyses that showed that measures of life satisfaction and positive affect loaded on a separate factor from measures of anxiety and depression (Headey, Kelley, & Wearing, 1993). Thus, studies reveal that mental health is not merely the absence of mental illness symptoms, nor is it simply the presence of high levels of subjective well-being.

The measures of subjective well-being shown previously in Table 13.1 fall into two clusters of symptoms. Whereas measures of emotional well-being comprise a cluster that reflects symptoms of emotional vitality, measures of psychological well-being and social well-being reflect a cluster of symptoms of positive functioning. Both clusters of mental health symptoms mirror the cluster of symptoms used in the *DSM-III-R* (American Psychiatric Association, 1987) to diagnose a major depressive episode (MDE). That is, depression consists of symptoms of depressed mood (e.g., or anhedonia: loss of pleasure derived from activities) and symptoms of malfunctioning (e.g., insomnia or hypersomnia). Of the nine symptoms of MDE, a diagnosis of depression is made when a respondent reports five or more symptoms (at least one symptom must be from the depressed mood cluster).

The diagnosis of states along the mental health continuum is based on the *DSM-III-R* (American Psychiatric Association, 1987) approach for major depression. In the study by Keyes (2002), respondents completed a structured scale of positive affect and an item on life satisfaction. Respondents also completed the six scales of psychological well-being and five scales of social well-being. Altogether, the study included two symptom scales of emotional vitality and 11 symptom scales of positive functioning (i.e., six psychological, five social, well-being). To be diagnosed as *languishing* in life, individuals must exhibit low levels (low = lower tertile) on one of the two scales of emotional well-being and low levels on six of the 11 scales of positive functioning. To be diagnosed as *flourishing* in life, individuals must exhibit high levels (high = upper tertile) on one of the two scales of emotional well-being and high levels on six of the 11 scales of positive functioning. Adults who are *moderately mentally healthy* are neither flourishing nor languishing in life. Individuals who are languishing or flourishing must therefore exhibit, respectively, low or high levels of emotional vitality and positive functioning on at least 50% or more of the symptom scales. As with the diagnosis of major depression, the symptoms of emotional vitality are considered essential for the diagnosis of mental health insofar as individuals must exhibit either a high level of satisfaction or a high level of positive affect.

In sum, mental health should be viewed as a complete state consisting of two dimensions: the mental illness continuum and the mental health continuum. As shown in Figure 13.1, each dimension respectively ranges from a high to a low level of symptoms of mental illness and mental health. When both dimensions are crossed together, two states of mental illness and three states of mental health emerge. Individuals who are flourishing in life are completely mentally healthy because they are not only free of major depression, they also fit the diagnostic criteria for the presence of mental health. Individuals who fit the criteria for moderate mental health and for languishing have incomplete mental health; although these individuals are not depressed, they do not have sufficiently high levels of well-being to fit the criteria for mental health. In turn, there are individuals with incomplete mental illness such as those who fit the *DSM* criteria for major depression but who have at least moderate or even higher levels of subjective well-being. Although such individuals may have other comorbid mental illnesses, they are classified as having a "pure" episode of mental illness,

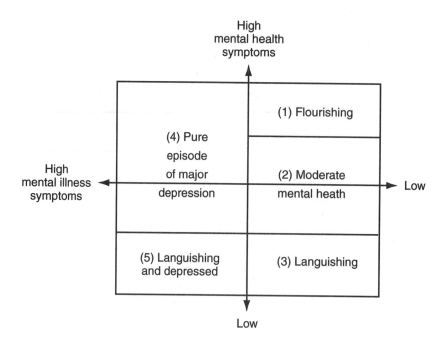

Figure 13.1. The complete mental health model and diagnostic categories.

because they are not also languishing in life. Last, individuals who fit the criteria for major depression and for languishing have complete mental illness, because they are mentally ill *and* devoid of mental health.

MENTAL HEALTH IN THE UNITED STATES

Findings From the Study of Midlife in the United States

The Midlife in the United States (MIDUS) study comprises a nationally representative sample of 3,032 adults between the ages of 25 and 74. This study was conducted in 1995 by an interdisciplinary team of scholars convened and supported by the John D. and Catherine T. MacArthur Foundation to study successful aging and human development (see Brim, Ryff, & Kessler, in press). MIDUS is an exemplary study for many reasons, two of which are relevant to this chapter. First, MIDUS used structured *DSM-III-R* categories (American Psychiatric Association, 1987) to diagnose mental illness. MIDUS used the Composite International Diagnostic Interview Short Form scales (CIDI-SF; Kessler, Andrews, Mroczek, Ustun, & Wittchen, 1998), which has shown excellent diagnostic sensitivity and specificity compared with diagnoses based on the complete CIDI in the National Comorbidity Study (Kessler, DuPont, Berglund, & Wittchen, 1999). During the telephone interview that was part of the research, the CIDI-SF was used to assess whether respondents exhibited symptoms indicative of MDE during the past 12 months. Second, the MIDUS measured the emotional, psychological, and social well-being of adults. Thus—using the mental health diagnosis described earlier—MIDUS permits the investigation of languishing and flourishing in comparison with *DSM* diagnoses of mental illnesses. What follows is based on MIDUS and research reported in Keyes (2002).

Mental Health: Prevalence and Comorbidity

Most adults, 85.9%, did not have a depressive episode. However, only 21.6% of adults fit the criteria for flourishing in life. More than half of the sample (i.e., 58.7%) had moderate mental health, and nearly 20% of adults fit the criteria for languishing in life. Cross-tabulation of the depression diagnosis and the mental health diagnosis revealed a strong dose–response relationship. About 5% of flourishing adults and 13% of adults with moderate mental health had a depressive episode in the past year. However, 28% of languishing adults had major depression during the past year. Thus, moderately mentally healthy individuals were two times more likely than flourishing adults to have had a depressive episode; languishing adults were five times more likely than flourishing adults and two times as likely as moderately mentally healthy adults to have had a depressive episode.

The combination of depression and mental health diagnoses permitted the assessment of the complete mental health status of respondents. Of the 14.1% of adults who had a depressive episode, 9.4% had a pure episode of depression (i.e., incomplete mental illness),[7] and the remaining 4.7% of depressed adults were also languishing (i.e., completely mentally ill). Of the 85.9% of nondepressed cases, 56.6% were moderately mentally healthy, 17.2% were completely mentally healthy (i.e., flourishing), and 12.1% had incomplete mental health (i.e., pure languishing).

Mental Health: Psychosocial Functioning

Respondents were asked to evaluate their "mental or emotional health" on a scale from "poor," "fair," "good," "very good," to "excellent." Figure 13.2 reveals that the diagnosis of complete mental health corresponds with individuals' self-reported mental, emotional health. More than half of the adults who were languishing and had an episode of depression evaluated their emotional health as "poor" or "fair." In contrast, fewer than 1% of flourishing and just under 6% of adults with moderate mental health said their emotional health was "poor" or "fair." However, almost 18% of adults with a pure languishing (i.e., languishing but not depressed) and 22% of adults with pure depressive episode (i.e., depressed but not languishing) saw their emotional health as "poor" or "fair."

Almost all of the flourishing adults and more than half of adults with moderate mental health felt that their emotional health was "very good" or "excellent." In contrast, only a third of adults with pure languishing and a third of adults with pure depression felt that their emotional health was "very good" or "excellent." Only 15% of adults who were languishing and had a depressive episode saw their emotional health as "very good" or "excellent." Conversely, more than half of the adults who languished and had depression said their emotional health was "poor" or "fair." Nearly as many adults with pure languishing—about one third—as those with pure depression said their emotional health was "poor" or "fair." Less than 6% of adults with moderate mental health and less than 1% of flourishing adults said their emotional health was "poor" or "fair."[8]

---

[7] Of the 14.1% depressed adults, 0.9% were also flourishing and 8.5% were also moderately mentally healthy.

[8] The association of mental health with perceived emotional health was unchanged in multivariate models that include adjustment for a host of sociodemographic variables (i.e., sex, age, race, education, marital status, employment status).

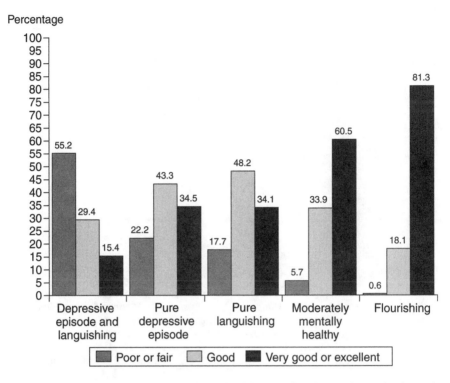

Percentage

Figure 13.2. Self-rated mental, emotional health by major depressive episode and mental health status.

Respondents also evaluated how much their health limited them from doing any of nine instrumental activities of daily life. The activities included such things as lifting and carrying groceries, climbing several flights of stairs, walking several blocks, and moderate activity such as vacuuming. The analysis focused on whether a respondent reported at least one activity that was limited "a lot" by their health, which denoted a "severe" limitation. Nearly 70% of adults who were languishing and had a depressive episode had at least one severe limitation, whereas 64% of adults with pure languishing had at least one severe limitation. About 55% of moderately well and 55% of individuals with pure depression had at least one severe limitation. Only 42% of flourishing adults reported at least one severe limitation. Thus, flourishing adults also appeared to be the most physically healthy subpopulation. However, more adults with pure languishing showed signs of physical health problems than adults with pure depression. By comparison, almost three quarters of adults who were languishing and had a depressive episode showed signs of physical health problems.

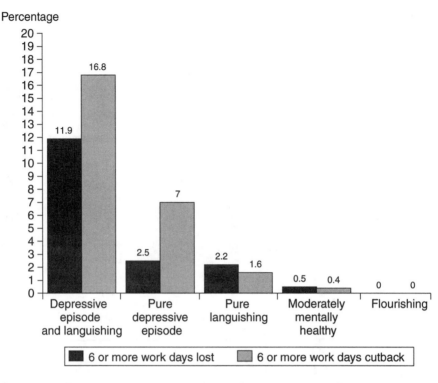

Percentage

Depressive episode and languishing — 6 or more work days lost: 11.9, 6 or more work days cutback: 16.8
Pure depressive episode — 2.5, 7
Pure languishing — 2.2, 1.6
Moderately mentally healthy — 0.5, 0.4
Flourishing — 0, 0

■ 6 or more work days lost   ▨ 6 or more work days cutback

Figure 13.3. Severe work impairment over past 30 days by major depressive episode and mental health status.

Data were collected regarding the number of days of work in the past 30 days individuals either cut back on the work they could get done or were completely unable to go to work or carry out normal household activities (i.e., days of lost work). Follow-up questions assessed whether the work cutbacks and lost days of work were a result of problems with physical health, mental health, or a combination of mental and physical health. Analyses reported focused on work loss and cutbacks because of mental health or the combination of mental and physical health (cutbacks and days lost solely because of physical health were omitted from the analysis). Moreover, the analyses focused on "severe" cutbacks and lost work, operationalized as six or more days (during the past 30 days) cut back or lost.

Figure 13.3 illustrates that mental health and mental illness were also associated with impairments in work attendance and productivity. None of the flourishing adults had a severe work cutback or a severe loss of workdays in the past 30 days. Moreover, fewer than 1% of the moderately mentally healthy adults had a severe cutback of productivity or a severe loss of workdays. However, nearly as many adults with pure languishing as adults with pure depression had a severe loss of workdays. More than three times as many adults with pure depression as with pure languishing had severe cutbacks in productivity. Finally, adults with the comorbid condition of languishing and depression were especially likely to have severe loss of workdays and severe cutbacks of productivity when compared with adults with pure depression and pure languishing.[9]

In short, flourishing and moderate mental health are associated with superior profiles of psychosocial functioning when compared with pure languishing and pure depression. The comorbid condition of languishing with a depressive episode was associated with the most psychosocial impairment relative to all other states of complete mental health. Pure languishing, or the absence of mental health, appears to be as burdensome to psychosocial functioning as an episode of pure depression. It is noteworthy that pure languishing is not subclinical depression. Adults who had "pure" languishing (i.e., no MDE) had an average of 0.1 (SD = 0.6) symptoms of depression, indicating that most of these individuals did not have even one symptom of depression.

CONCLUSION

Only recently has mental illness received the dubious but important distinction of being a disability as well as a disease of the brain. Based on data from 1990, the economic burden of major depression alone was estimated at $43.7 billion because of work absenteeism, diminished productivity, and treatment (Greenberg, Stiglin, Finkelstein, & Berndt, 1993). As a class, mental disorders were the third most costly condition in the United States in 1999, with combined direct and indirect costs of nearly $160 billion (Keyes & Lopez, 2002). Globally, depression in 1996 was ranked among the top five causes of disability and premature mortality, and depression is projected to become the second leading cause of disability and premature mortality by the year 2020 (Murray & Lopez, 1996). The treatment and prevention of mental illness, particularly major depression, are pressing issues facing many countries.

However, research reviewed in this chapter indicates that there are equally grave reasons for concern about the absence of mental health (i.e., languishing). Languishing corresponds with substantial psychosocial impairment. Languishing is associated with poor emotional health, with high limitations of daily living, and with a high likelihood of a severe number (i.e., six or more) of lost days of work (because of mental health). Although

---

[9]The association of mental health with psychosocial functioning and impairment was unchanged in multivariate models that include adjustment for a host of sociodemographic variables (i.e., sex, age, race, education, marital status, employment status).

it was not associated with severe work cutback, languishing was associated with more days of work cutback compared with moderately well adults. Pure depression was a burden that impaired psychosocial functioning; it was not, however, any more of a burden than pure languishing. Like languishing, a major depressive episode was associated with poor emotional health, high limitations of activities of daily living, and a high likelihood of severe work cutbacks and lost days of work.

Functioning was considerably worse when languishing was comorbid with a major depressive episode—in other words, individuals who were languishing and had depression in the past year. These individuals had the worst self-reported emotional health, the most limitations of activities of daily living, the most days of work lost, and the greatest cutback of productivity. In contrast, functioning was markedly improved among moderately well and flourishing adults. These adults reported the best emotional health, the fewest days of work loss, and the fewest days of work productivity cutbacks. Moreover, flourishing adults reported even fewer limitations of activities of daily living than adults who were moderately well. In short, research indicates that there are clear benefits to be obtained if we seek the objective of promoting complete mental health.

Pure languishing was more prevalent than a pure episode of major depression. Moreover, fewer than 2 in 10 adults between the ages of 25 and 74 were flourishing, and just more than one half had moderate mental health. When a major depressive episode was cross-classified with the mental health diagnosis, findings showed that languishing adults were at much greater risk for a depressive episode than adults who were flourishing or had moderate mental health. Because the MIDUS data are cross-sectional, however, causality between languishing and depression cannot be discerned and remains a topic for future investigation.

When extrapolated to the target population based on the 1995 U.S. Census Bureau's estimates (i.e., 154.5 million adults, aged 25 to 74), the prevalence estimates suggest that about 7.3 million adults were completely mentally ill with a depressive episode and languishing in life. Another 14.5 millions adults had pure depression, and 18.6 million had pure languishing. About 26.6 million adults were completely mentally healthy—in other words, flourishing in life. To put these estimates into perspective, the estimated number of individuals with pure languishing would literally replace the entire population of the state of New York, which had 18.9 million residents as of the most recent census.[10] Moreover, the number of mentally healthy, flourishing individuals would just replace the combined state popu-

---

[10] State populations are taken from the year 2000 U.S. Census Bureau's "geographic comparison tables" at http://factfinder.census.gov/servlet/BasicFactsServlet

lations of Texas (i.e., 20.9 million in 2000) and Missouri (i.e., 5.6 million in 2000).

What, in conclusion, should be the priorities of mental health policy, practice, and research in the 21st century? The modus operandi of the NIMH is supporting research related to identifying, treating, and preventing mental illnesses (see U.S. Department of Health and Human Services, 1995) to promote the mental health of the U.S. population. Proponents of the study of mental health, and the implications of this chapter, suggest that the current modus operandi of the NIMH is incomplete. Mental illness and mental health are correlated but separate continua. As such, prevention and treatment of mental illness will not necessarily result in more mentally healthy individuals. In fact, by focusing solely on mental illness, the NIMH cannot improve this nation's mental health. It can, however, reduce this nation's mental illness, which is a profoundly important step toward the objective of a mentally healthy population. A second and equally important step is to engage in genuine mental health promotion, which includes the objectives of reducing the amount of languishing adults and increasing the number of flourishing individuals in the population.

The study of mental health also raises new questions for the objectives and the nature of mental illness treatment and prevention. Treatment objectives for mental illness are symptom reduction and prevention of relapse (Gladis, Gosch, Dishuk, & Crits-Christoph, 1999; U.S. Department of Health and Human Services, 1999). However, findings summarized in this chapter suggest that mental health promotion is the ideal objective of treatment. Future research should also investigate whether and how languishing adults are at risk for depression. Most interventions to prevent mental illness are based on findings of the study of risk and protective factors for mental illness (i.e., "at risk" populations). Another source of prevention knowledge may be gleaned from the study of the life course and social contexts of mentally healthy youth and adults. Understanding the nature and etiology of the strengths and competencies of flourishing individuals may provide therapeutic insights for promoting strengths and competencies in mentally ill patients (see, e.g., Fava, 1999).

To achieve its goal of "improving this nation's health," the NIMH should marshal the political will and economic support in Congress to build a science of mental health in the same way it has, since 1946, built the science of mental illness. The promotion of flourishing, if nations are to thrive socially and economically, must also be an objective for the World Health Organization's public mental health efforts (see World Health Organization, 2001). The study and promotion of mental health can be a solution, not merely a slogan, for the future. In sum, it is time to truly pursue the study and promotion of mental health, and this is can be achieved with a more positive psychology as well as a more positive sociology.

REFERENCES

American Psychiatric Association. (1987). *Diagnostic and statistical manual of mental disorders* (3rd ed., rev.). Washington, DC: Author.

Andrews, F. M., & Withey, S. B. (1976). *Social indicators of well-being: Americans' perceptions of life quality.* New York: Plenum Press.

Bradburn, N. M. (1969). *The structure of psychological well-being.* Chicago: Aldine.

Brim, O. G., Ryff, C. D., & Kessler, R. C. (Eds.). (in press). *A portrait of midlife in the United States.* Chicago: University of Chicago Press.

Bryant, F. B., & Veroff, J. (1982). The structure of psychological well-being: A sociohistorical analysis. *Journal of Personality and Social Psychology, 43,* 653–673.

Cushman, P. (1990). Why the self is empty: Toward a historically situated psychology. *American Psychologist, 45,* 599–611.

Diener, E. (1984). Subjective well-being. *Psychological Bulletin, 95,* 542–575.

Diener, E., Sandvik, E., & Pavot, W. (1991). Happiness is the frequency, not the intensity, of positive versus negative affect. In F. Strack, M. Argyle, & N. Schwarz (Eds.), *Subjective well-being: An interdisciplinary perspective* (pp. 119–139). Oxford: Pergamon Press.

Diener, E., Suh, E. M., Lucas, R. E., & Smith, H. L. (1999). Subjective well-being: Three decades of progress. *Psychological Bulletin, 125,* 276–302.

Fava, G. A. (1999). Well-being therapy: Conceptual and technical issues. *Psychotherapy and Psychosomatics, 68,* 171–179.

Frisch, M. B., Cornell, J., Villanueva, M., & Retzlaff, P. J. (1992). Clinical validation of the Quality of Life Inventory: A measure of life satisfaction for use in treatment planning and outcome assessment. *Psychological Assessment, 4,* 92–101.

Frontline. (2002). The lost children of Rockdale County. Retrieved July 15, 2002, at http://www.pbs. org/wgbh/pages/frontline/shows/georgia/etc/script.html

Funk, M. M. (1998). *Thoughts matter: The practice of the spiritual life.* New York: Continuum.

Gladis, M. M., Gosch, E. A., Dishuk, N. M., & Crits-Christoph, P. (1999). Quality of life: Expanding the scope of clinical significance. *Journal of Consulting and Clinical Psychology, 67,* 320–331.

Greenberg, P. E., Stiglin, L. E., Finkelstein, S. N., & Berndt, E. R. (1993). The economic burden of depression in 1990. *Journal of Clinical Psychiatry, 54,* 405–418.

Headey, B. W., Kelley, J., & Wearing, A. J. (1993). Dimensions of mental health: Life satisfaction, positive affect, anxiety, and depression. *Social Indicators Research, 29,* 63–82.

Jahoda, M. (1958). *Current concepts of positive mental health.* New York: Basic Books.

Kessler, R. C., Andrews, G., Mroczek, D, Ustun, B., Wittchen, H-U. (1998). The World Health Organization Composite International Diagnostic Interview

Short Form (CIDI-SF). *International Journal of Methods in Psychiatric Research, 7*, 171–185.

Kessler, R. C., DuPont, R. L., Berglund, P., & Wittchen, H-U. (1999). Impairment in pure and comorbid generalized anxiety disorder and major depression at 12 months in two national surveys. *The American Journal of Psychiatry, 156*, 1915–1923.

Kessler, R. C., McGonagle, K. A., Zhao, S., Nelson, C. B., Hughes, M., et al. (1994). Lifetime and 12 month prevalence of DSM-III-R psychiatric disorders in the United States: Results from the National Comorbidity Survey. *Archives of General Psychiatry, 51*, 8–19.

Keyes, C. L. M. (1998). Social well-being. *Social Psychology Quarterly, 61*, 121–140.

Keyes, C. L. M. (2002). The mental health continuum: From languishing to flourishing in life. *Journal of Health and Social Behavior, 43*, 207–222.

Keyes, C. L. M., & Lopez, S. J. (2002). Toward a science of mental health: Positive directions in diagnosis and interventions. In C. R. Snyder & S. J. Lopez (Eds.), *The handbook of positive psychology* (pp. 45–59). New York: Oxford University Press.

Keyes, C. L. M., & Ryff, C. D. (1999). Psychological well-being in midlife. In S. L. Willis & J. D. Reid (Eds.), *Middle aging: Development in the third quarter of life* (pp. 161–180). Orlando, FL: Academic Press.

Keyes, C. L. M., Ryff, C. D., Lee, Y-H. (in press). Somatization and mental health: A comparative study of the idiom of distress hypothesis. *Social Science and Medicine*.

Keyes, C. L. M., & Shapiro, A. (in press). Social well-being in the United States: A descriptive epidemiology. In O. G. Brim, C. D. Ryff, & R. C. Kessler (Eds.), *A Portrait of Midlife in the United States*. Chicago: University of Chicago Press.

Keyes, C. L. M., Shmotkin, D., & Ryff, C. D. (2002). Optimizing well-being: The empirical encounter of two traditions. *Journal of Personality and Social Psychology, 82*, 1007–1022.

Keyes, C. L. M., & Waterman, M. B. (2003). Dimensions of well-being and mental health in adulthood. In M. Bornstein, L. Davidson, C. L. M. Keyes, & K. A. Moore (Eds.), *Well-being: Positive development throughout the life course* (pp. 481–501). Mahwah, NJ: Erlbaum.

Levy, S. T. (1984). Psychoanalytic perspectives on emptiness. *Journal of the American Psychoanalytic Association, 32*, 387–404.

Mechanic, D. (1989). *Mental health and social policy*. Englewood Cliffs, NJ: Prentice Hall.

Mechanic, D. (1999). Mental health and mental illness: Definitions and perspectives. In A. V. Horwitz & T. L. Scheid (Eds.), *A handbook for the study of mental health: Social contexts, theories, and systems* (pp. 12–28). New York: Cambridge University Press.

Mrazek, P. J., & Haggerty, R. J. (Eds.). (1994). *Reducing risks for mental disorders*. Washington, DC: National Academy Press.

Murray, C. J. L., & Lopez, A. D. (Eds.). (1996). *The global burden of disease: A comprehensive assessment of mortality and disability from diseases, injuries, and risk factors in 1990 and projected to 2020.* Cambridge, MA: Harvard School of Public Health.

Myers, D. G. (2000). *The American paradox: Spiritual hunger in an age of plenty.* New Haven, CT: Yale University Press.

"The Oprah Winfrey Show." (1998, Oct. 13). *Finding your authentic self.* Transcript produced by Burrelle's Information Services, Livingston, NJ.

Oxford English Dictionary, 2nd Edition. (1991). Oxford: Oxford University Press.

Rebellon, C., Brown, J., & Keyes, C. L. M. (2001). Suicide and mental illness. In C. E. Faupel & P. M. Roman (Eds.), *The encyclopedia of criminology and deviant behavior (Vol. 4): Self destructive behavior and disvalued identity* (pp. 426–429). London: Taylor and Francis.

Robins, L. N., & Regier, D. A. (Eds.). (1991). *Psychiatric disorders in America: The Epidemiological Catchment Area study.* New York: Free Press.

Ryff, C. D. (1989). Happiness is everything, or is it? Explorations on the meaning of psychological well-being. *Journal of Personality and Social Psychology, 57,* 1069–1081.

Ryff, C. D., & Keyes, C. L. M. (1995). The structure of psychological well-being revisited. *Journal of Personality and Social Psychology, 69,* 719–727.

Ryff, C. D., & Singer, B. (1998). The contours of positive human health. *Psychological Inquiry, 9,* 1–28.

Spitzer, R. L., & Wilson, P. T. (1975). Nosology and the official psychiatric nomenclature. In A. Freedman, H. Kaplan, & B. Sadock (Eds.), *Comprehensive textbook of psychiatry* (pp. 826–845). Baltimore: Williams and Wilkins.

Sutera, J. (1999). Acedia revisited: New case for an old sin. *American Monastic Newsletter, 29,* 3–5.

Tolstoy, L. (1951). *A confession: The gospel in brief and what I believe* (Trans. A. Maude). London: Oxford University Press. (Original published 1882)

U.S. Department of Health and Human Services. (1995). *Basic behavioral science research for mental health: A report of the national advisory mental health council.* Rockville, MD: Author.

U.S. Department of Health and Human Services. (1998). *Suicide: A report of the Surgeon General.* Rockville, MD: Author

U.S. Department of Health and Human Services. (1999). *Mental health: A report of the Surgeon General.* Rockville, MD: Author.

Watson, D., & Tellegen, A. (1985). Toward a consensual structure of mood. *Psychological Bulletin, 98,* 219–235.

World Health Organization. (1948). World Health Organization constitution. In *Basic documents.* Geneva: Author.

World Health Organization. (2001). *The world health report 2001. Mental Health: New understanding, new hope.* Geneva: Author.

AUTHOR INDEX

Numbers in italics refer to listings in the references sections.

Grob, A., 141, *156*
Gross, J. J., 139, *155*
Gruenewald, T. L., 149, *158*
Guilford, J. P., 172, *179, 180*
Gurung, R. A. R., 149, *158*
Guthman, E. O., 6, *12*

Habermas, T., 257, *271*
Hackman, J. R., 186, 287, 188, *201, 202*
Haggerty, R. J., 293, *312*
Haidt, J., 3, 10–11, 37n, 105n, 275, 276,
    276n, 280, 281, 282, 284, 285,
    286, *288, 289*
Hallahan, M., 68, *76*
Hamilton, S. F., 234, *244*
Hamilton, V. L., 277, *288*
Hanson, K. A., 261, *268*
Hansson, R. O., 264, *266*
Harned, D. B., 121–122, *125*
Harrington, D. M., 164, 172, *179, 180*
Harris, M. B., 228, *244*
Harris, S. D., 59, *74*
Harris, T. O., 40, 48, *52*
Hart, H. M., 39, *52*
Harter, J. K., 205, 208, 217, 218, 220,
    222
Hartnett, S. A., 64, *76*
Hartup, W. W., 130, *155*
Hartwick, J., 186, 187, *202*
Haselager, W. F. G., 262, *270*
Haslam, N., 121, *125*
Hayes, T. L., 208, 217, 218, *222*
Headey, B. W., 301, *310*
Heatherton, T., 39, *52*
Heavey, C. L., 137, *153*
Heckhausen, H., 256, *270*
Heckhausen, J. , 28, *35*, 256, 257, 258,
    262, *270*
Hedin, D., 232, *244*
Heider, K., 135, *156*
Heidrich, S. M., 21, 22, *32*
Heine, S. J., 68, 69, *76*
Helson, H., 137, *155*
Henderson, S. A., 197, *201*
Heng, B. H., 63, *76*
Henry, W., 84, *102*
Herbert, T. B., 130, *153*
Herling, S., 231, *243*
Hersh, M. A., 280, *288*
Hervig, L. K., 59, *77*

Herzberg, F., 187, *202*
Herzog, A. R., 238, 239, 231, *245*
Herzog, T., 68, *76*
Hewitt, L. N., 236, *247*
Heyman, R. E., 150, *152*
Hidi, S., 87, *102*
Higgins, A., 286, *288*
Higgins, E. T., 131, 141, *155*, 258, *270*
Higgins, G. O., 29, *33*
Higgins, P., 117, 119, *124*
Hjelle, L. A., 62, *76*
Ho, M. L., 63, *76*
Hobfoll, S. E., 258, *270*
Hoggson, N., 231, *243*
Holmes, C. S., 39, 42, *53*
Holmes, T. H., 130, *155*
Hoobler, G. D., 145, *155*
Horn, L., 37n
Horwitz, R. I., 29, *35*
Houlihan, D., 284, *287*
House, J. S., 130, *155*, 236, 238, 239,
    241, *244, 245*
Houts, R. M., 133, 149, *155*
Hovecar, D., 173, *180*
Hsieh, K. H., 139, *152*
Hughes, M., 233, *244*, 294, *311*
Hull, J. G., 62, *76*
Hunt, J., 89, *102*
Hunter, J. E., 211, 212, 214, *222, 223*
Huselid, M. A., 212, *222*
Huston, T. L., 133, 149, *155*

Iaffaldano, M. T., 207, *222*
Igreja, I., 111, *126*
Imada, S., 196, 198, *203*
Inghilleri, P., 84, 91, 92, *102*
Insel, T. R., 149, *155*
Isaacowitz, D. M., 147, *153*
Isen, A. M., 205, 210, *222*
Ito, T. A., 137, *155*

Jackson, J. M., 168, *180*
Jackson, S., 90, 91, *102*
Jacobson, N. S., 137, *155*
Jahoda, M., 294, 295, 300, 301, *310*
James, S. A., 64, *76*
James, W., 16, *33*, 84, 85, *102*
Janda, L. H., 171, *180*
Janikula, J., 231, 232, 232n, *247*

McCormick, C., 168, *182*
McCrae, R. R., 141, *156*, 175, *180*, 190, *202*
McCullough, M. E., 121, 122, *127*, *128*, 285, *288*
McEwen, B. S., 29, *34*, *35*, 149, *157*
McGonagle, K. A., 294, *311*
McGregor, I., 21, *34*
McKee, B., 38, *52*
McKenna, C., 150, *152*
McKenzie, R. C., 212, *223*
McMahon, K., 238, 242, *246*
Meacham, J. A., 257, *269*
Mead, G. H., 8, 84, 85, 86, 88, *103*
Mechanic, D., 293, 298, *311*
Mednick, M. T., 173, *181*
Mednick, S. A., 173, *181*
Medvec, V. H., 145, *154*
Meijer, Z., 275n, 282, *288*
Meir, E. I., 194, *202*
Melamed, S., 194, *202*
Mendolia, M., 62, *76*
Merriefield, P. R., 172, *179*
Merton, R. K., 176, *182*
Metalsky, G. I., 60, 61, *74*, *78*
Meyer, D., 69, *77*
Midlarksy, E., 237, 238n, 242, *245*
Mieder, W., 263, *271*
Milburn, N., 235, *243*
Miller, G. A., 259, *271*
Miller, J., 187, *202*, 234, *245*
Miller, K. A., 187, *202*
Miller, L. E., 194, *202*
Millman, L., 285, *288*
Miringoff, M., 5, *12*
Mischel, W., 260, *272*
Mish, F. C., 171, *181*
Mockros, C., 98, *103*
Moen, P., 238, *245*
Moffitt, T. E., 18, *34*
Moody, S. W., 233, *244*
Moore, C. W., 230, 231, *245*
Moos, R. H., 39, 50, 51, *52*
Morse, N. C., 187, *202*
Mortimer, J. T., 232, 234, *245*
Mortimore, P., 17, *34*
Moskowitz, D. S., 111, 112, *124*
Mrazek, P. J., 293, *312*
Mroczek, D., 41, *52*, 303, *310*
Muchinsky, P. M., 207, *222*
Muldoon, K., 234, *244*

Muldrow, T. W., 212, *223*
Muraven, M., 121, *124*
Murch, R. L., 39, 40, *52*
Murray, C. J. L., 206, *223*, 293, 207, *312*
Murray, H. A., 174, *181*
Musick, M. A., 238, 239, 231, *245*
Myers, D. G., 5, *12*, 68, *77*, 111, 113, 130, *156*, 297, *312*
Myers-Lipton, S. J., 234, *245*, 236

Nagata, D. K., 70, *76*
Nakamura, J., 7, 8, 83, 88, 92, 93, *101*, *103*
Nelson, C. B., 294, *311*
Nemeroff, C., 285, *288*
Nepps, P., 130, *157*
Nesselroade, J. R., 255
Newman, S., 228, *246*
Newmann, F. A., 232, *246*
Nichols, P. A., 39, *52*
Nisbett, R. E., 263
Noelle-Neumann, E., 92, *103*
Nord, W. R., 186, 187, *202*
Norem, J. K., 68, 71, *77*
Noriega, V., 59, *74*
Norman, C. C., 150, *152*
Notarius, C., 134, 137, *156*
Nowlis, V., 229, *246*
Nozick, R., 123, *127*
Nunally, J., 169, *181*
Nussbaum, M. C., 249, *272*

Oelmüller, W., 251, *272*
Oettingen, G., 68, *77*, 256, 260, *271*, 27
Oishi, S., 109, *127*
Oldham, G. R., 186, 187, 188, *201*, *202*
Olson, J. M., 137, *156*
Oman, D., 238, 242, *246*
Omoto, A. M., 242, *246*
Onawola, R., 228, *246*
Ong, Y. W., 63, *76*
Oppenheimer, L., 87, *103*
Osguthorpe, R. T., 233, *246*
Ostrop, G., 263, *272*
Ottenbacher, K. J., 118, *128*
Ouston, J., 17, *34*
Owen, J. F., 59, *78*

Smith, B. K., 278, 287
Smith, H. L., 109, *125*, 130, *153*, 299, *310*
Smith, J., 251, 252, 254, 256, 260, 263, 267, 269, 272, 273
Smith, M. L., 108, *124*
Smith, N. D., 251, 271
Smith, N. K., 137, *155*
Smith, R. S., 17, 36
Smith, S. E., 133, 149, *155*
Smither, J. W., 209, *223*
Snyder, C. R., 55, 79, 121, 122, *127*, *128*, 163, *182*
Snyder, M., 228, 232, 234, 235, 242, 244, 245, 246
Snyderman, B. B., 187, *202*
Solomon, R. L., 136, *158*
Sorokin, P. A., 176, *182*
Sosik, J. J., 207, *221*
Spearman, C., 173, *182*
Spector, P. E., 206, 207, *223*
Spielman, L., 106, *126*
Spitzberg, B. H., 145, *155*
Spitzer, R. L., 293, *312*
Srivastava, S., 108, *126*
Stall, S., 280, 289
Stang, D. J., 145, *156*
Stanley, S. M., 260, *271*
Stattin, H., 85, *103*
Staudinger, U. M., 20, 35, 249, 251, 252, 254–255, 259, 261, 262, 263, 267, 273
Staw, B. M., 187, 190, *203*, 207, *224*
Stearns, P., 197, *203*
Steele, J. D., 280, 289
Steen, T. A., 55, 57, 78
Stein, M. I., 165, *182*
Stellar, E., 29, 34
Stern, D., 62n, 78
Sternberg, R. J., 172, 174, *182*, *183*, 251, 273
Stetsenko, A., 260, *271*
Stevens, N., 130, *155*
Stich, M. H., 229, 247
Stiglin, L. E., 307, *310*
Storaasli, R. D., 260, *271*
Stouhamer-Loeber, M., 18, 34
Strack, S., 59, 79
Strand, M., 89–90
Streitman, S., 17, 32
Stroebe, M. S., 130, *158*

Stroebe, W., 130, *158*
Stukas, A. A., 228, 234, 235, 242, *244*, *246*
Suh, E. M., 109, *125*, *127*, 130, 141, *153*, *156*, 299, *310*
Sullivan, W. M., 188, *201*
Sulloway, F. J., 175, *182*
Sutera, J., 295, *312*
Sutton, K. J., 24, *31*, 40, 49, 52
Sutton, S. K., 140, *158*
Suzuki, T., 68, 76
Swank, A. B., 112, *126*
Sweeney, P. D., 58, 79
Swidler, A., 188, *201*
Syme, S. L., 58, 75

Tam, A., 275n, 282, 288
Tardiff, T. Z., 174, *183*
Taylor, E., 5, *12*
Taylor, R. D., 19, 36
Taylor, S. E., 62n, 69, 79, 134, 135, 136, 145, 149, *154*, *158*
Teasdale, J. D., 60, 74
Tedeschi, R. G., 24, 36
Tehrani, K., 112, *125*
Tellegen, A., 17, 18, *32*, 139, 150, *158*, 299, *312*
Tennen, H., 25, 35, 36, 63, 79, 117, 119, *124*
Terman, L. M., 171, 172, 173, *183*
Tesser, A., 115, 116, *124*
Thibaut, J. W., 137, *158*
Thoits, P. A., 27, 36, 39, 51, 53, 228, 236, 242, *246*, 247
Thompson, C. P., 145, *158*
Thoresen, C. J., 207, *222*
Thoresen, E., 238, 242, *246*
Thurnher, M., 38, 40, 53
Tiger, L., 57, 73, 79
Tillich, P., 113, *128*
Tipton, S. M., 188, *201*
Todd, P. M., 255, 269
Tolstoy, L., 151, *158*, 295–296, 296n, *312*
Tomlinson-Keasey, C., 171, *183*
Tooby, J., 135, *153*
Trepiccione, M., 37n
Triandis, H. C., 69, 79
Turner, R. J., 40, 53
Turner, V., 90, *103*

SUBJECT INDEX

Collective agency, 69
Collectivist culture, 69
Comforts, 199–200
Common good, 286
Community relocation, 21, 22, 26
Community service, 227–243
    adult, 235–236, 240–241
    college student, 228–229, 230–235
    defined, 227
    elderly, 236–238, 240–241
    long-term effects, 229–241
    moderating and mediating factors,
        238–239
    motivation, 228
    psychoneuroimmulogic benefits,
        228
    theoretical view, 227–228
Compassion, 283
Compensatory model, 194
Completeness, 166
Composite International Diagnostic Inter-
    view Short Form scales (CIDI–
    SF), 303
Conflict, 132–133, 148
Confucianism, 90
Conscientiousness, 190
Content Analysis of Verbatim Explana-
    tions (CAVE), 61, 62
Control beliefs, 260
Coping strategies, 23, 40–41
Creative genius, 163–179
Creative products, 168–169
Creativity
    criteria, 165–166
    biography and, 173–175
    defined, 165–166
    fulfillment, 8–9
    genius and, 163–179
    measurement, 168–175
    personality, 173–175
    positive nature, 163–165
    productivity, 168–169
    sociocultural, 175–177
Creativity in Later Life Project, 83n, 89,
    89n
Criticism, 148
Cross-age tutoring, 233
Cross-cultural studies. *See* Cultural
    context
Cross-generational interconnectedness,
    164

Cultural context
    Asian elevation, 282–283
    creativity, 170, 175–177
    eating habits, 196–198
    extrinsic goals, 114
    optimism and pessimism, 68–72
    purity and pollution, 277–283
Cultural knowledge, 259, 263
Cultural psychology, 286
Cumulative life adversity, 22
Customer satisfaction–loyalty, 215

Defensive pessimism, 71–73
Depression
    adult rates, 4
    cognition and, 209–210
    demographics, 308–309
    diagnosis, 300–301
    health impacts, 113, 293
    languishing and, 294, 308
    productivity impact, 206, 293, 307
    relapse prevention, 30
    self-worth and, 48
    troubled relationships and, 130
    volunteering and, 235
    youth rates, 4
Dieting, 196
Disability, 22–23, 117–120, 233
Disgust, 280–281
Dispositional optimism, 58–59, 63,
    64–65
Divergent thinking tests, 173
Doing good. *See* Volunteering
Domain, 97–98
Downsizers, 5
Down syndrome, 21
Drug use, 280
DSM-III-R, 301, 302, 303
Dual-task allocations, 264–265

Eastern cultures, 69
Eating, 194–199
Ego development, 18–19
Ego resiliency, 18, 20
Elder(s). *See also* Aging
    community service, 230, 236–238,
        240–241
    disability, 22
    mental health, 236–237

morbidity and mortality, 237–238
resilience, 25–27, 28
transitions, 21, 22
Elective selection, 258
Elevation
basic features, 281–282
described, 10, 276
disgust versus, 281, 285
India and Japan, 282–283
positive moral emotion and, 275–287
Emergent meaning, 97–98
Emergent motivation, 92, 93
Eminence, 169
Emotion, 131, 135, 139–140, 210–212
Emotion theory, 284
Employee well-being, 9, 213, 205–221
Enculturation, 95
Enjoyment, 88
Environment, 83, 84, 211 213
EPQ, 175
Estrangement, 86
Eudaimonia, 7, 249, 251, 286
European Americans, 70
Evolutionary adaptation, 135–136
Evolutionary psychology, 135
Experience, 84–88
Expectancy violation process, 137, 138–139
Expectations, 58, 212
Experience of meaning, 94–100
Experience Sampling Method (ESM), 91, 96
Explanatory style, 60–61, 65
Extraversion, 141
Extremity bias, 144
Extrinsic goals, 113–115
Extrinsic motivation, 187
Eysenck Personality Questionnaire, 174

Factual knowledge, 252
Feedback, 209
Fiction, 90
Field, 97–100
Flatland, 276–277
Flourishing
described, 6, 94
diagnosis, 301–302
measurements, 27–28
mental health benefits, 294

optimism and, 55–74
resilience and, 15–31
thriving versus, 25
Flow, 89–94
Flow activity, 89, 89n
Food, 194–199
Food ambivalence, 196, 198
Forgiveness, 133
Frankl's logotherapy, 24
French paradox, 196–199
Friendships, 213
Fulfillment, 8–9, 185–186
Full involvement, 88–94

Gallup Organization, 205n, 208, 214
Gallup Workplace Audit (GWA), 208–209, 213–219, 221
Generativity, 38, 111, 110–112
Genius
creativity and, 163–179
criteria, 165–166
defined, 166–167
heritability, 176
measurement, 168–175
positive nature, 163–165
sociocultural, 175–177
Goal(s), 105–107
disability and, 117–120
intrinsic and extrinsic, 113–115
life meaning and, 107–109
resilience and, 21
virtue and, 120–122
Goal content, 110–113
Goal-focused group psychotherapy, 106
Goal orientation, 115–117
Goal striving, 120–122
Guilford's Alternate Uses Test, 172

Happiness, 249
Health maintenance, 49
Helplessness, 60
Heritage High School, 297
Hindu culture, 278–279
HIV status, 111
Hobbies, 191
Hostility, 64
Humanistic psychology, 5, 164
Hypertension, 64

Mood, 228–229, 229n
Moral beauty, 284
Moral emotions, 276, 276n
Morality, 275–287
Moral judgment, 280
Motivation, 106, 140, 228
Music, 90
Muslim cultures, 69, 278

Narcissism, 113
National Comorbidity Study, 303
National Death Index, 239
National Institute of Mental Health
    (NIMH), 11, 15n, 293, 309
Need to belong, 146
Negative expectation, 65, 60
Negative feedback, 92
Negativity bias, 137, 139, 143n, 145
Neuromuscular disease (NMD), 117–120
Neuroticism, 141
Novelty, 165–166
Nurturance, 149
Nurturing ties, 26

Obesity, 195–196
Occam's razor, 284
Ocytocin, 149
Opponent process models, 136
Optimism
    Asian, 70–73
    callings and, 190
    comparisons and contrasts, 62–65
    cultural context, 68–72
    current view, 55
    defined, 56
    dispositional, 58–59, 63, 64–65
    flourishing and, 55–74
    measurement, 66–68
Optimistic bias, 63
Originality. See Creativity
Ortgeist, 175–176

Passions, 148, 192–194
Patience, 121–122
Peak experience, 286
Peers, 98–99
Peer tutoring, 233
Perceived health, 240–241

Perfectionism, 64
Perseverance, 122
Personal goals, 105–107, 117–120
Personal growth, 7
Personality
    Big 5 model, 141
    creative genius, 173–175
    in MIDUS analyses, 42–43
Personal Strivings Assessment Packet,
    118
Person–environment fit theory, 205, 212
Person–object interaction, 87
Pessimism, 56–61, 71–73
Pessimistic explanatory style, 65
Physical health
    avoidant striving and, 116
    perceived, 240–241
    positive, 26
    resilience and, 21
Play, 90, 191–194
Pleasure, 185, 199–200
Pleasure–eating link, 195
Poetry, 89–90
Positive life, 109
Positive moral emotions, 275–287, 276n
Positive physical health, 26
Positive psychology
    aim, 3, 6
    described, 3–4, 6, 109
    mental health and, 309
    optimism research, 55–74
    of relationships, 129–152
Post-polio syndrome (PPS), 117–120
Posttraumatic growth (PTG), 24
Posttraumatic stress disorder (PTSD), 24
Power, 110, 111, 167
Practical wisdom, 249, 251, 255, 263
Practice, 260
Prevention, 141
Primogeniture, 174–175
Problem-focused coping, 22
Procedural knowledge, 252
Procrastination, 64
Productivity, 8–9, 168–169
Profitability, 219
Promotion, 141
Protective factors, 17–18, 26
Protective resources, 26
Prudence, 121
Psychological Experiences Study (PTP),
    43–50

Successful Midlife Development Research
Network (MIDMAC), 293n

Talent, 163
TAT test, 174, 175
Teen Outreach Program, 231
Terman's Gifted Children, 129, 171
Terman's intelligence study, 171, 173
Theoretical wisdom, 249, 251–252
Third dimension, 276–283
Thriving, 25
Time, losing track of, 92
Trait interest, 87
Trauma, 24–25, 26–27, 130
Turning points. *See* Psychological turning
    points
Turnover, 207, 215, 217–218
Type A behavior, 64

Uncertainty management, 253
Uniqueness, 166–167

Value-related life priorities, 253
Valued Youth Program, 231, 233
Virtues, 120–122
Vital engagement, 83–100
    environment and, 211
    experience and, 84–88
    experience of meaning, 94–100
    as psychological concept, 86–87
    subjective experience, 88–94
Voluntary association membership, 235
Volunteering. *See also* Community
        service
    for the common good, 286
    decline in, 5
    effect on the volunteer, 10, 228–
        229, 230–235
    motivation, 228
    roles, 228
    as societal fulfillment, 193
Well-being
    described, 206, 300
    goals, 110

symptoms, 298–300
wisdom and, 251
workplace, 205–221
youth, 232–233
Well-being therapy, 30, 106
Wisconsin Longitudinal Study (WLS),
    22, 23
Wisdom, 249–266
    meta-heuristic, 255
    practical, 249, 251, 255, 263
    SOC and, 256–265
    theoretical, 249, 251–252
WIST categories, 109
Withdrawal, 49
Women
    food ambivalence, 196, 198
    pessimistic explanatory style, 65
    resilience, 23
    spiritual strivings, 112
Work
    as a calling, 96, 186–190, 207
    impairment or loss, 306
    intrinsic–extrinsic motivation, 186–
        187
    involvement, 186–187
    values, 186–187
Work centrality, 186–187
Work orientation, 188–190
Workplace well-being, 9, 205–221
    business outcomes meta-analysis,
        205–221
    employee expectations, 211–212
    employee turnover–retention, 215,
        217–218
    management practices, 208–209
    pay and benefits, 219
    short-term satisfiers, 220
    tangible rewards, 219
    theoretical foundations, 209–213
World Health Organization, 309

Youth. *See* Adolescent(s)
Youth Development Study, 231

Zeitgeist, 176
Zung depression inventory, 300

ABOUT THE EDITORS

Corey L. M. Keyes is a social psychologist. He received his PhD in sociology from the University of Wisconsin, Madison. He has been a member of the Emory University faculty since 1997, where he holds joint appointments in the Department of Sociology and in the Department of Behavioral Sciences and Health Education of the Rollins School of Public Health. He is a member of the steering committee of the Society for the Study of Human Development, the John D. and Catherine T. MacArthur Foundation's Research Network on Successful Midlife Development, and the Positive Psychology Network. His research focuses broadly on the domains of successful human development and aging and the diagnosis and etiology of mental health and illness.

Jonathan Haidt is a social and cultural psychologist. He received his PhD from the University of Pennsylvania in 1992 and then did postdoctoral research at the University of Chicago and in Orissa, India. He has been on the faculty of the University of Virginia since 1995. His research focuses on morality, and he began his career studying the negative moral emotions, such as disgust, shame, and vengeance. In 1998 he had his awakening to positive psychology with the realization that there was almost no research on the positive moral emotions—the emotions people feel when other people do kind, heroic, or otherwise virtuous acts. He now studies these emotions, including elevation, awe, admiration, and gratitude. He is the 2001 winner of the Templeton Prize in Positive Psychology.